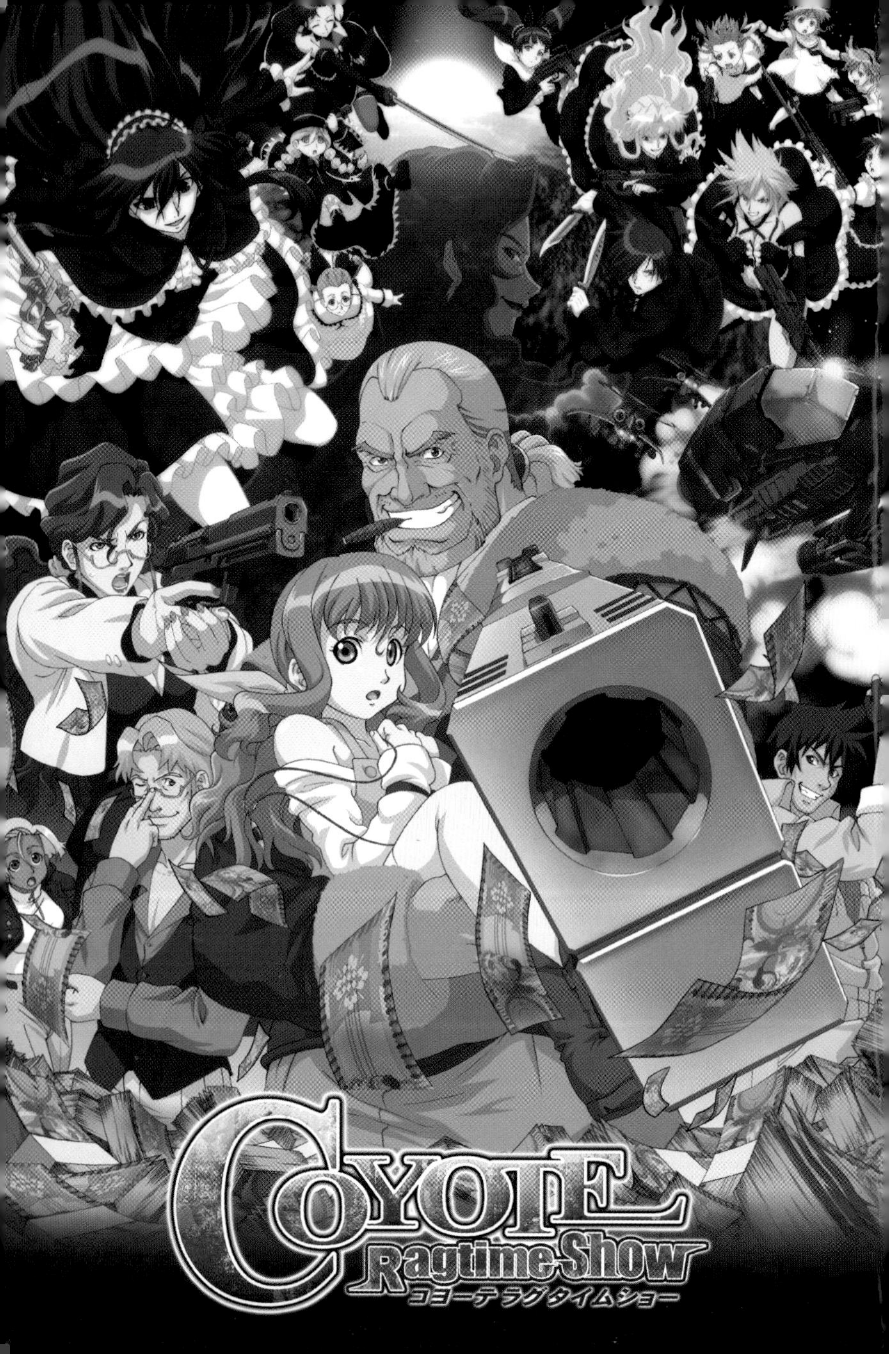
COYOTE
Ragtime Show
コヨーテラグタイムショー

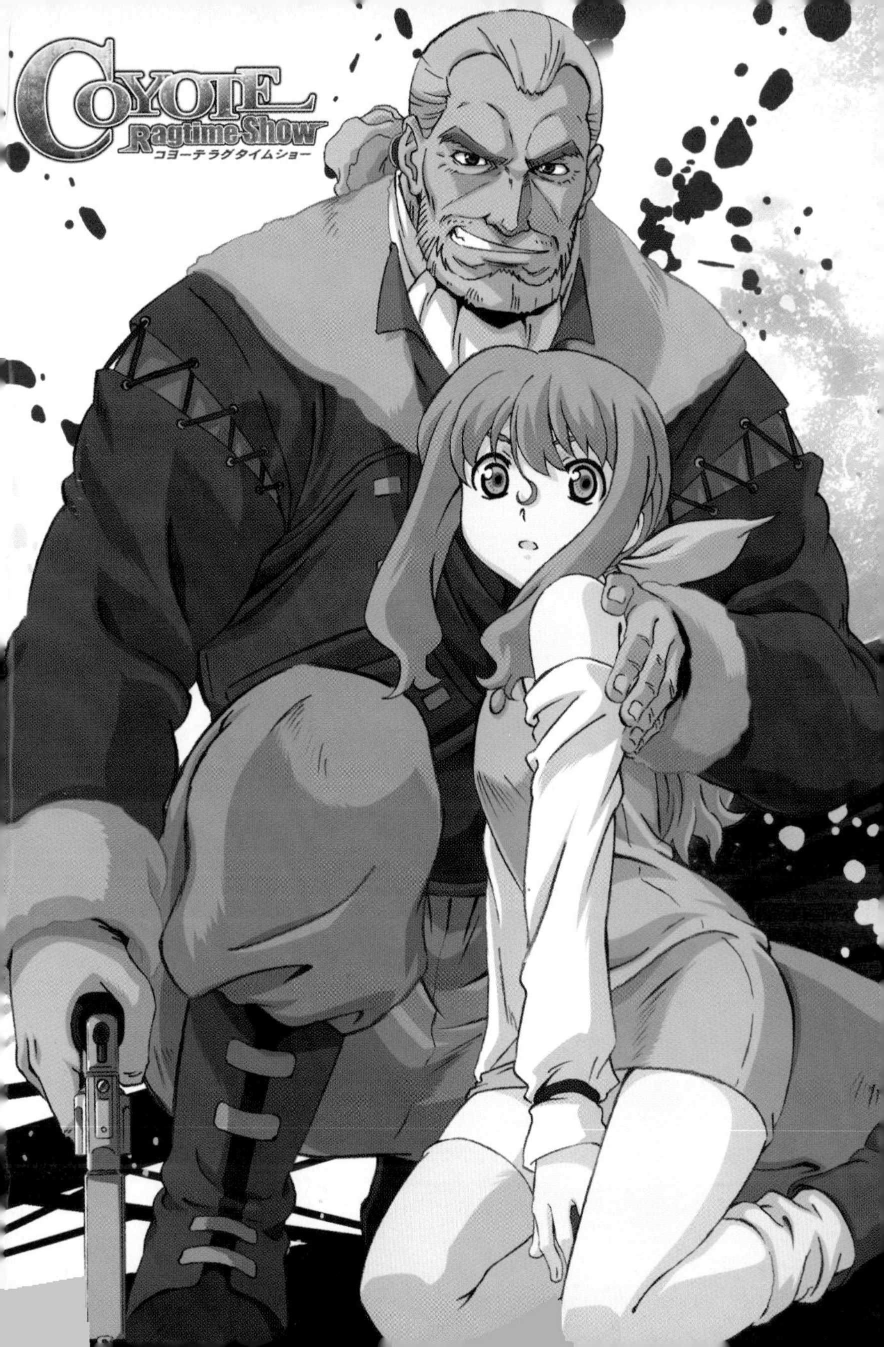
COYOTE Ragtime Show
コヨーテラグタイムショー

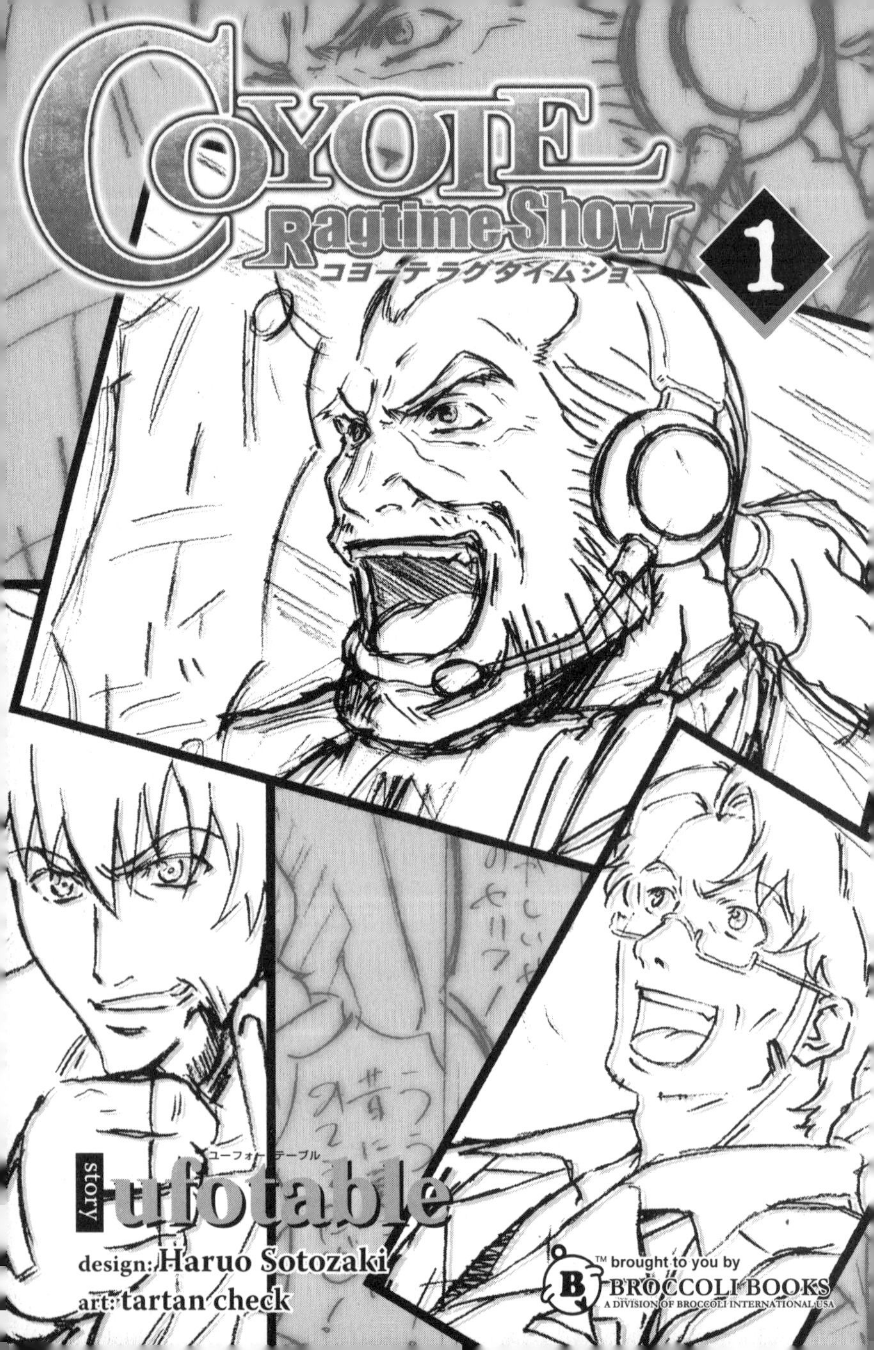
COYOTE
Ragtime Show
コヨーテラグタイムショー
1
story
ユーフォーテーブル
ufotable
design: Haruo Sotozaki
art: tartan check
TM brought to you by
BROCCOLI BOOKS
A DIVISION OF BROCCOLI INTERNATIONAL USA

Other titles available from Broccoli Books

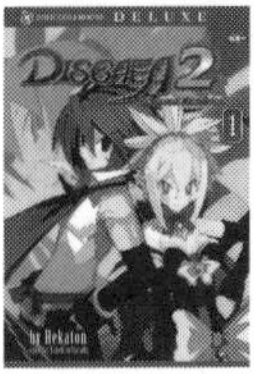
DELUXE
DISGAEA 2

Disgaea® 2
❑Volume 1 (ongoing)

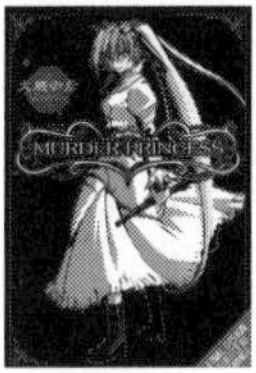
MURDER PRINCESS

Murder Princess
❑Volume 1 (of 2)

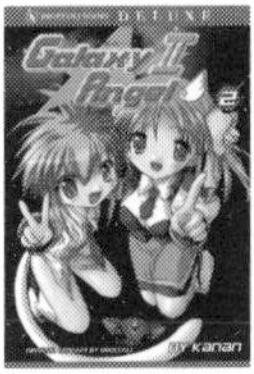
DELUXE
Galaxy Angel II

Galaxy Angel II
❑Volume 1 (of 6)
❑Volume 2

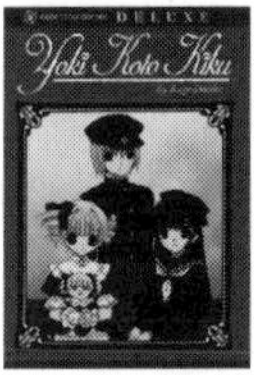
DELUXE
Yoki Koto Kiku

Yoki Koto Kiku
❑Volume 1 (of 1)

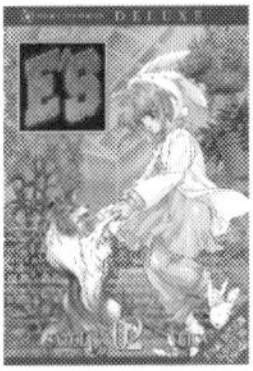
DELUXE
E'S

E'S
❑Volume 1 (ongoing)
❑Volume 2

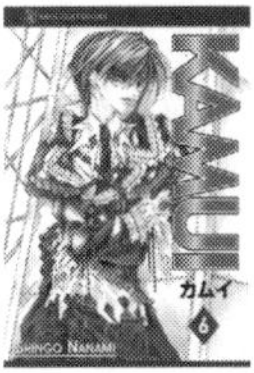
KAMUI
カムイ
SHINGO NANAMI

KAMUI
❑Volume 1 (of 11)
❑Volume 2
❑Volume 3
❑Volume 4
❑Volume 5
❑Volume 6
❑Volume 7

Aquarian Age – Juvenile Orion
❑Volume 1 (of 5)
❑Volume 2
❑Volume 3
❑Volume 4
❑Volume 5

Di Gi Charat Theater
❑Dejiko's Summer Vacation
❑Piyoko is Number One!

Di Gi Charat Theater – Dejiko's Adventure
❑Volume 1 (of 3)

Disgaea®
❑Volume 1 (of 1)

Galaxy Angel
❑Volume 1 (of 5)
❑Volume 2
❑Volume 3
❑Volume 4
❑Volume 5

Galaxy Angel Beta
❑Volume 1 (of 3)
❑Volume 2
❑Volume 3

Galaxy Angel Party
❑Volume 1 (ongoing)
❑Volume 2

For more information about Broccoli Books titles,
check out **bro-usa.com!**

Coyote Ragtime Show Volume 1

English Adaptation Staff
Translation: Satsuki Yamashita
English Adaptation: Melissa Gima
Touch-Up & Lettering: Keiran O'Leary
Cover & Graphic Supervision: Christopher McDougall

Editor: Dietrich Seto
Sales Manager: Ardith D. Santiago
Managing Editor: Shizuki Yamashita
Publisher: Kaname Tezuka

Email: editor@broccolibooks.com
Website: www.broccolibooks.com

A BROCCOLI BOOKS Manga
Broccoli Books is a division of Broccoli International USA, Inc.
1728 S. La Cienega Blvd., Los Angeles, CA 90035

ISBN13: 978-1-5974-1155-4
ISBN10: 1-59741-155-8

Published by Broccoli International USA, Inc.
First printing, April 2007
Cover illustration by Seiya Numata, color direction by Emi Chiba
Page 1 insert illustration by Tomonori Sudou, color direction by Emi Chiba
Page 2 insert illustration by Haruo Sotozaki, color direction by Emi Chiba

Distributed by Publishers Group West

ANIME GAMERS   BROCCOLI INTERNATIONAL USA
www.bro-usa.com

10 9 8 7 6 5 4 3 2 1
Printed in Canada

characters

MISTER
First class felon with countless aliases. Mister is respected by fellow coyotes for his loyalty to his friends and subordinates. He was one of Pirate King Blues' best friends.

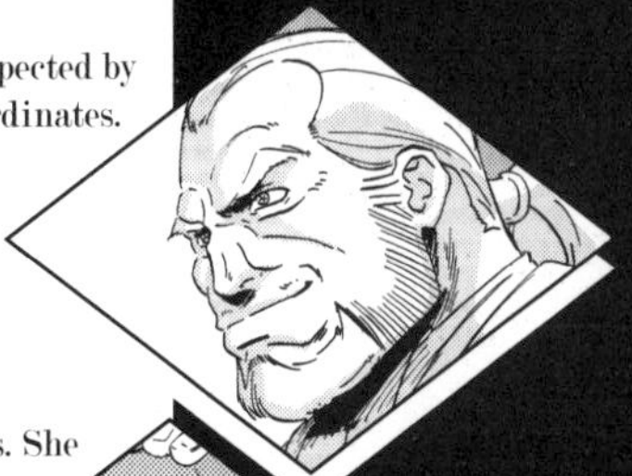

FRANCA
Franca is the daughter of the late Pirate King Blues. She was taken in by Mister after her father's death, and operates a bar in Mister's absence.

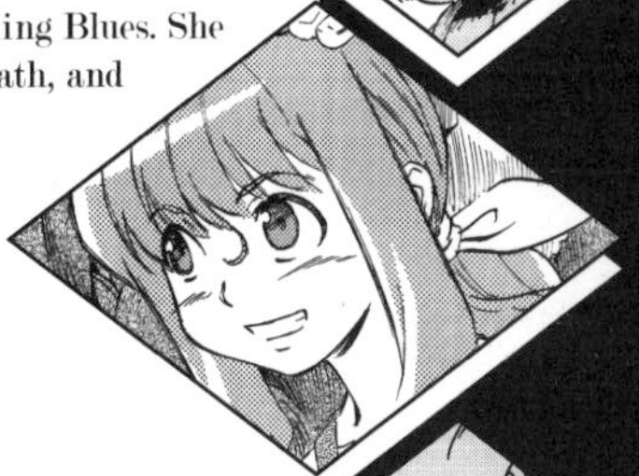

BLUES
Pirate King and father of Franca, he is a legendary coyote who stole 10 billion space dollars from the Central Bank. He was killed three years ago, and hid the money on Planet Graceland.

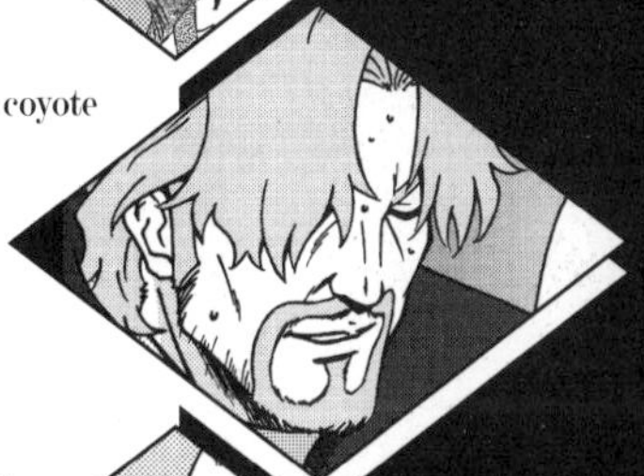

BISHOP
Bishop is a talented con artist who uses his good looks and smooth talk to gain the trust of others.

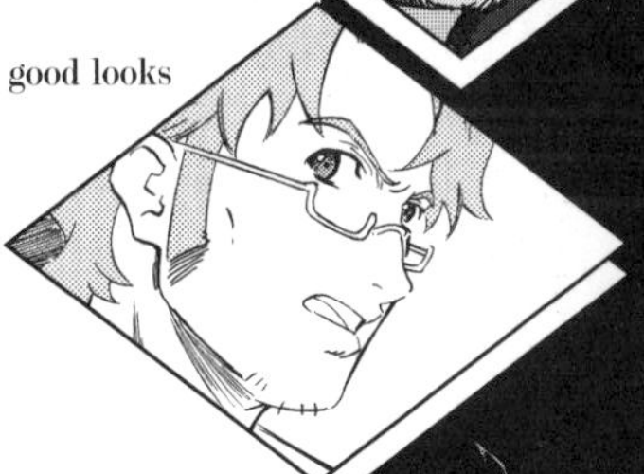

KATANA
Katana is a top-notch driver with over 50 citations for reckless driving, and illegal transport of dangerous substances and people.

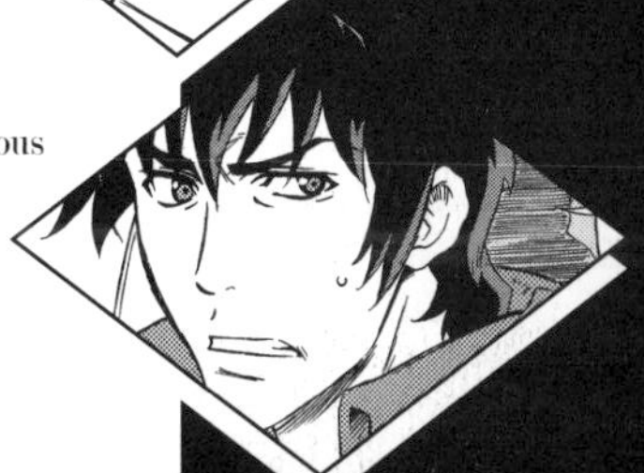

coyote ragtime show 1

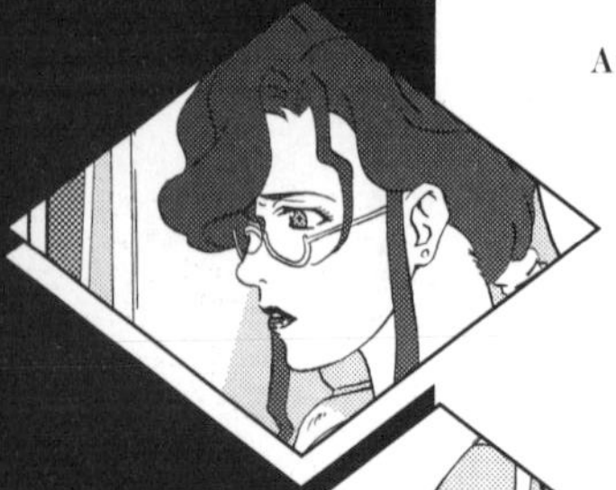

ANGELICA

Angelica is an investigator with the Space Federation Police who has been chasing after Mister for the past four years.

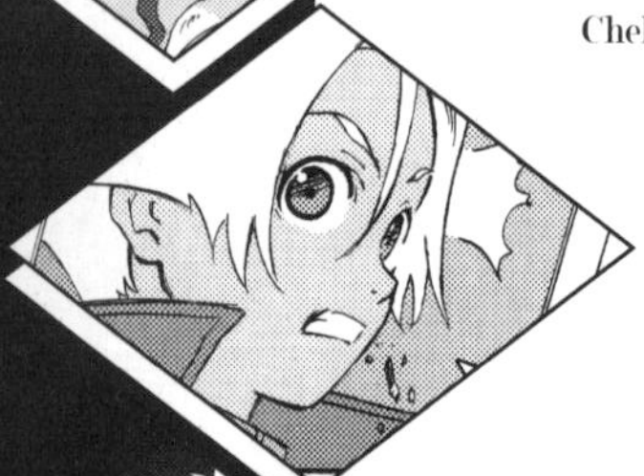

CHELSEA

Chelsea is a ditzy, young police officer working under Angelica.

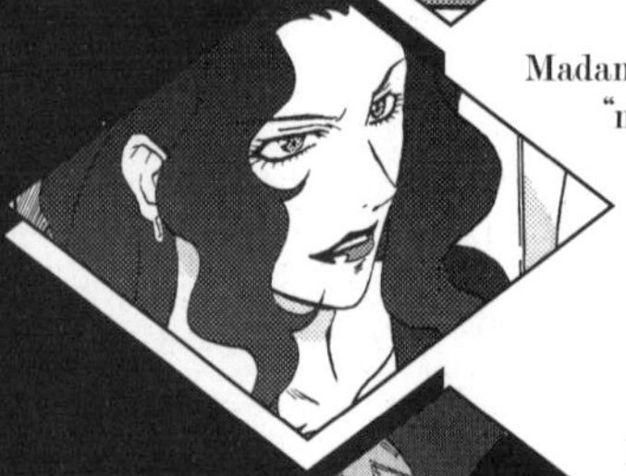

MADAME MARCIANO

Madame Marciano is a member of the Criminal Guild and "mother" to the 12 SISTERs. She carries a mysterious grudge against Mister.

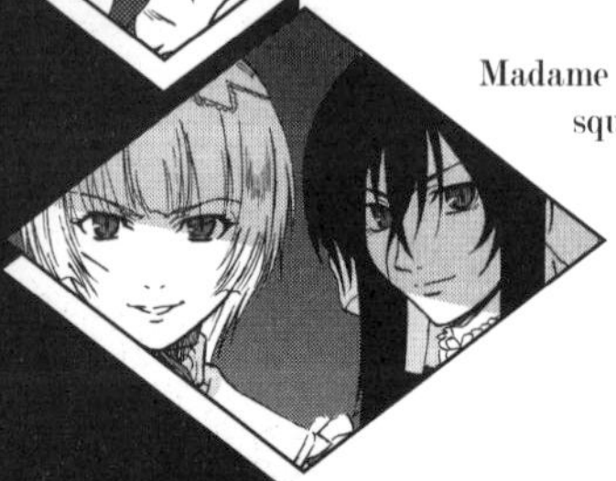

12 SISTERs

Madame Marciano's 12 "daughters" and personal hit squad. Each is named after a month from the Gregorian calendar.

CONTENTS

COYOTE Ragtime Show Vol.01
007
COMIC RUSH
012006

COYOTE Ragtime Show Vol.02
057
COMIC RUSH
022006

COYOTE Ragtime Show Vol.03
087
COMIC RUSH
032006

COYOTE Ragtime Show Vol.04
113
COMIC RUSH
042006

COYOTE Ragtime Show Vol.05
145
COMIC RUSH
052006

COYOTE ENCYCLOPEDIA
— Marciano's 12 SISTERs —
180

COYOTE Ragtime Show ❶

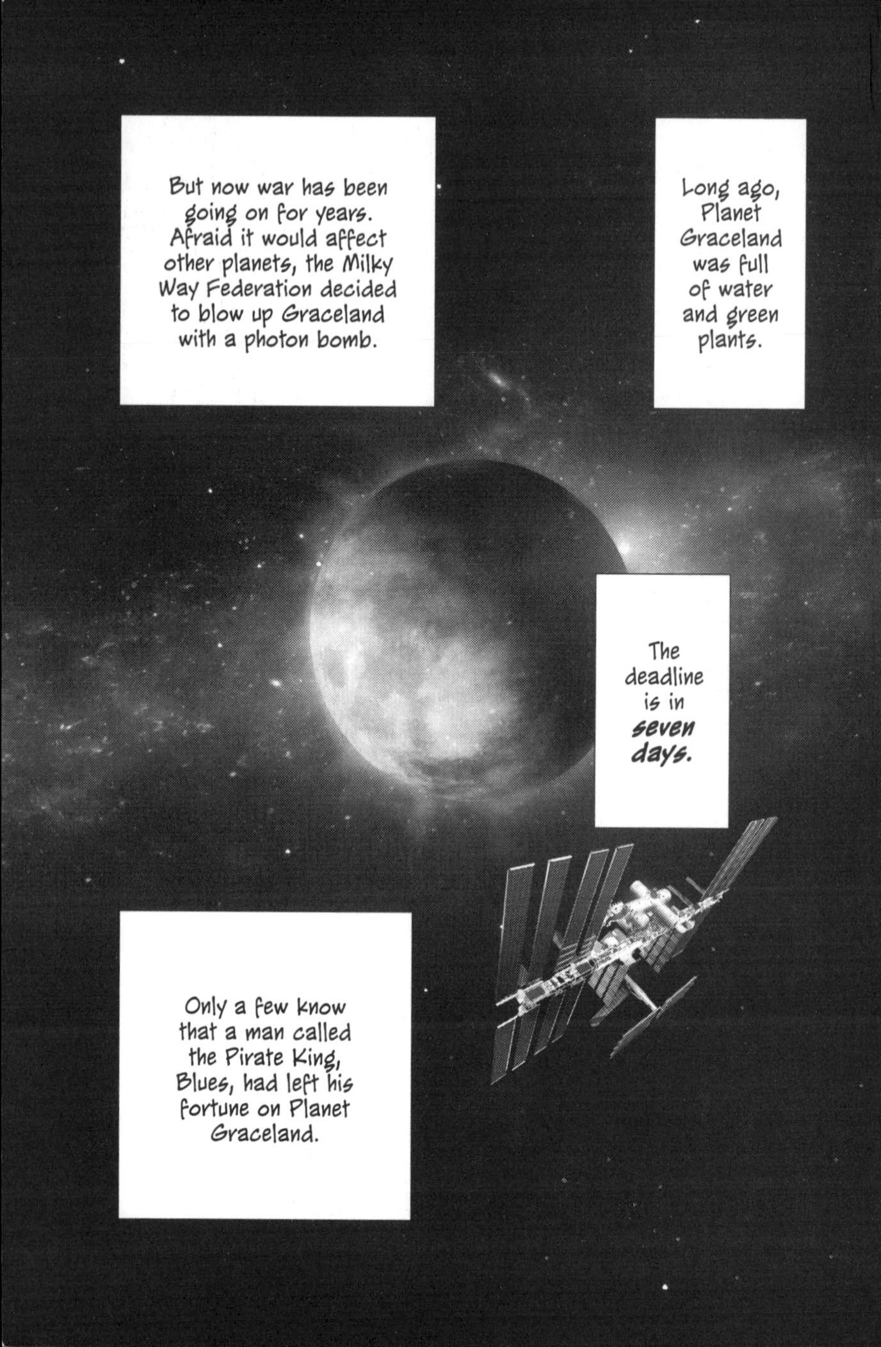
Long ago, Planet Graceland was full of water and green plants.
But now war has been going on for years. Afraid it would affect other planets, the Milky Way Federation decided to blow up Graceland with a photon bomb.
The deadline is in seven days.
Only a few know that a man called the Pirate King, Blues, had left his fortune on Planet Graceland.

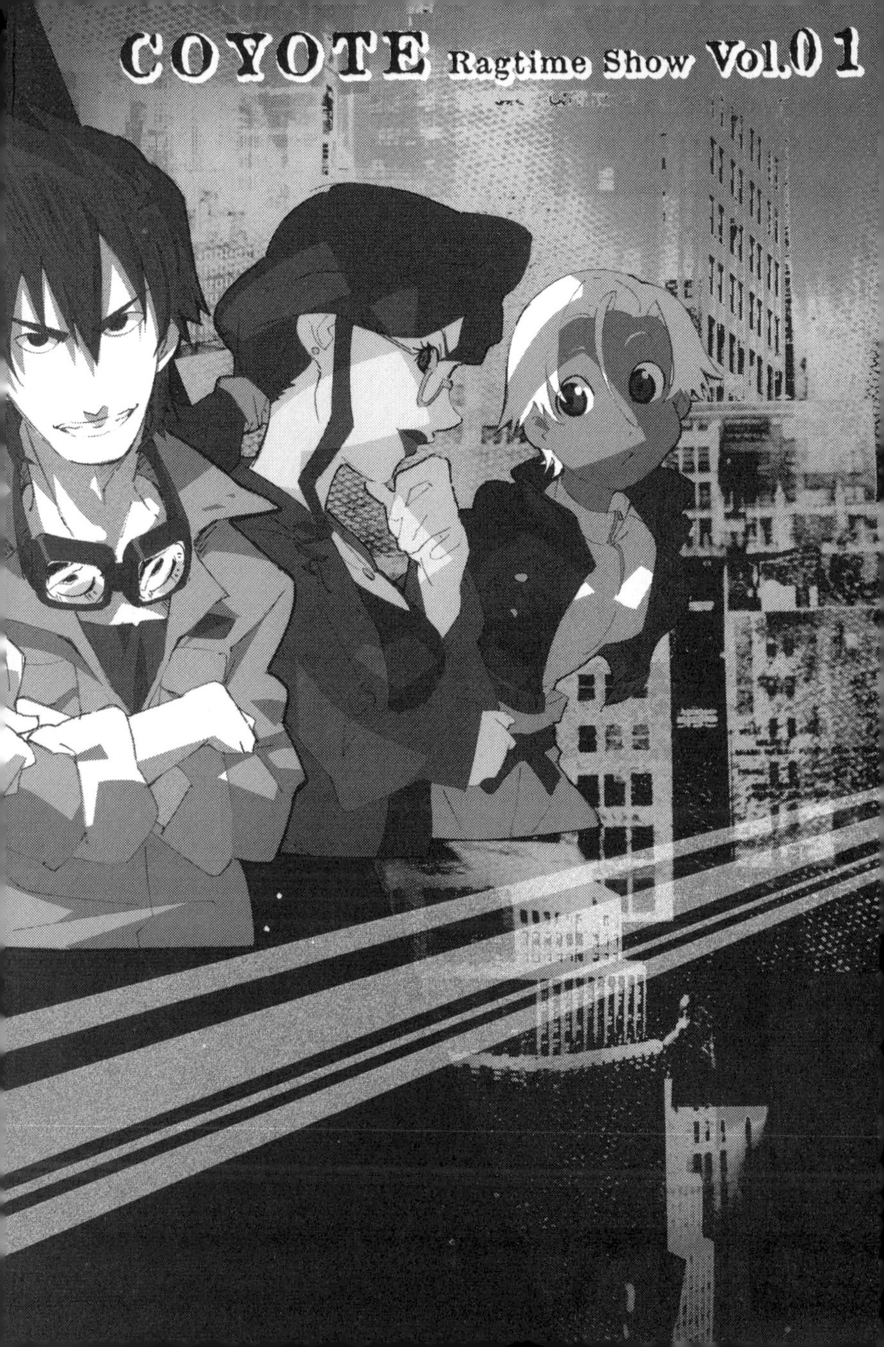
COYOTE Ragtime Show Vol.01

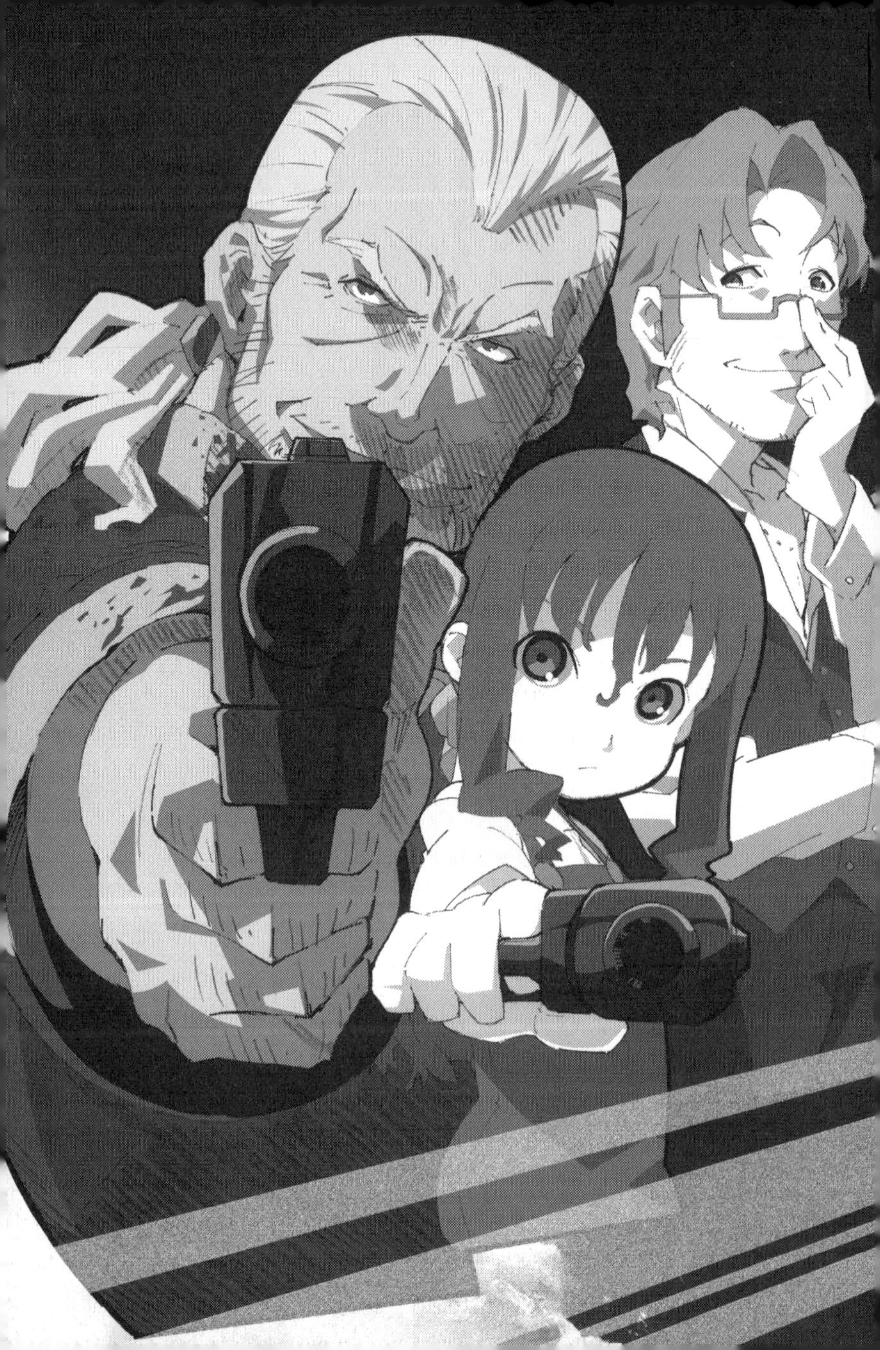

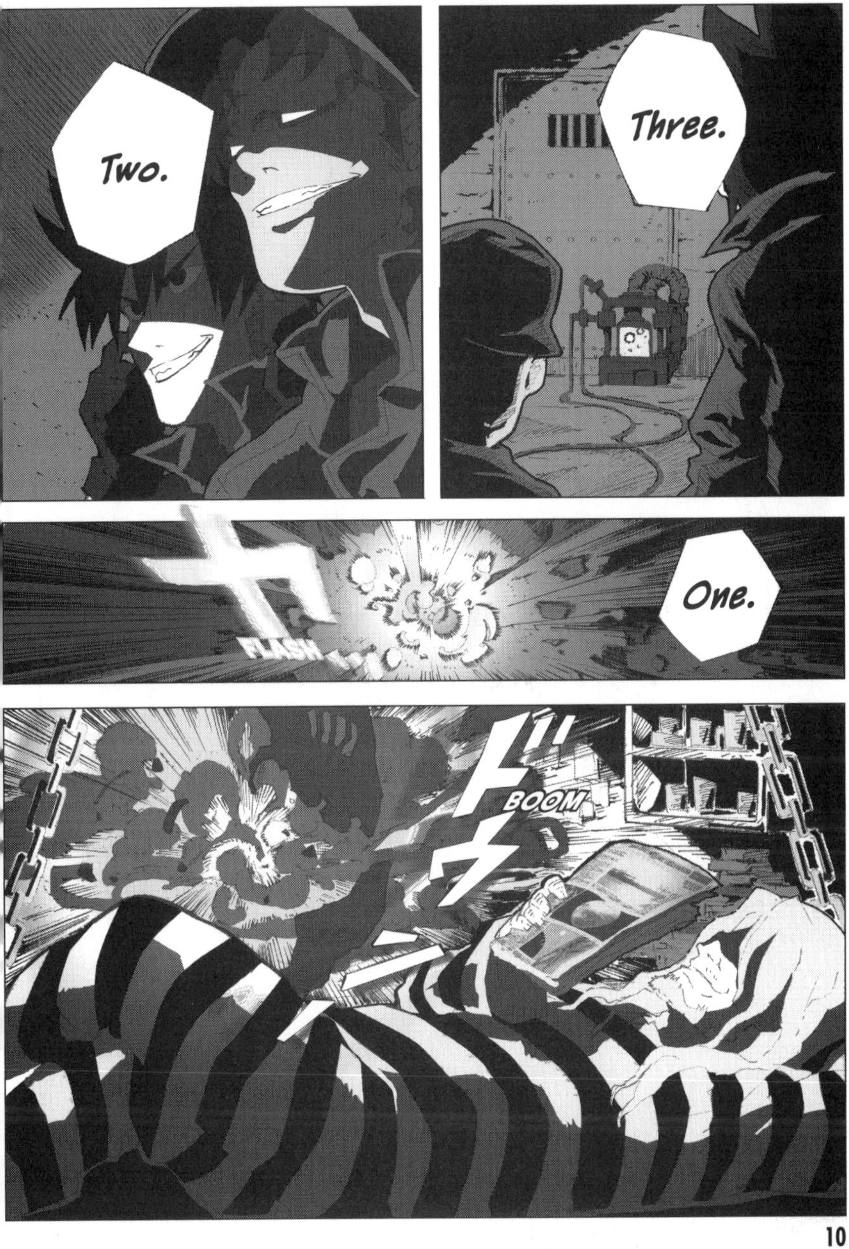
Three.
Two.
One.
FLASH
BOOM

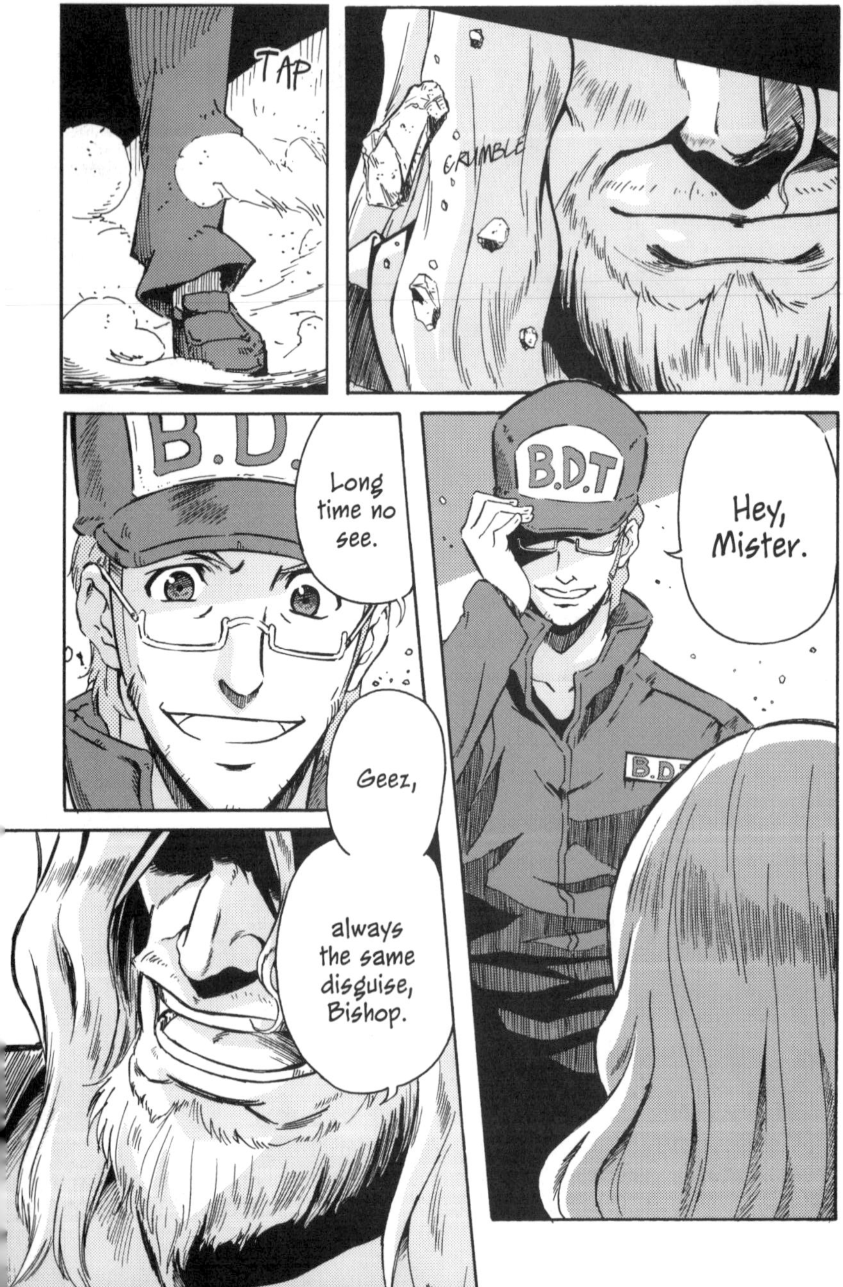
CRUMBLE
TAP
B.D.T
Hey, Mister.
Long time no see.
Geez,
always the same disguise, Bishop.

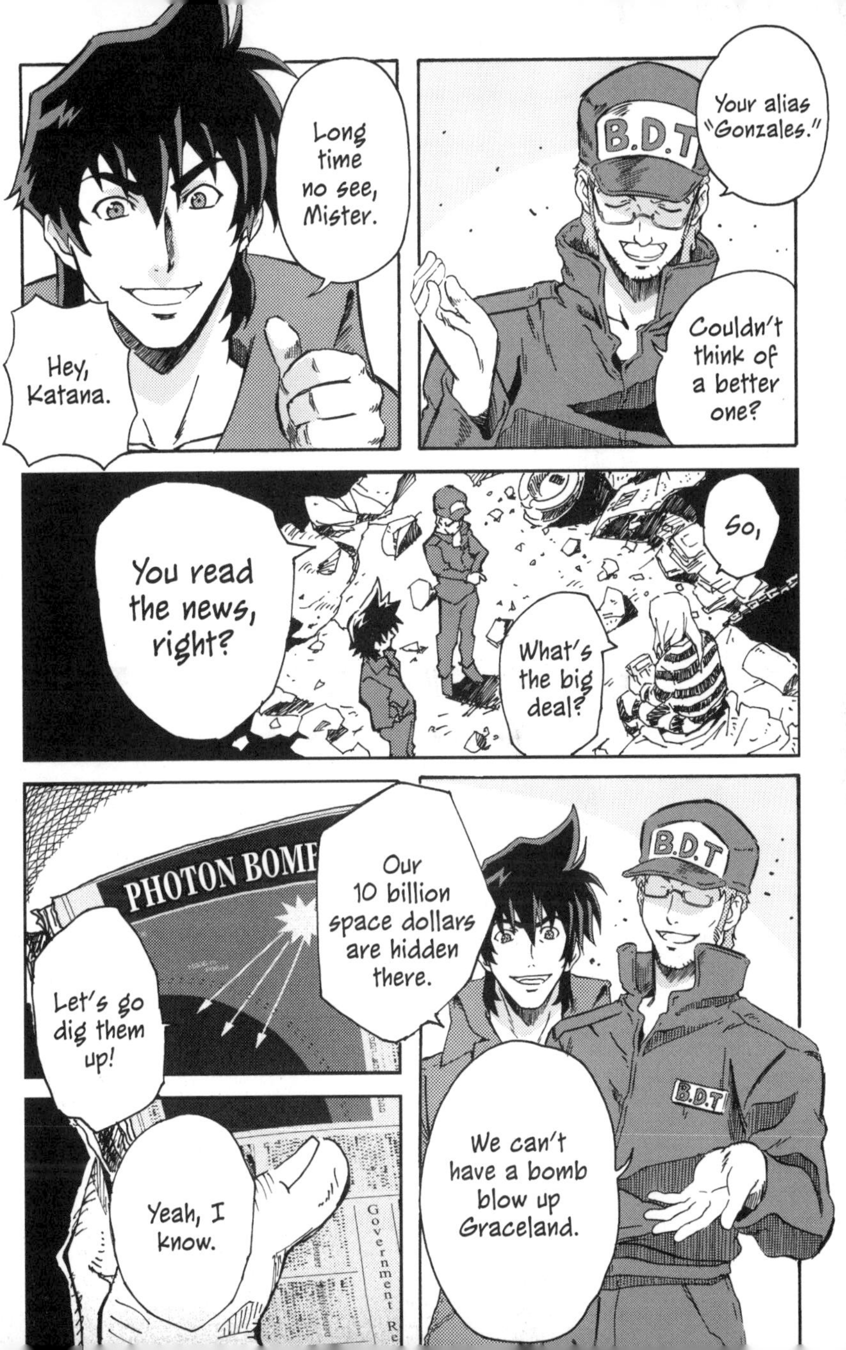

Your alias "Gonzales."
Couldn't think of a better one?
Long time no see, Mister.
Hey, Katana.
B.D.T
So,
What's the big deal?
You read the news, right?
Our 10 billion space dollars are hidden there.
We can't have a bomb blow up Graceland.
B.D.T
B.D.T
PHOTON BOM
Let's go dig them up!
Yeah, I know.
Government

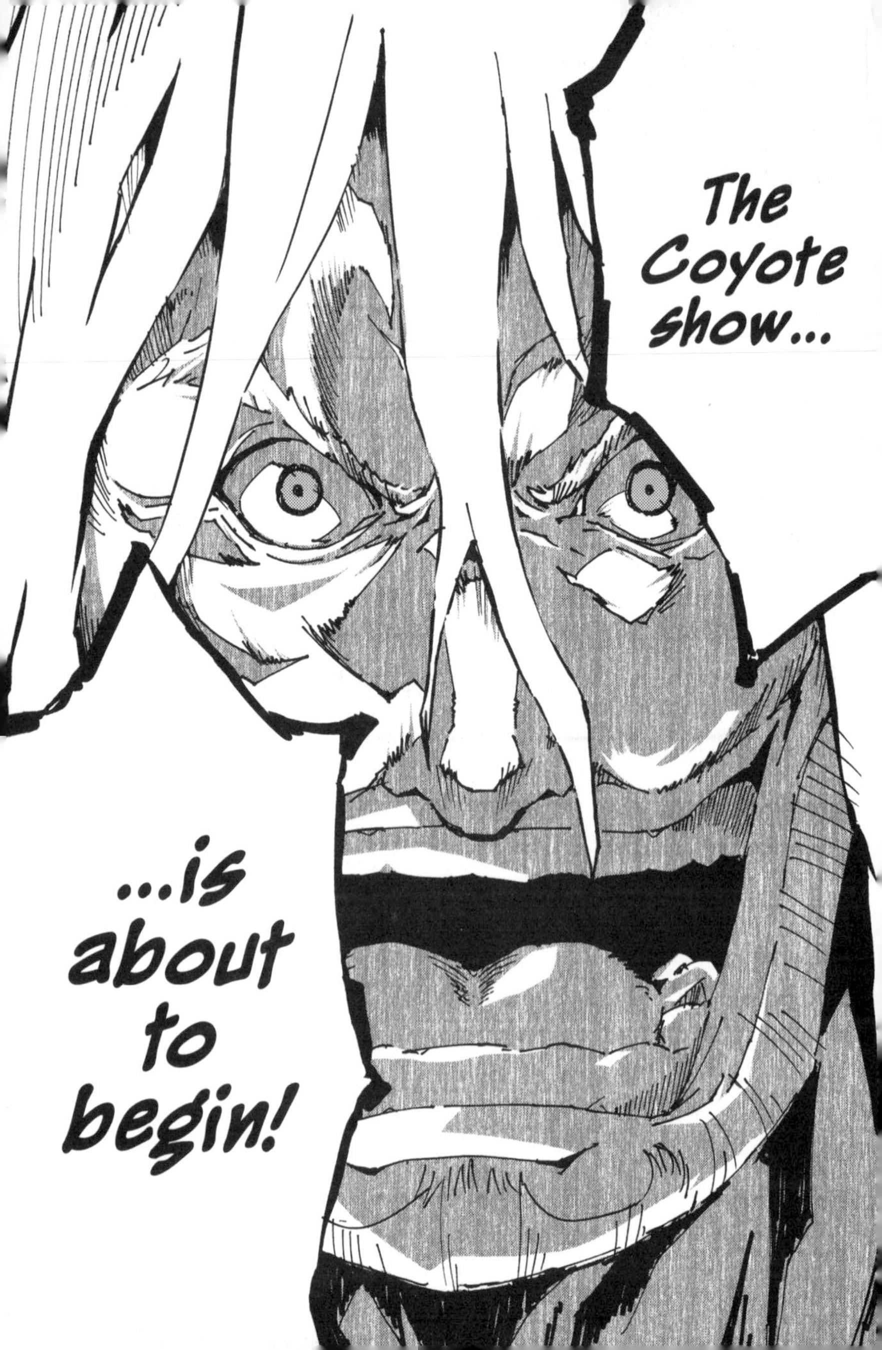
The Coyote show...
...is about to begin!

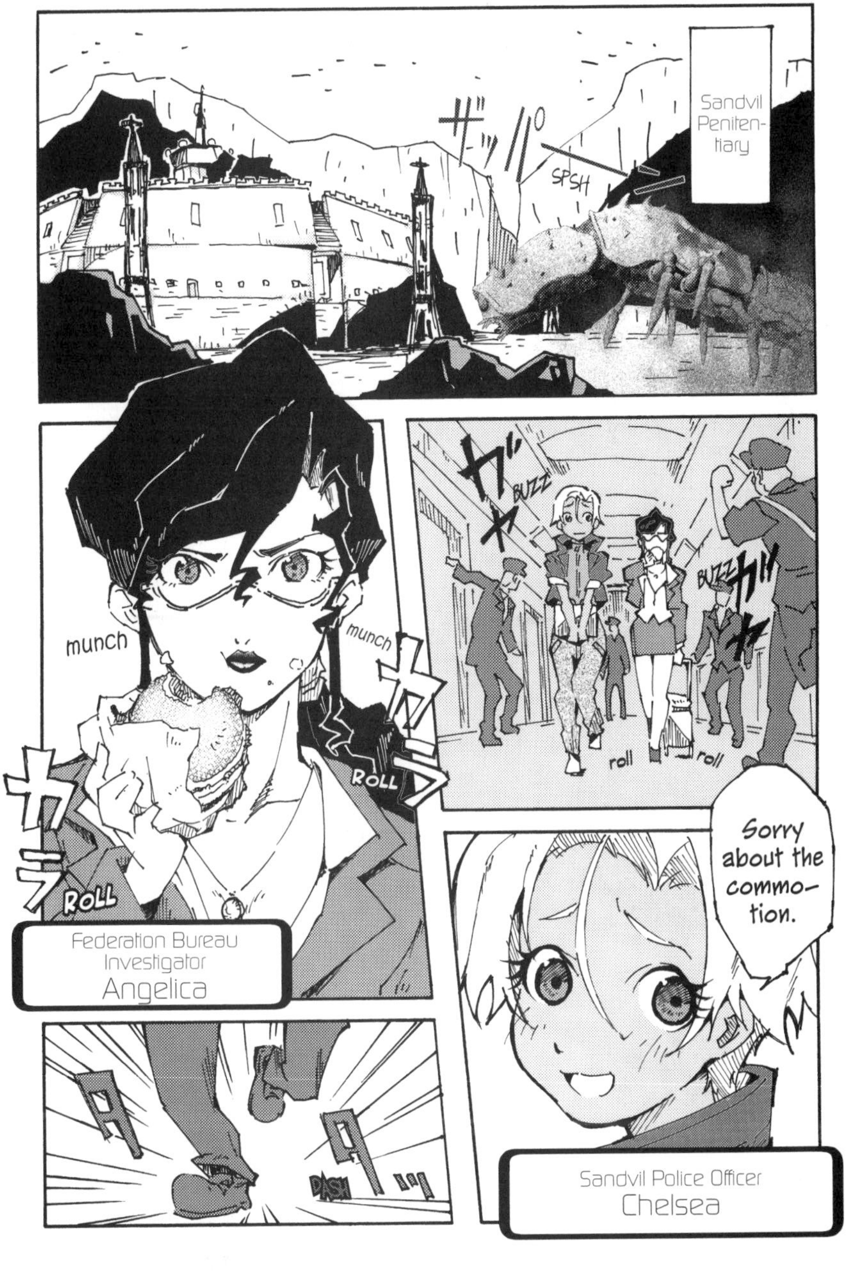

Sandvil Penitentiary
SPSH
BUZZ
BUZZ
roll
roll
Sorry about the commotion.
Sandvil Police Officer
Chelsea
munch
munch
ROLL
ROLL
Federation Bureau Investigator
Angelica
DASH

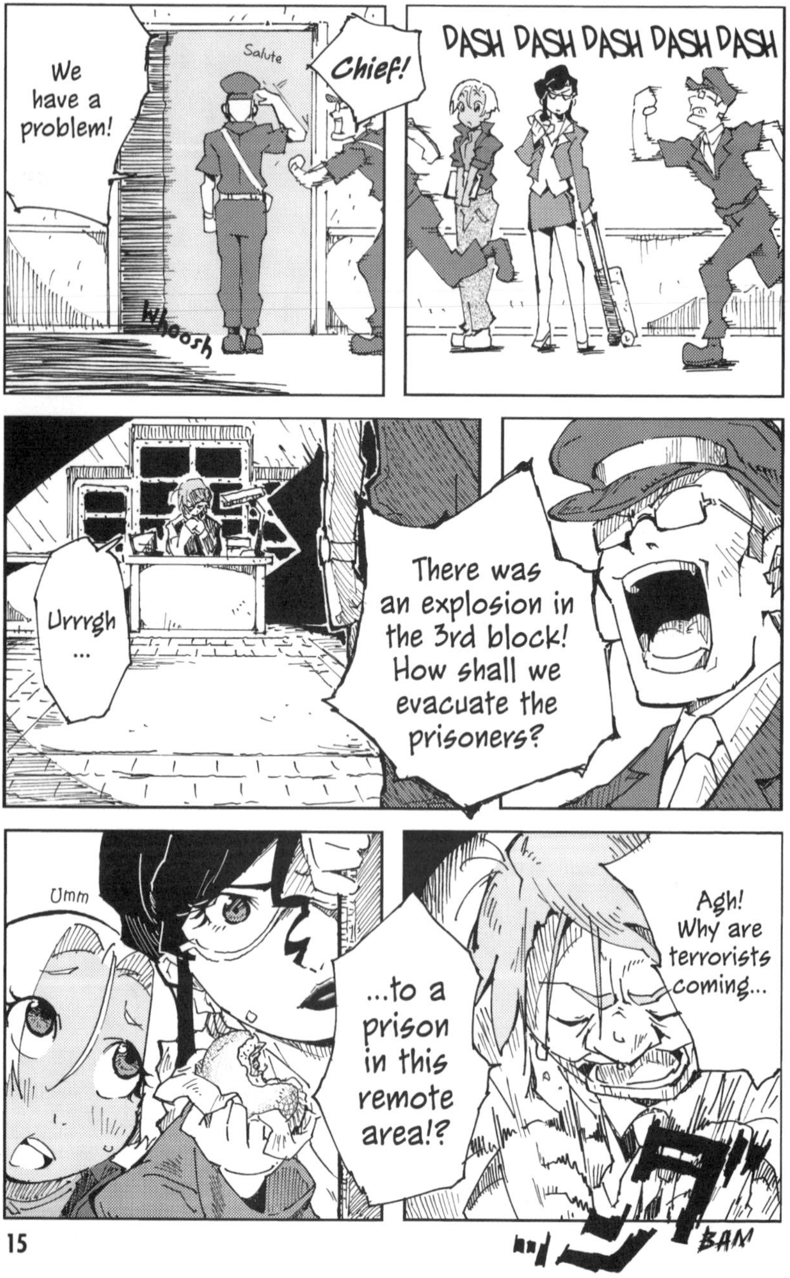
DASH DASH DASH DASH DASH
Chief!
Salute
We have a problem!
Whoosh
There was an explosion in the 3rd block! How shall we evacuate the prisoners?
Urrrgh ...
Agh! Why are terrorists coming...
BAM
...to a prison in this remote area!?
Umm

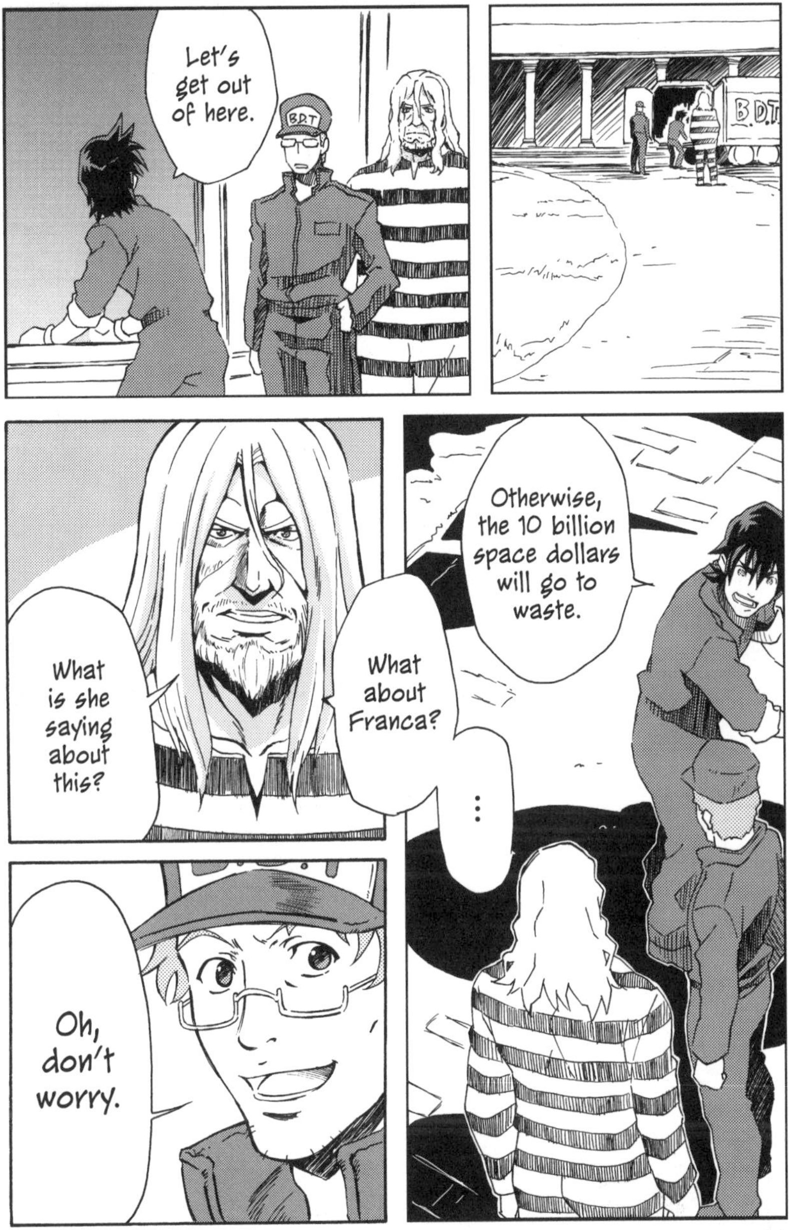
Let's get out of here.
Otherwise, the 10 billion space dollars will go to waste.
...
What about Franca?
What is she saying about this?
Oh, don't worry.

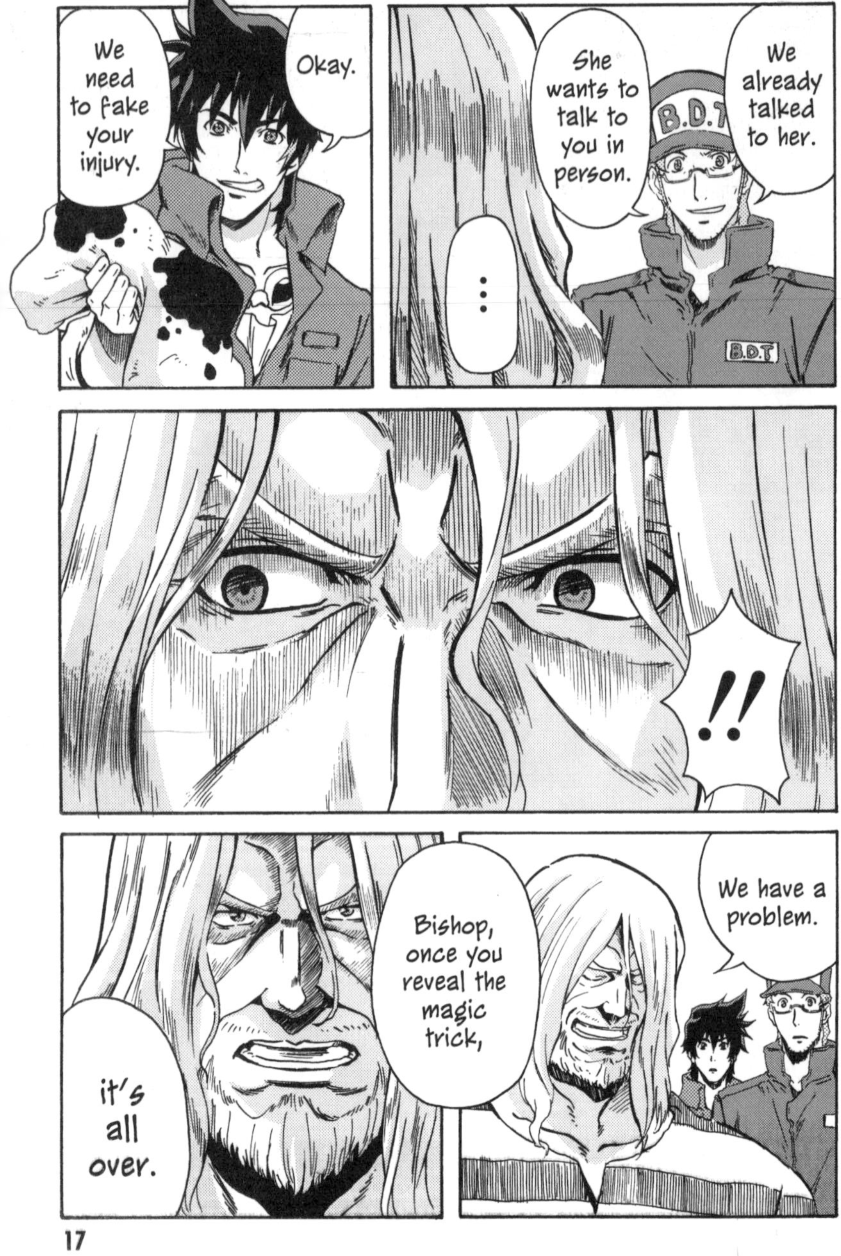
We already talked to her.
She wants to talk to you in person.
...
Okay.
We need to fake your injury.
!!
We have a problem.
Bishop, once you reveal the magic trick,
it's all over.

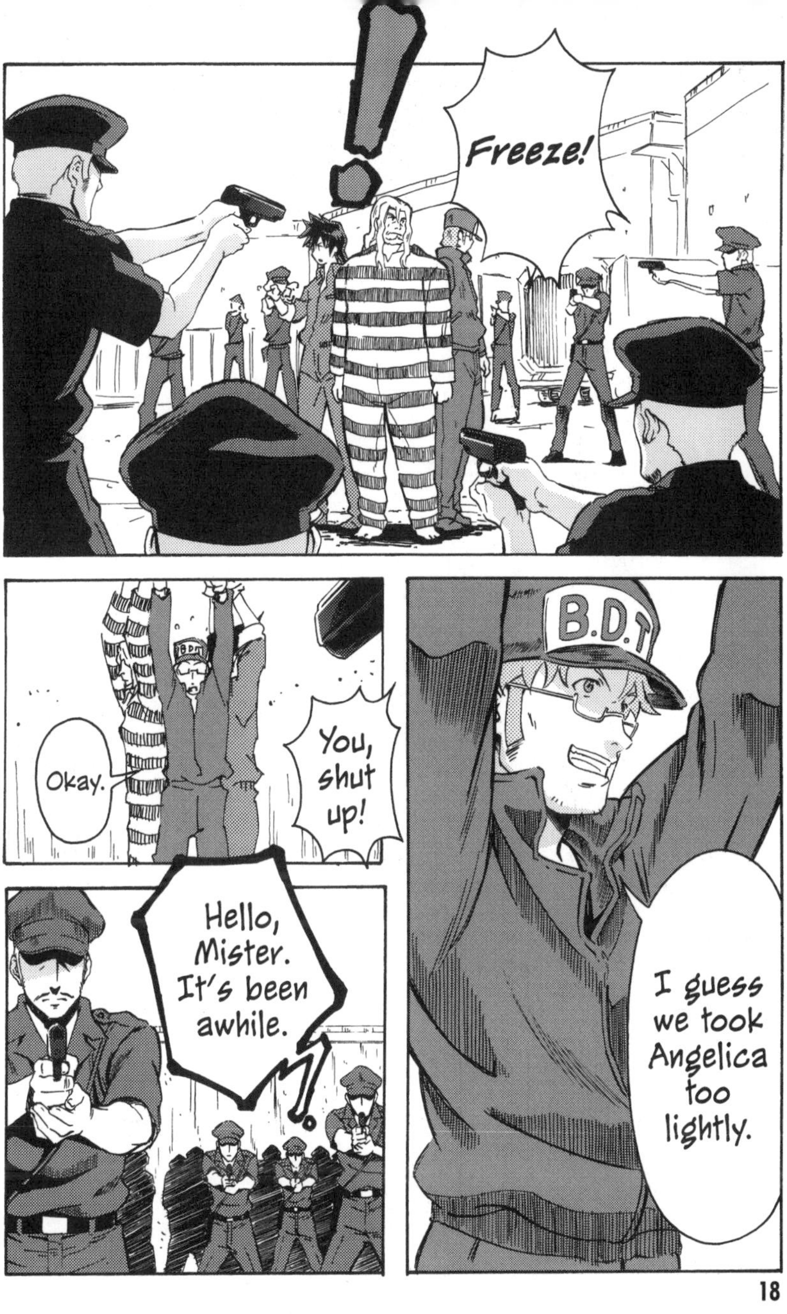
Freeze!
I guess we took Angelica too lightly.
You, shut up!
Okay.
Hello, Mister. It's been awhile.

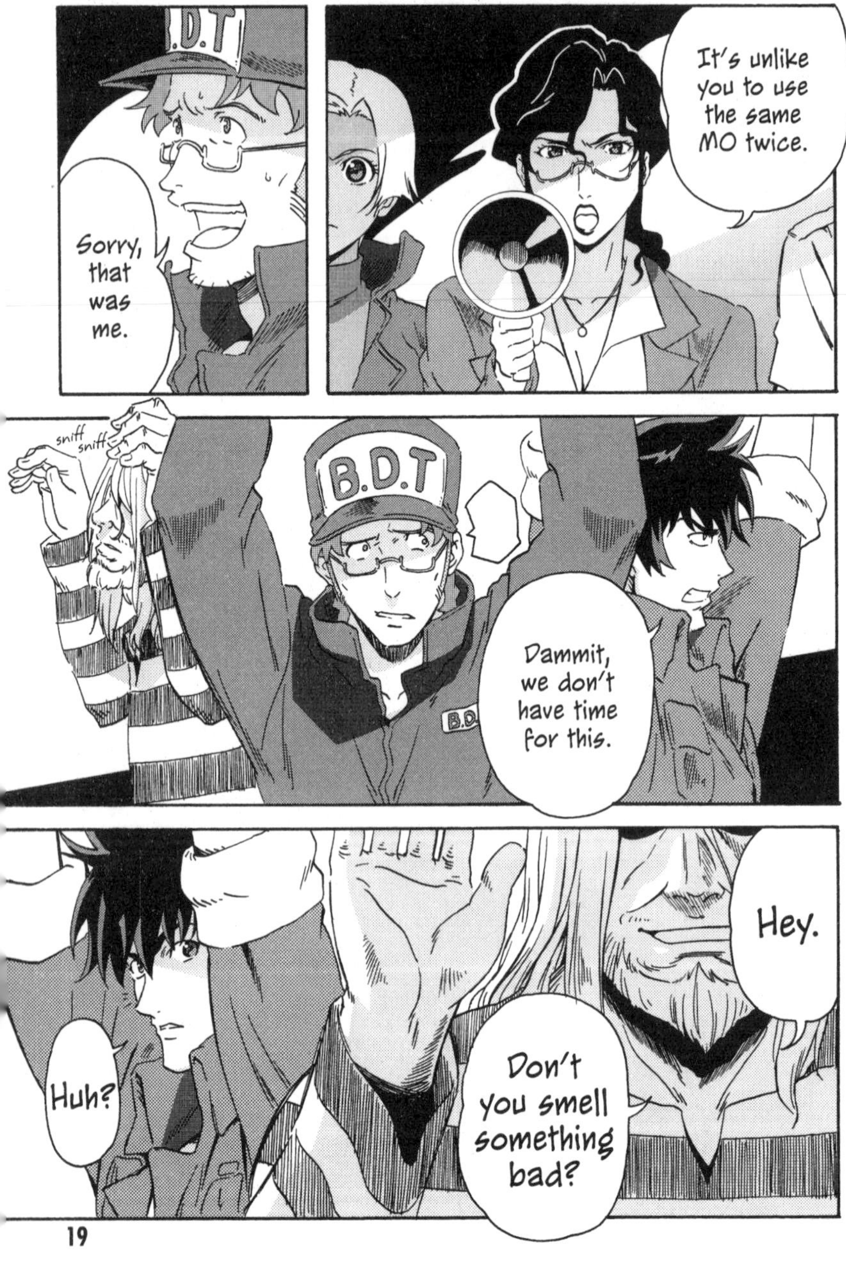
It's unlike you to use the same MO twice.
Sorry, that was me.
sniff sniff
Dammit, we don't have time for this.
Hey.
Don't you smell something bad?
Huh?

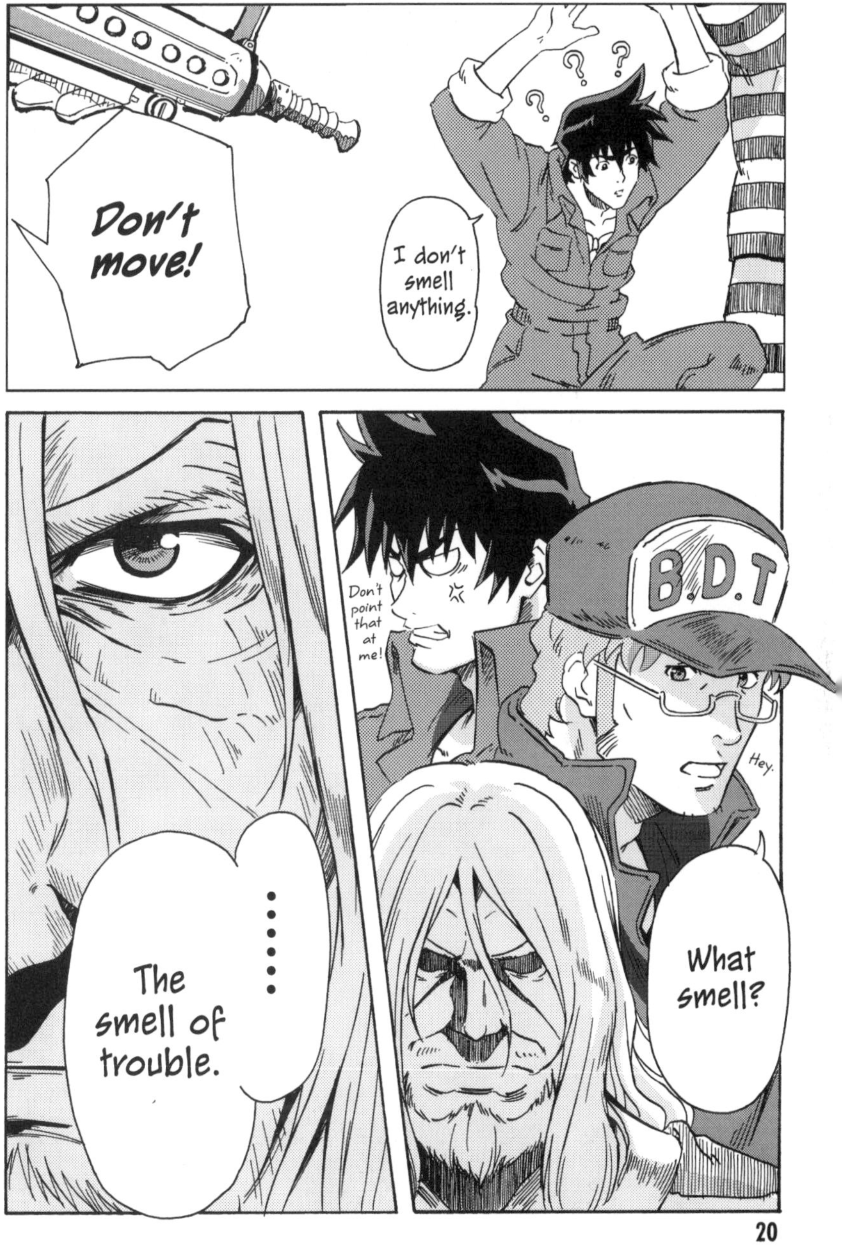
I don't smell anything.
Don't move!
Don't point that at me!
Hey.
What smell?
...... The smell of trouble.

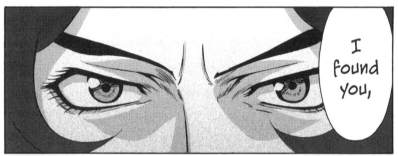

I found you,

MISTER!

21

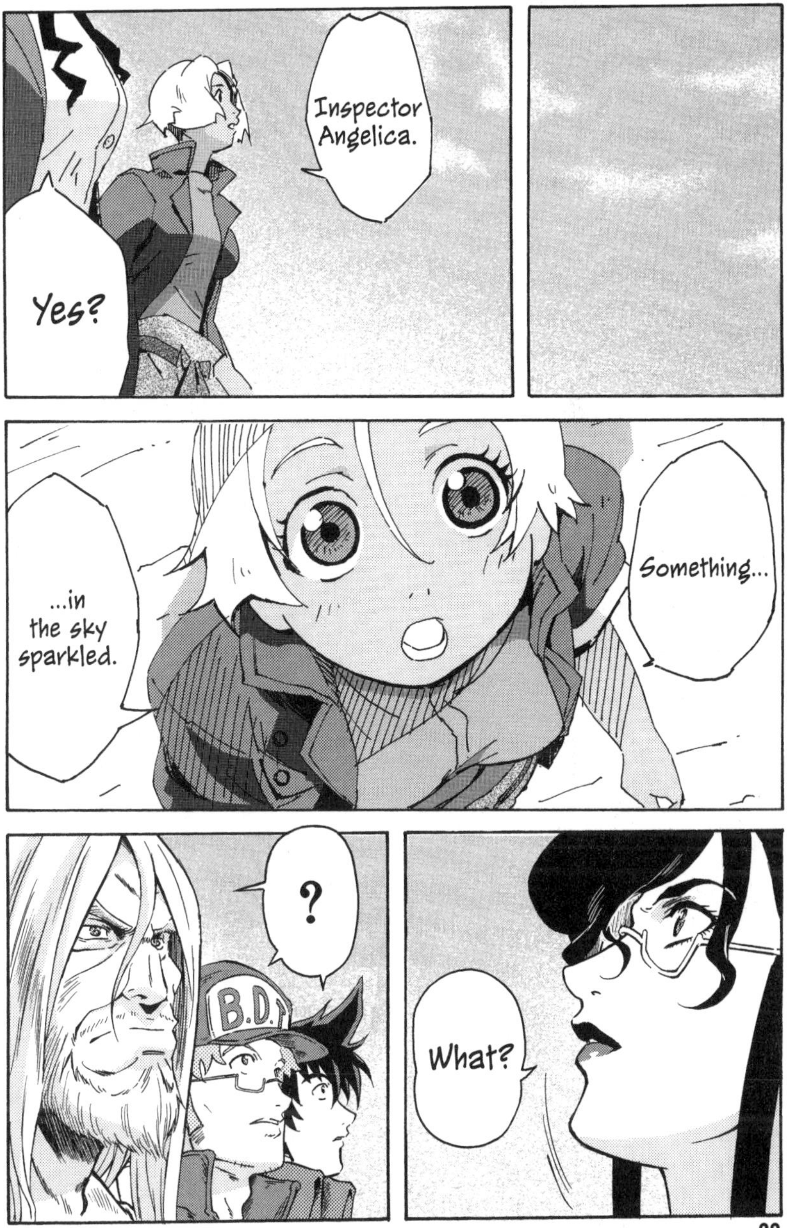
Inspector Angelica.
Yes?
Something...
...in the sky sparkled.
What?
?

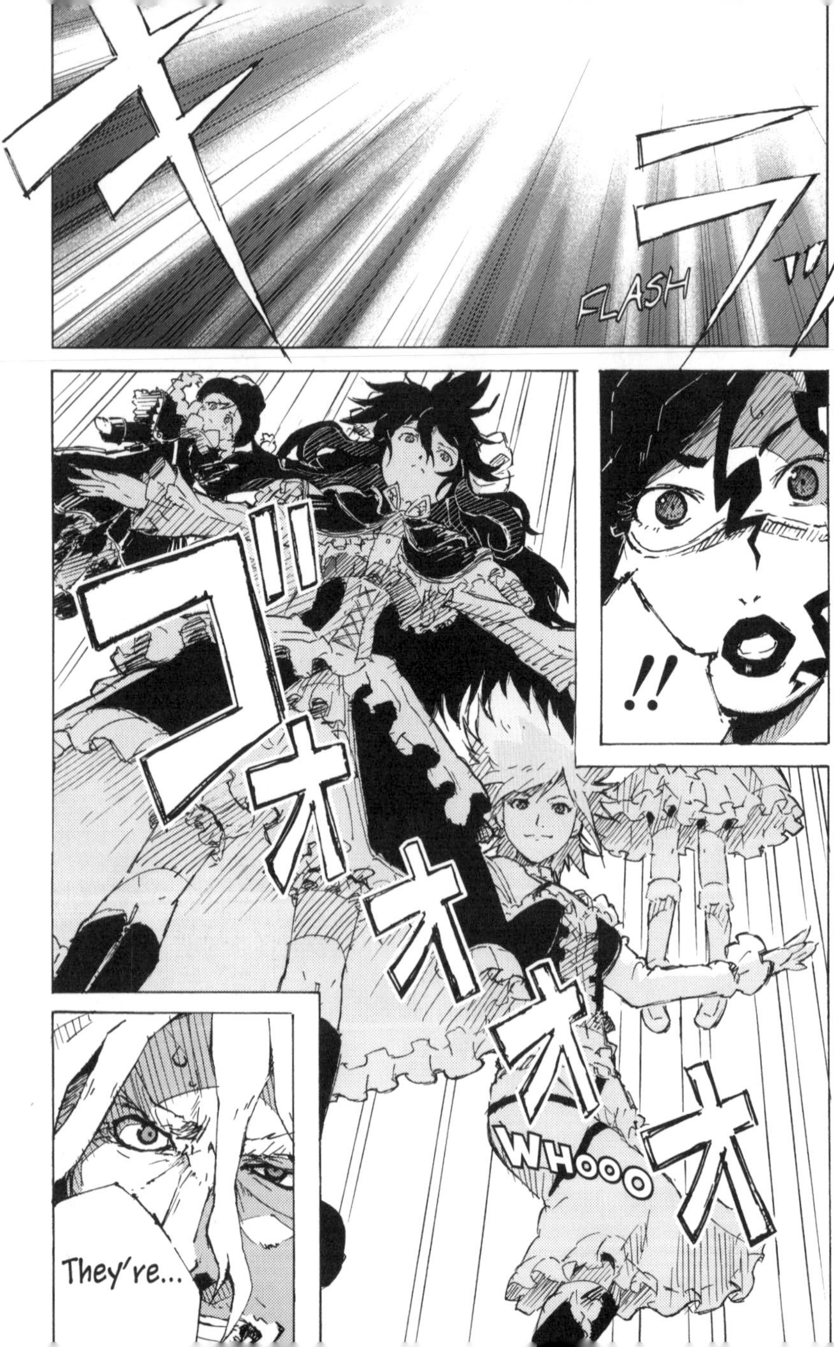

FLASH
!!
WHOOOO
They're...

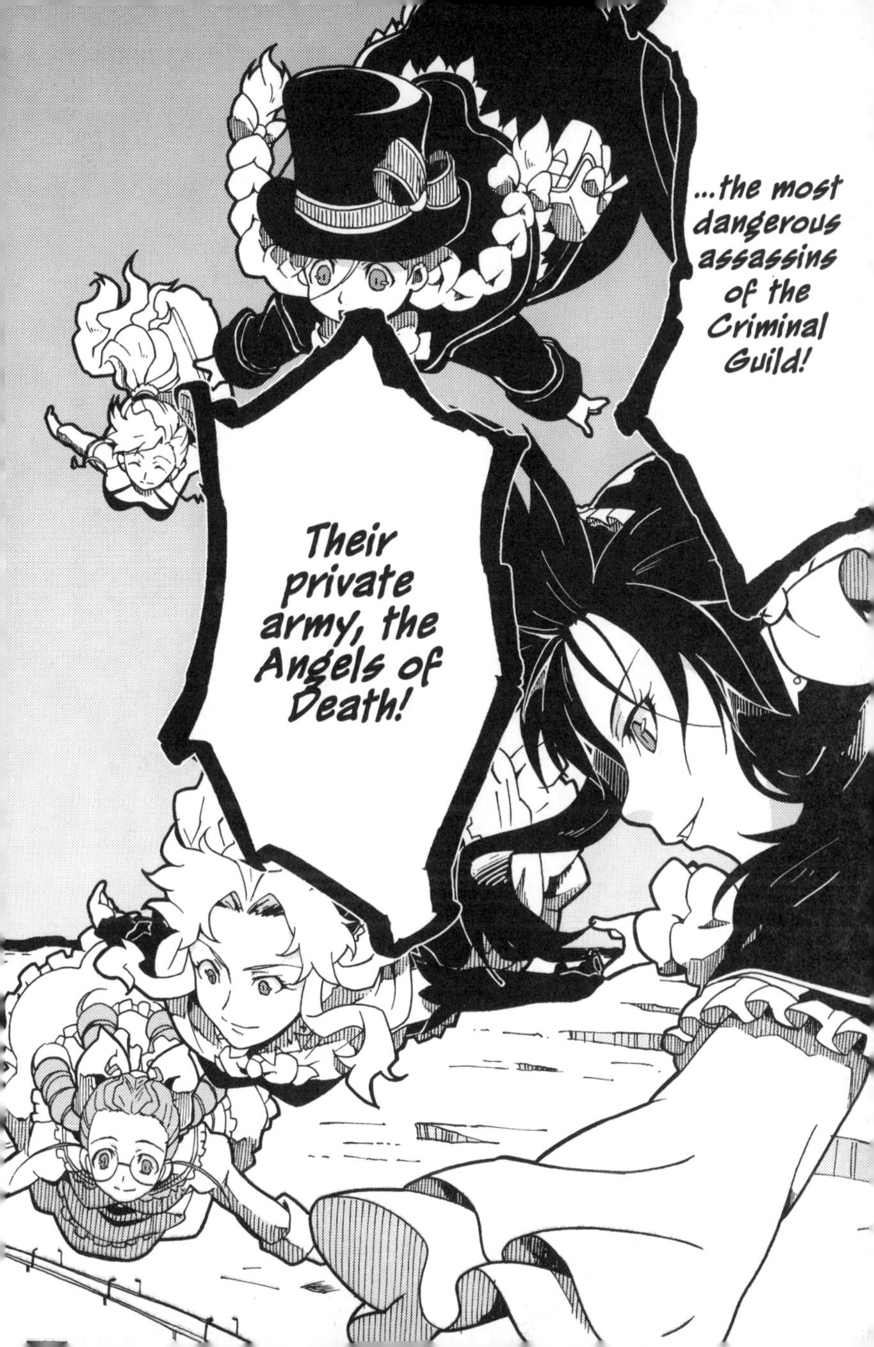
...the most dangerous assassins of the Criminal Guild!
Their private army, the Angels of Death!

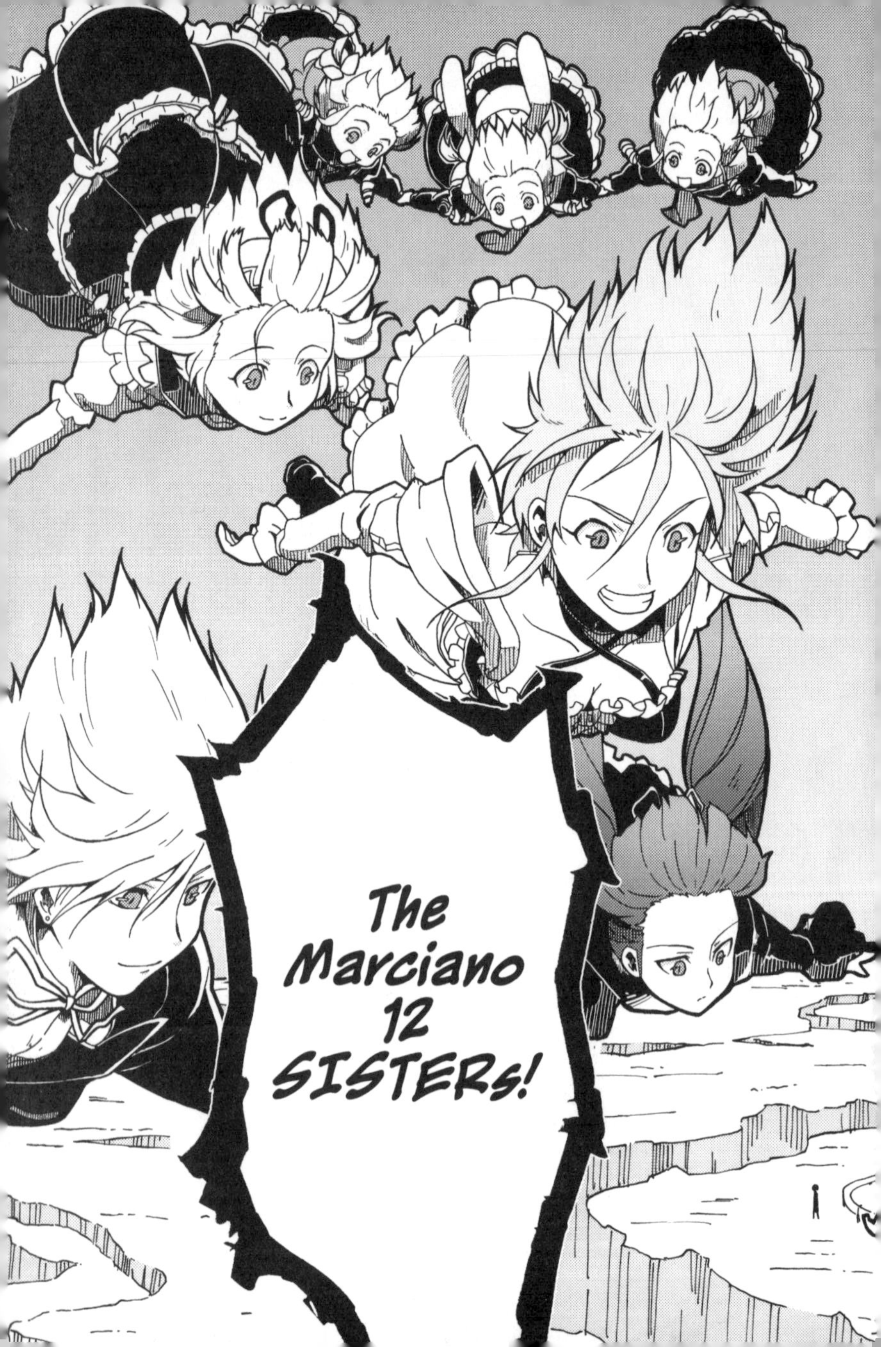
The Marciano 12 SISTERs!

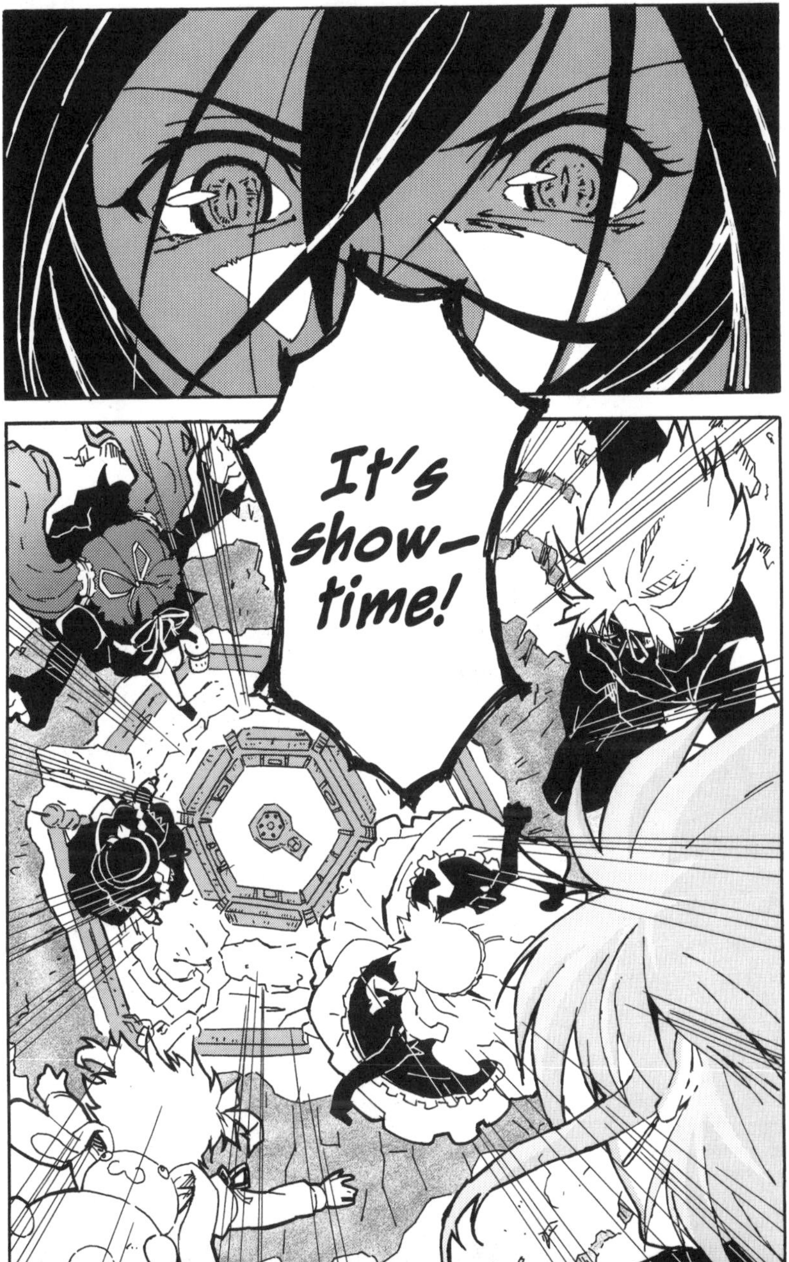
It's show-time!

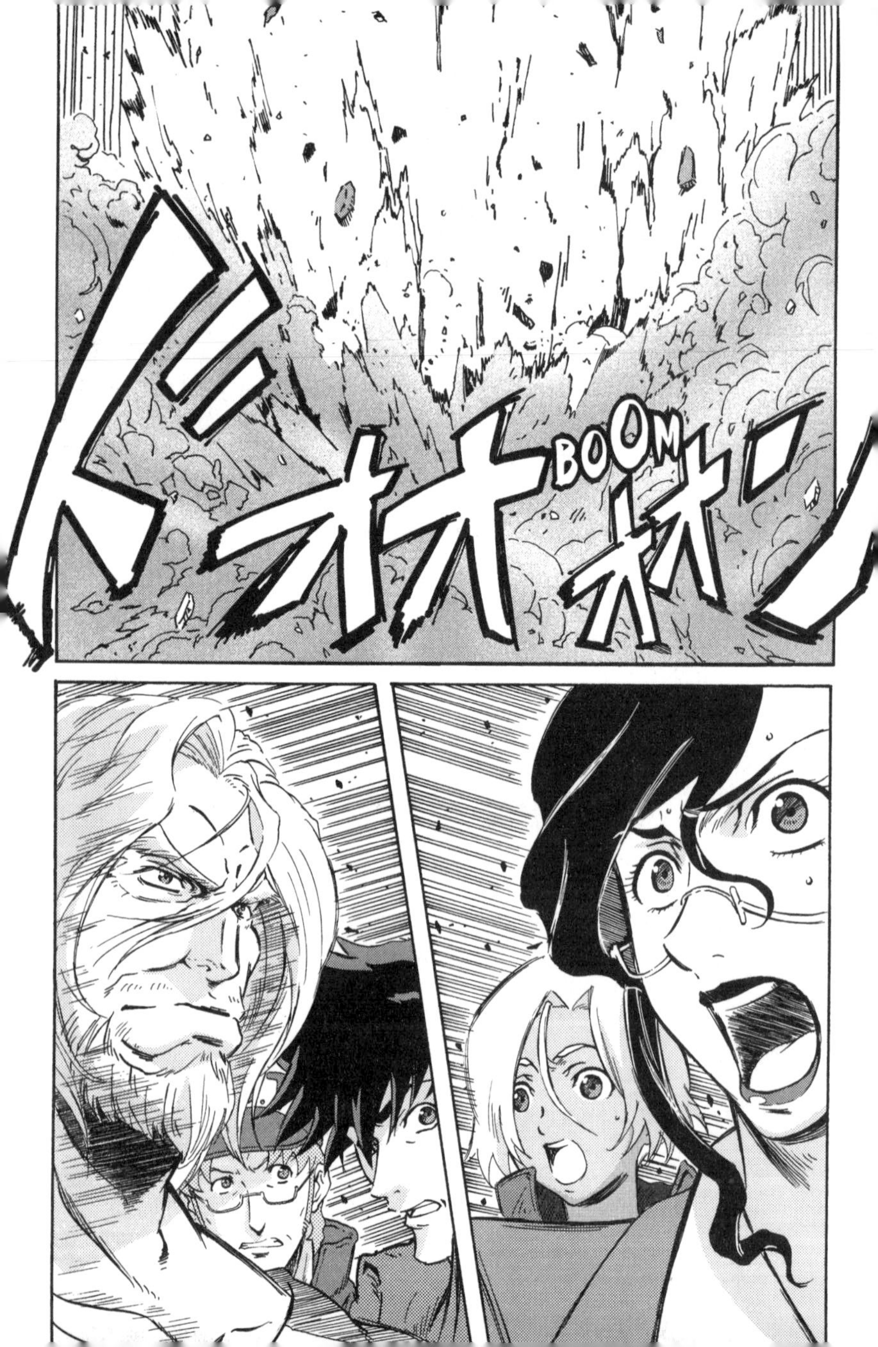
ドオオオン
BOOM

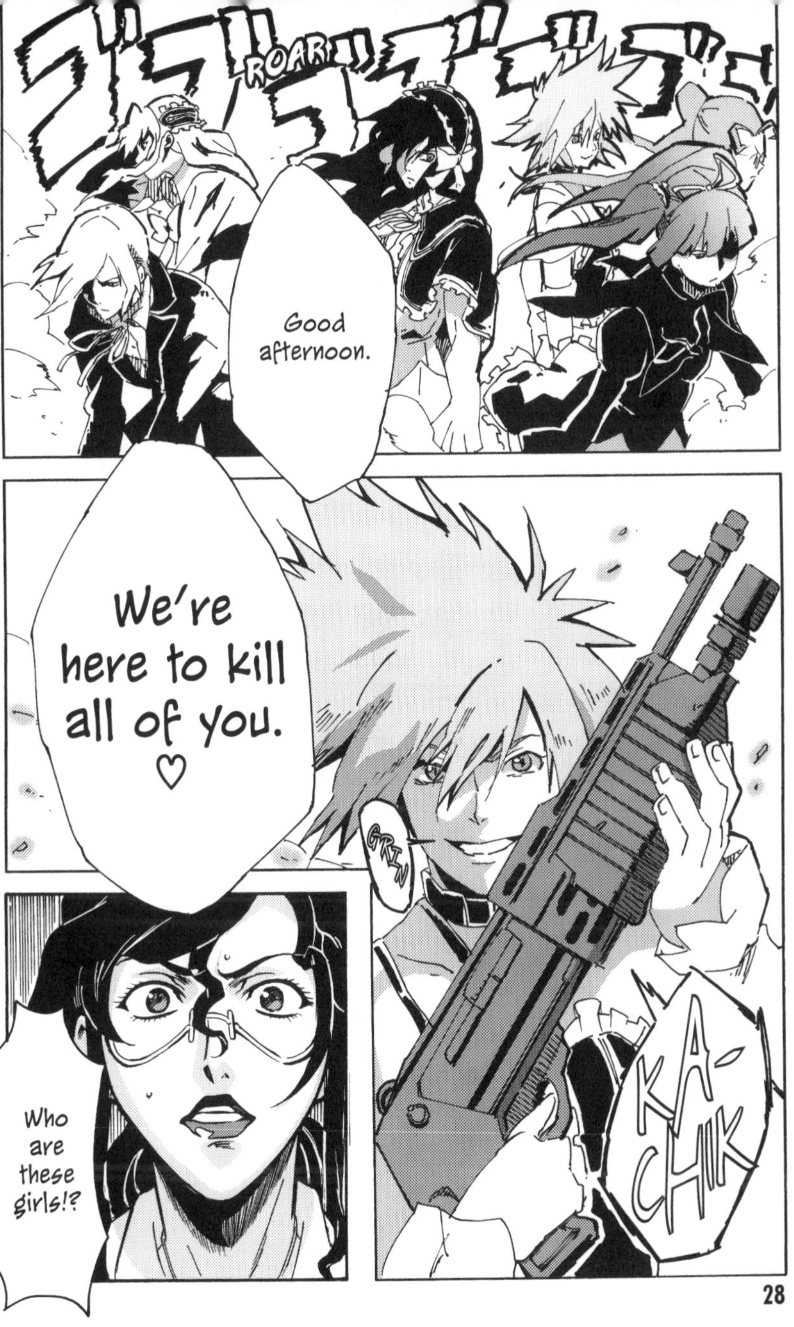
ROAR
Good afternoon.
We're here to kill all of you. ♡
GRIN
KA-CHIK
Who are these girls!?

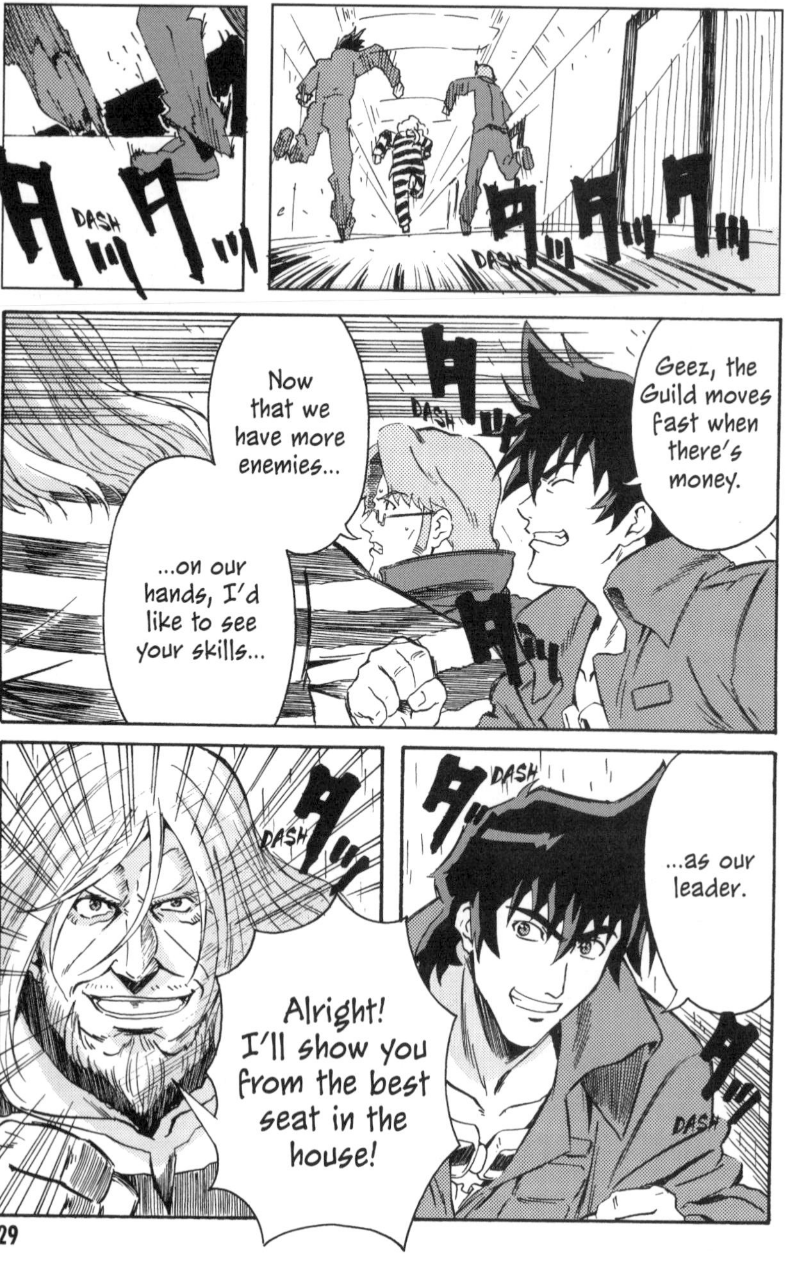
DASH
DASH
Geez, the Guild moves fast when there's money.
Now that we have more enemies...
DASH
...on our hands, I'd like to see your skills...
DASH
...as our leader.
DASH
DASH
Alright! I'll show you from the best seat in the house!

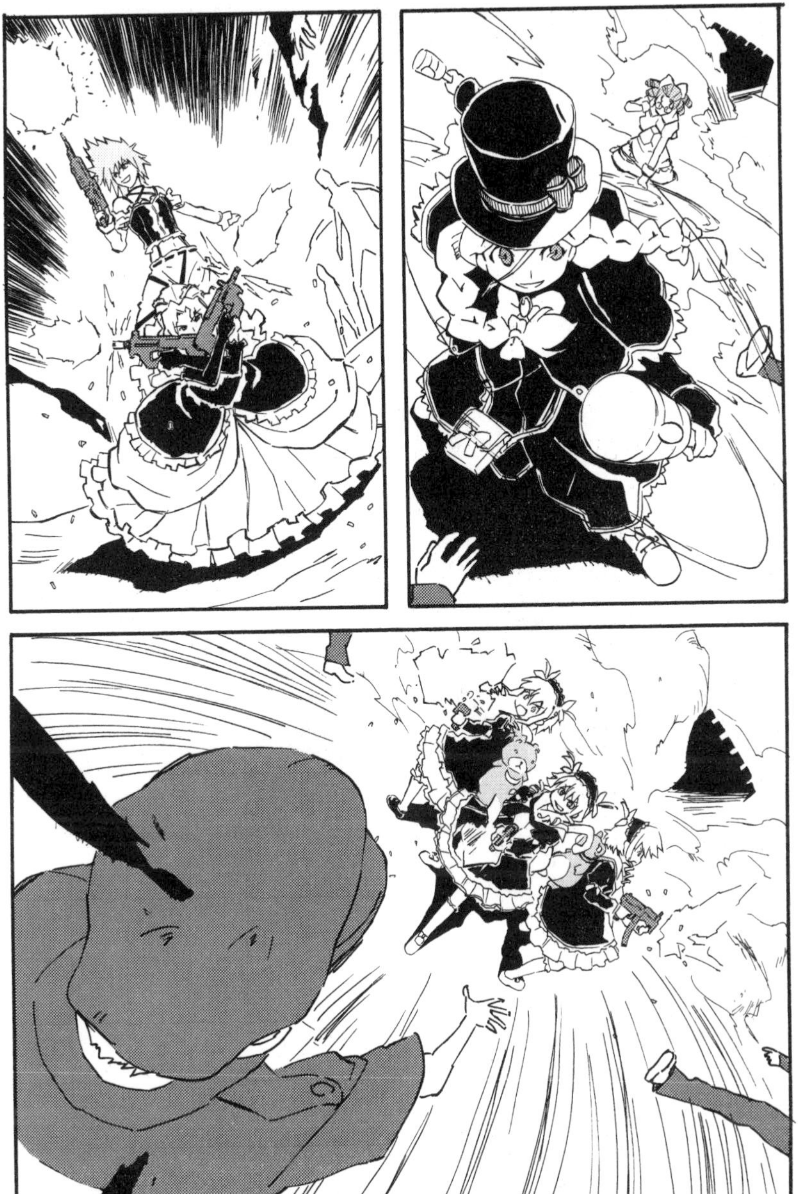

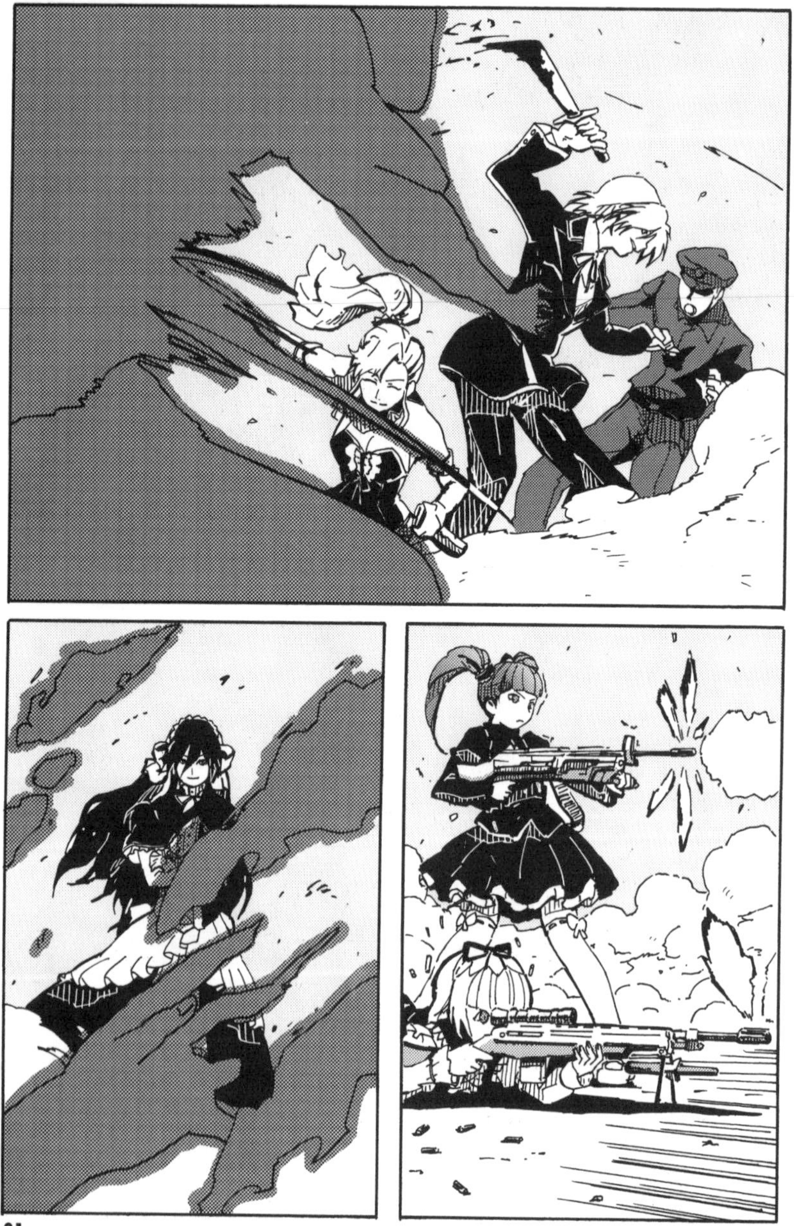

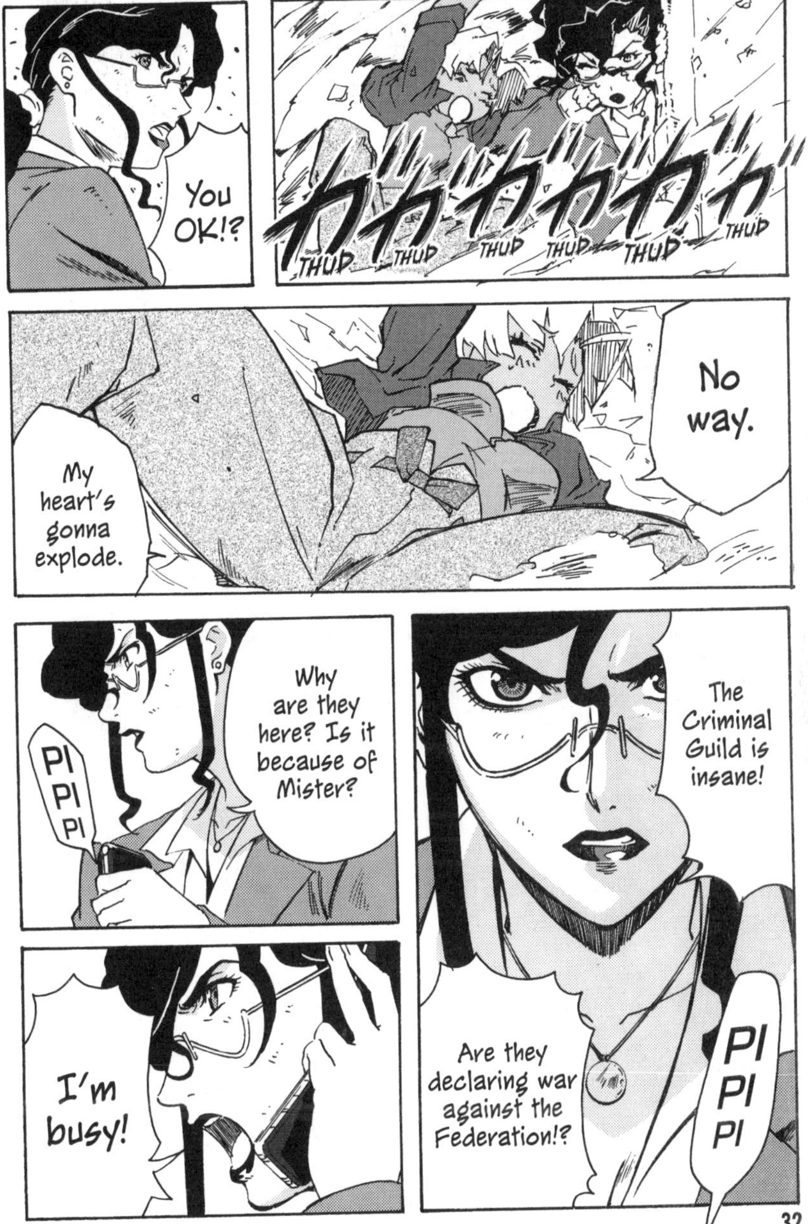
THUD THUD THUD THUD THUD THUD
You OK!?
No way.
My heart's gonna explode.
The Criminal Guild is insane!
Are they declaring war against the Federation!?
PI PI PI
Why are they here? Is it because of Mister?
PI PI PI
I'm busy!

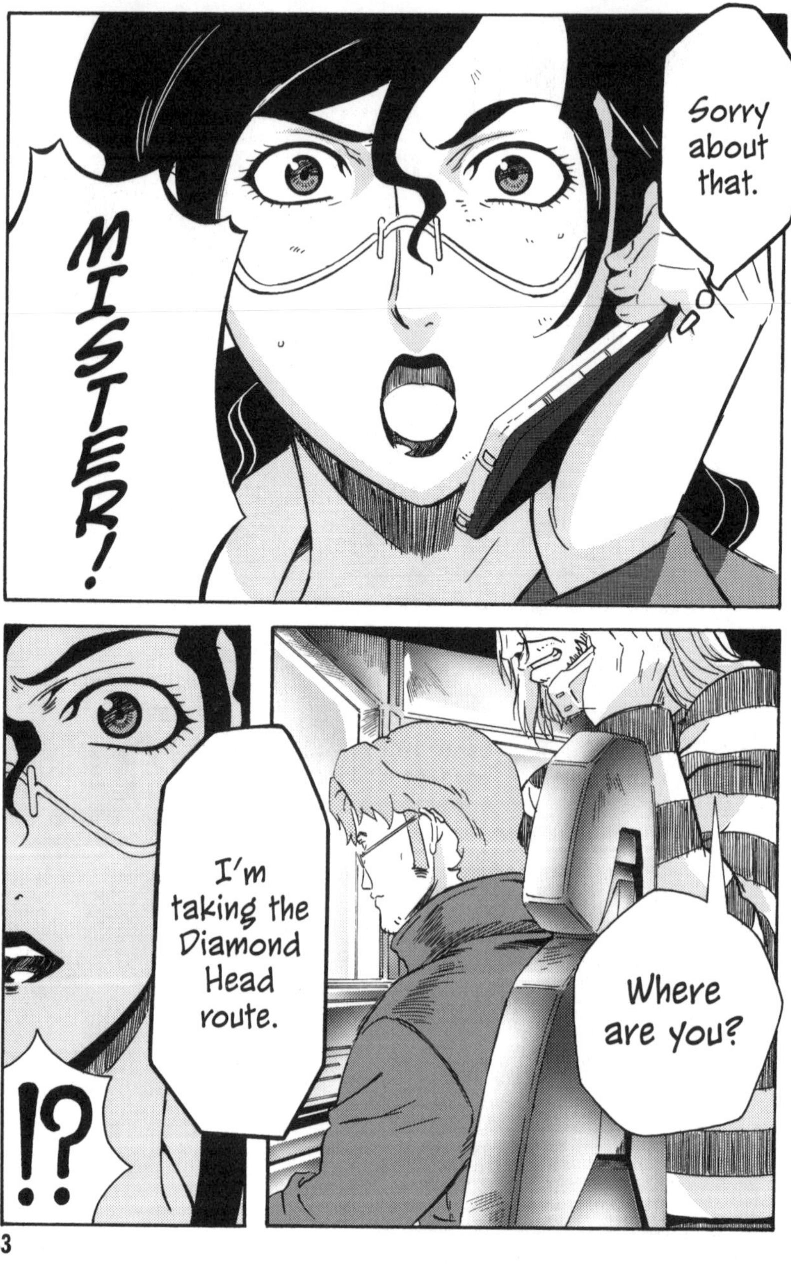
Sorry about that.
MISTER!
Where are you?
I'm taking the Diamond Head route.
!?

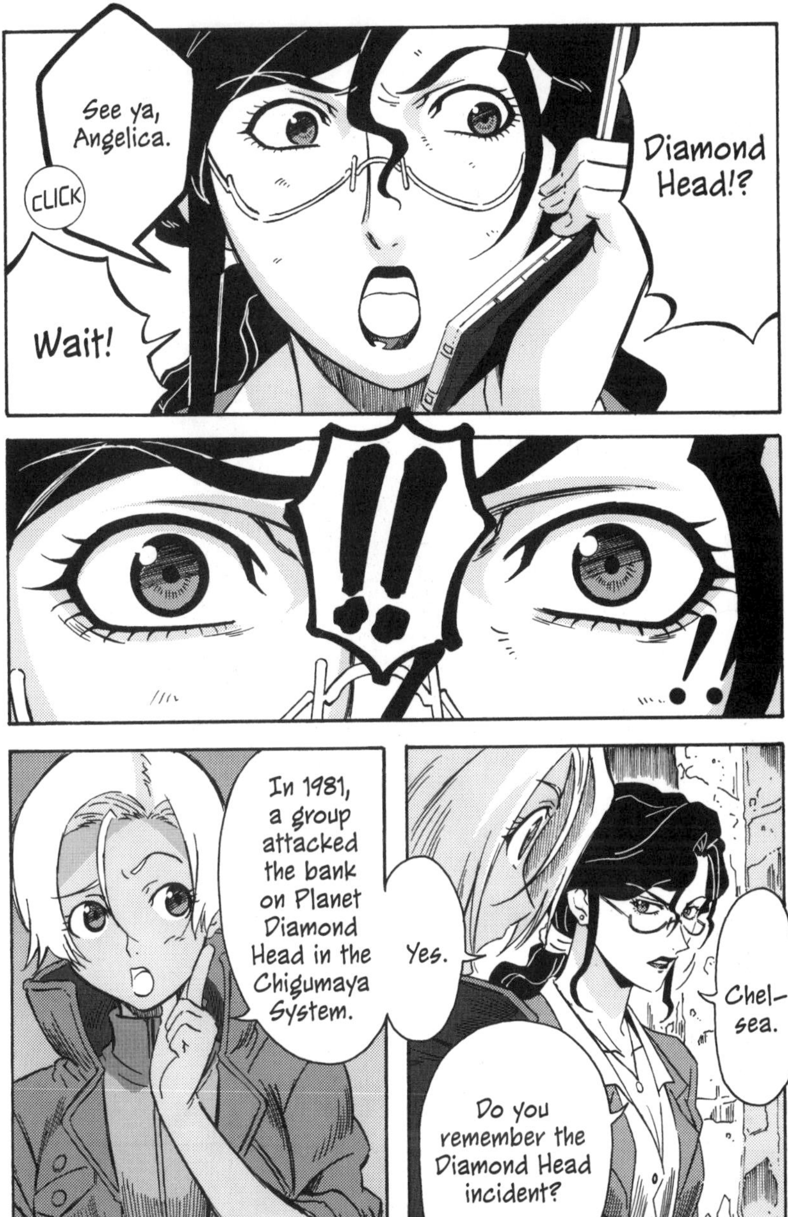
Diamond Head!?
See ya, Angelica.
CLICK
Wait!
!!
!..
Chel-sea.
Do you remember the Diamond Head incident?
Yes.
In 1981, a group attacked the bank on Planet Diamond Head in the Chigumaya System.

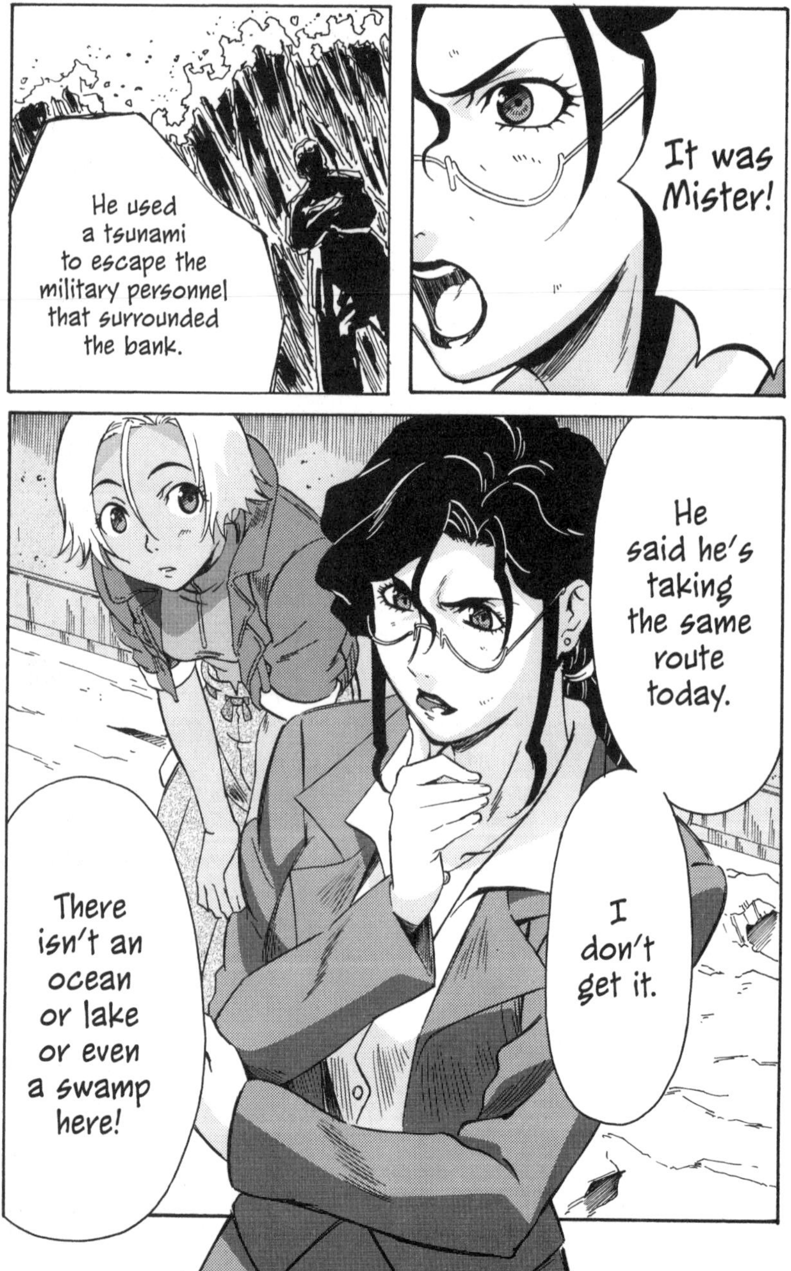
It was Mister!
He used a tsunami to escape the military personnel that surrounded the bank.
He said he's taking the same route today.
I don't get it.
There isn't an ocean or lake or even a swamp here!

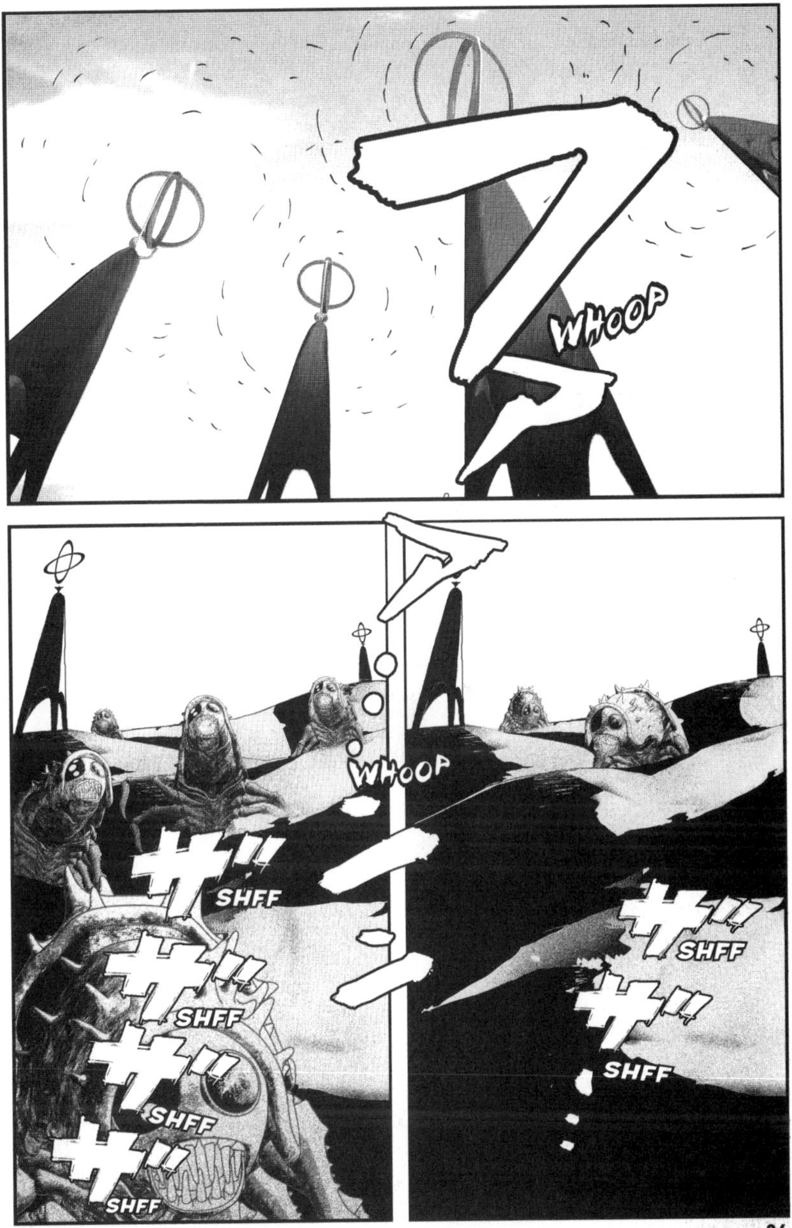
WHOOP
SHFF
SHFF
WHOOP
SHFF
SHFF
SHFF
SHFF

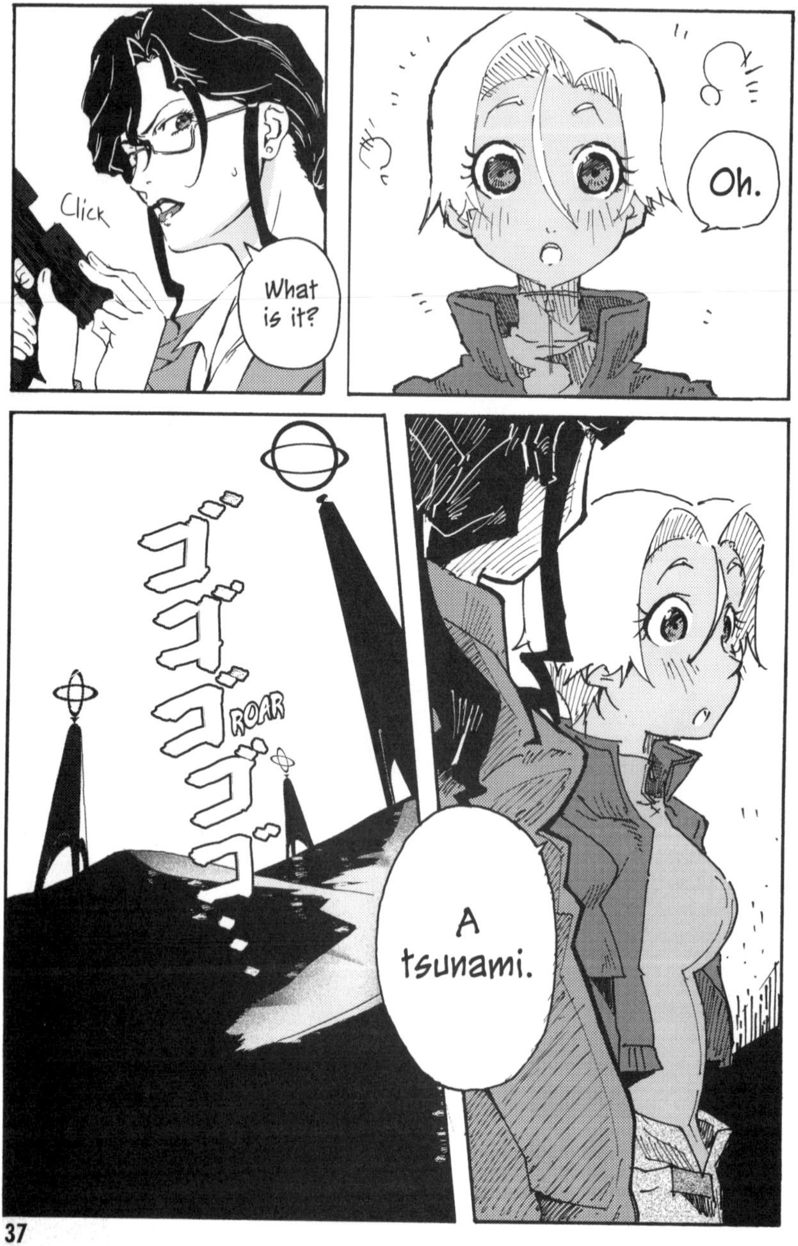
Oh.
Click
What is it?
A tsunami.
ROAR

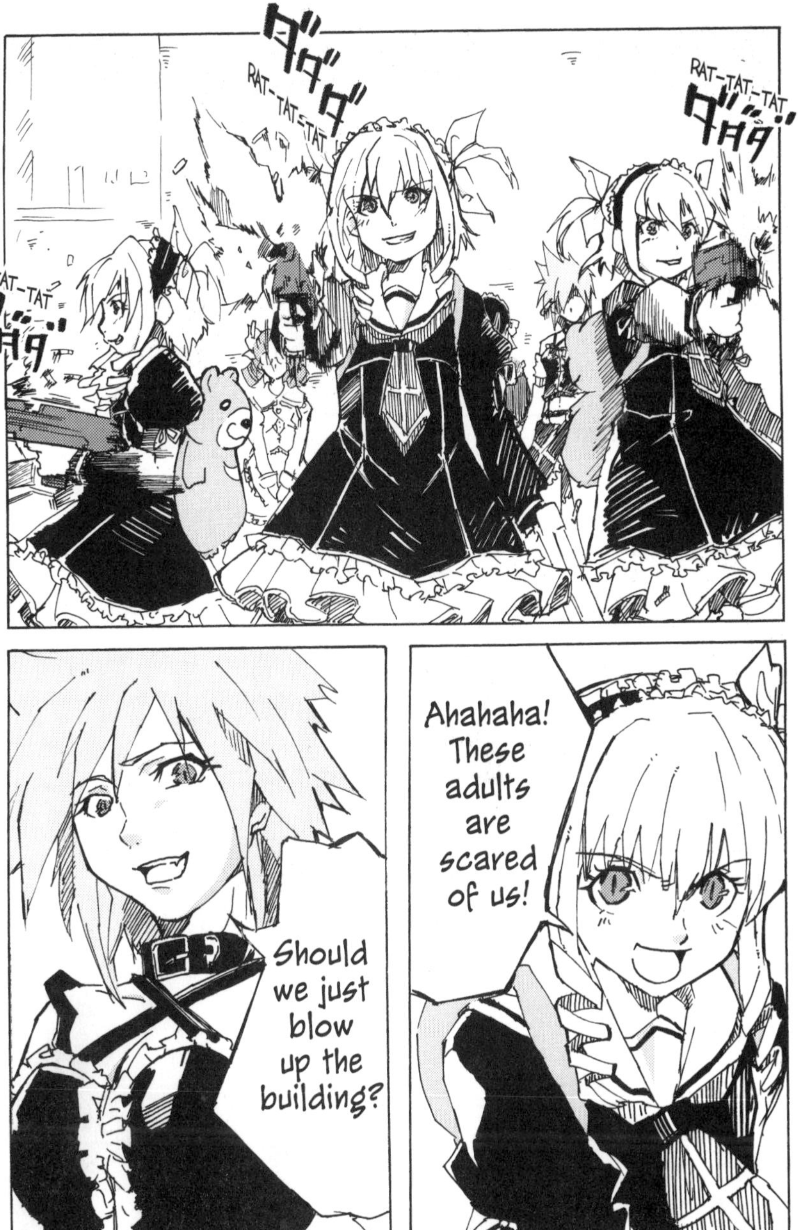
RAT-TAT-TAT
ダダダ
ダダダ
RAT-TAT-TAT
T-TAT-TAT
ダダダ
Ahahaha! These adults are scared of us!
Should we just blow up the building?

You can't find the target yet?

No.

Human data patterns are incomplete, so it takes awhile.

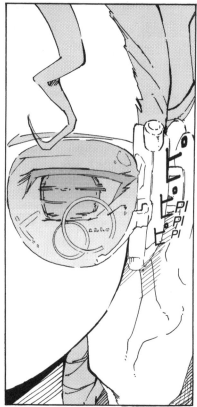

PI
PI
PI

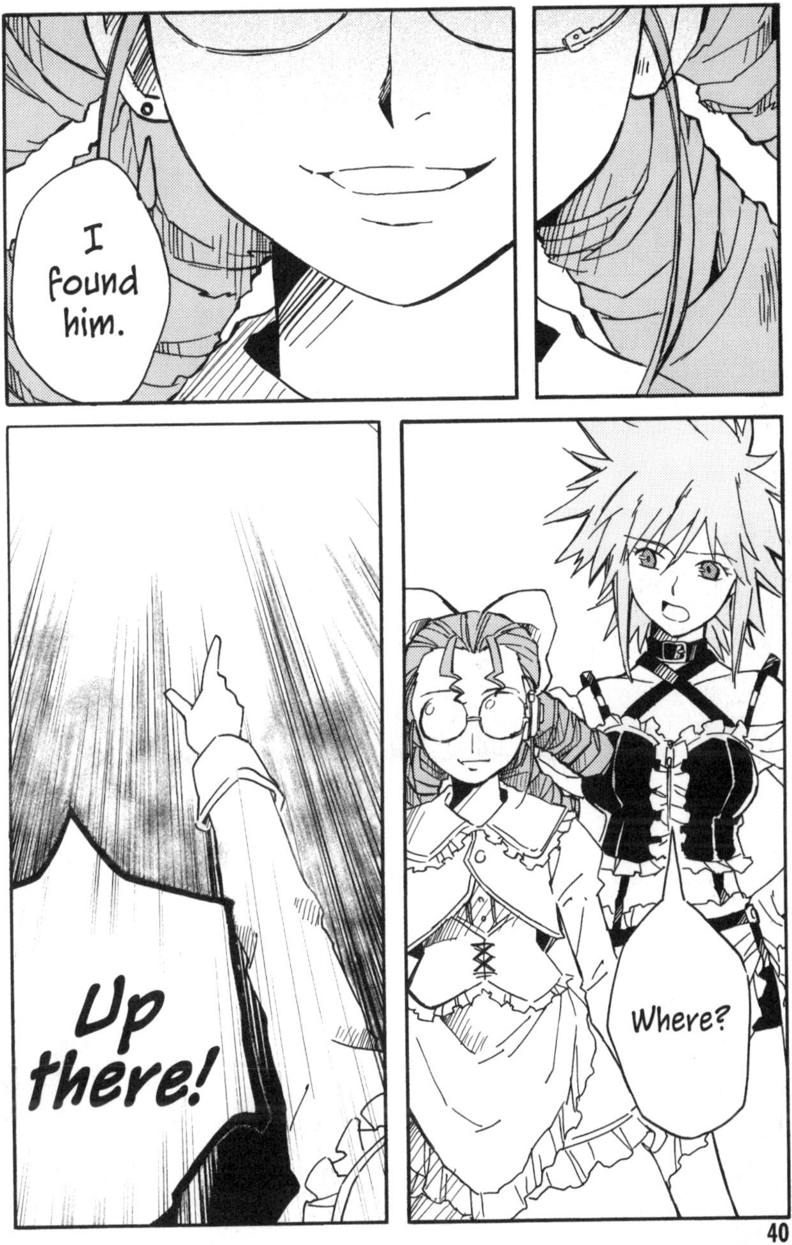
I found him.
Where?
Up there!

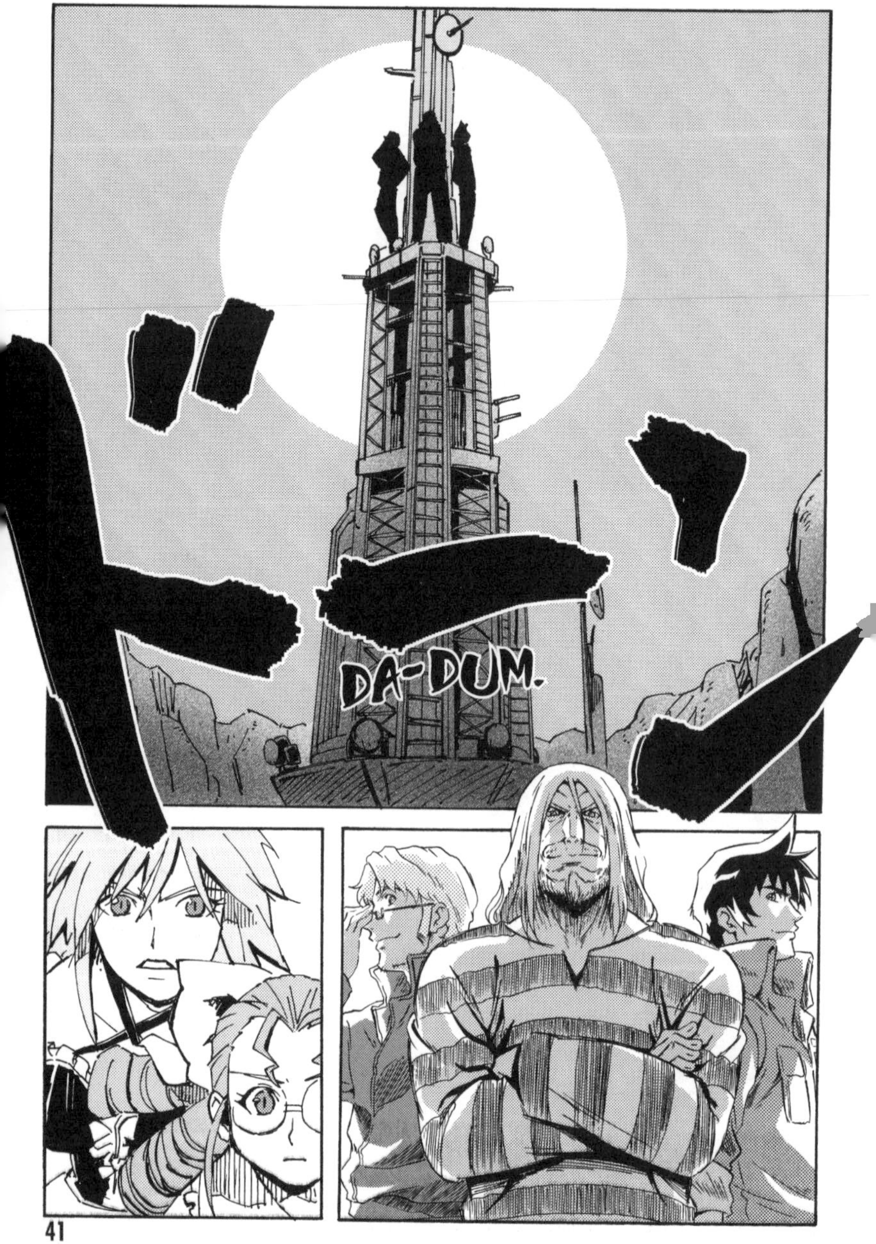
DA-DUM.

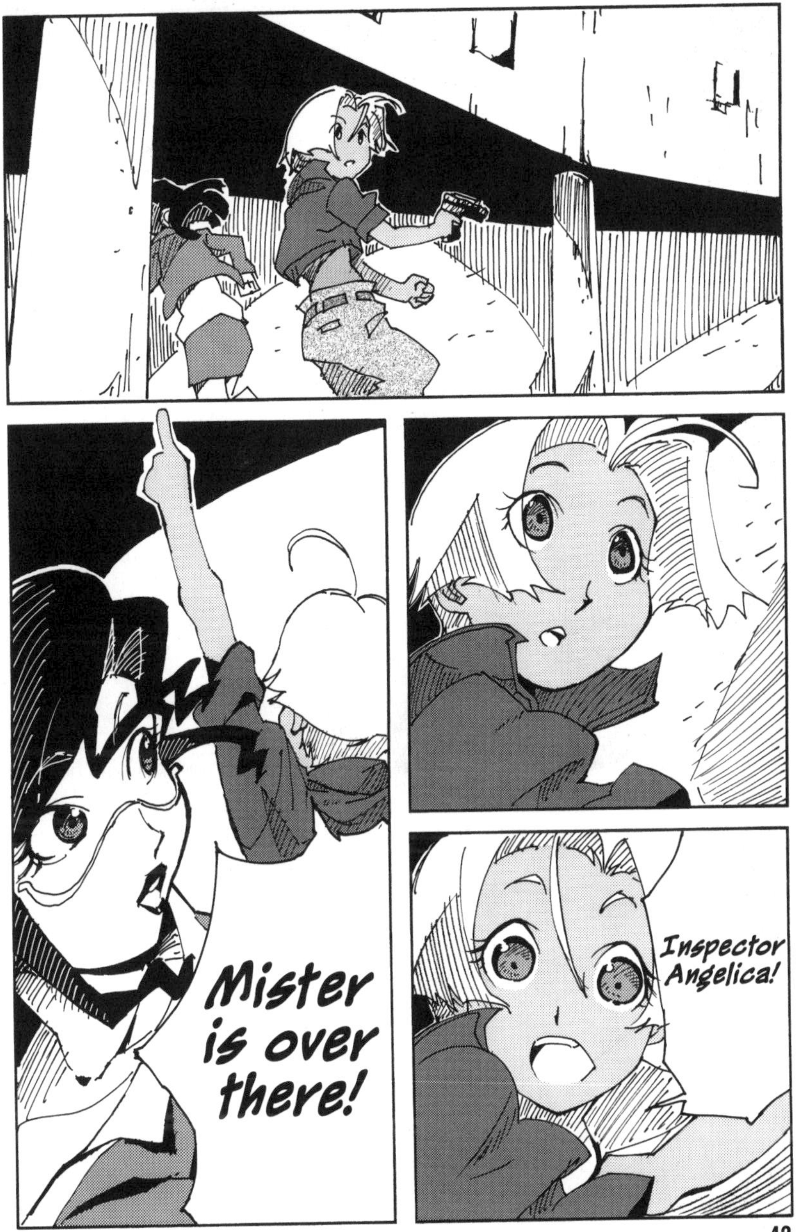
Inspector Angelica!
Mister is over there!

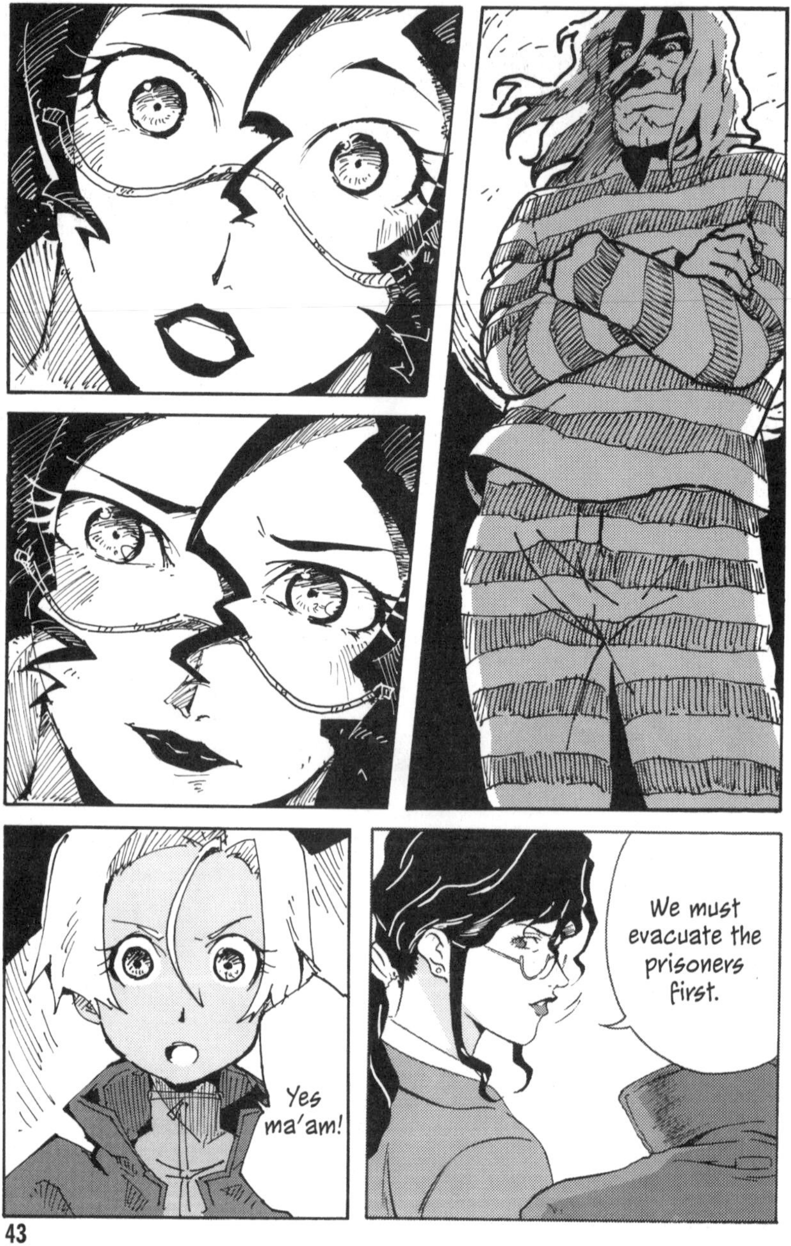
We must evacuate the prisoners first.
Yes ma'am!

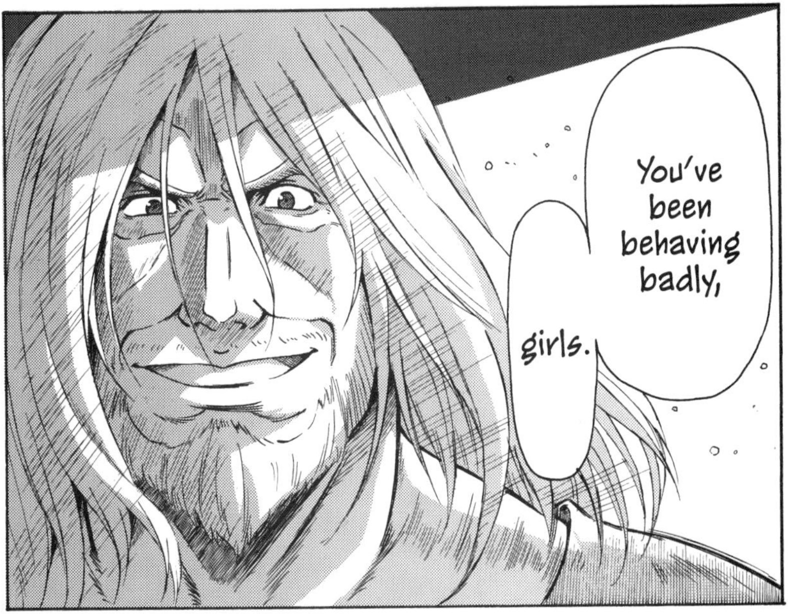
You've been behaving badly,
girls.

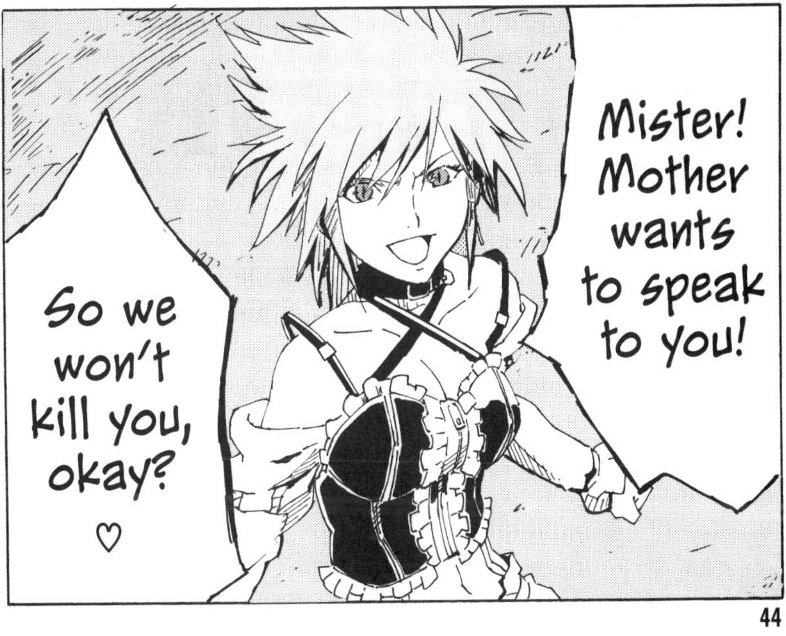
Mister! Mother wants to speak to you!
So we won't kill you, okay? ♡

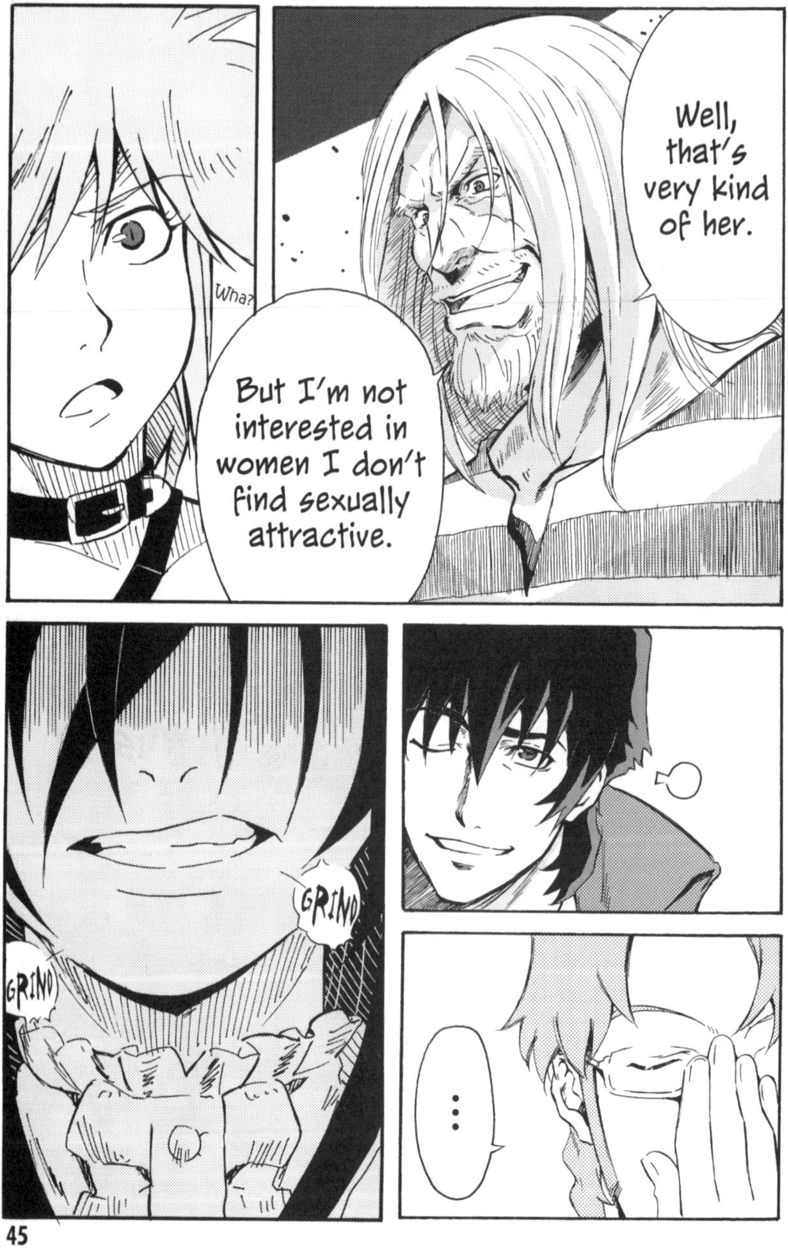
Well, that's very kind of her.
But I'm not interested in women I don't find sexually attractive.
Wha?
...
GRIND
GRIND

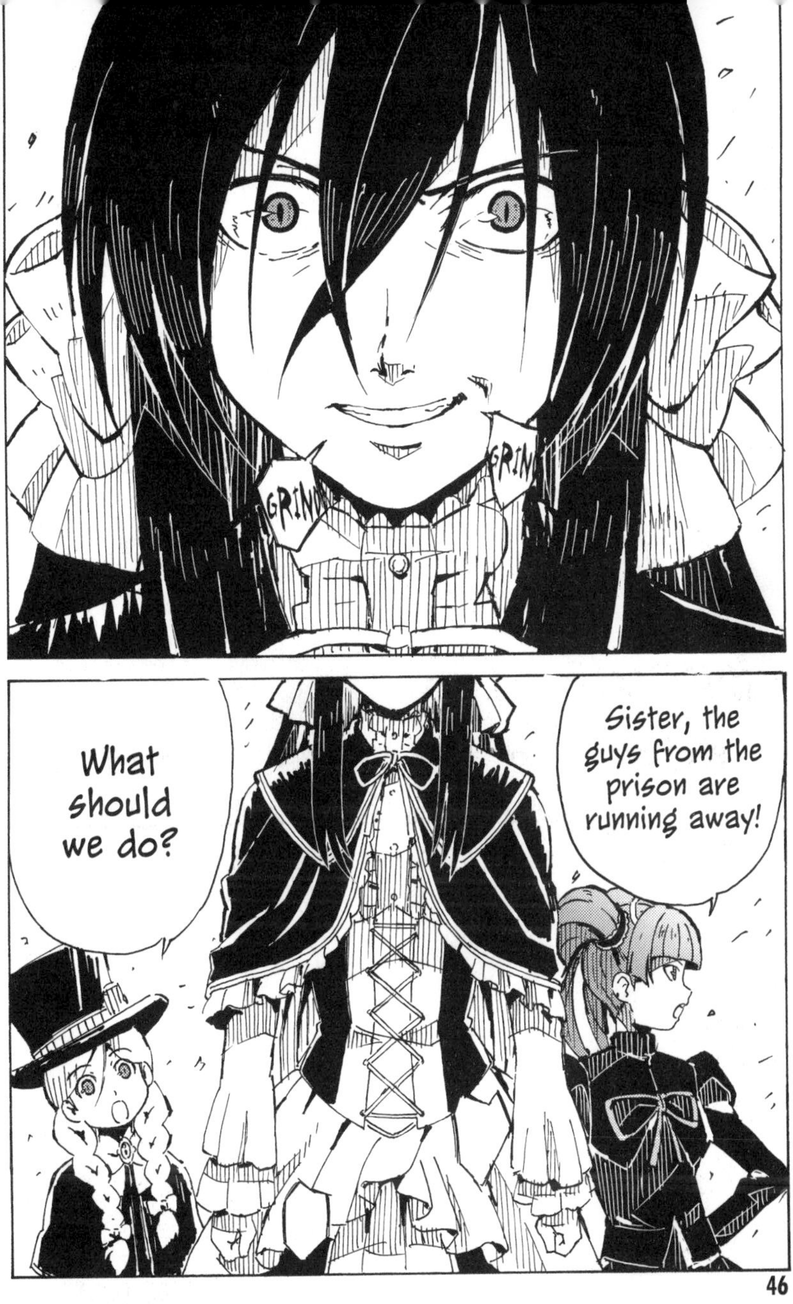
GRIN
GRIND
Sister, the guys from the prison are running away!
What should we do?

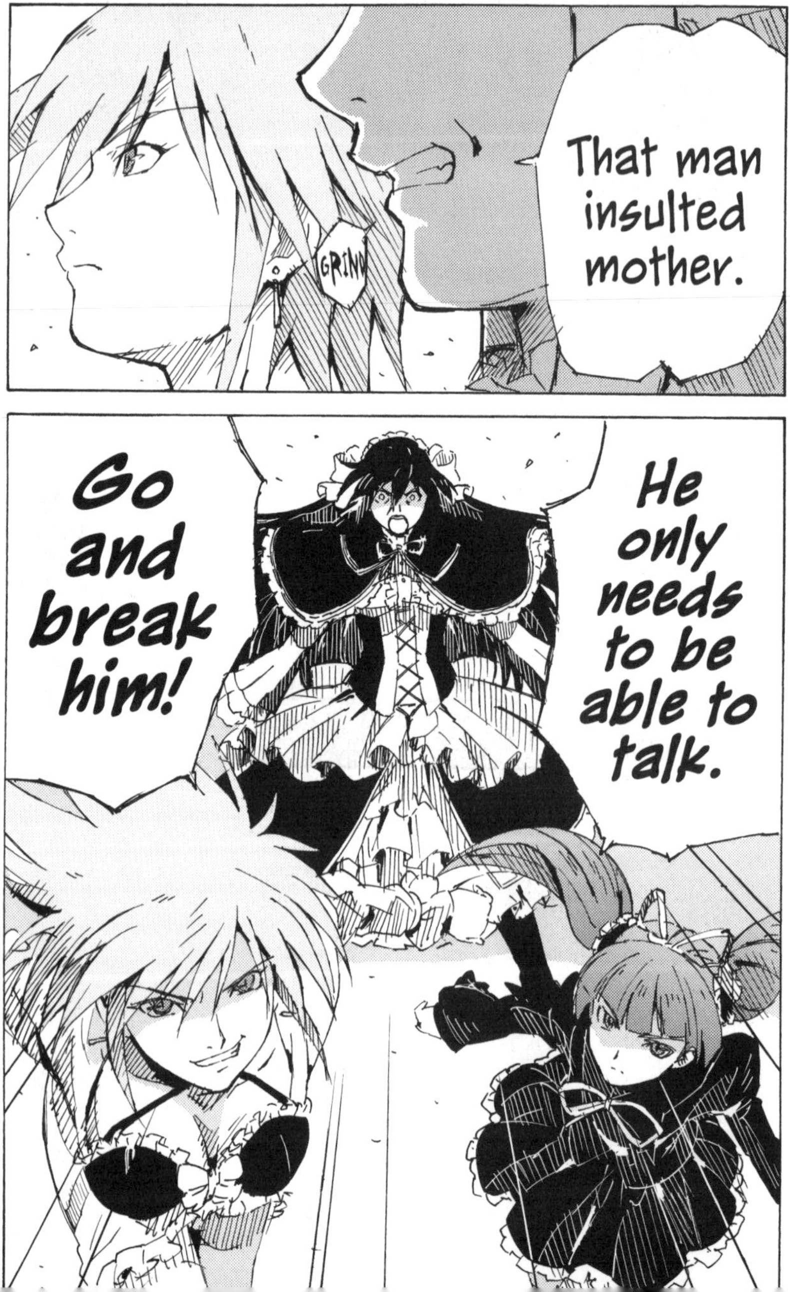
That man insulted mother.
GRIND
He only needs to be able to talk.
Go and break him!

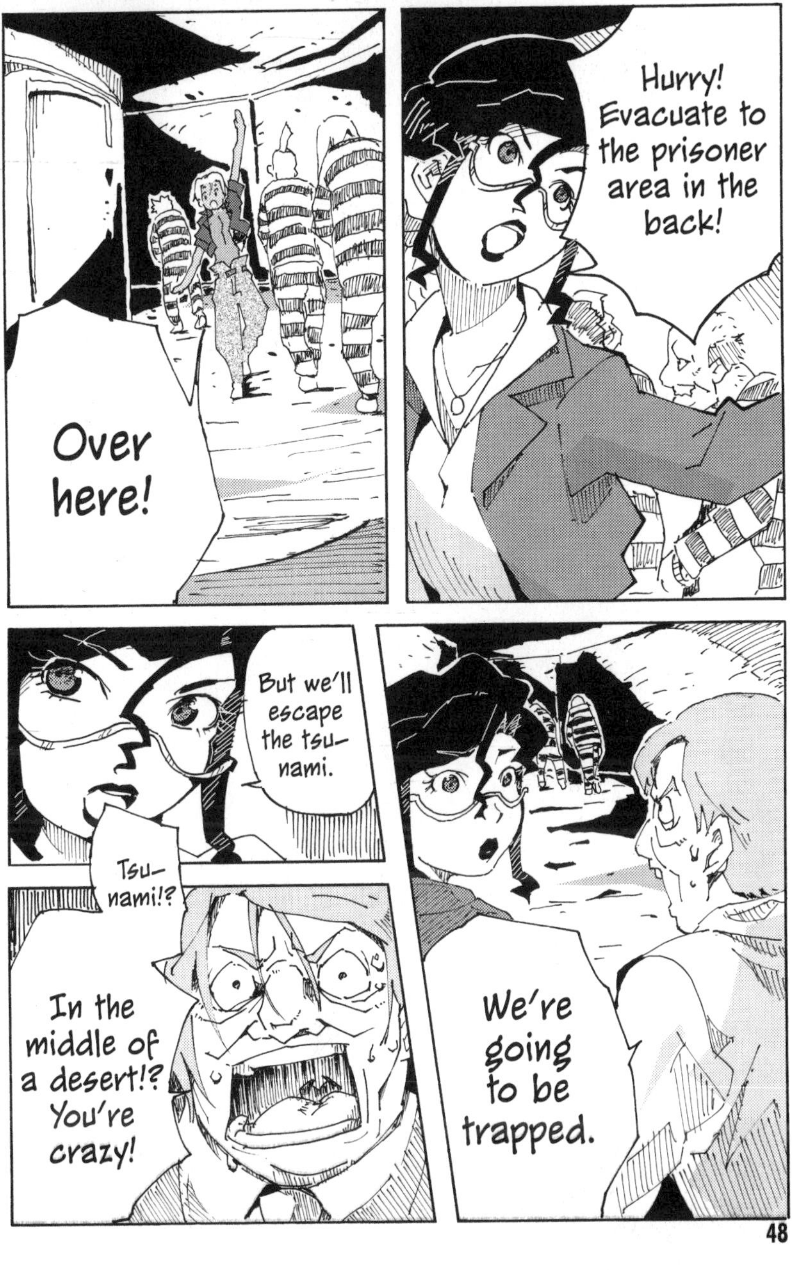
Hurry! Evacuate to the prisoner area in the back!
Over here!
We're going to be trapped.
But we'll escape the tsu-nami.
Tsu-nami!?
In the middle of a desert!? You're crazy!

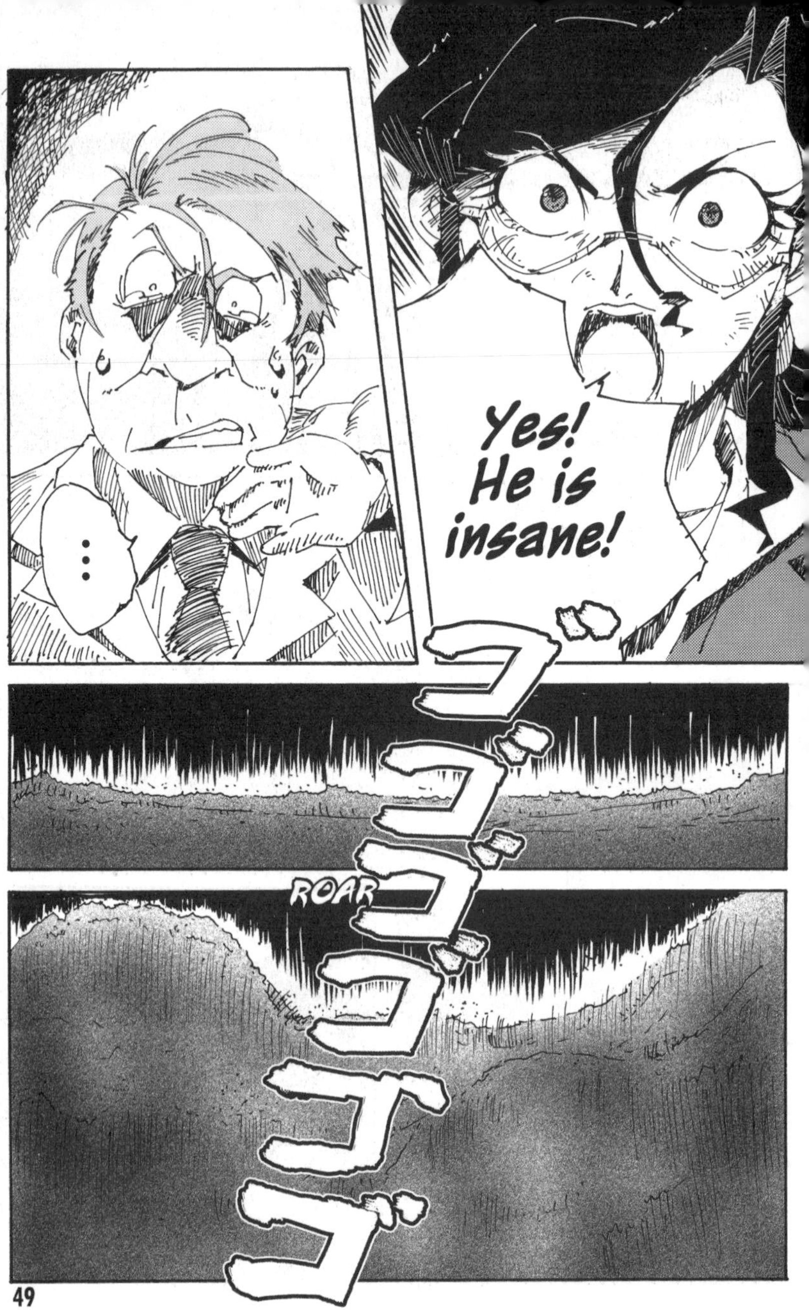
Yes! He is insane!
...
ROAR

A wave?

What was that?

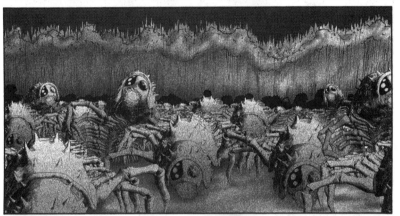

What a great show.

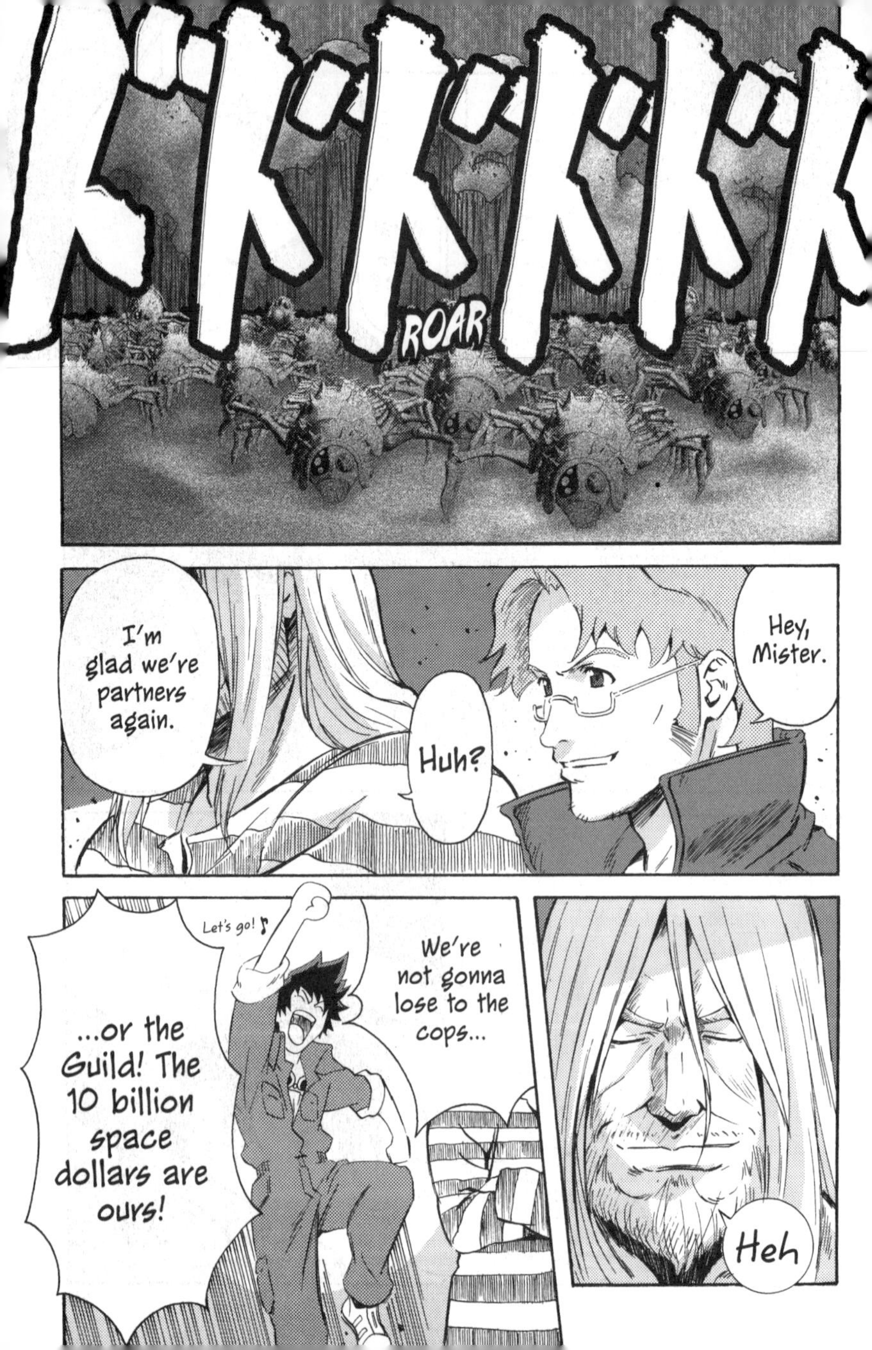
ROAR
Hey, Mister.
Huh?
I'm glad we're partners again.
Heh
We're not gonna lose to the cops...
Let's go! ♪
...or the Guild! The 10 billion space dollars are ours!

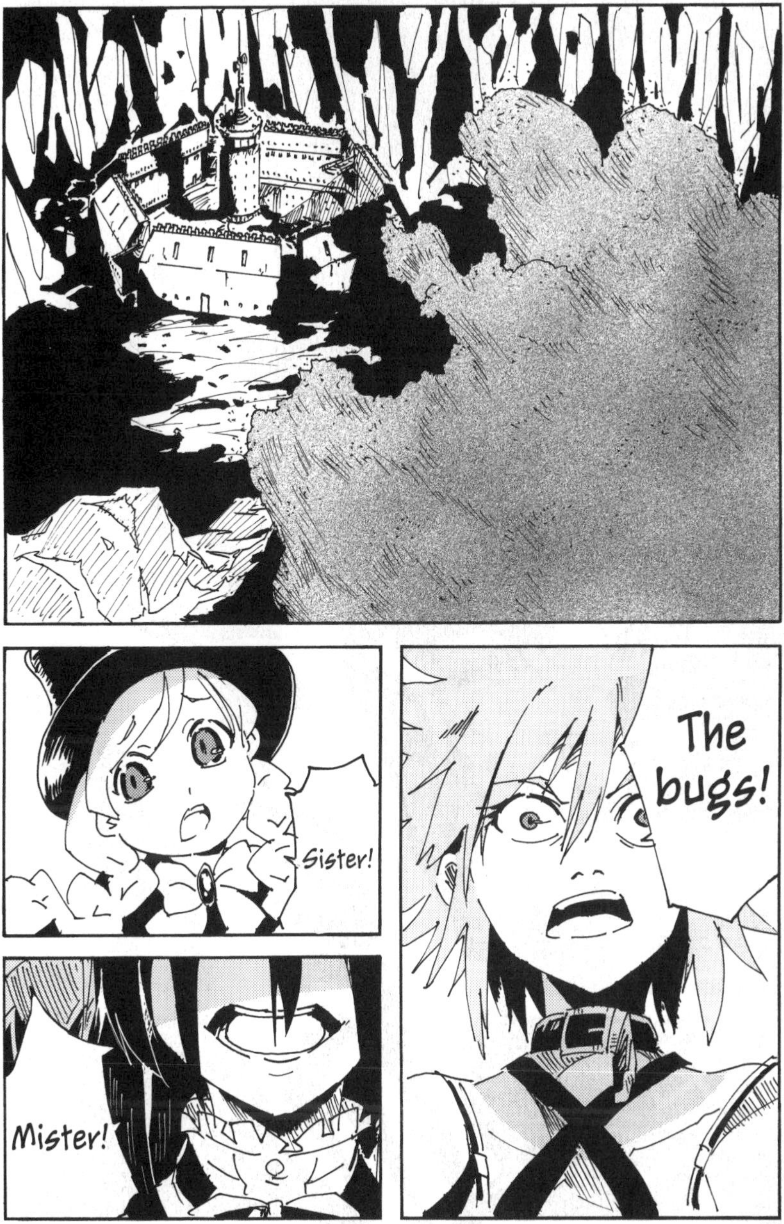
The bugs!
Sister!
Mister!

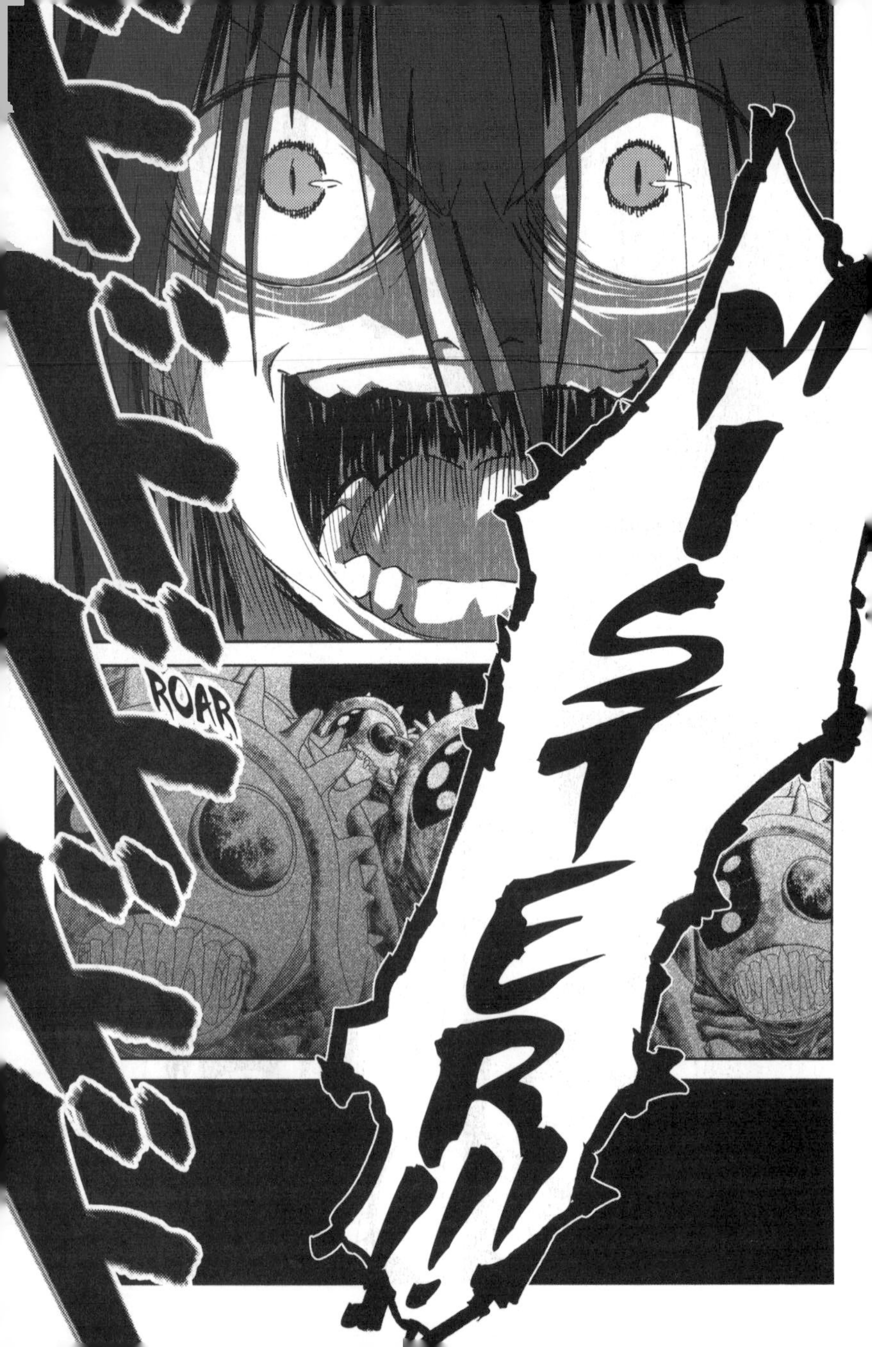
MISTER!!
ROAR

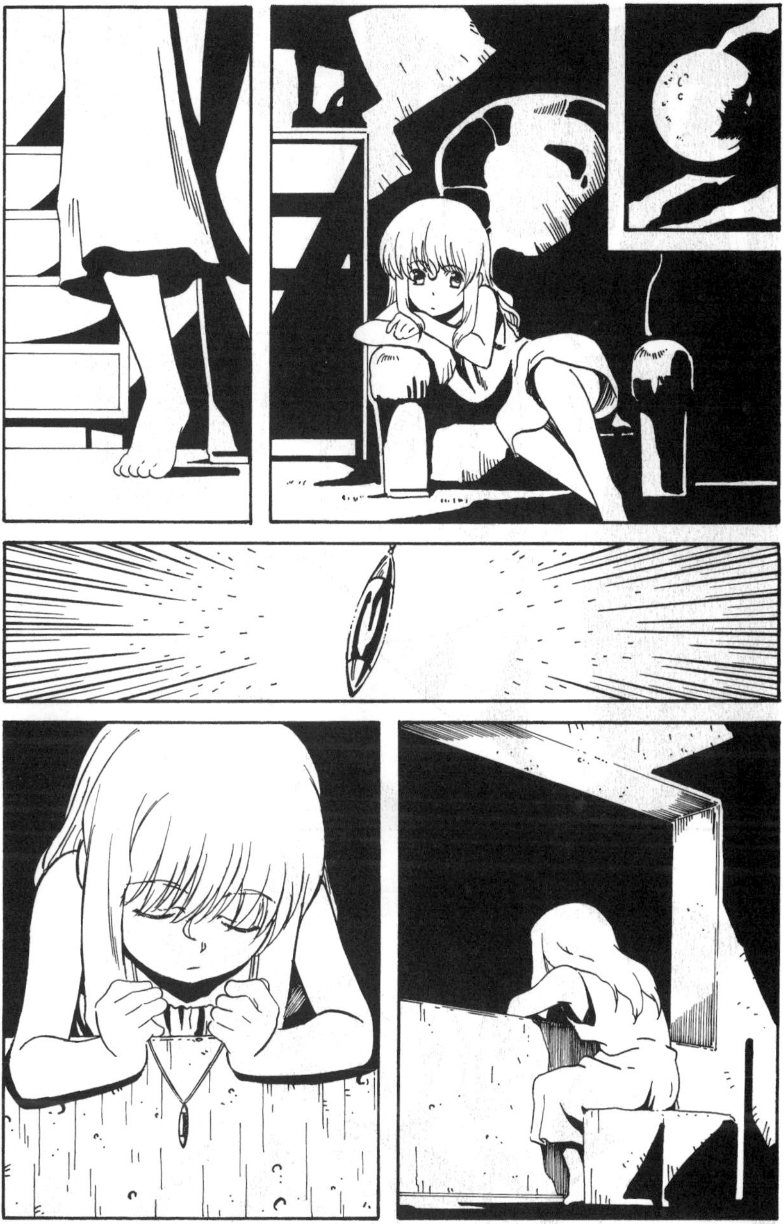

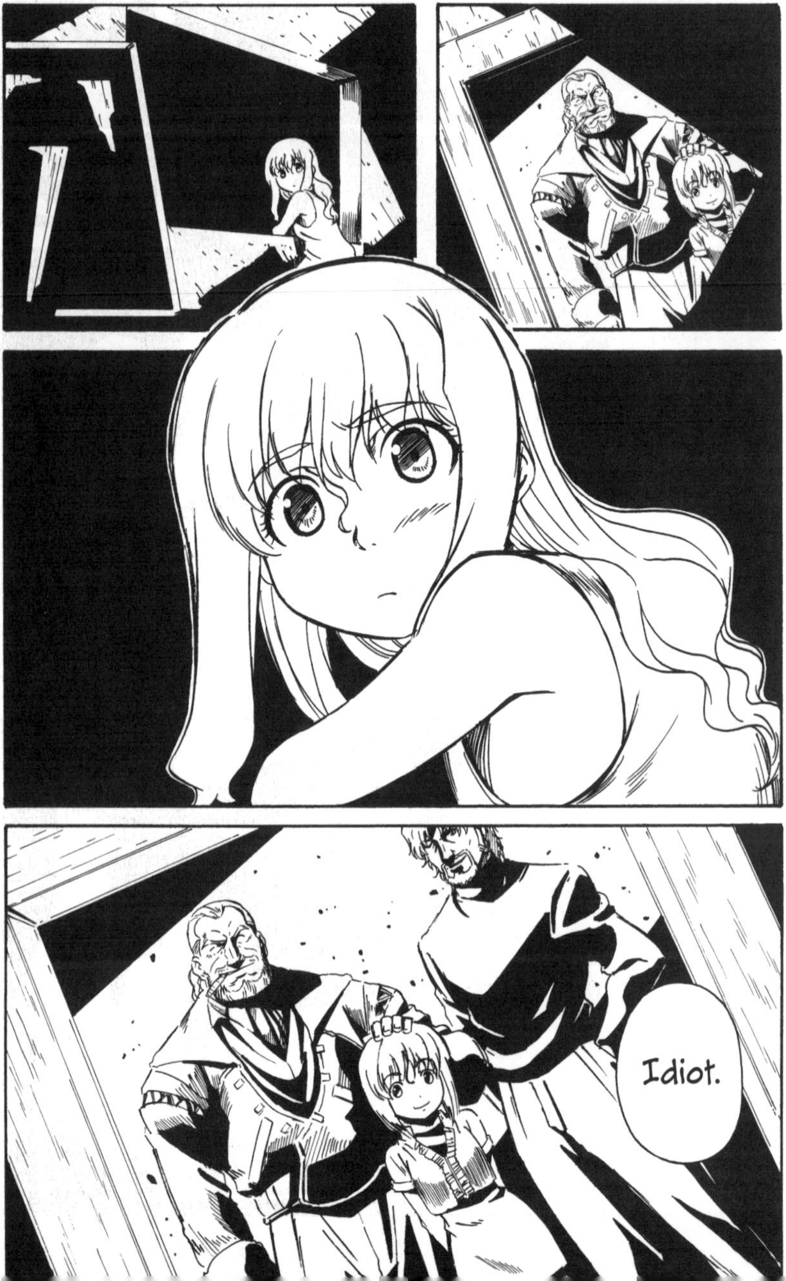
Idiot.

WANTED
wanted

MISTER
ミスター

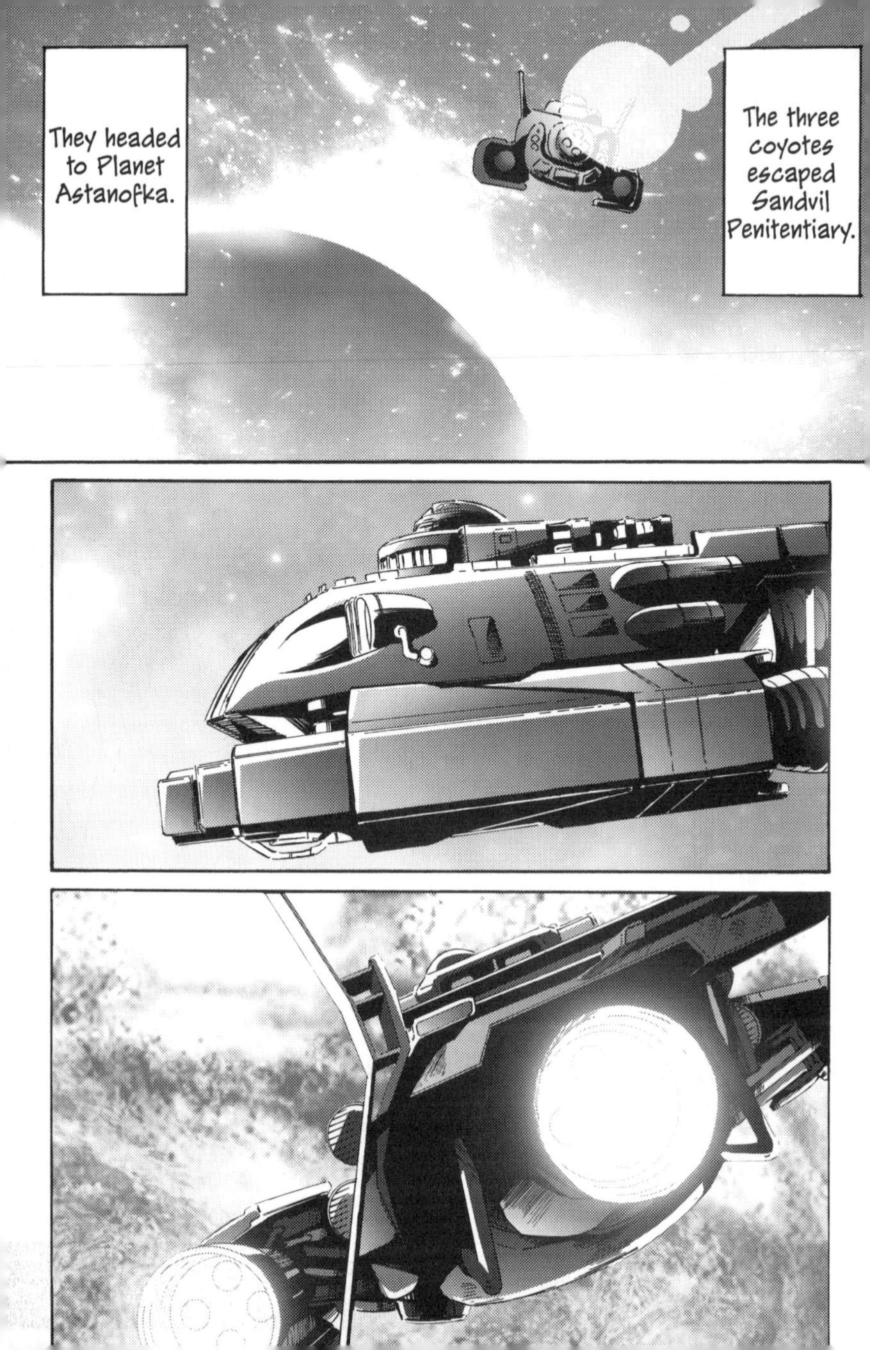
The three coyotes escaped Sandvil Penitentiary.
They headed to Planet Astanofka.

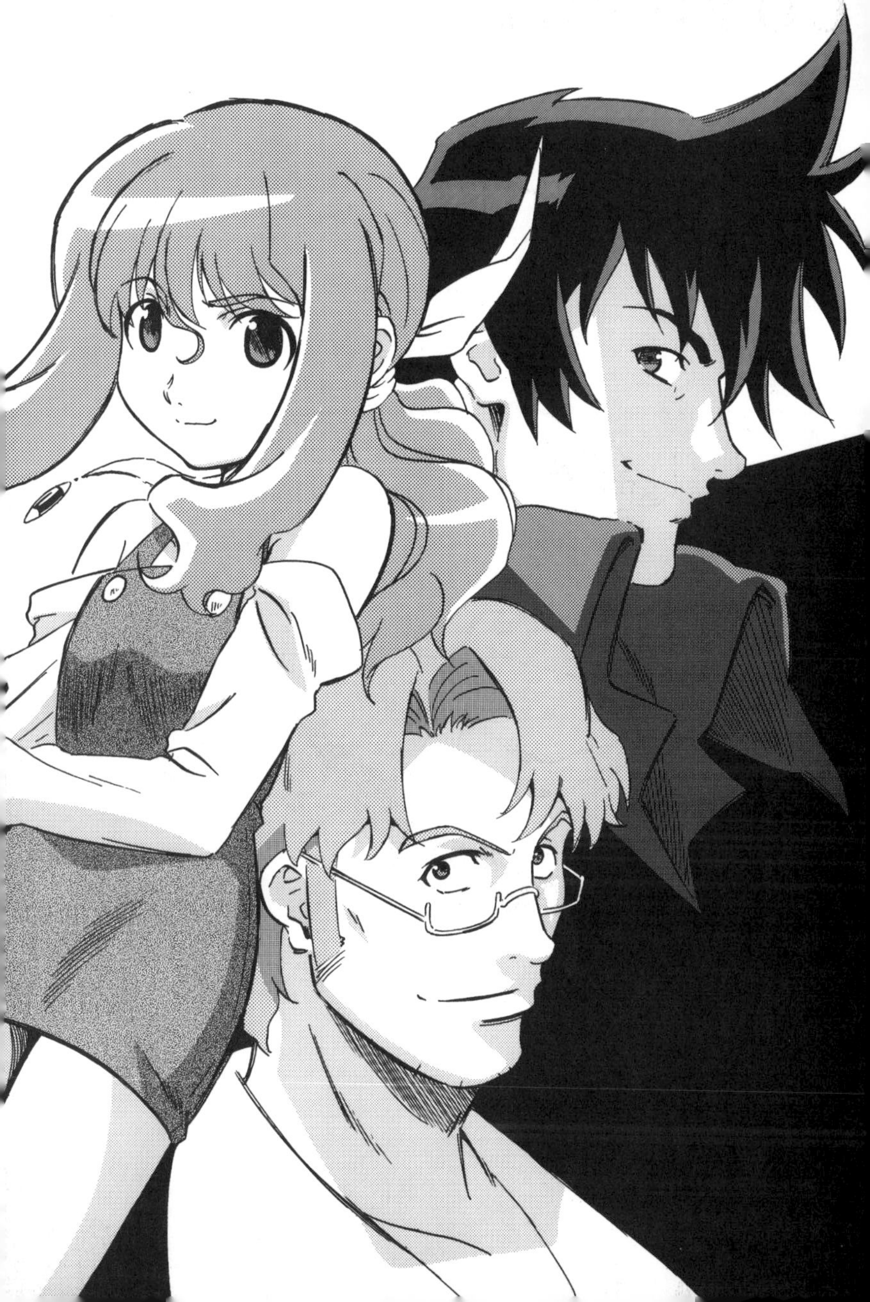

COYOTE Ragtime Show Vol.02

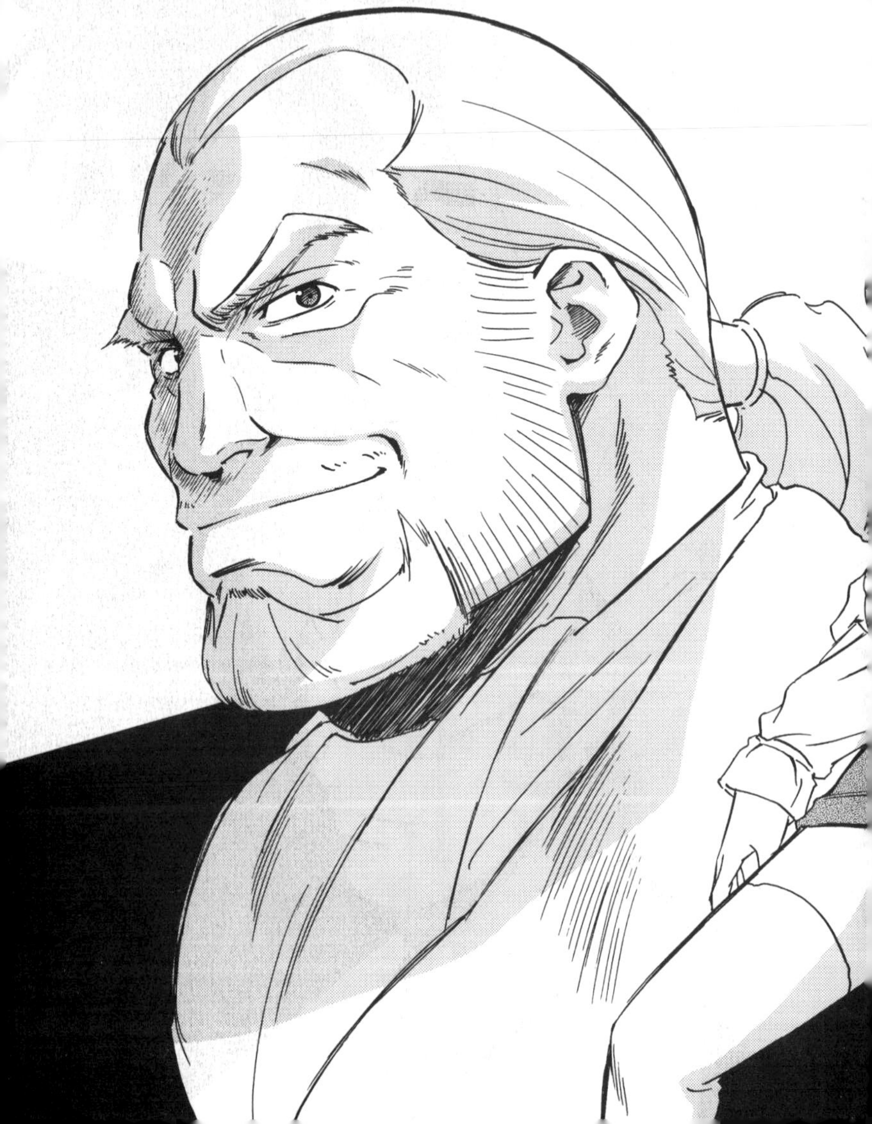

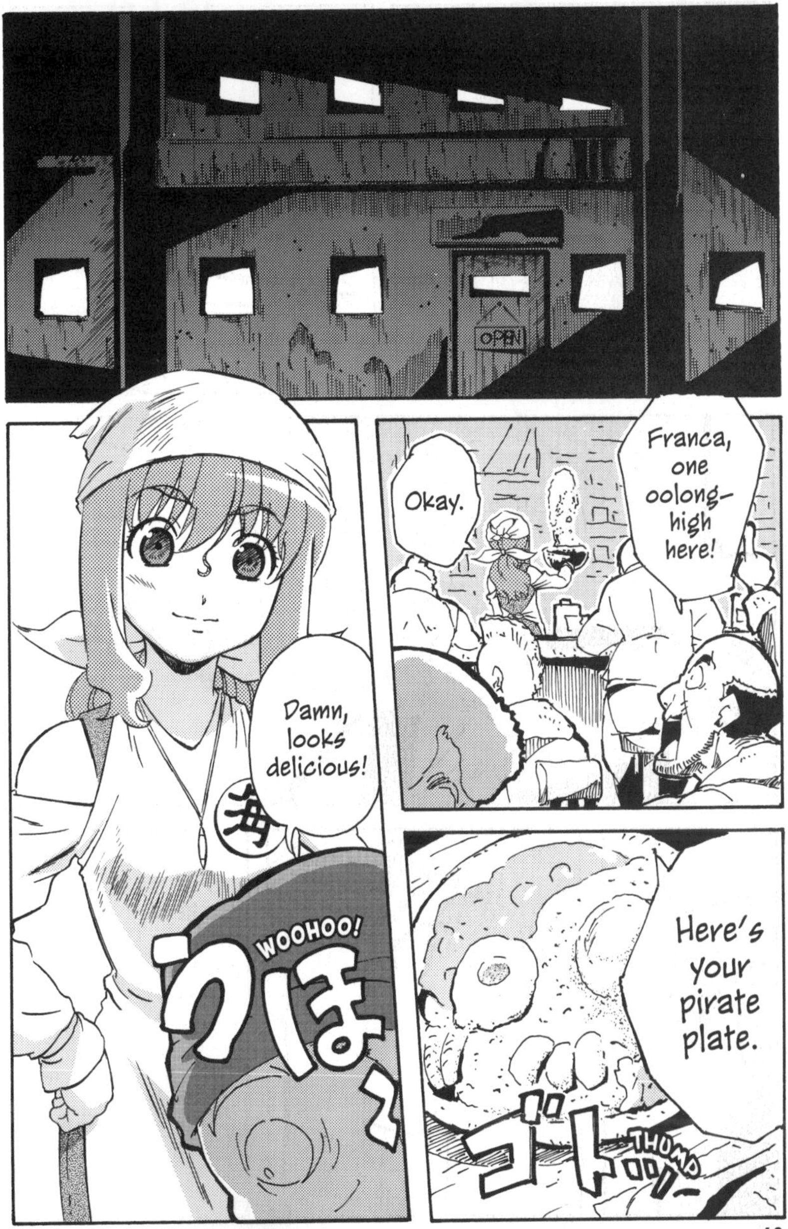
OPEN
Franca, one oolong-high here!
Okay.
Here's your pirate plate.
ゴトッ
THOMP
Damn, looks delicious!
うほっ
WOOHOO!

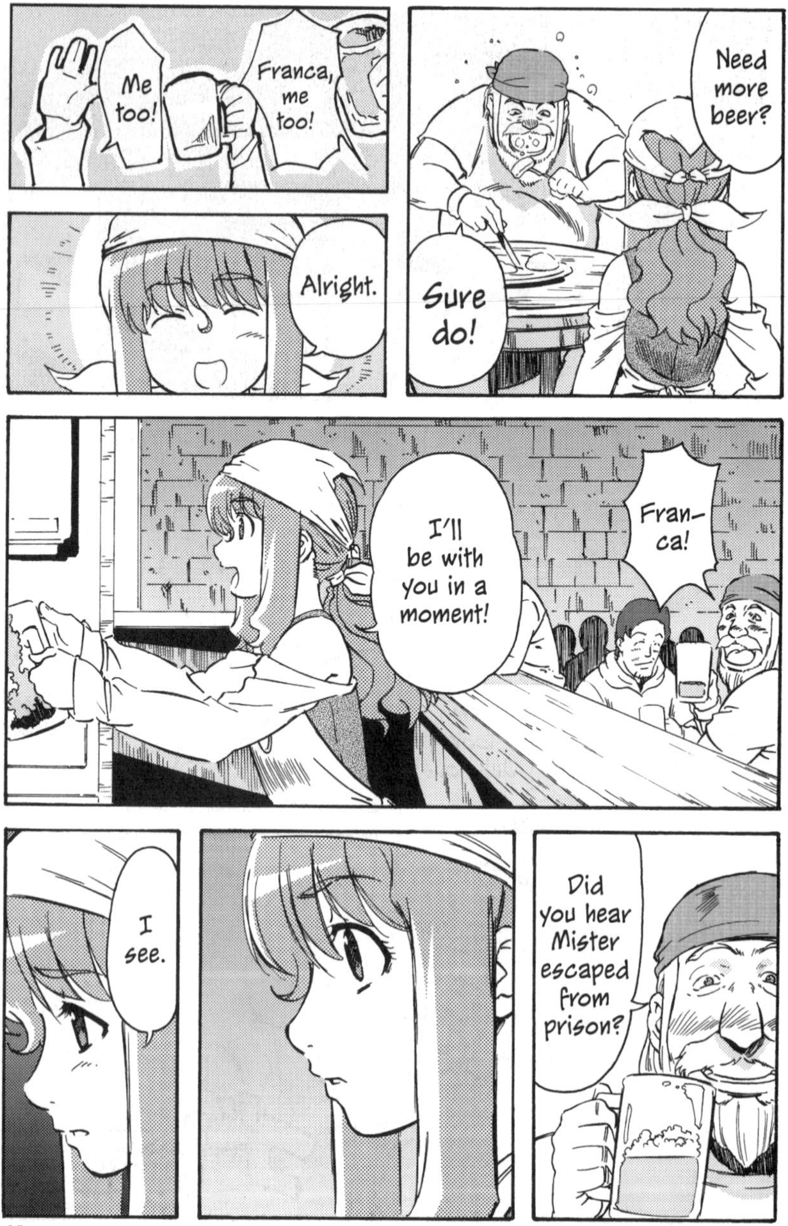
Need more beer?
Sure do!
Franca, me too!
Me too!
Alright.
Fran-ca!
I'll be with you in a moment!
Did you hear Mister escaped from prison?
I see.

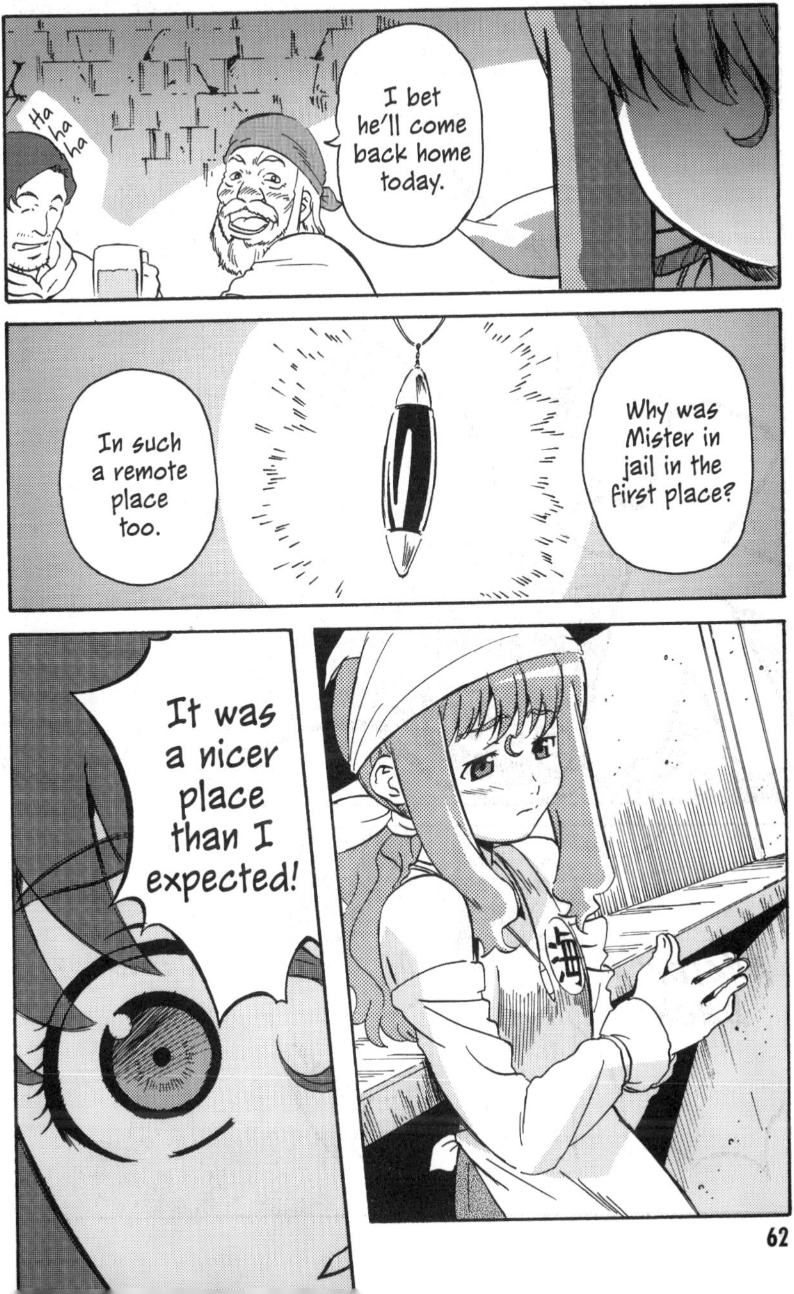
I bet he'll come back home today.
Ha ha ha
Why was Mister in jail in the first place?
In such a remote place too.
It was a nicer place than I expected!

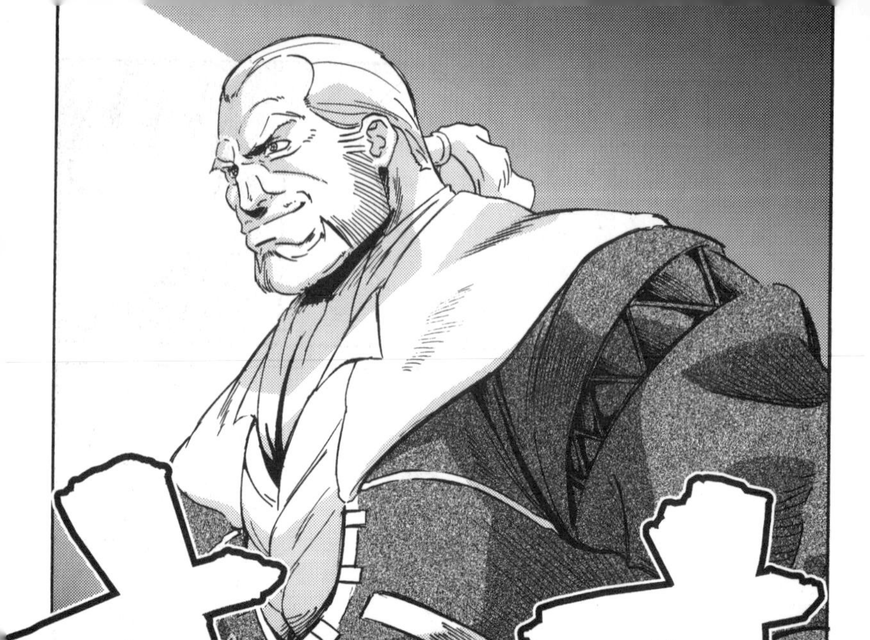
オオ
OOOH!
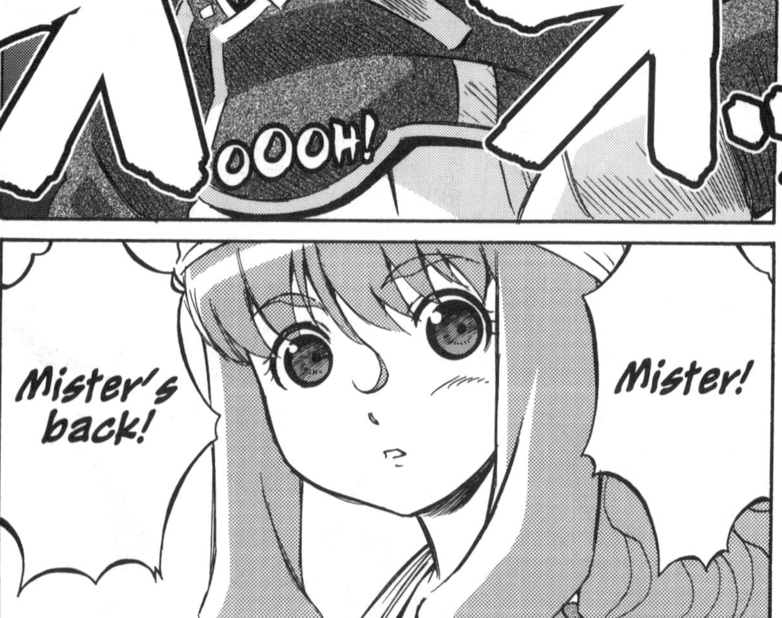
Mister!
Mister's back!

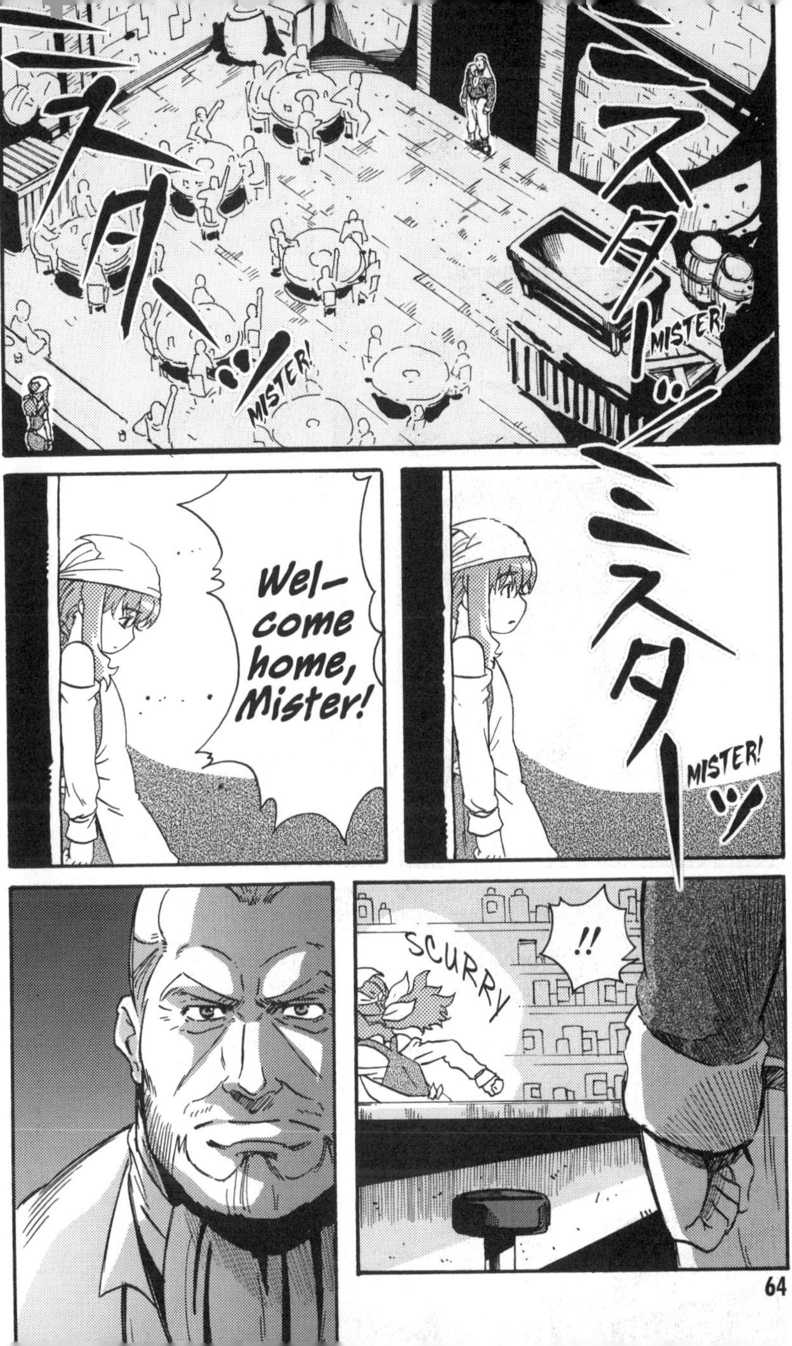
MISTER!
MISTER!
MISTER!
Wel-
come
home,
Mister!
!!
SCURRY

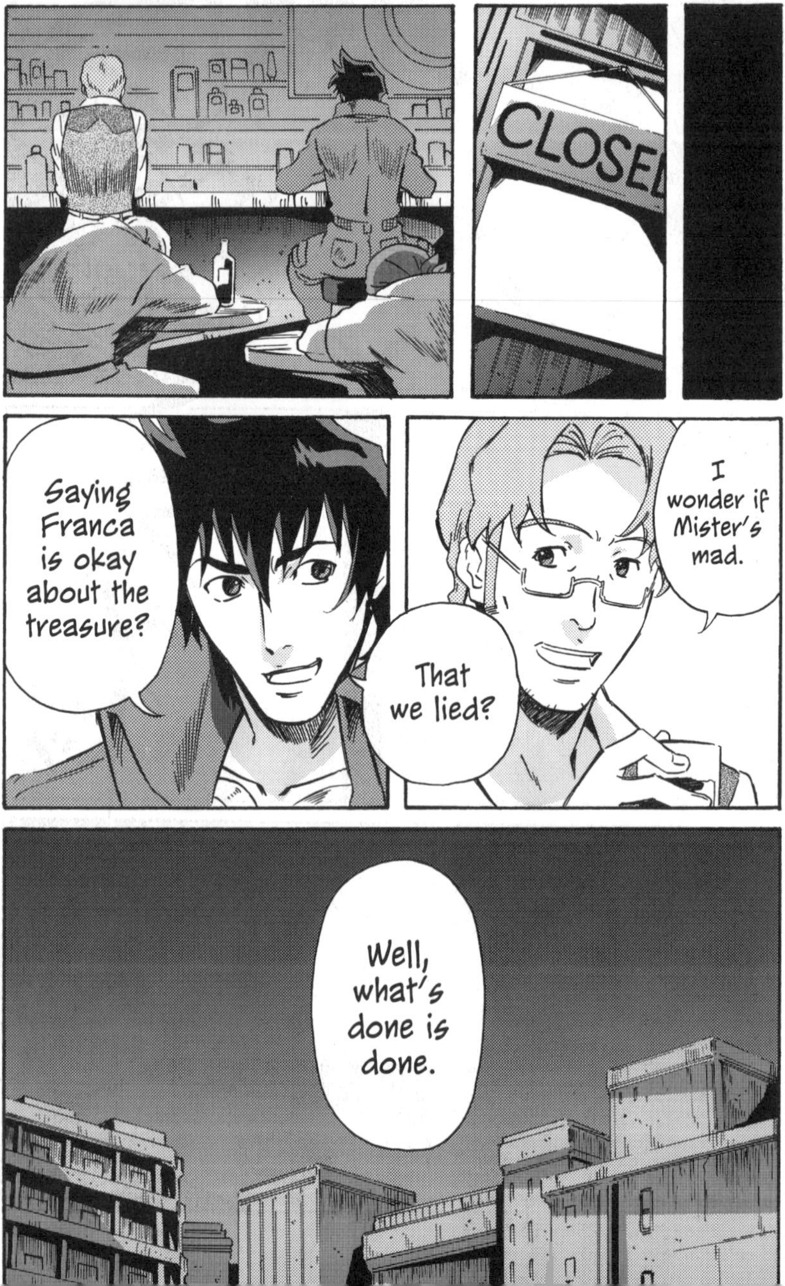
CLOSE
I wonder if Mister's mad.
That we lied?
Saying Franca is okay about the treasure?
Well, what's done is done.

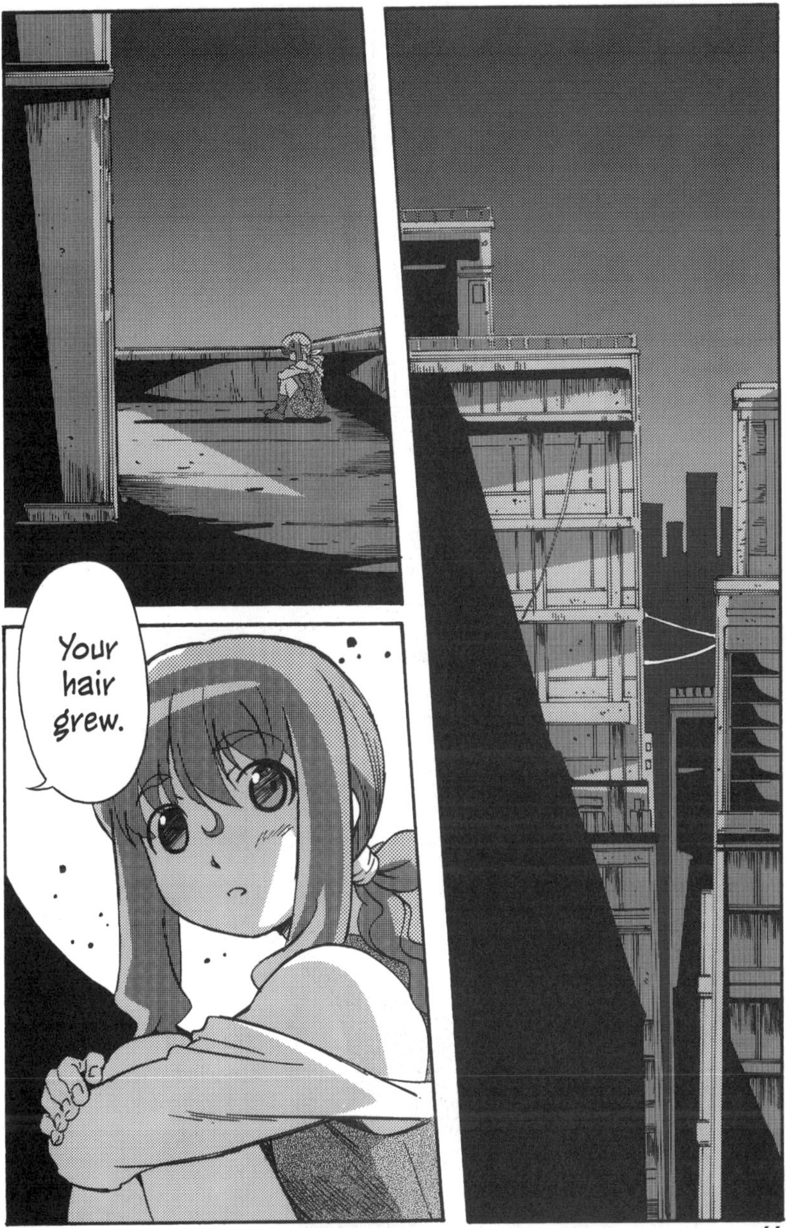
Your hair grew.

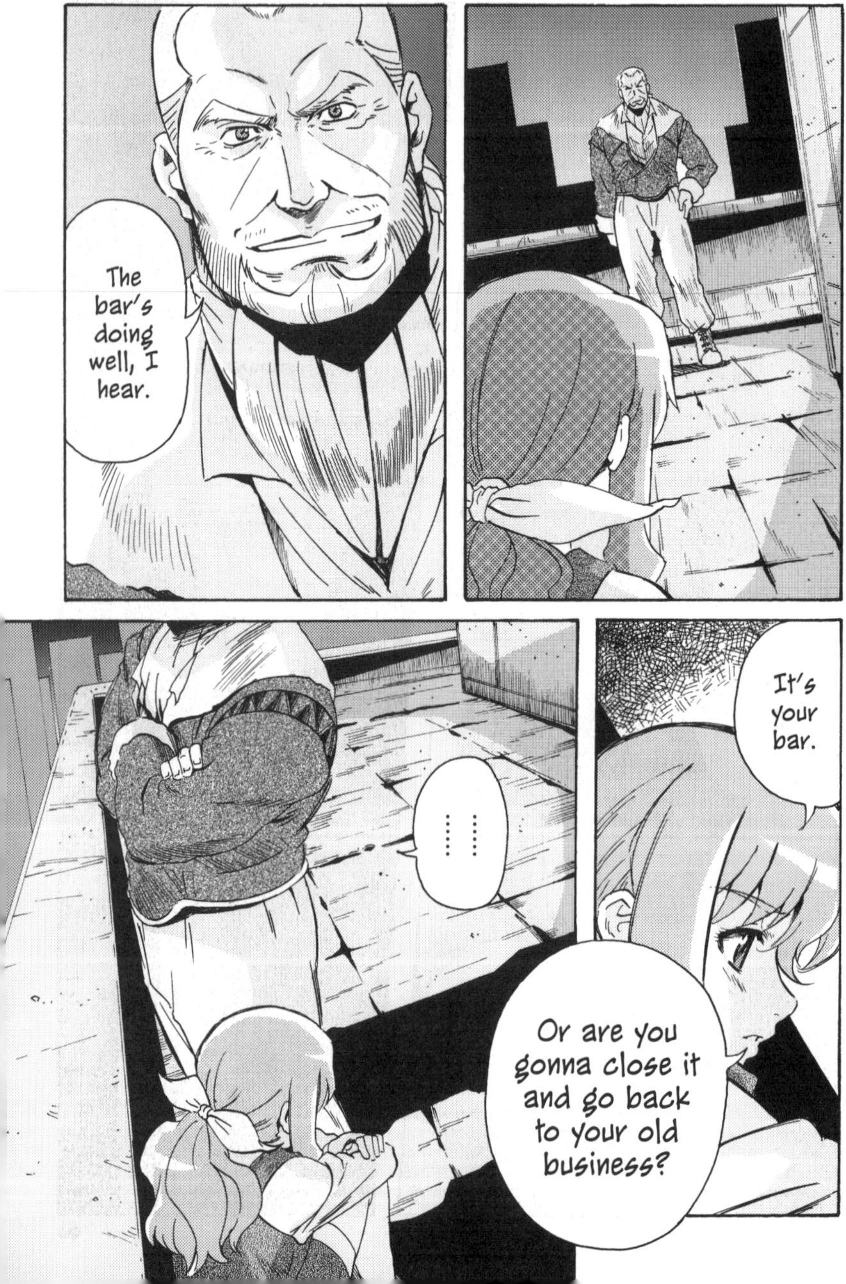
The bar's doing well, I hear.
It's your bar.
Or are you gonna close it and go back to your old business?
......

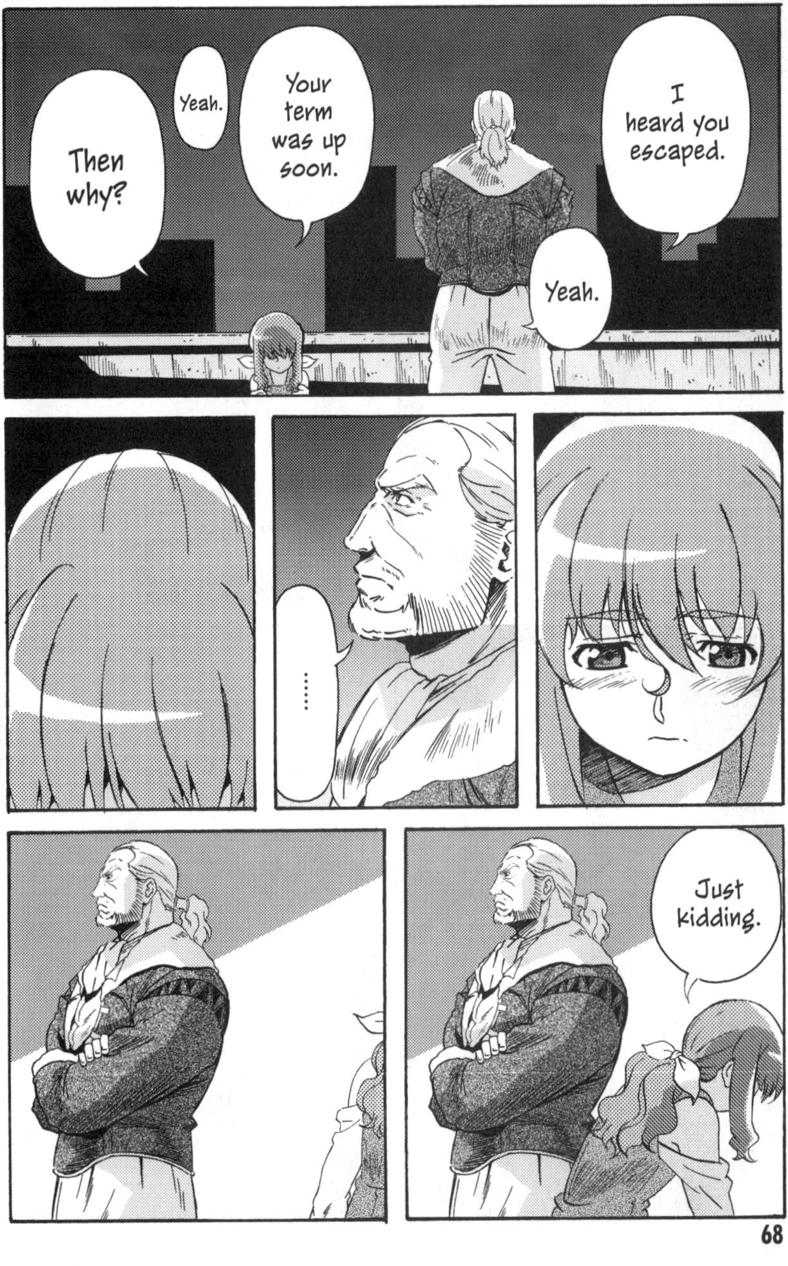

I heard you escaped.
Yeah.
Your term was up soon.
Yeah.
Then why?
......
Just kidding.

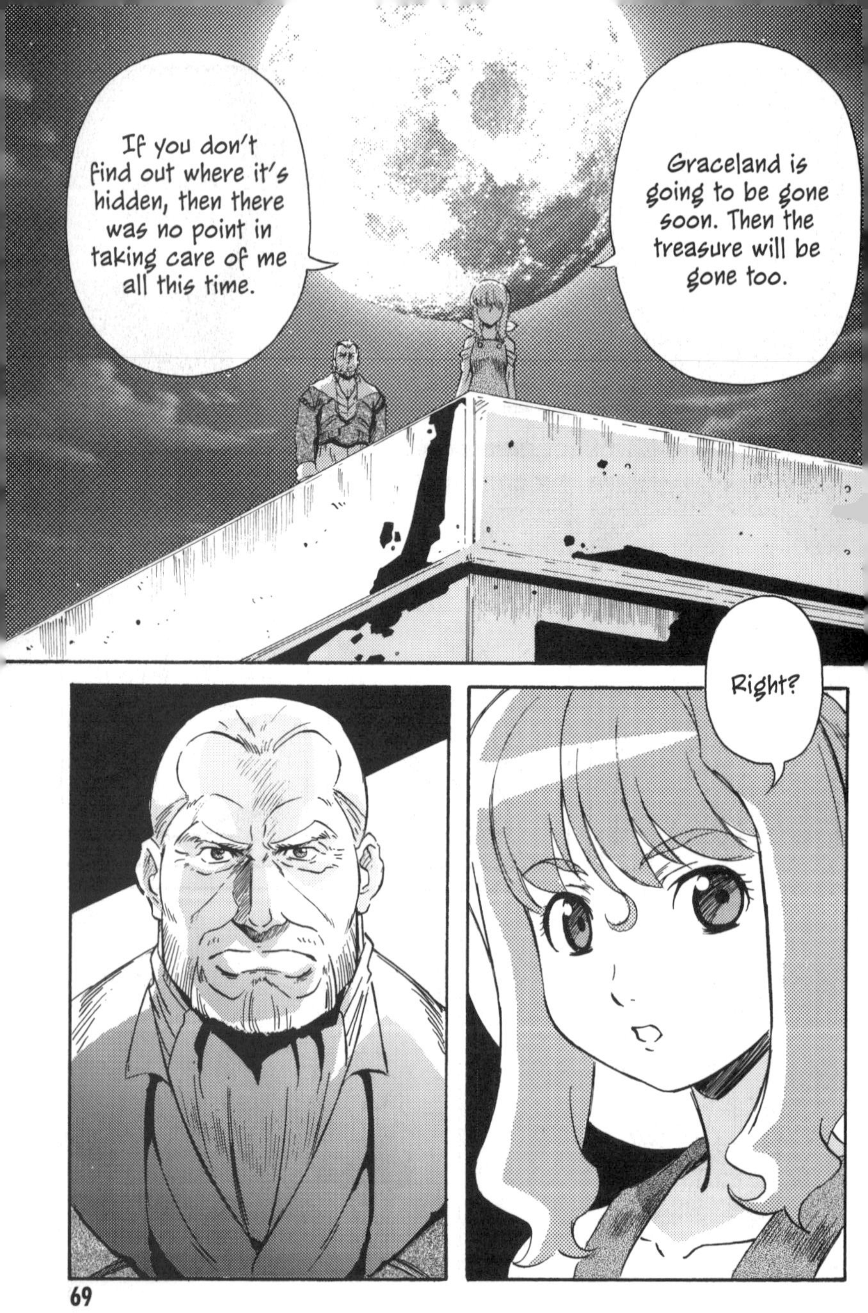
Graceland is going to be gone soon. Then the treasure will be gone too.
If you don't find out where it's hidden, then there was no point in taking care of me all this time.
Right?

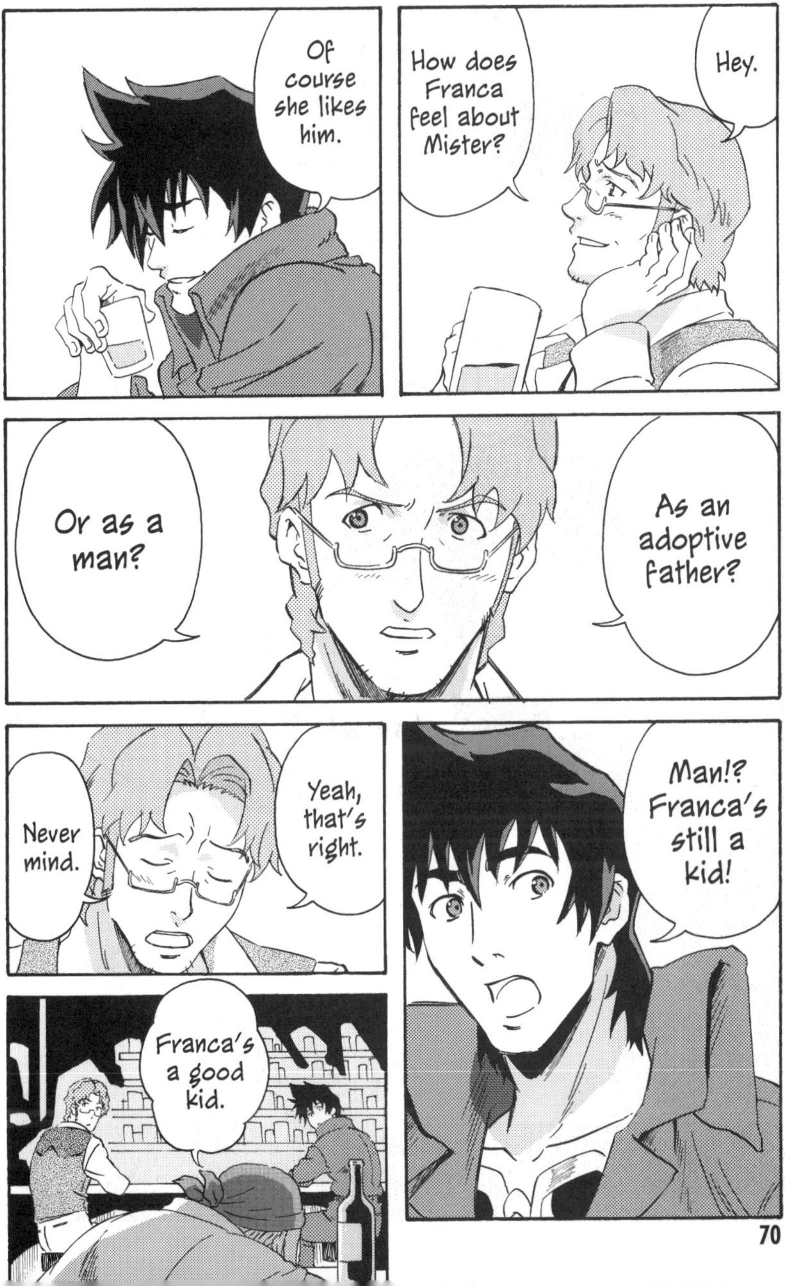
Hey.
How does Franca feel about Mister?
Of course she likes him.
As an adoptive father?
Or as a man?
Man!? Franca's still a kid!
Yeah, that's right.
Never mind.
Franca's a good kid.

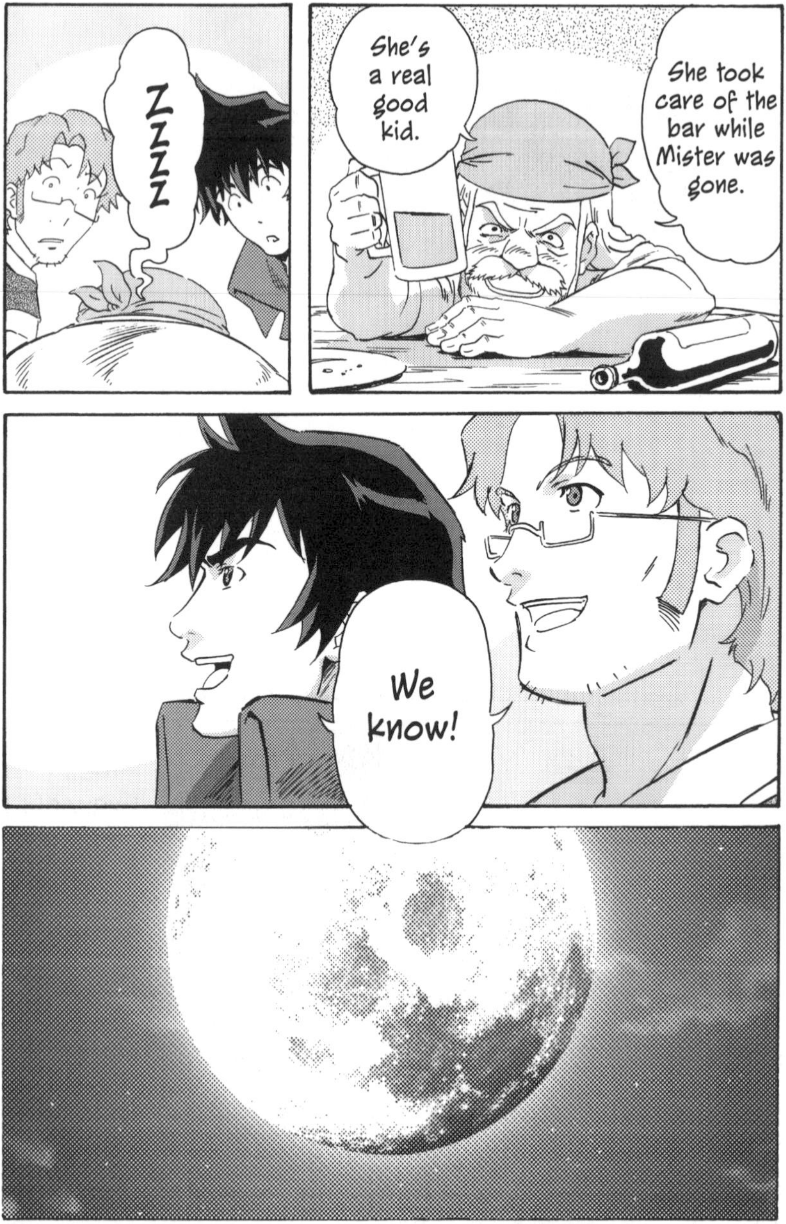
She took care of the bar while Mister was gone.
She's a real good kid.
ZZZZ
We know!

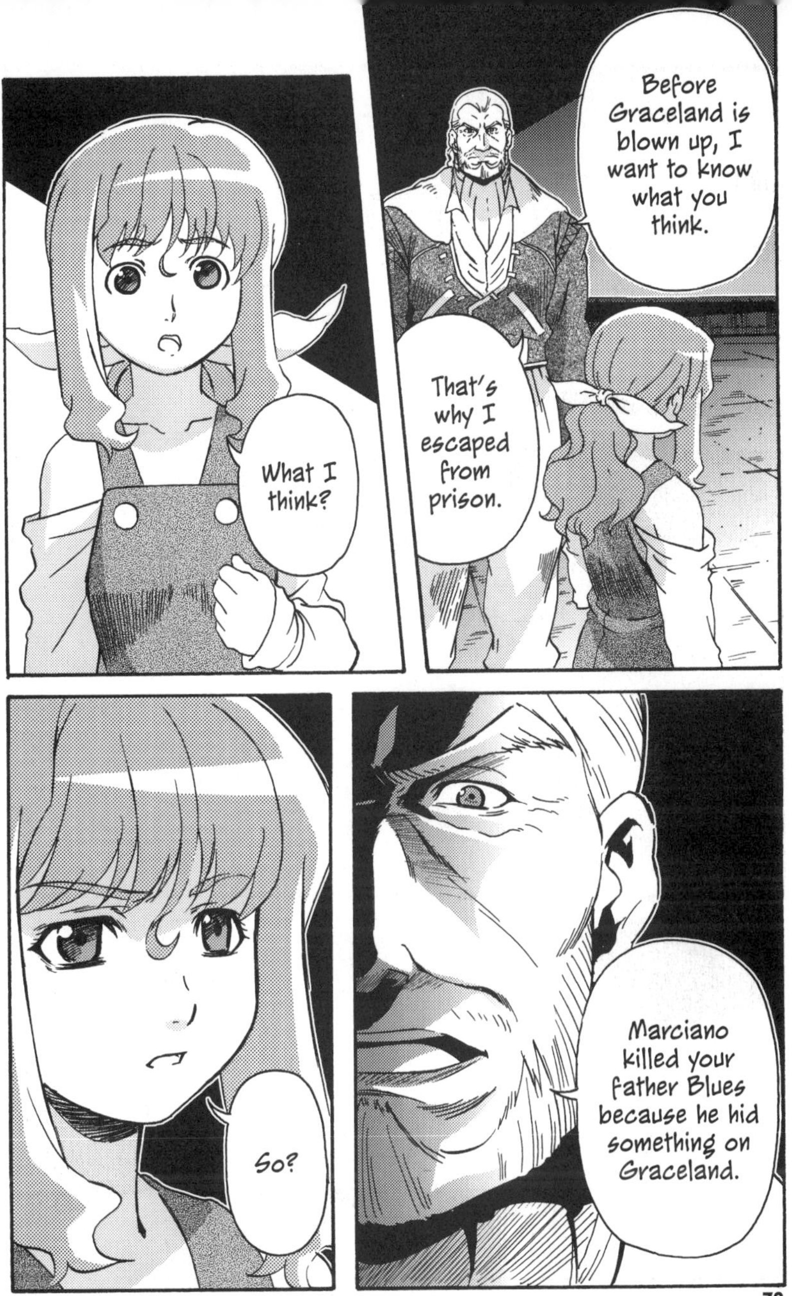
Before Graceland is blown up, I want to know what you think.
That's why I escaped from prison.
What I think?
Marciano killed your father Blues because he hid something on Graceland.
So?

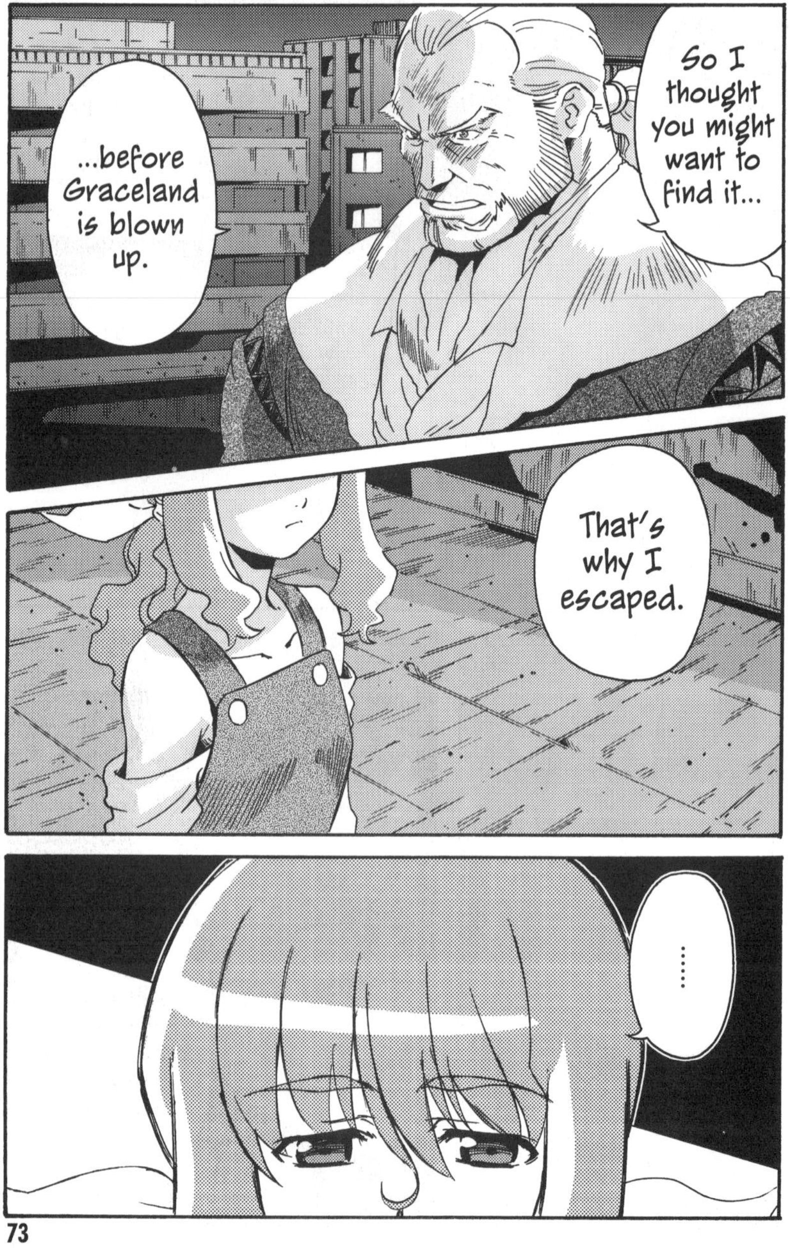
So I thought you might want to find it...
...before Graceland is blown up.
That's why I escaped.
......

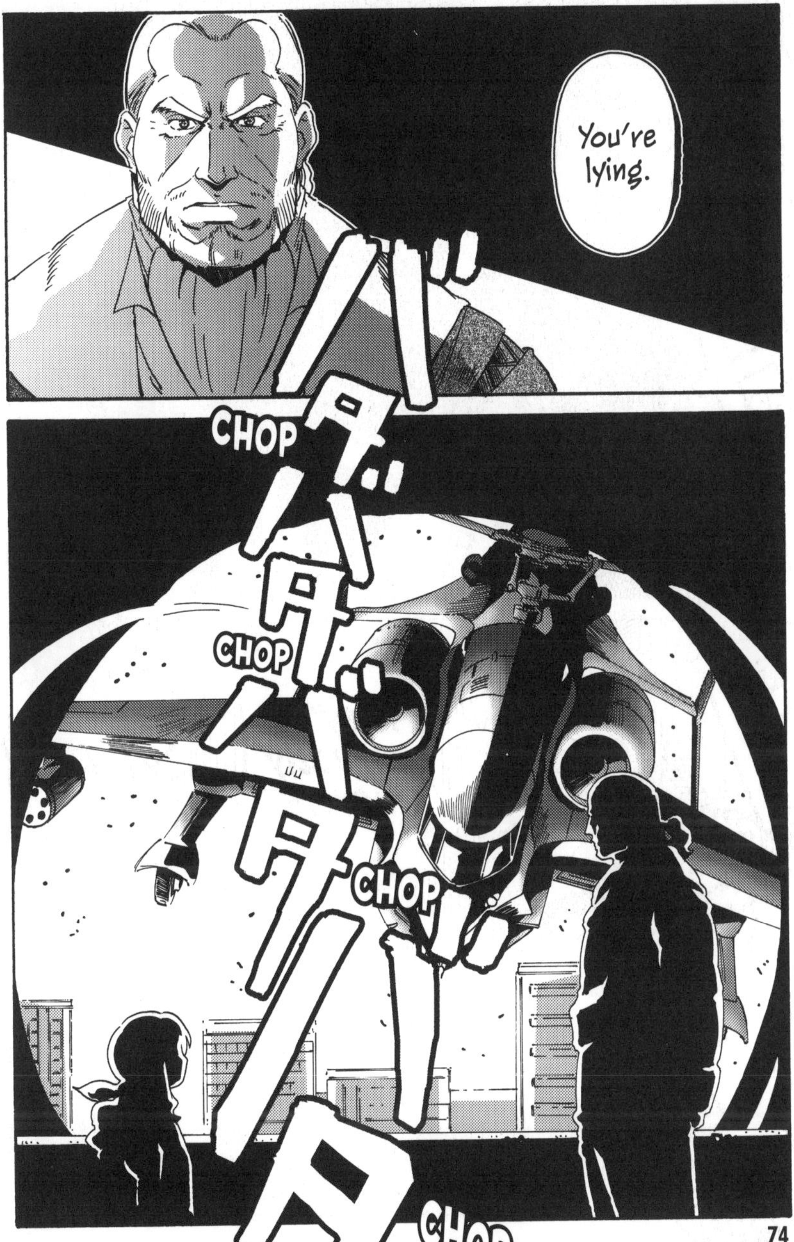
You're lying.
CHOP
CHOP
CHOP
CHOP

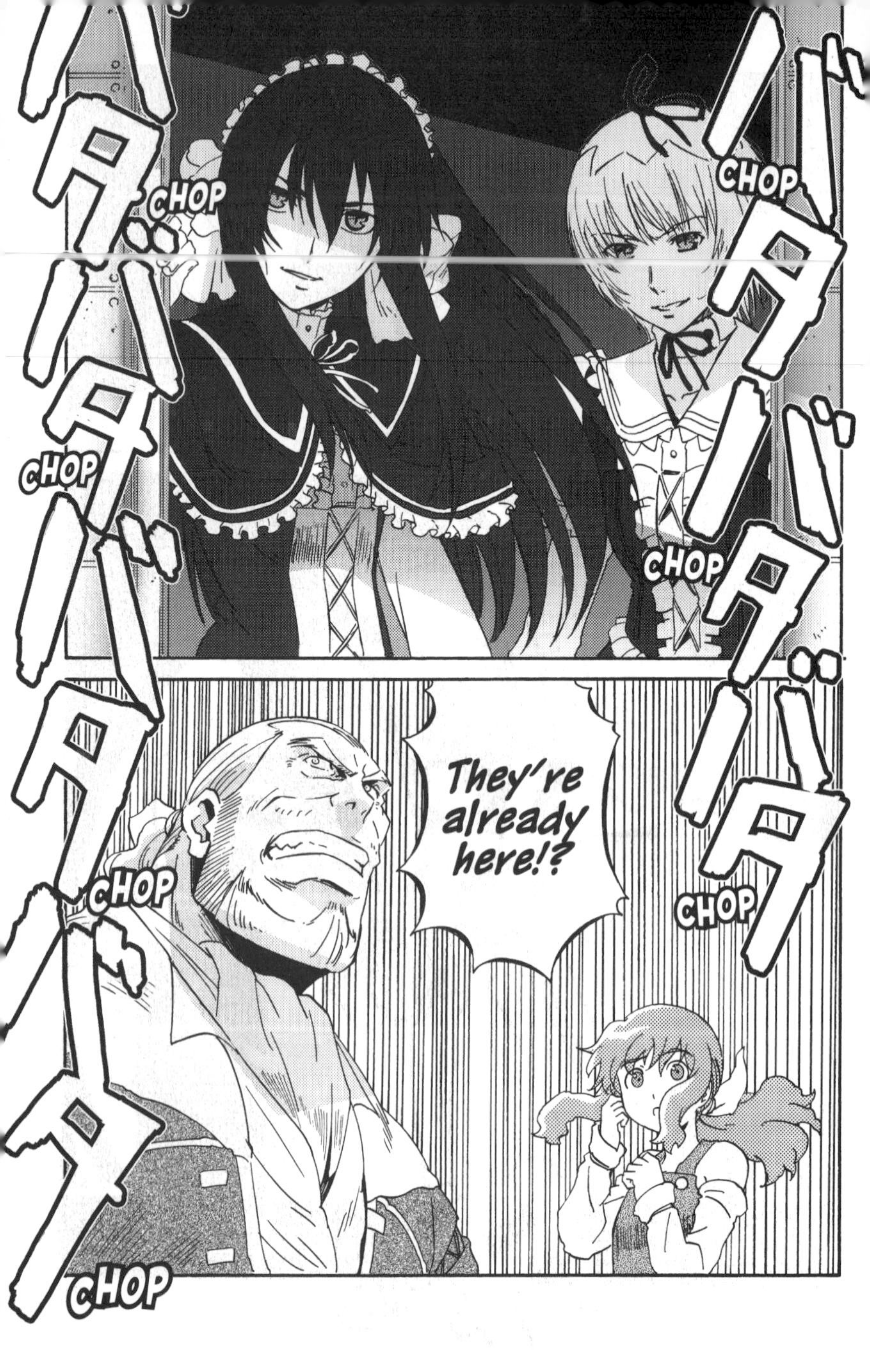
CHOP
CHOP
CHOP
CHOP
They're already here!?
CHOP
CHOP
CHOP

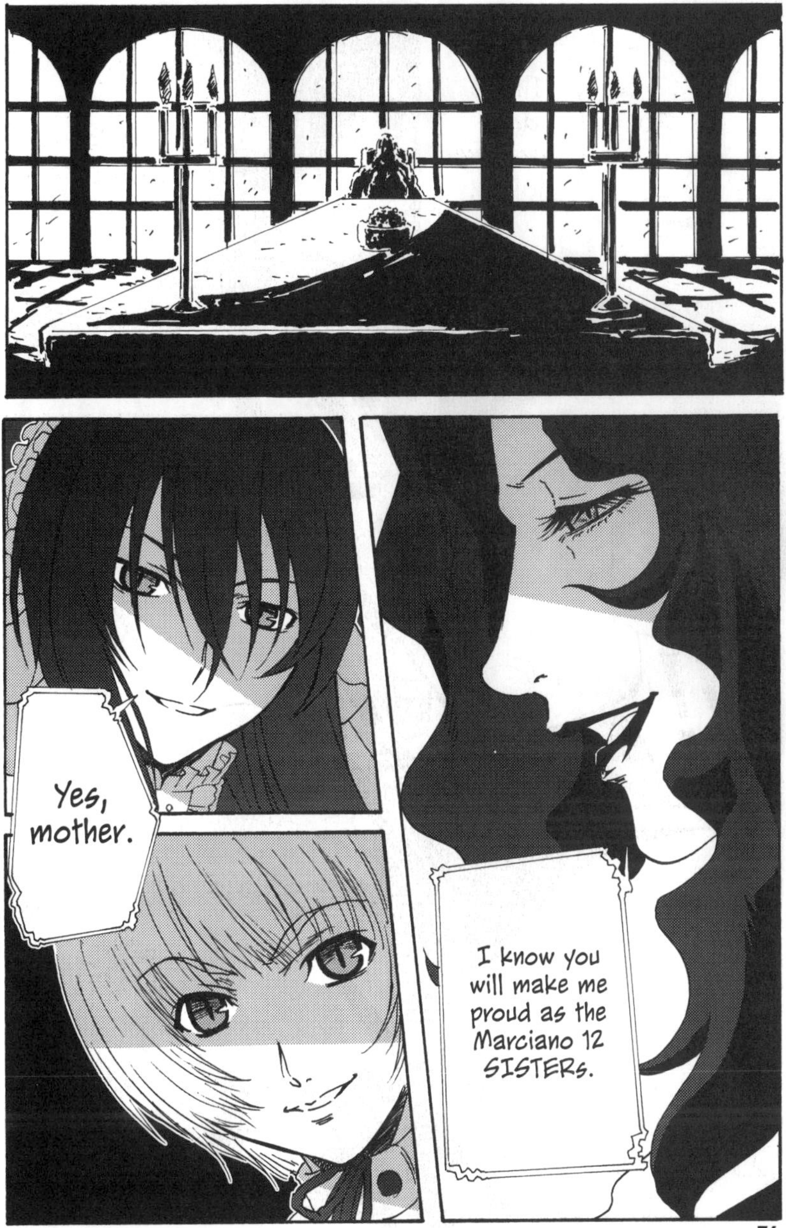
I know you will make me proud as the Marciano 12 SISTERs.
Yes, mother.

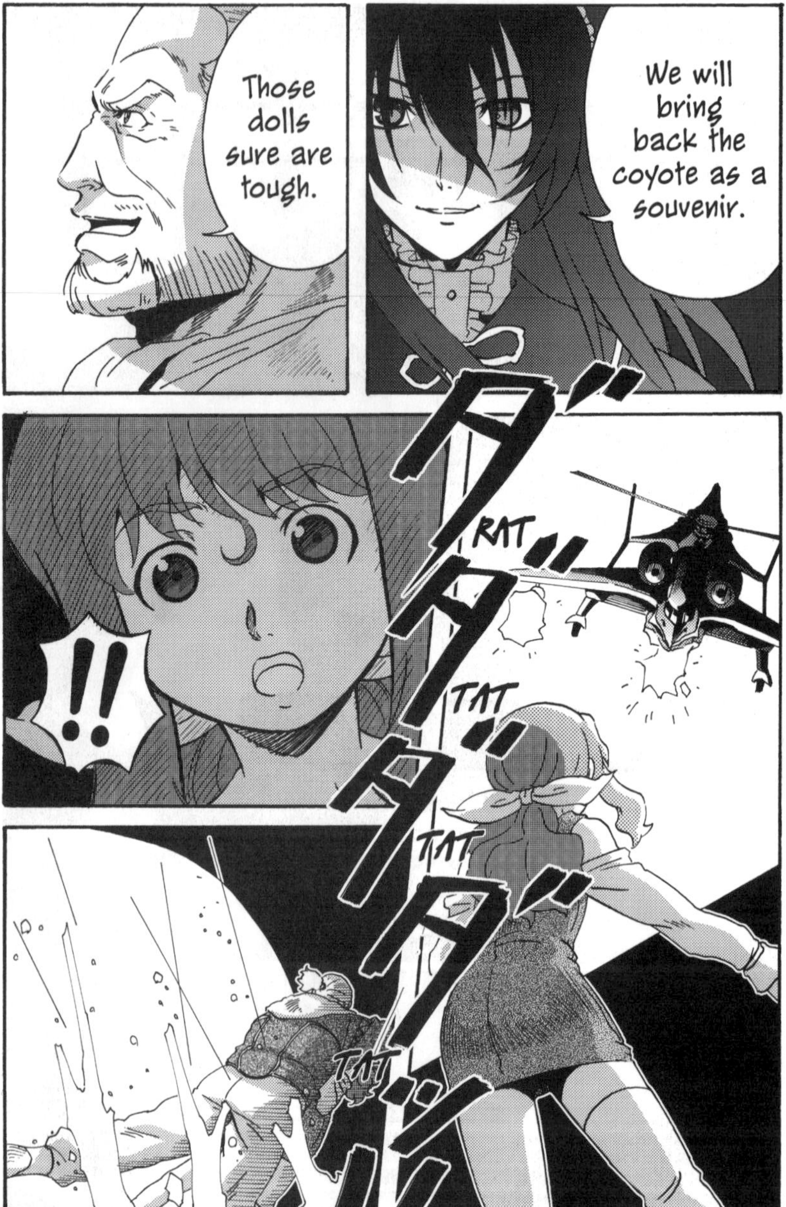

We will bring back the coyote as a souvenir.
Those dolls sure are tough.
RAT
TAT
!!
TAT
TAT

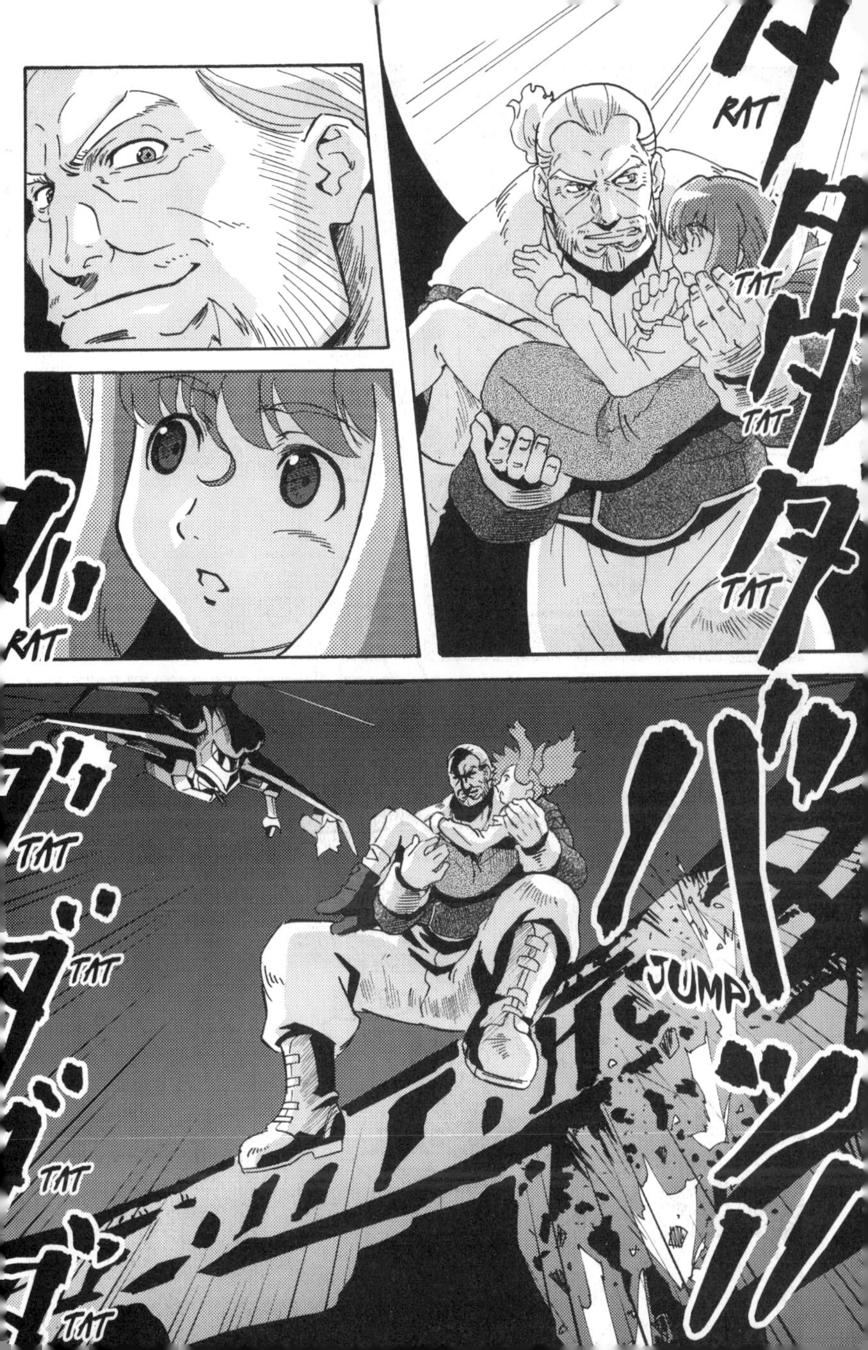
RAT
TAT
TAT
TAT
RAT
JUMP
TAT
TAT
TAT
TAT

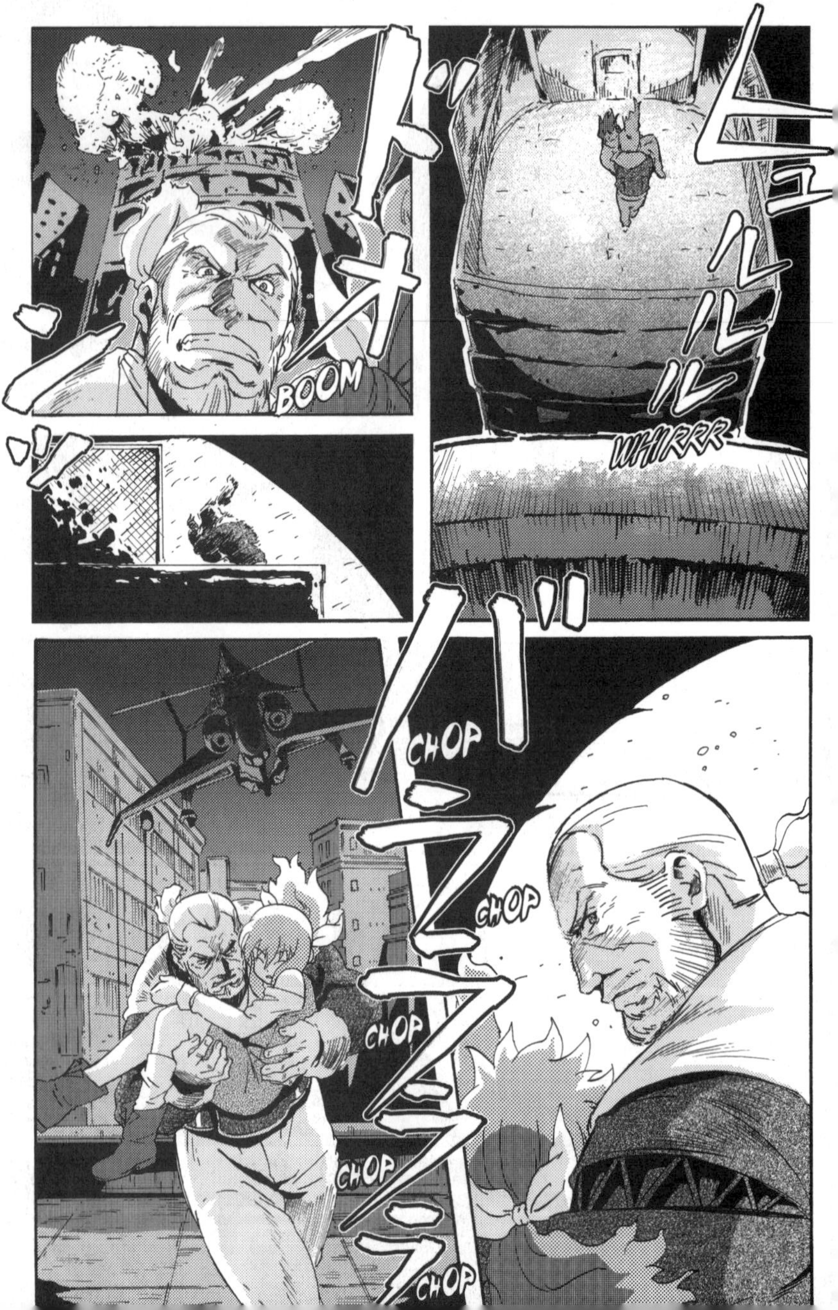
ヒュルルルル
WHIRRR
ドオ
BOOM
CHOP
CHOP
CHOP
CHOP
CHOP

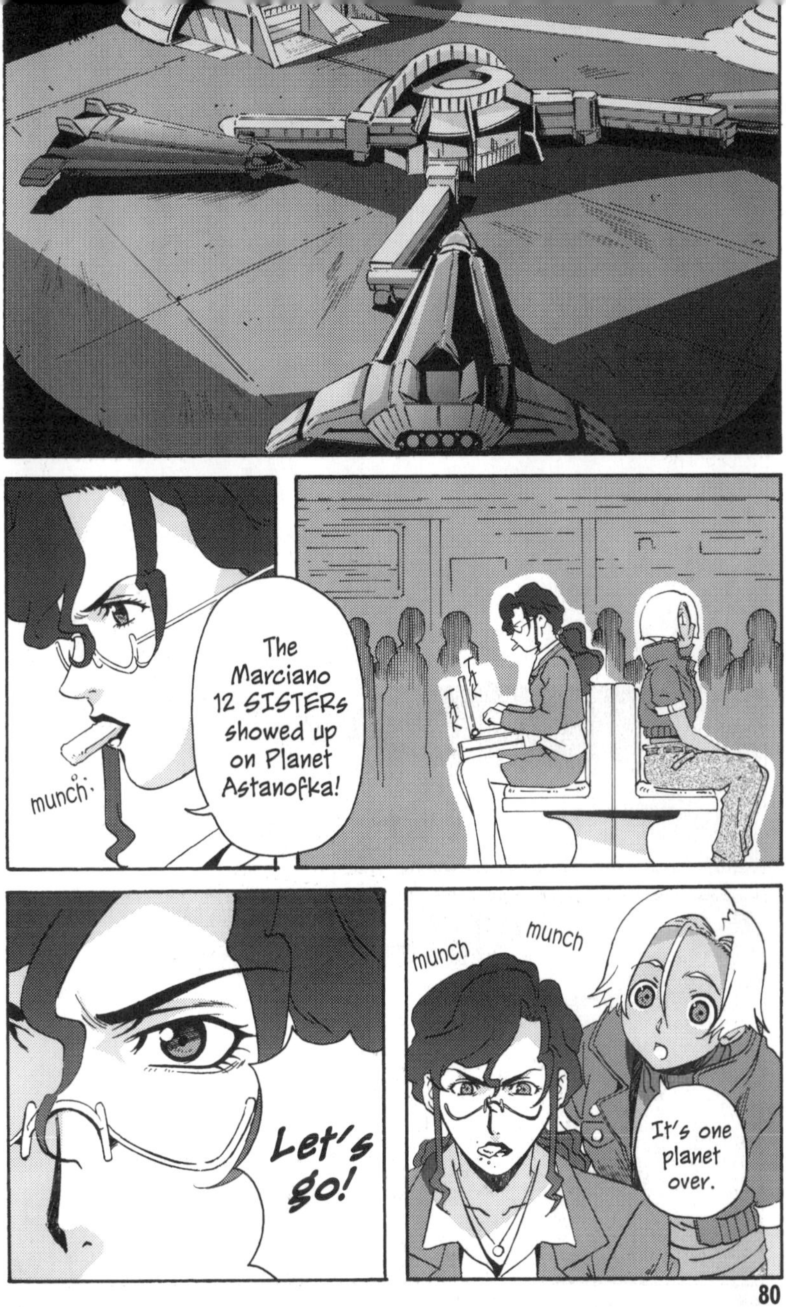
TAK TAK
The Marciano 12 SISTERs showed up on Planet Astanofka!
munch
munch
munch
It's one planet over.
Let's go!

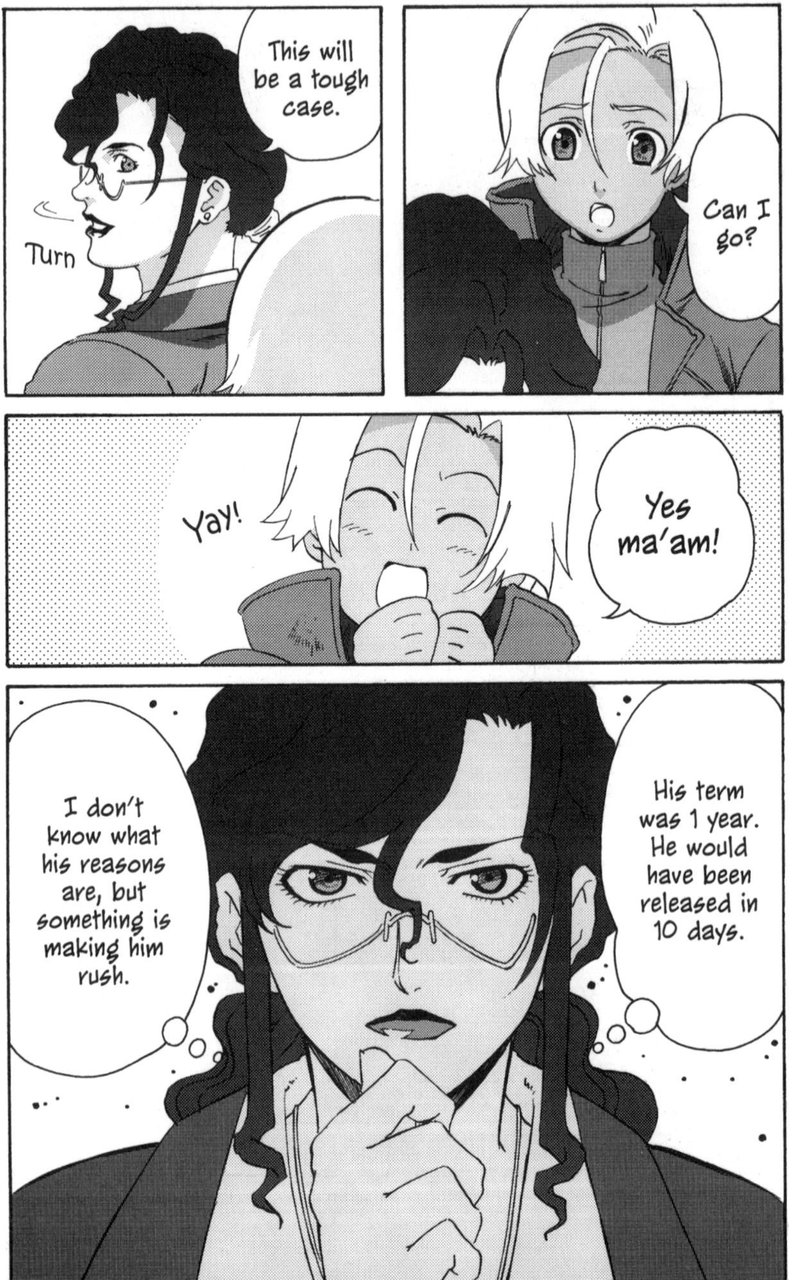
Can I go?
This will be a tough case.
Turn
Yes ma'am!
Yay!
His term was 1 year. He would have been released in 10 days.
I don't know what his reasons are, but something is making him rush.

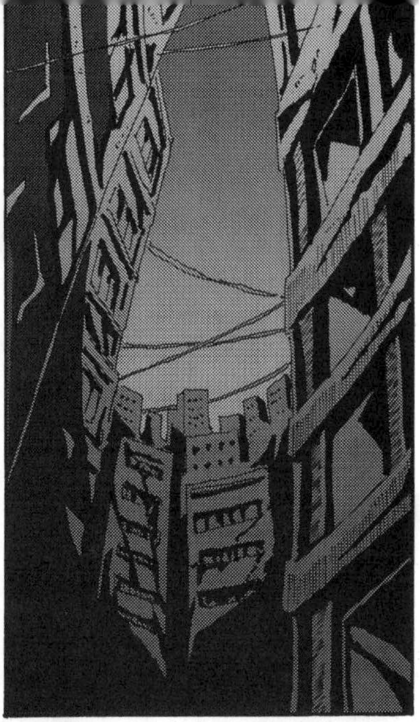
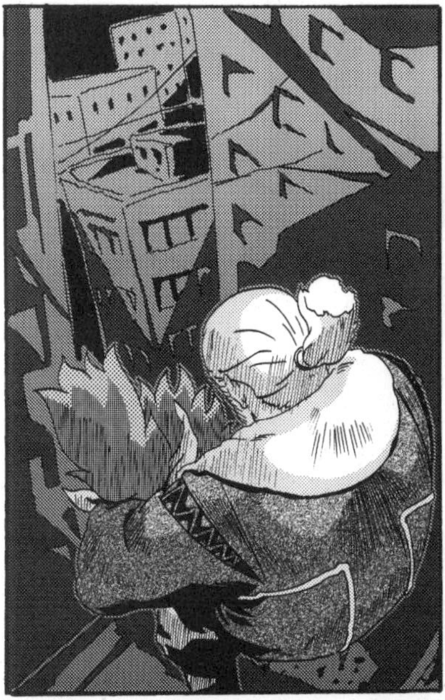
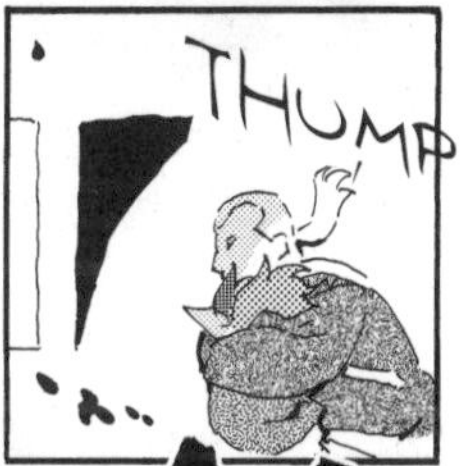
THUMP
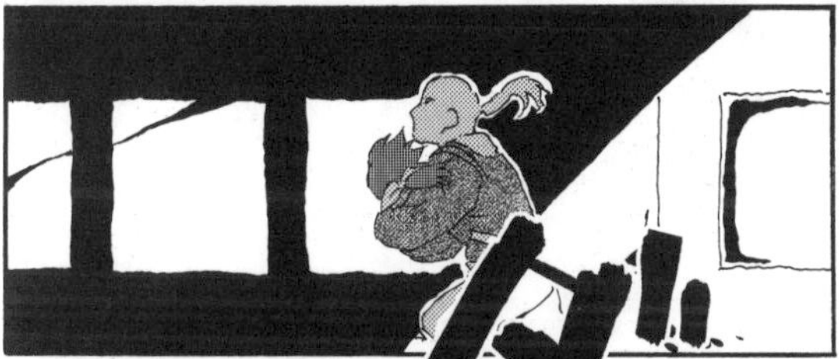
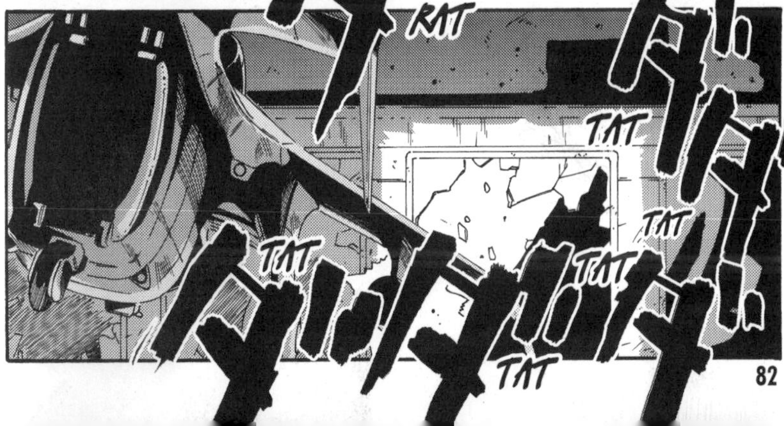
RAT
TAT
TAT
TAT
TAT
TAT

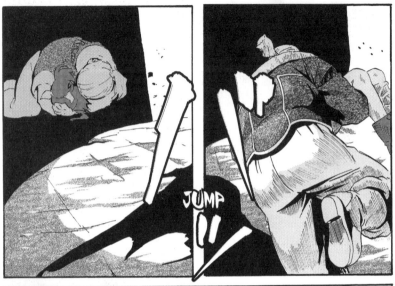

JUMP

Are you alright?

Push

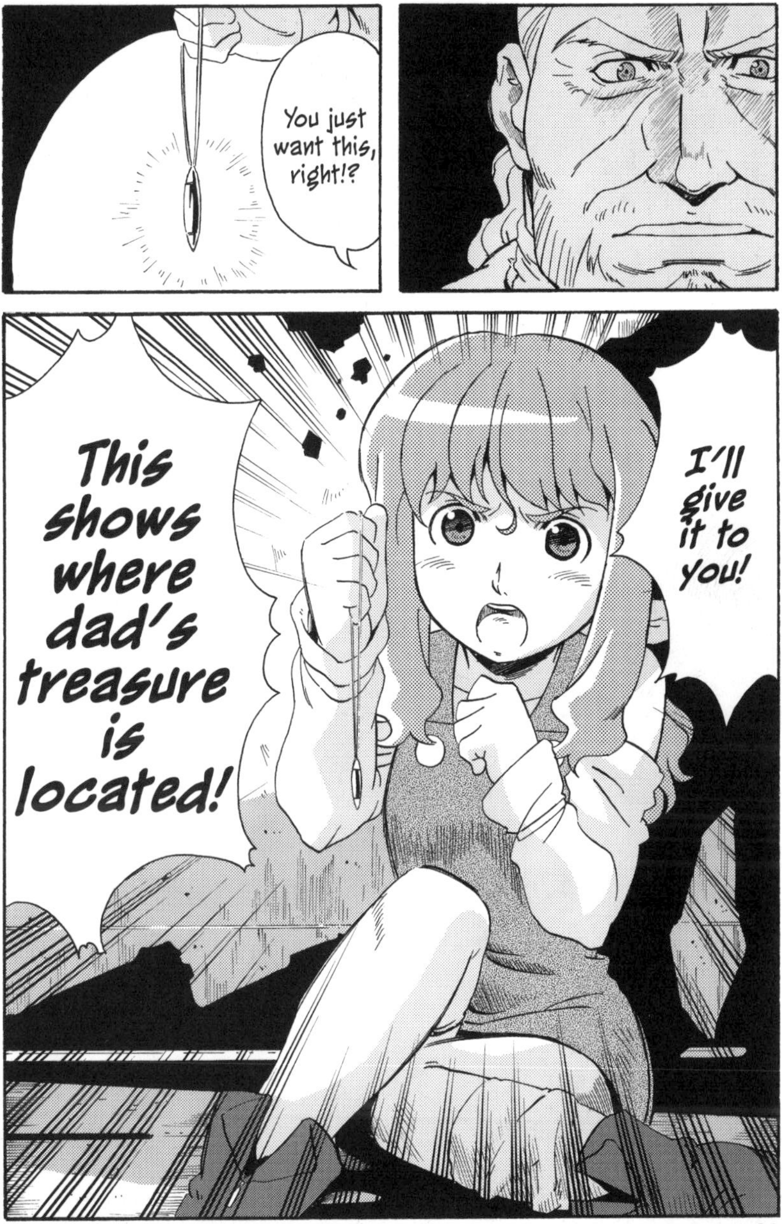
You just want this, right!?
I'll give it to you!
This shows where dad's treasure is located!

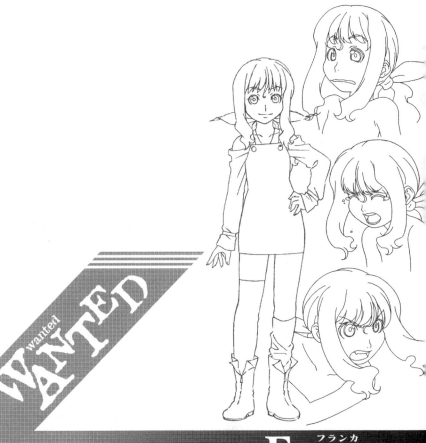

WANTED

wanted

FRANCA
フランカ

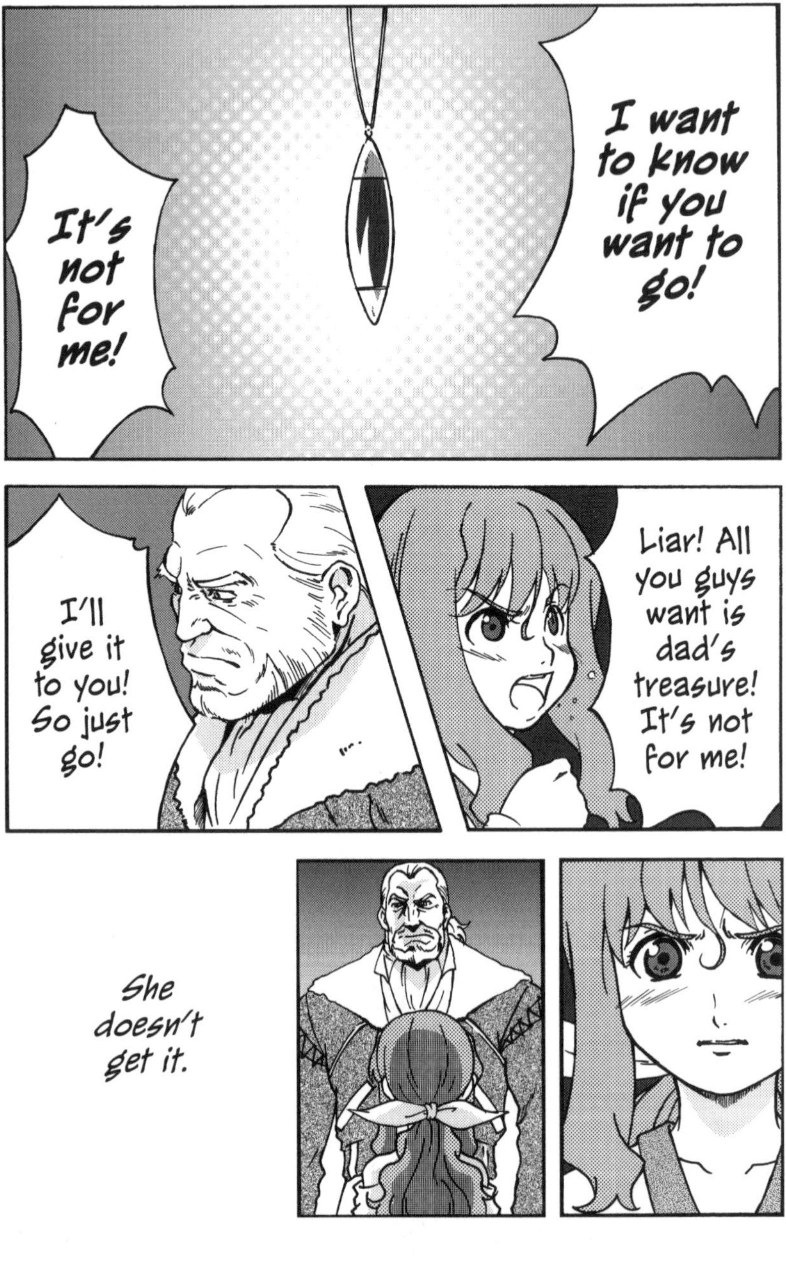
I want to know if you want to go!
It's not for me!
Liar! All you guys want is dad's treasure! It's not for me!
I'll give it to you! So just go!
...
She doesn't get it.

COYOTE Ragtime Show Vol.03

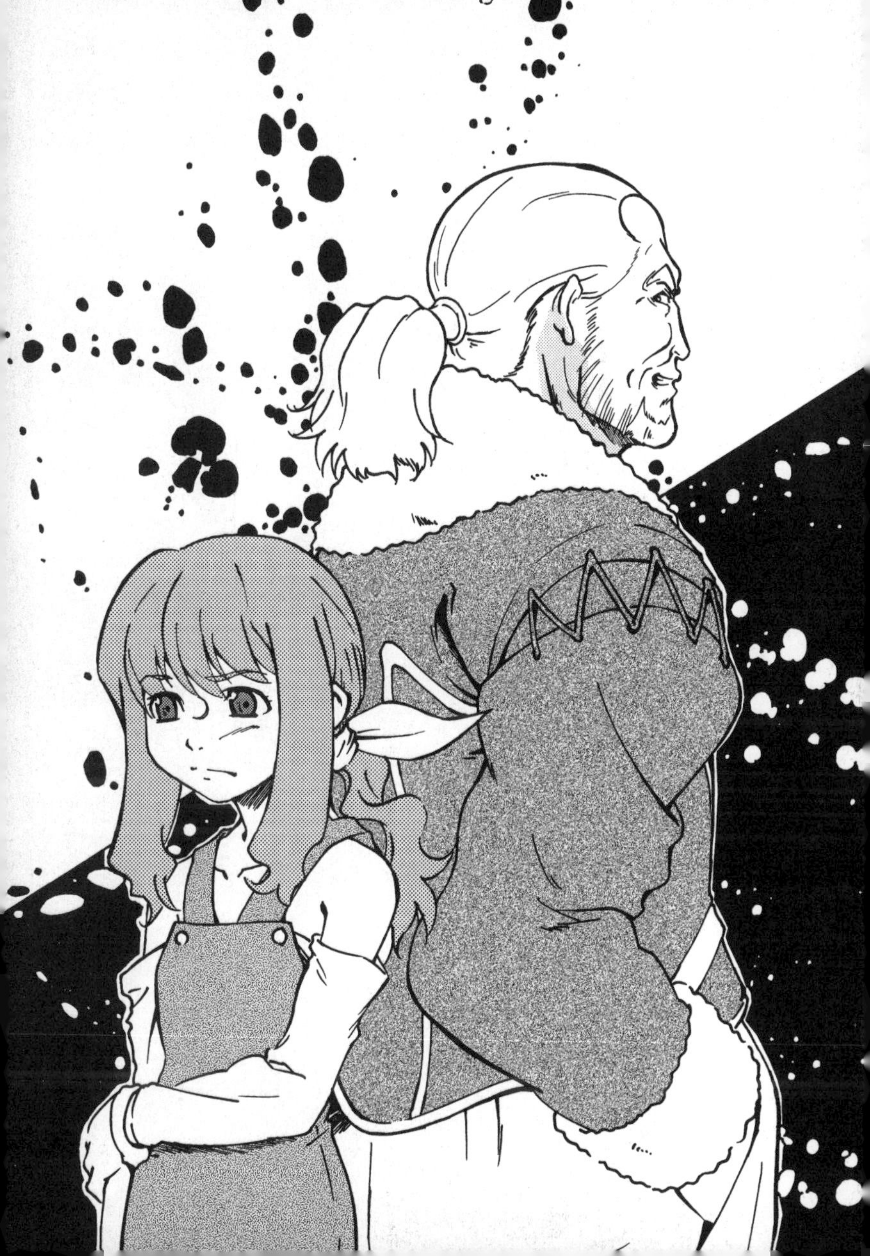

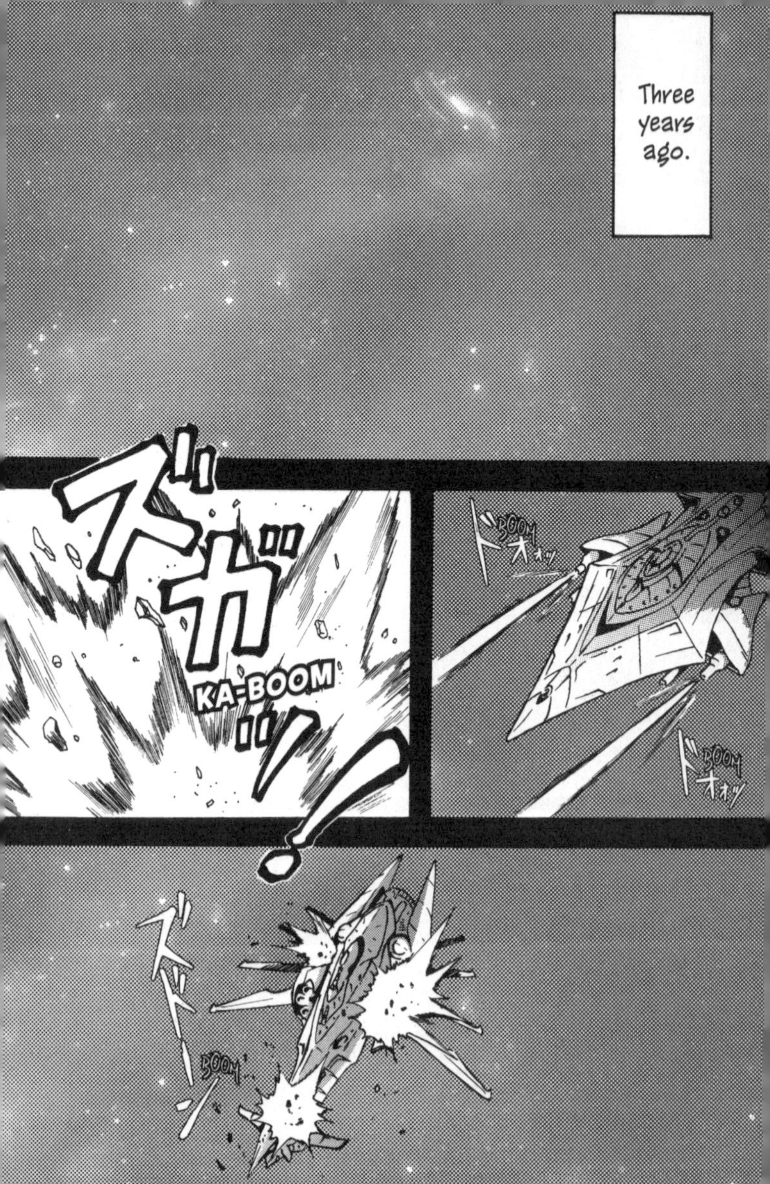
Three years ago.
BOOM
BOOM
KA-BOOM
BOOM

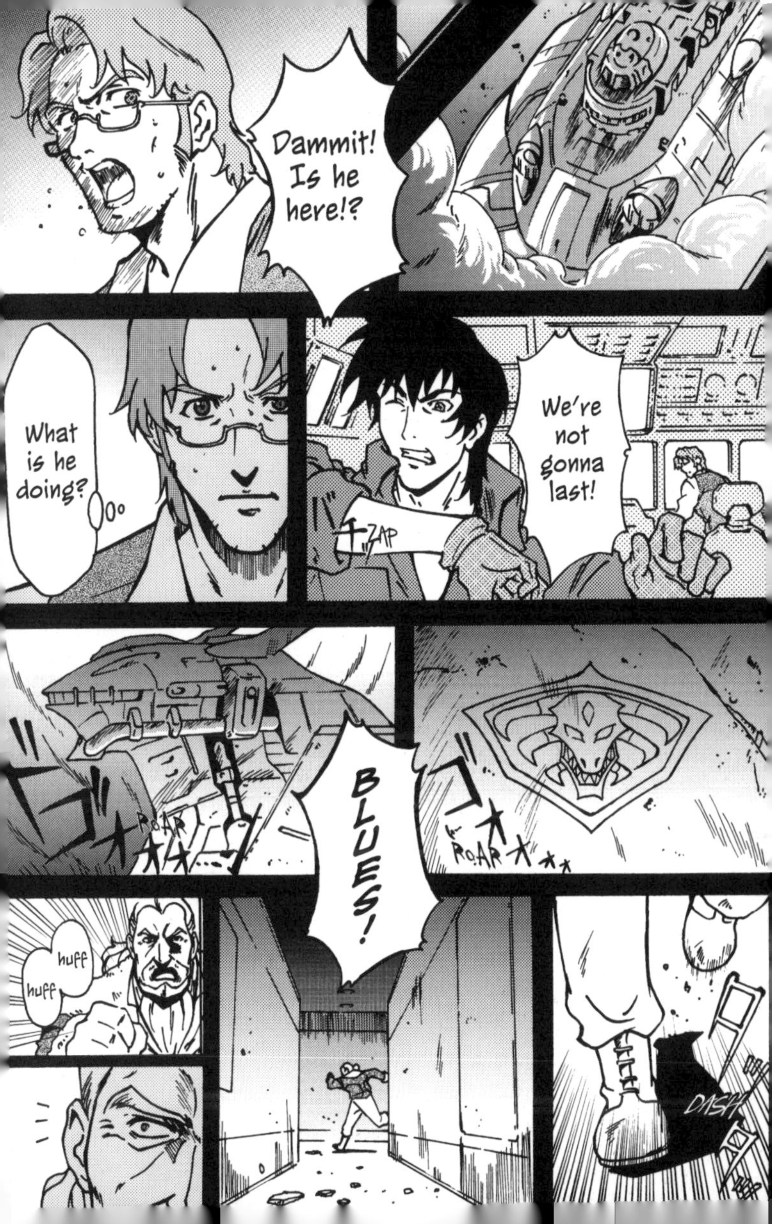

Dammit! Is he here!?
We're not gonna last!
ZAP
What is he doing?
ROAR
BLUES!
ROAR
DASH
huff
huff

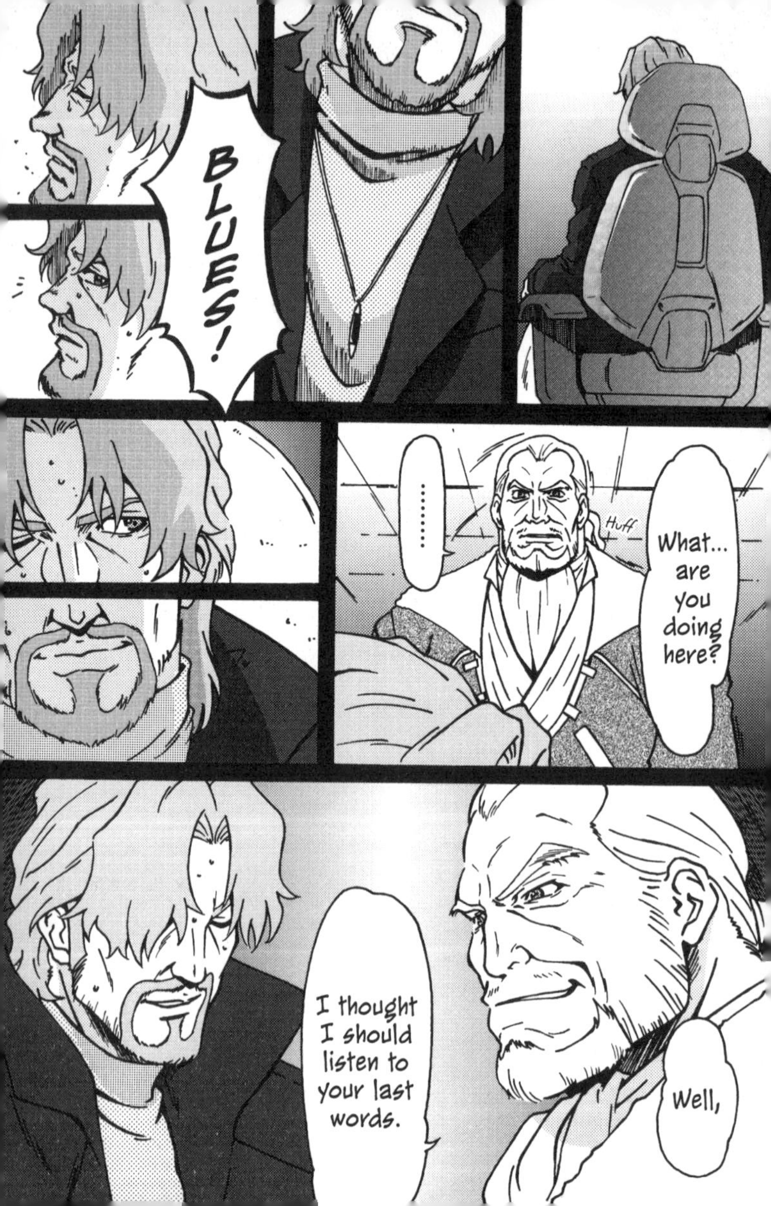
BLUES!
What... are you doing here?
Huff
......
Well,
I thought I should listen to your last words.

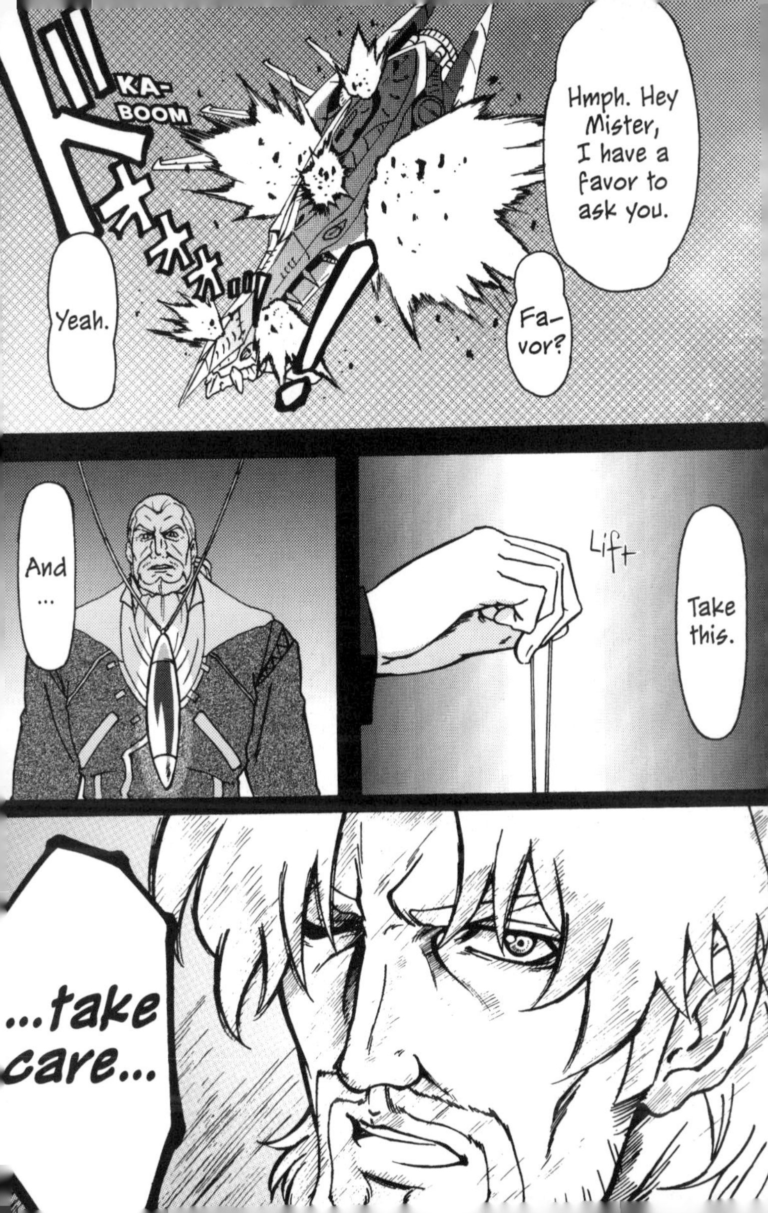
Hmph. Hey Mister, I have a favor to ask you.
Fa-vor?
KA-BOOM
Yeah.
Lift
Take this.
And ...
...take care...

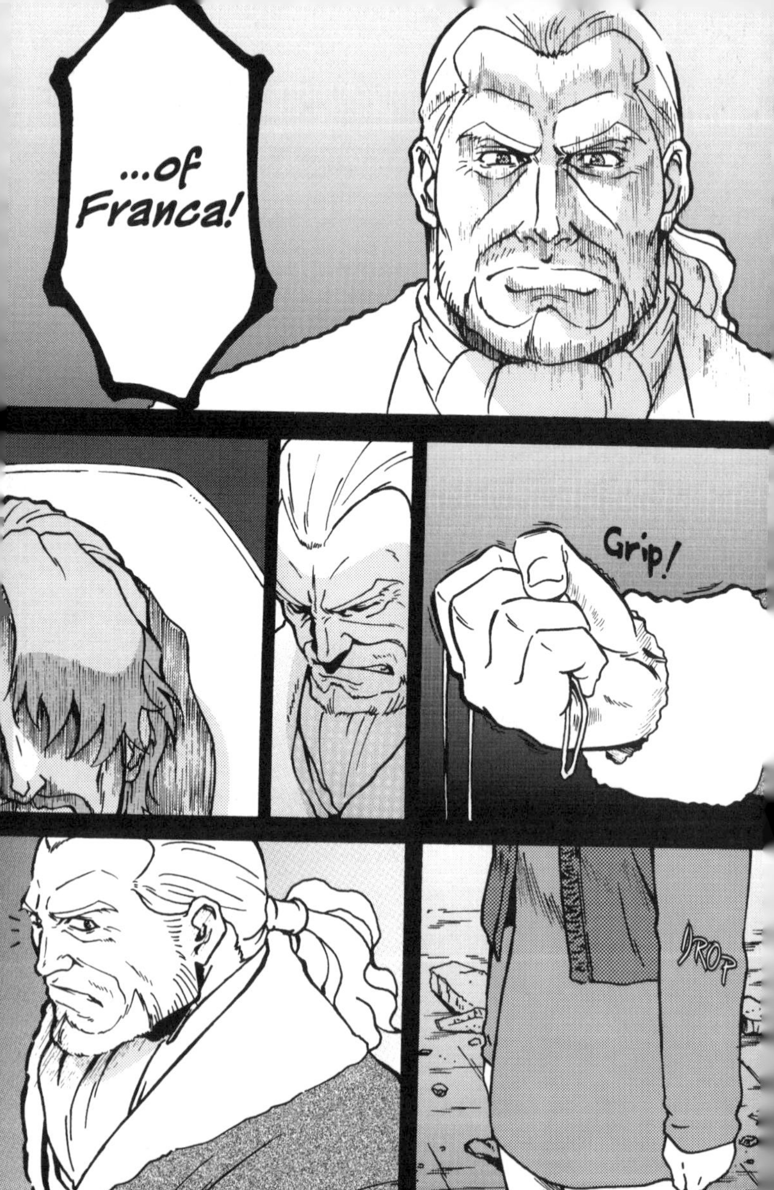
...of Franca!
Grip!
DROP

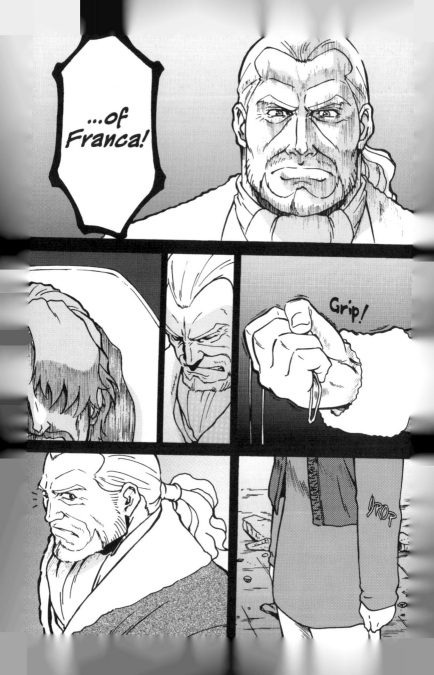

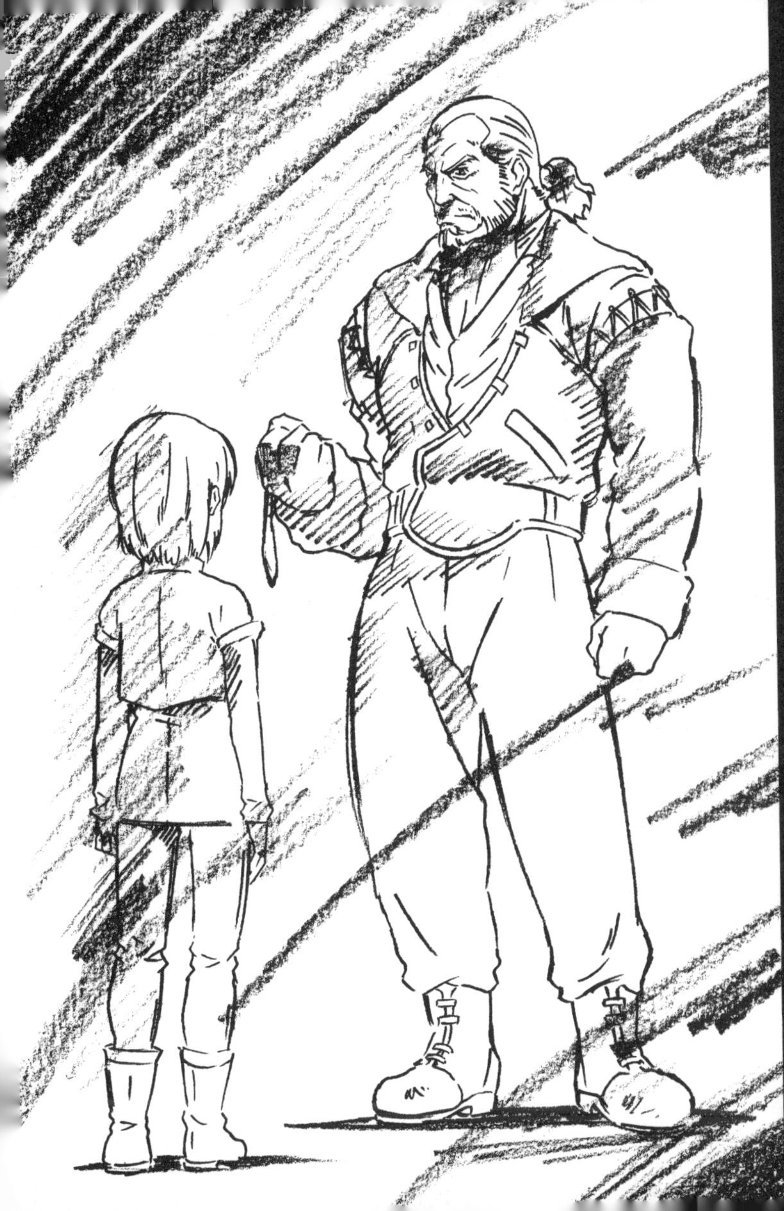

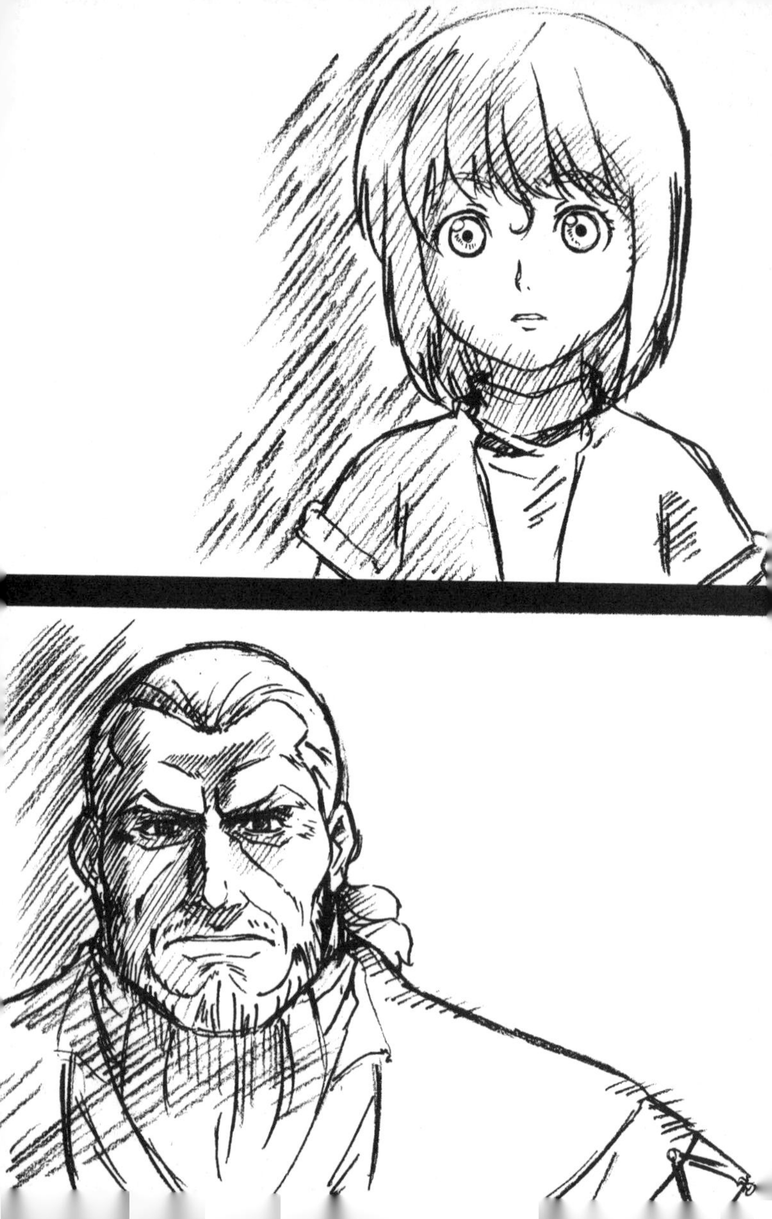

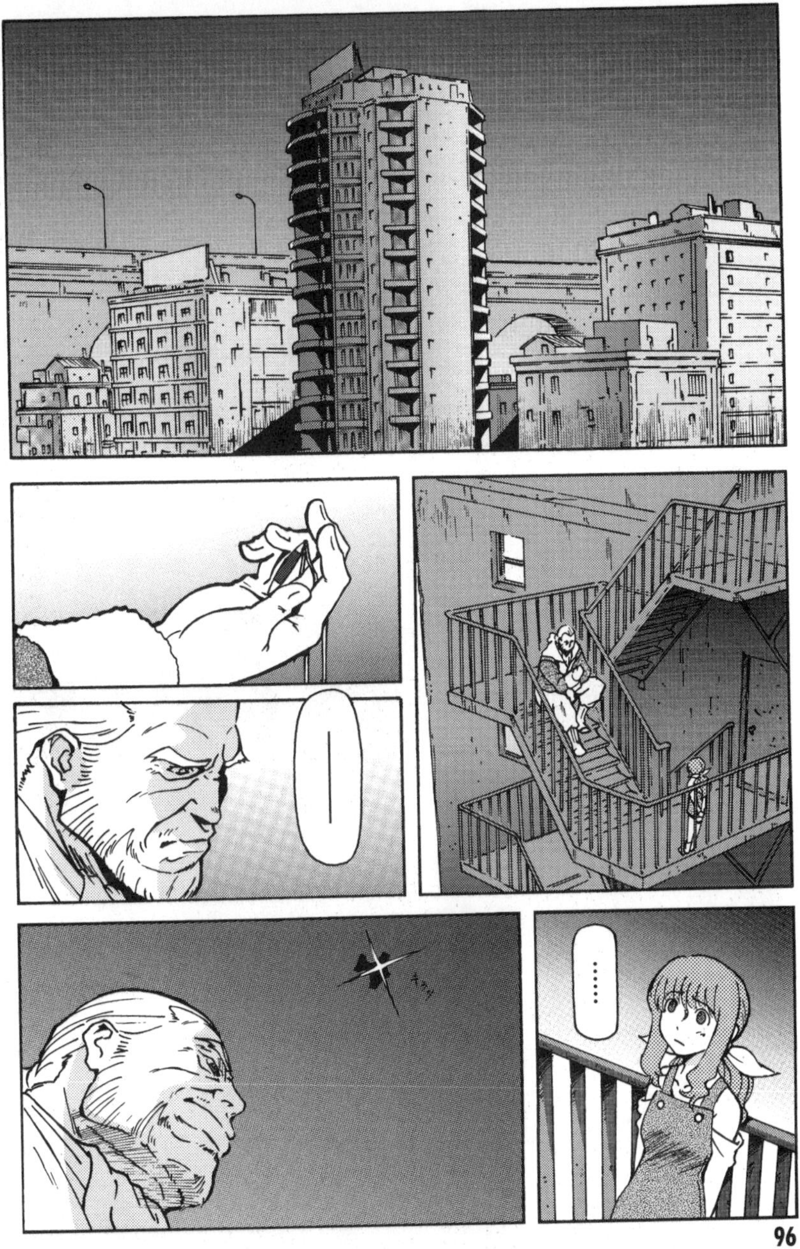
—
……

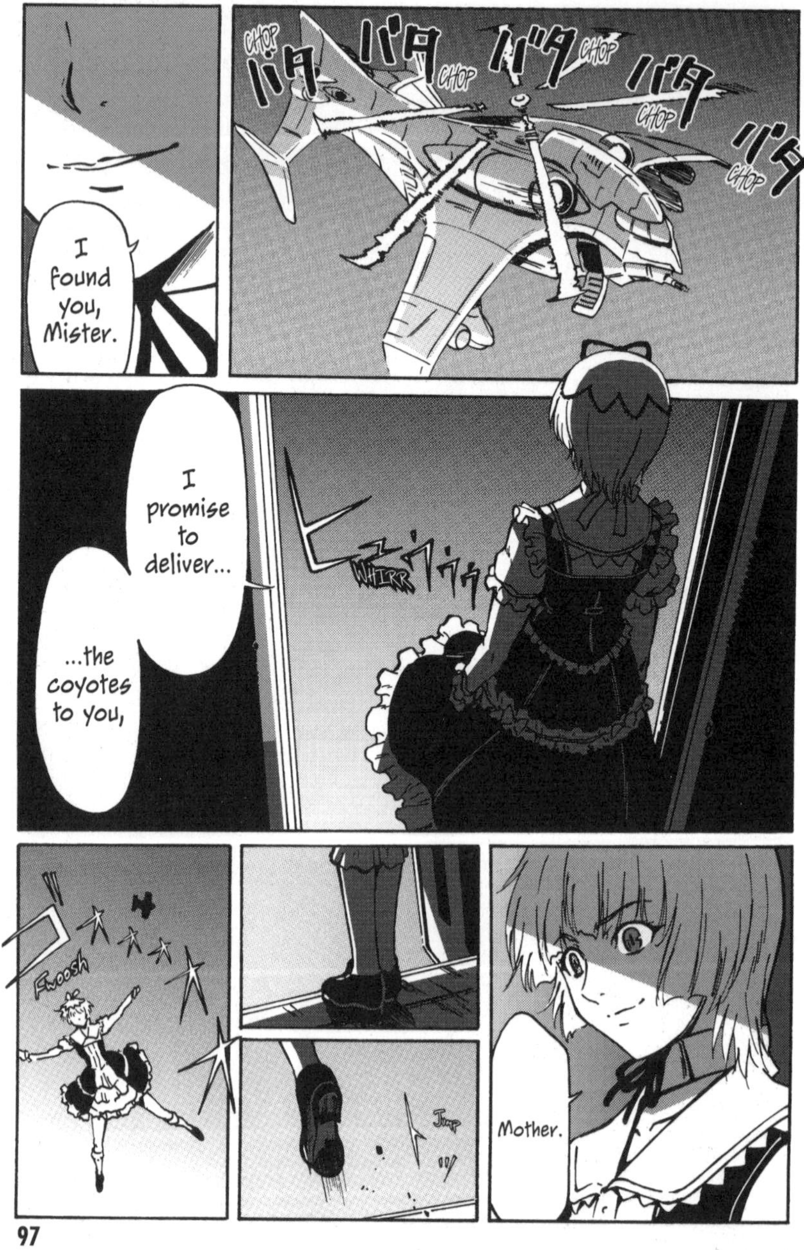

CHOP
バタ
バタ
CHOP
バタ
CHOP
バタ
CHOP
バタ
CHOP
I found you, Mister.
I promise to deliver...
...the coyotes to you,
WHIRR
Mother.
Jump
Fwoosh

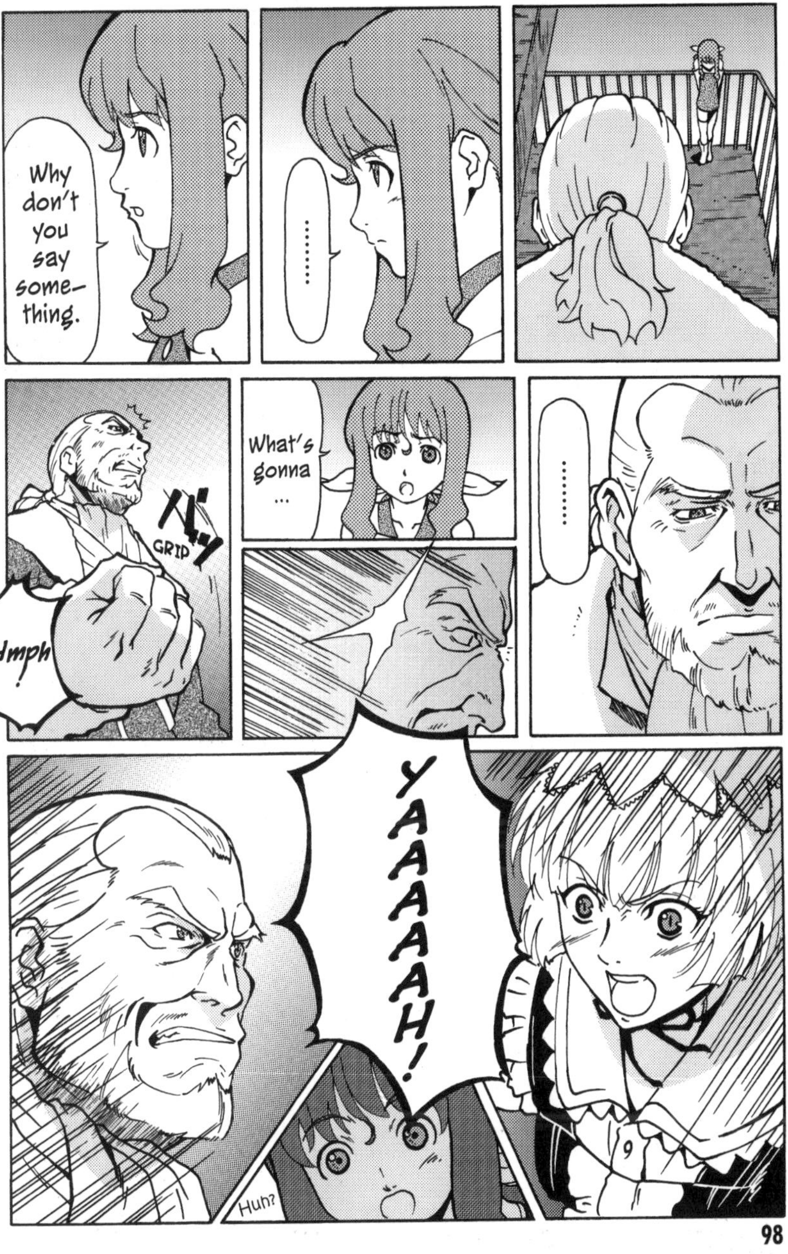

……
Why don't you say some-thing.
……
What's gonna ...
バッ
GRIP
Hmph!
YAAAAAAH!
Huh?

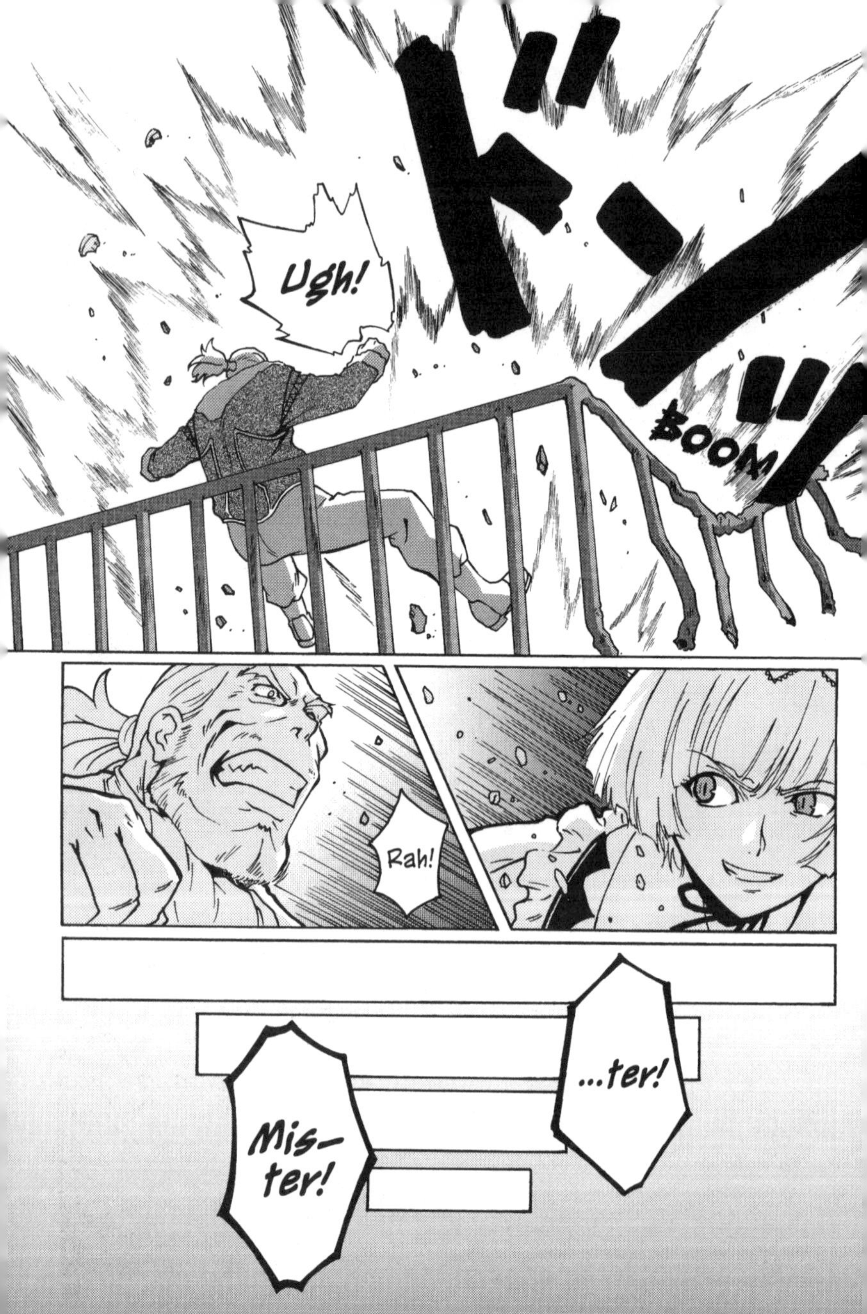
ドンッ
BOOM
Ugh!
Rah!
...ter!
Mis-ter!

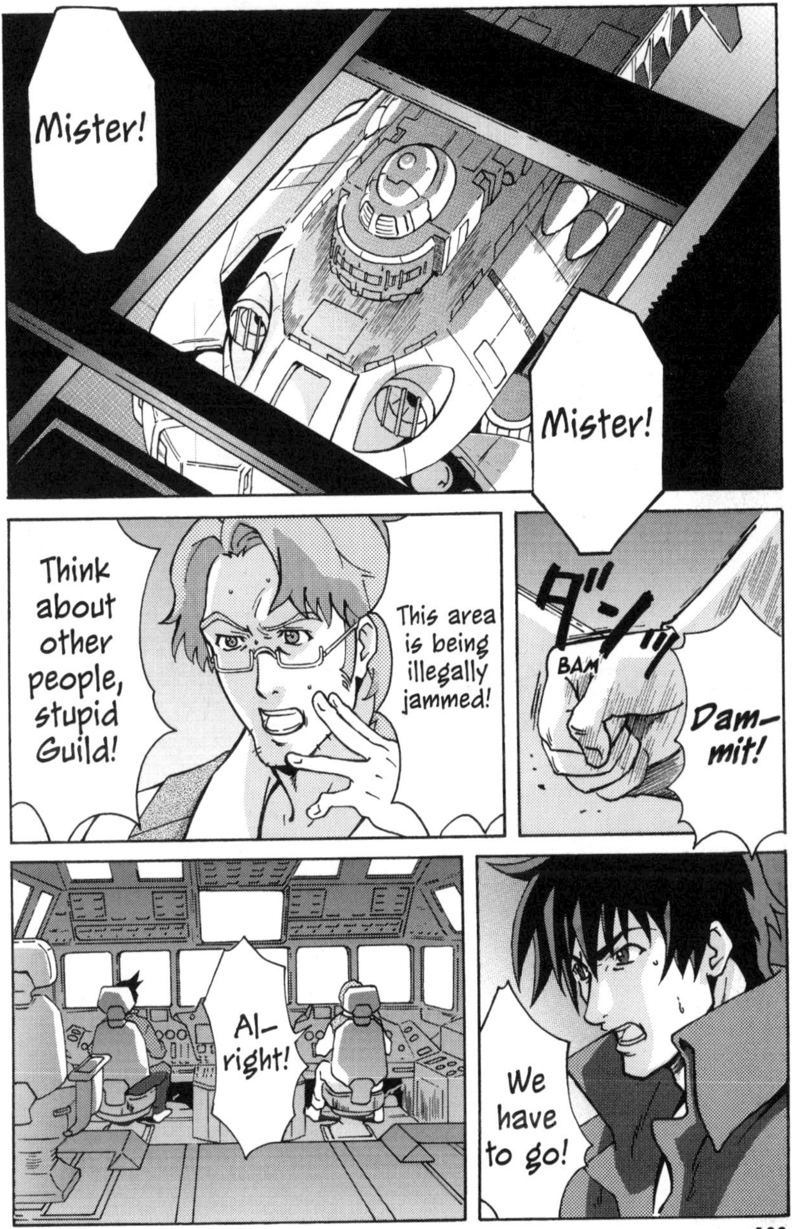
Mister!
Mister!
ダンッ
BAM
Dam-mit!
This area is being illegally jammed!
Think about other people, stupid Guild!
We have to go!
Al-right!

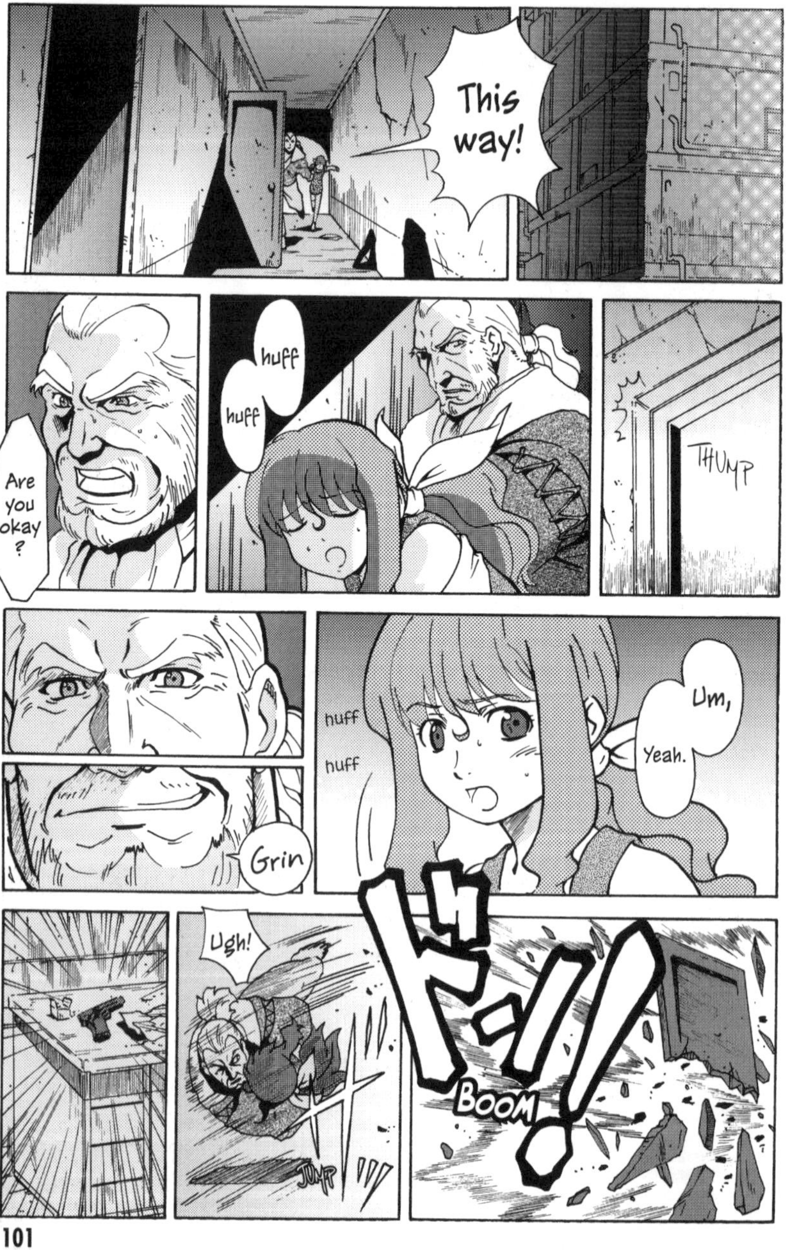
This way!
THUMP
huff
huff
Are you okay?
huff
huff
Um,
Yeah.
Grin
ドーン!!
BOOM
Ugh!
JUMP

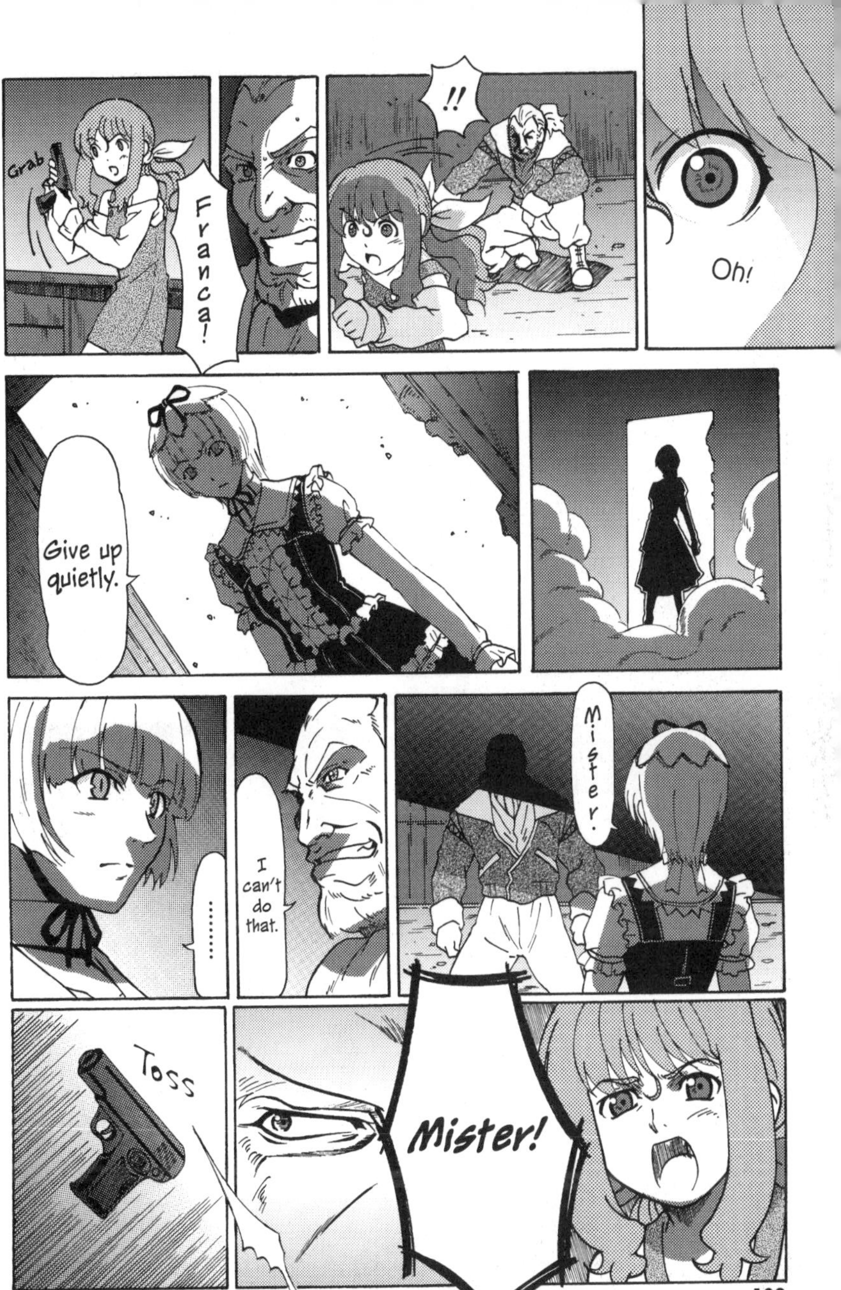
Oh!
!!
Franca!
Grab
Give up quietly.
Mister.
I can't do that.
....
Mister!
Toss

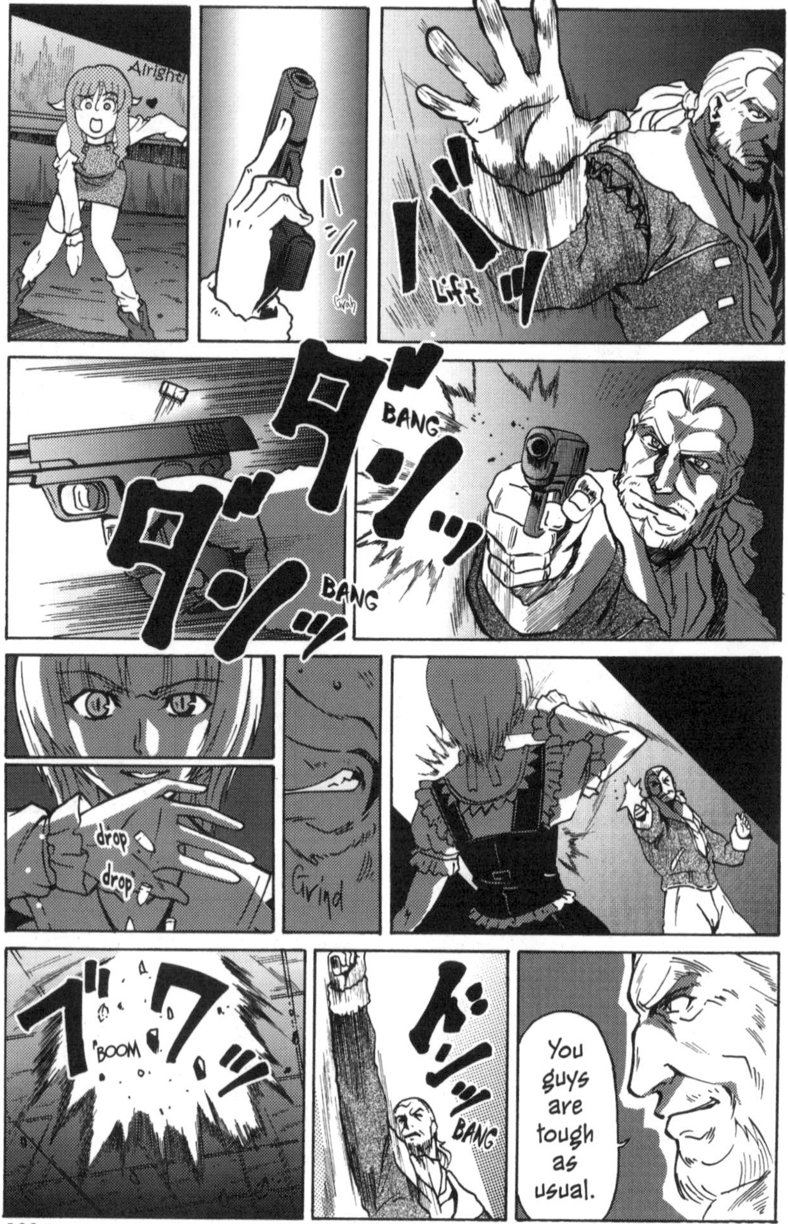

バッ
Lift
パシッ
Grab
Alright! ♥
ダンッ
BANG
ダンッ
BANG
Grind
drop
drop
You guys are tough as usual.
ドンッ
BANG
ブワッ
BOOM

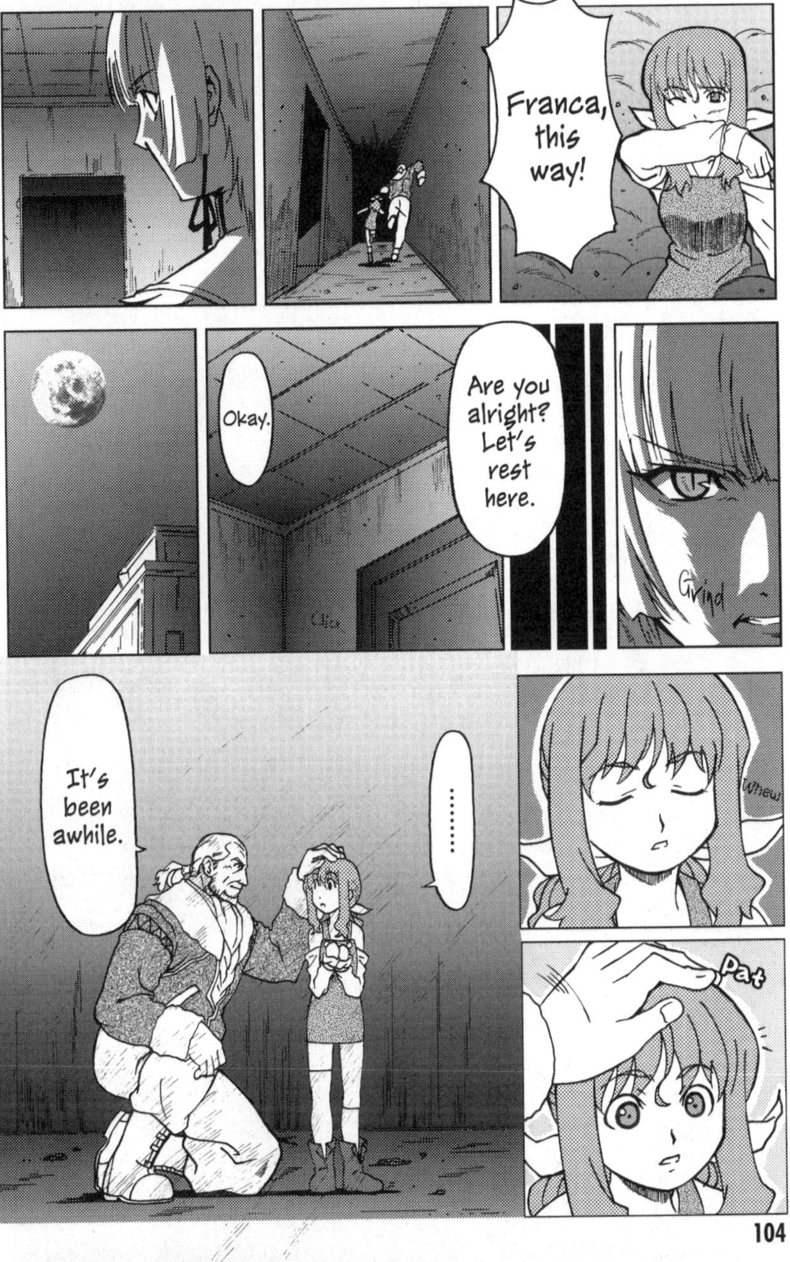
Franca, this way!
Grind
Are you alright? Let's rest here.
Okay.
Click
Whew
Pat
....
It's been awhile.

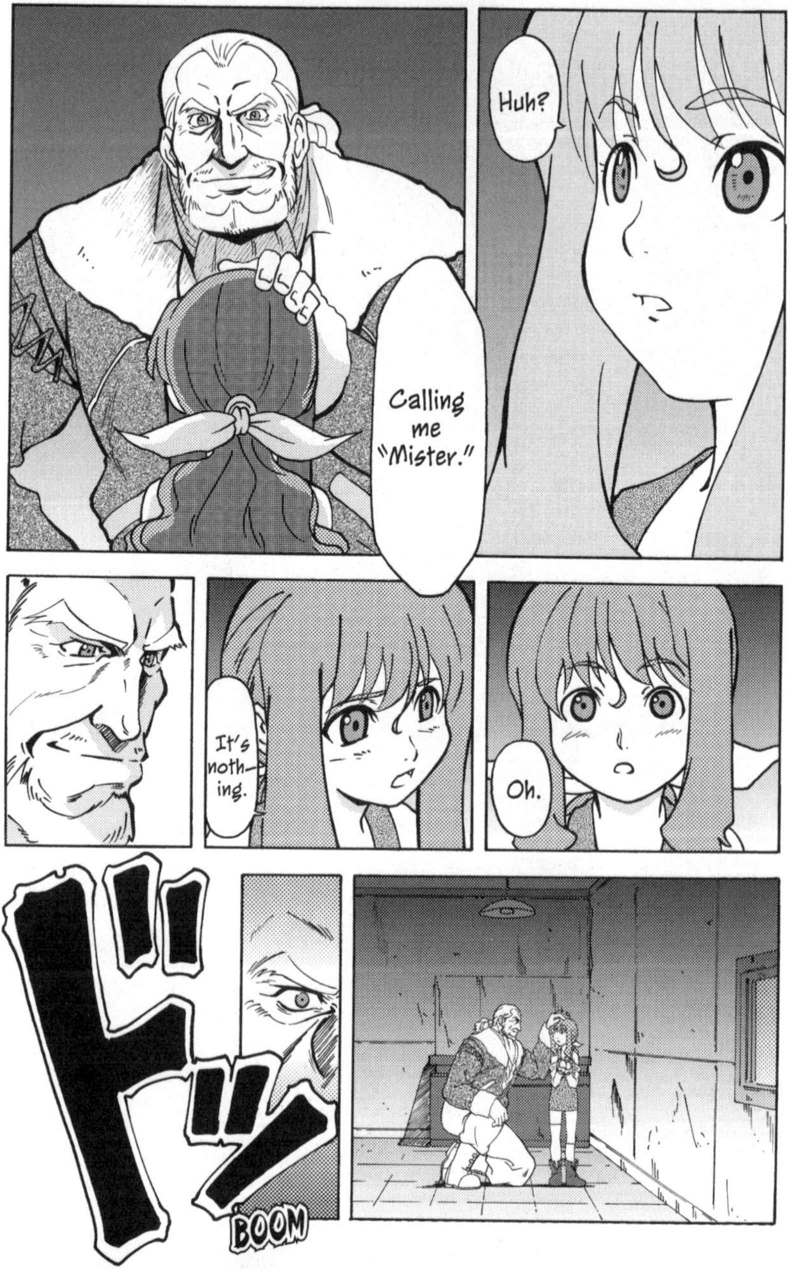
Huh?
Calling me "Mister."
Oh.
It's nothing.
ドッ
BOOM

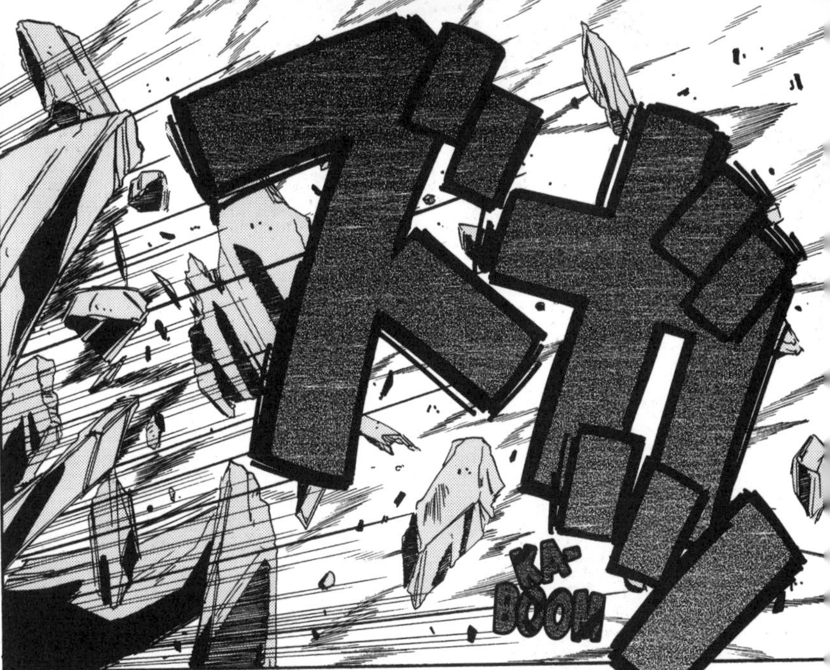
KA-BOOM
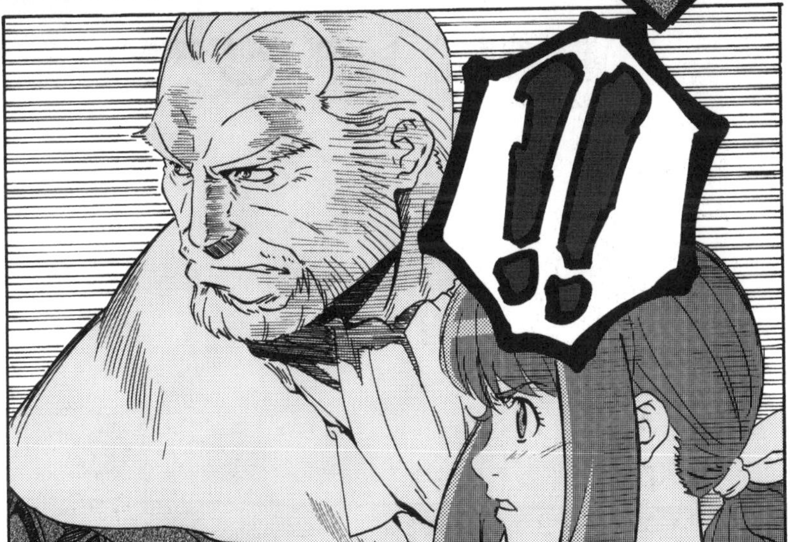
!!

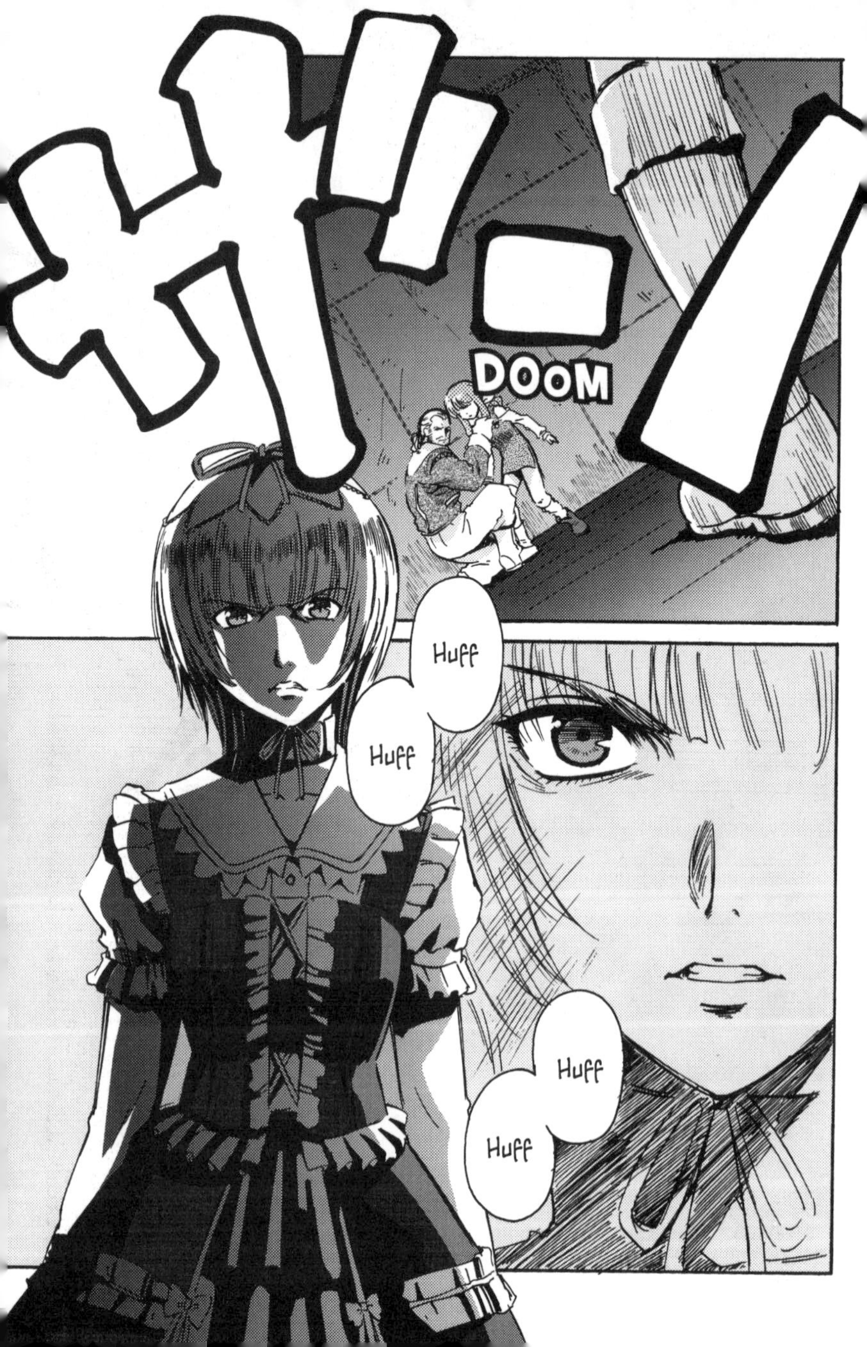
DOOM
Huff
Huff
Huff
Huff

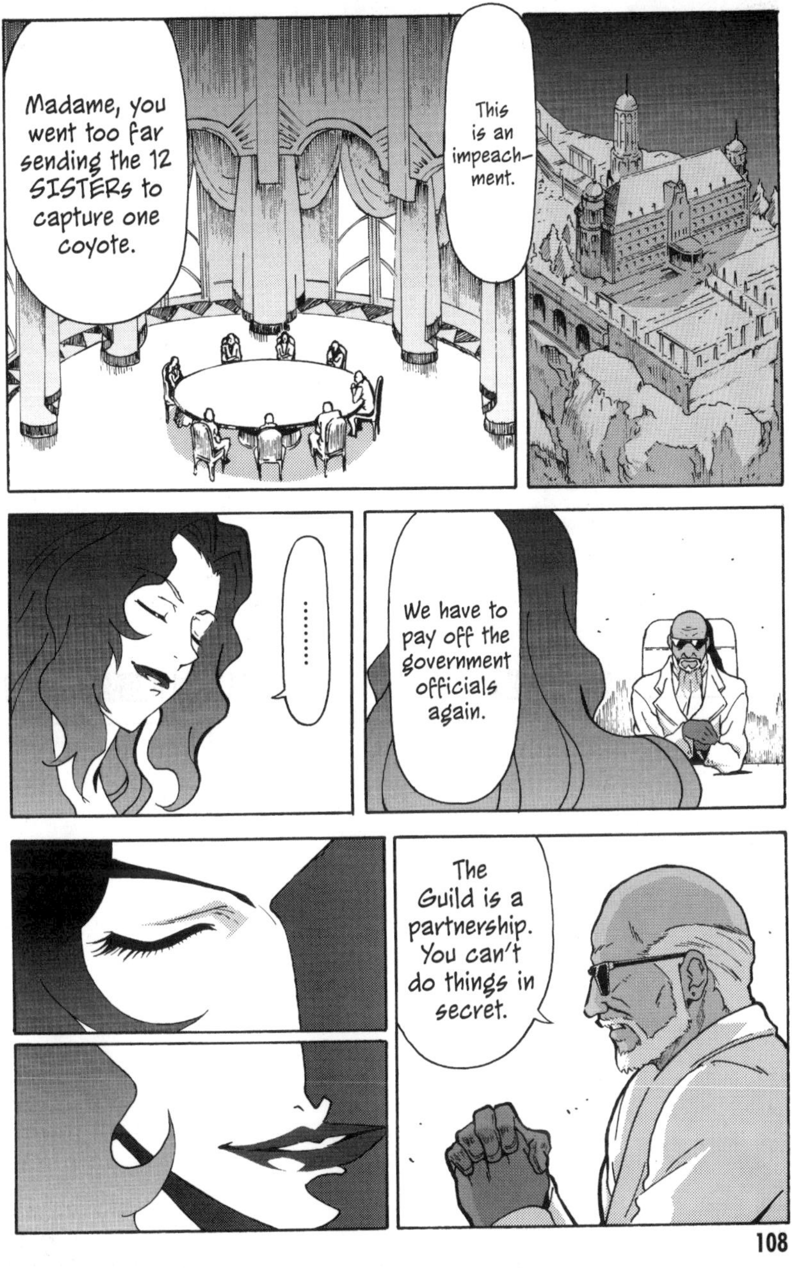
This is an impeach-ment.
Madame, you went too far sending the 12 SISTERs to capture one coyote.
We have to pay off the government officials again.
....
The Guild is a partnership. You can't do things in secret.

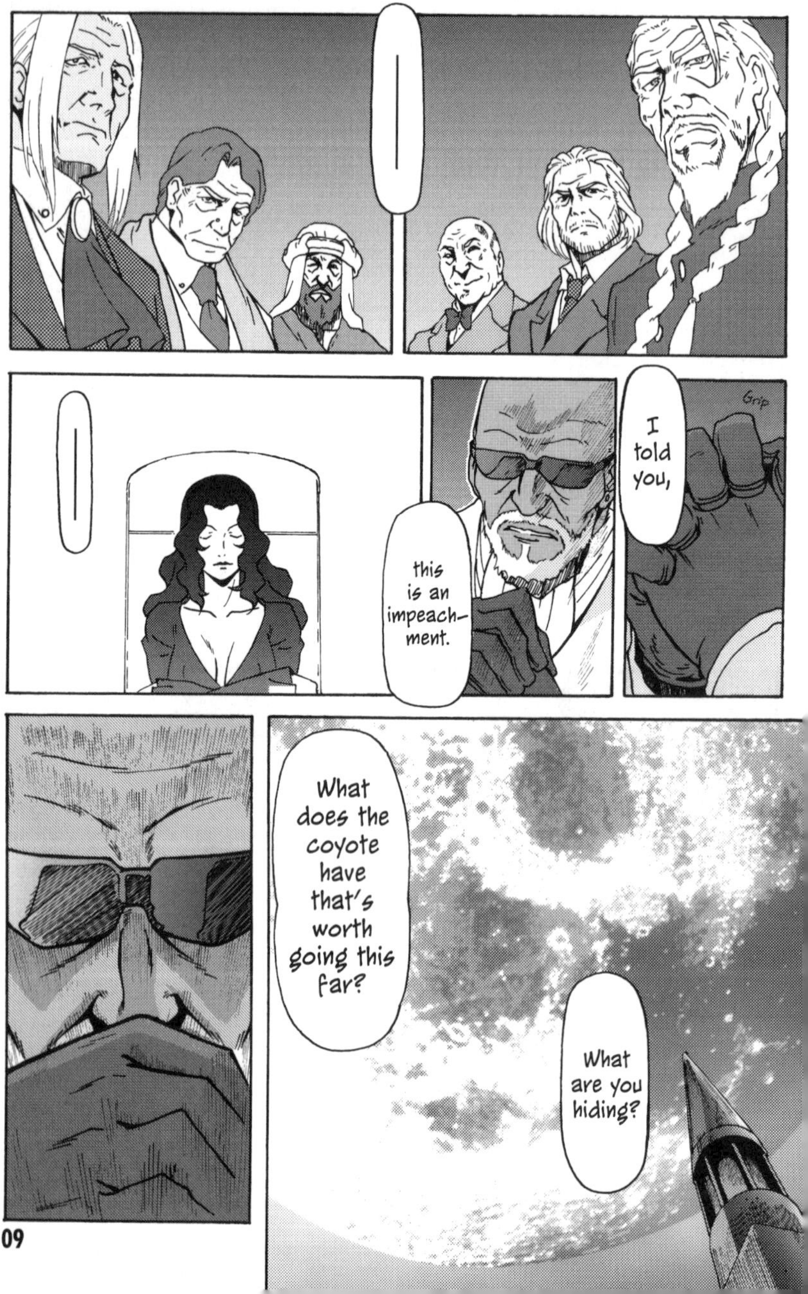
……
Grip
I told you,
this is an impeach-ment.
……
What does the coyote have that's worth going this far?
What are you hiding?

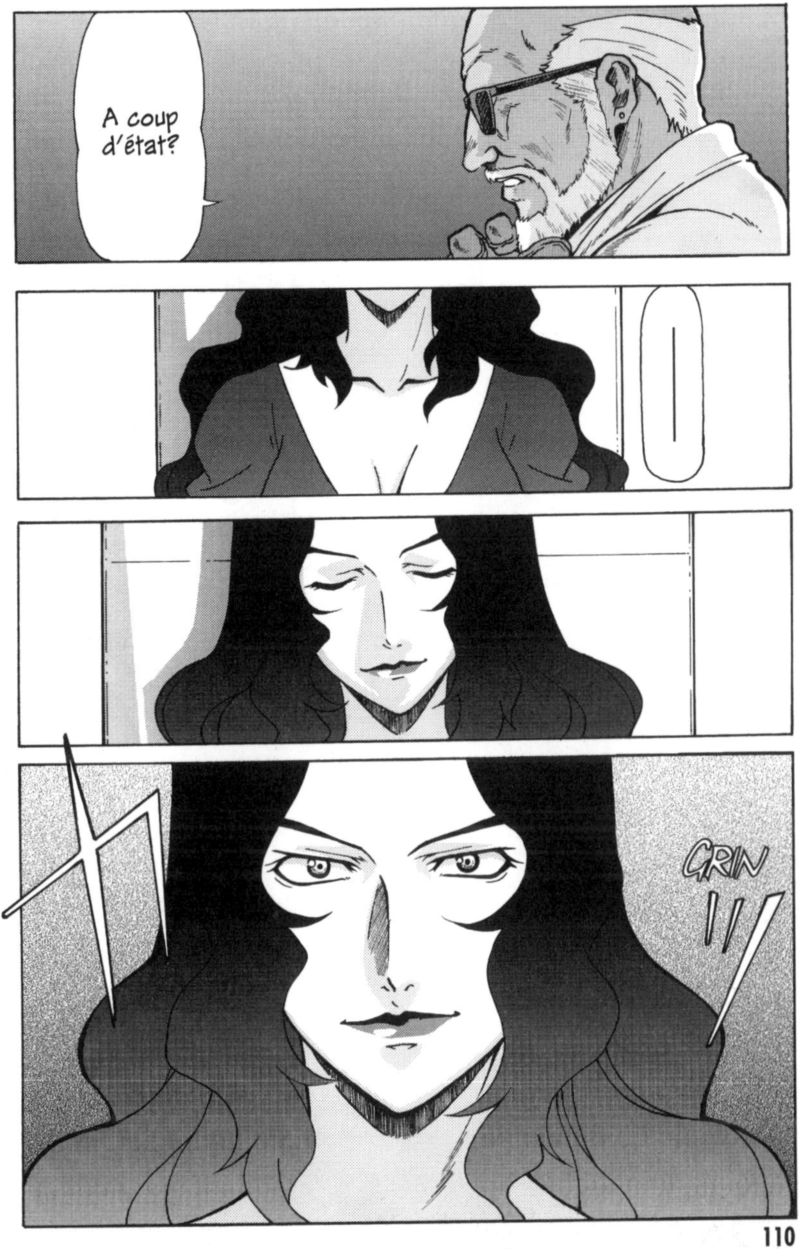
A coup d'état?
GRIN

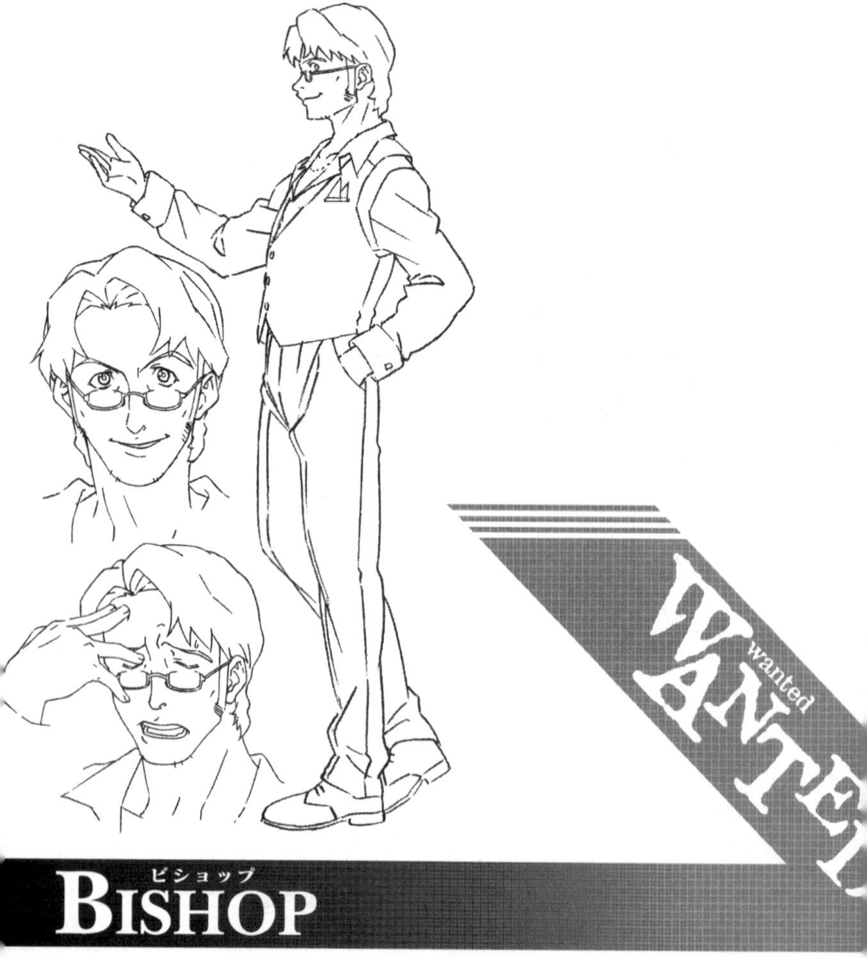

WANTED
wanted

ビショップ
BISHOP

WANTED

wanted

KATANA
カタナ

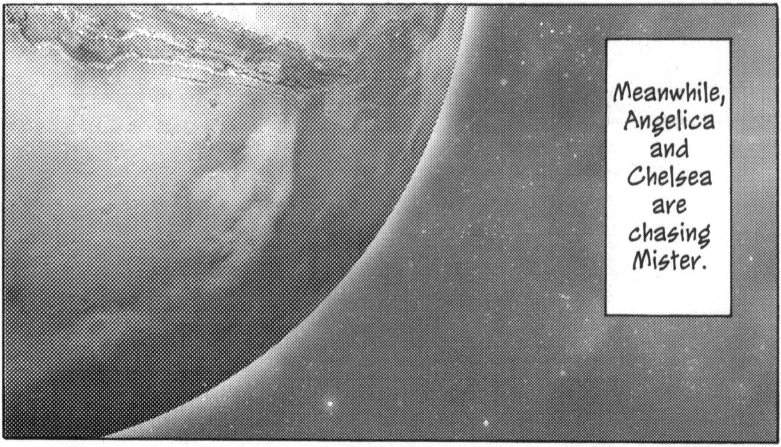
Meanwhile, Angelica and Chelsea are chasing Mister.
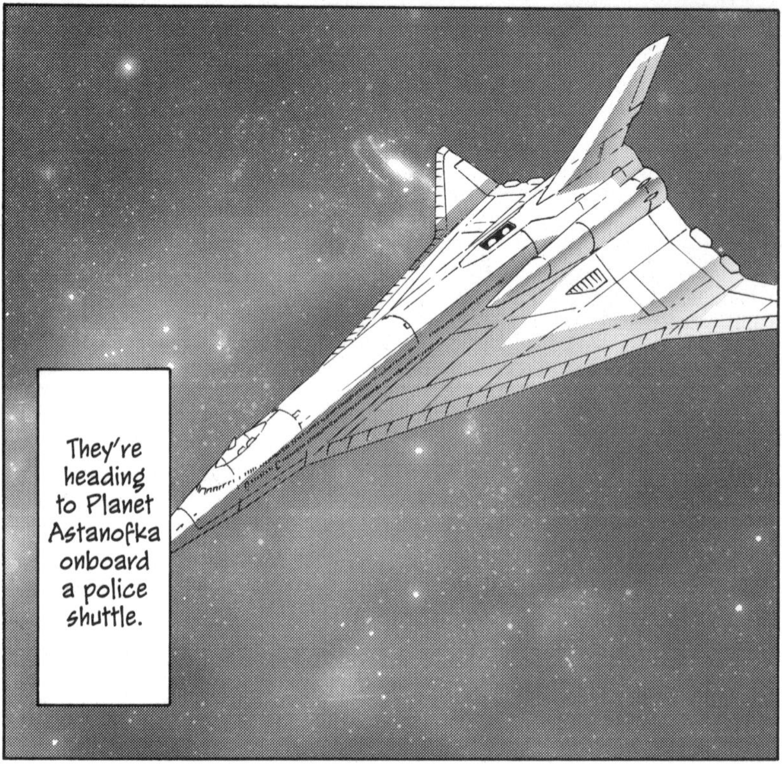
They're heading to Planet Astanofka onboard a police shuttle.

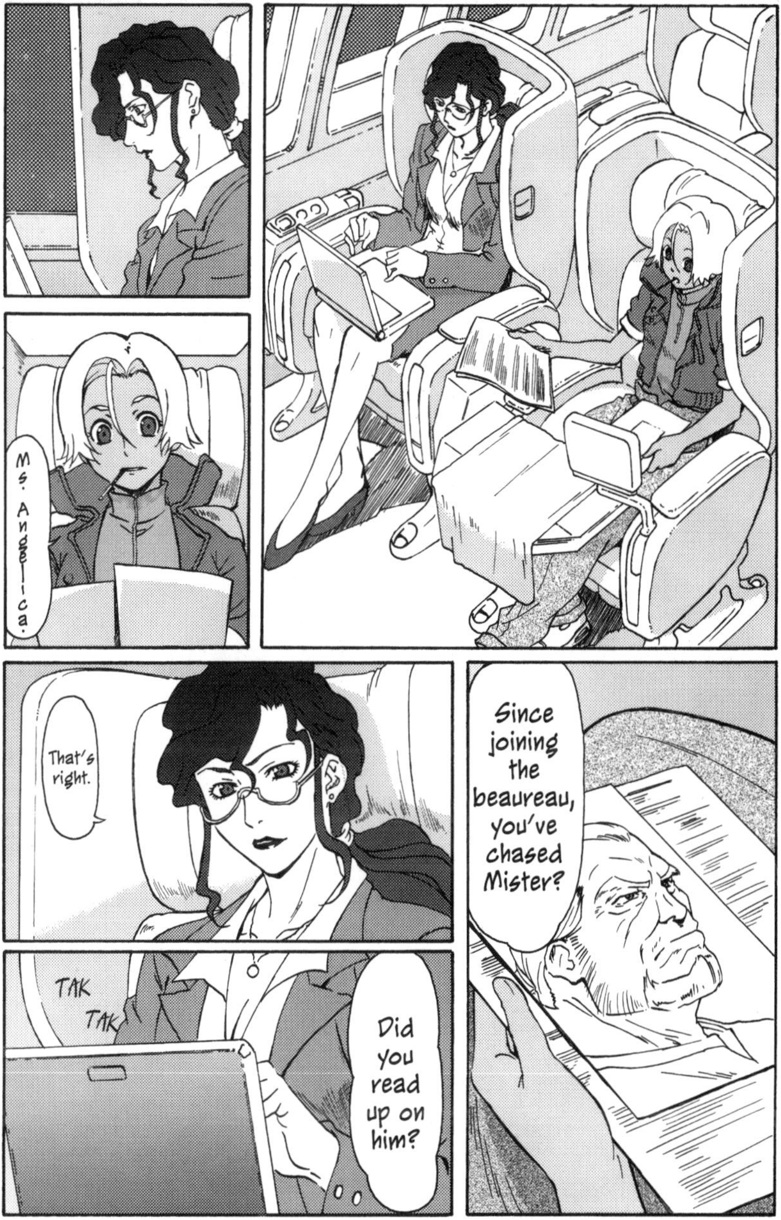
Ms. Angelica.
Since joining the beaureau, you've chased Mister?
That's right.
TAK TAK
Did you read up on him?

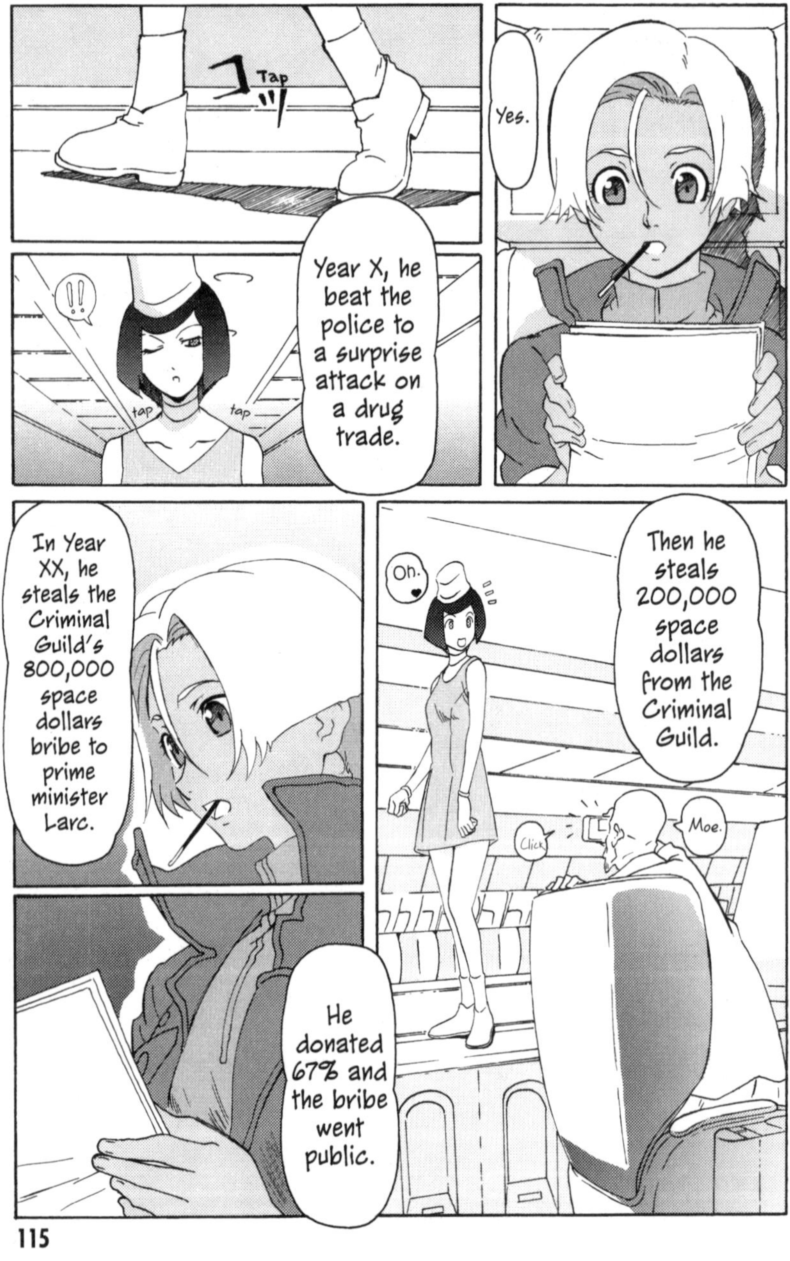

Yes.
Tap
!!
tap
tap
Year X, he beat the police to a surprise attack on a drug trade.
Then he steals 200,000 space dollars from the Criminal Guild.
Oh.
Moe.
Click
In Year XX, he steals the Criminal Guild's 800,000 space dollars bribe to prime minister Larc.
He donated 67% and the bribe went public.

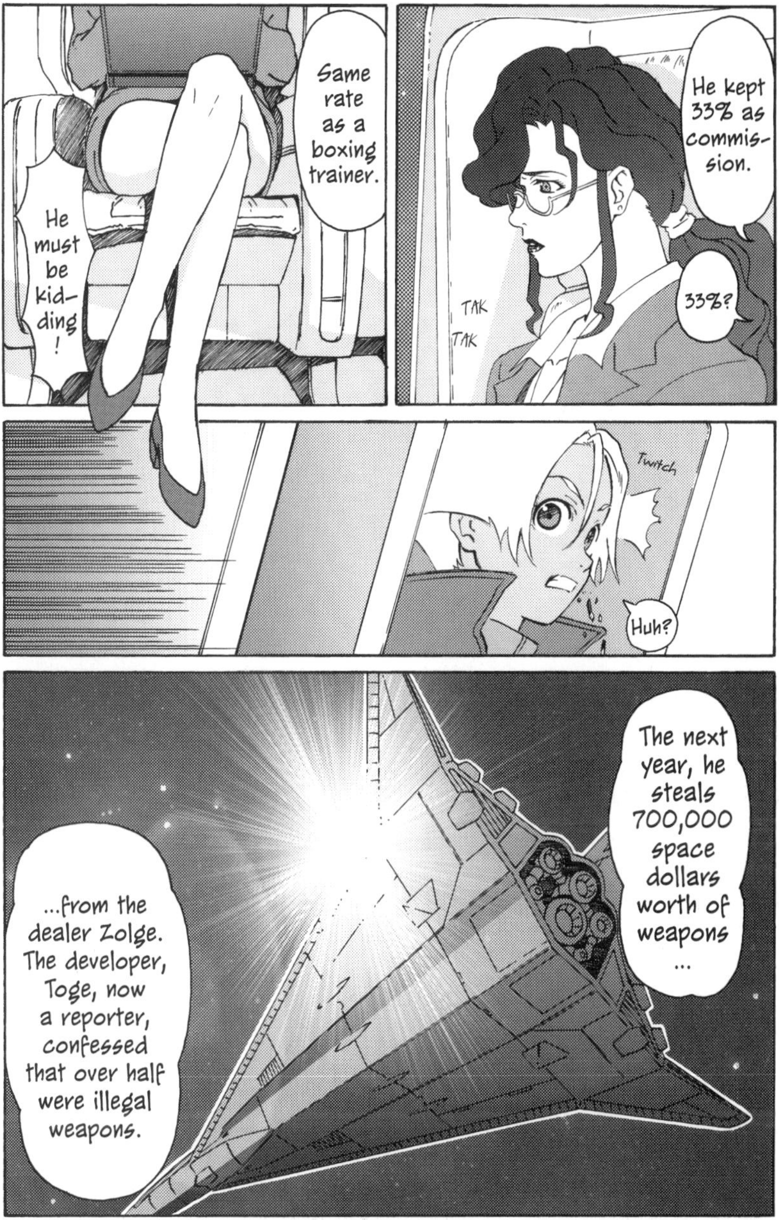
He kept 33% as commission.
33%?
TAK
TAK
Same rate as a boxing trainer.
He must be kidding!
Twitch
Huh?
The next year, he steals 700,000 space dollars worth of weapons...
...from the dealer Zolge. The developer, Toge, now a reporter, confessed that over half were illegal weapons.

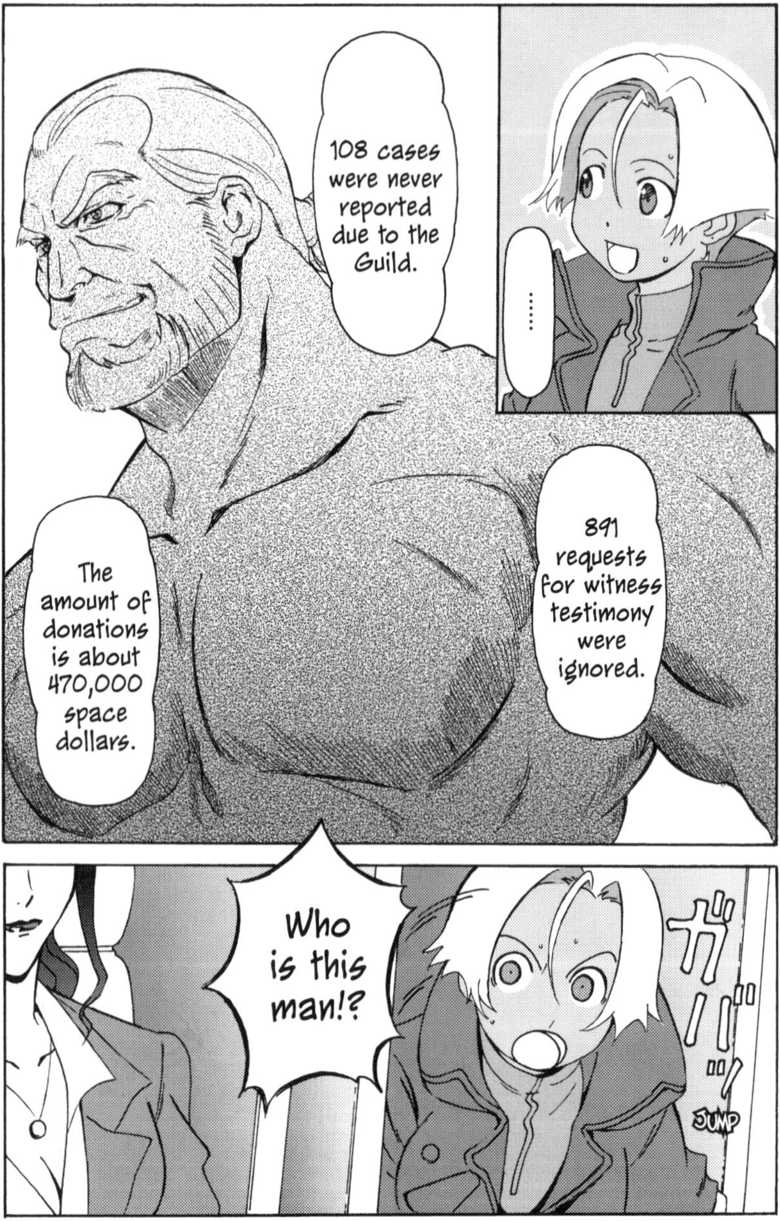
……
108 cases were never reported due to the Guild.
891 requests for witness testimony were ignored.
The amount of donations is about 470,000 space dollars.
Who is this man!?
JUMP

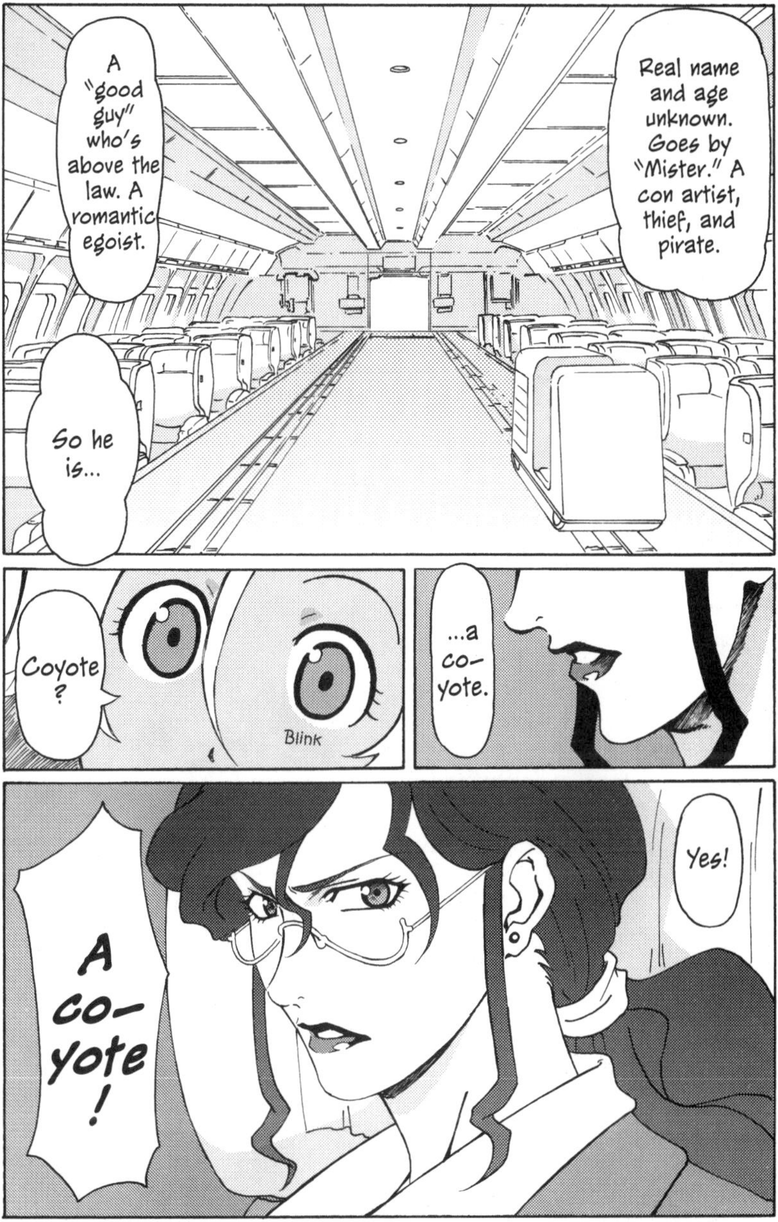
Real name and age unknown. Goes by "Mister." A con artist, thief, and pirate.
A "good guy" who's above the law. A romantic egoist.
So he is...
...a co-yote.
Coyote?
Blink
Yes!
A co-yote!

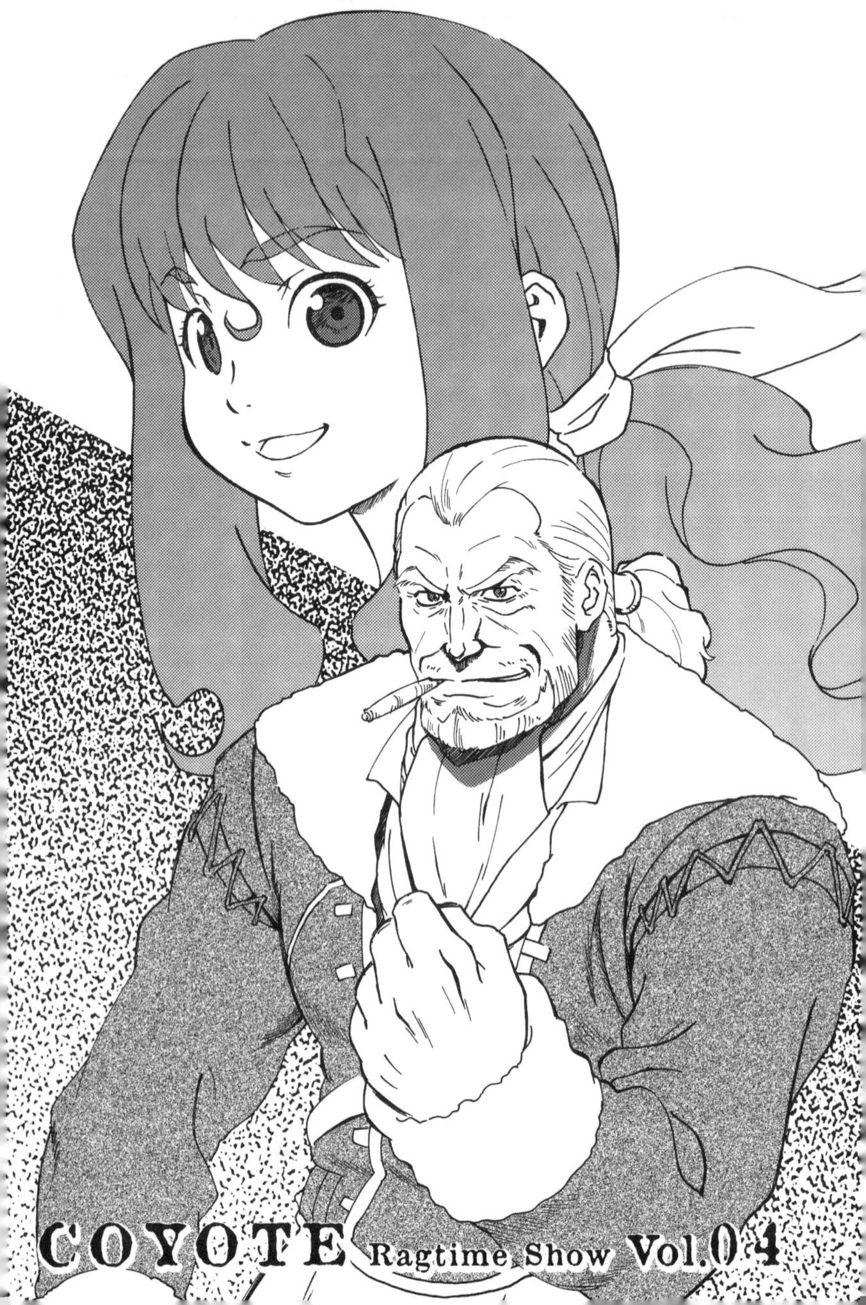
COYOTE Ragtime Show Vol.04

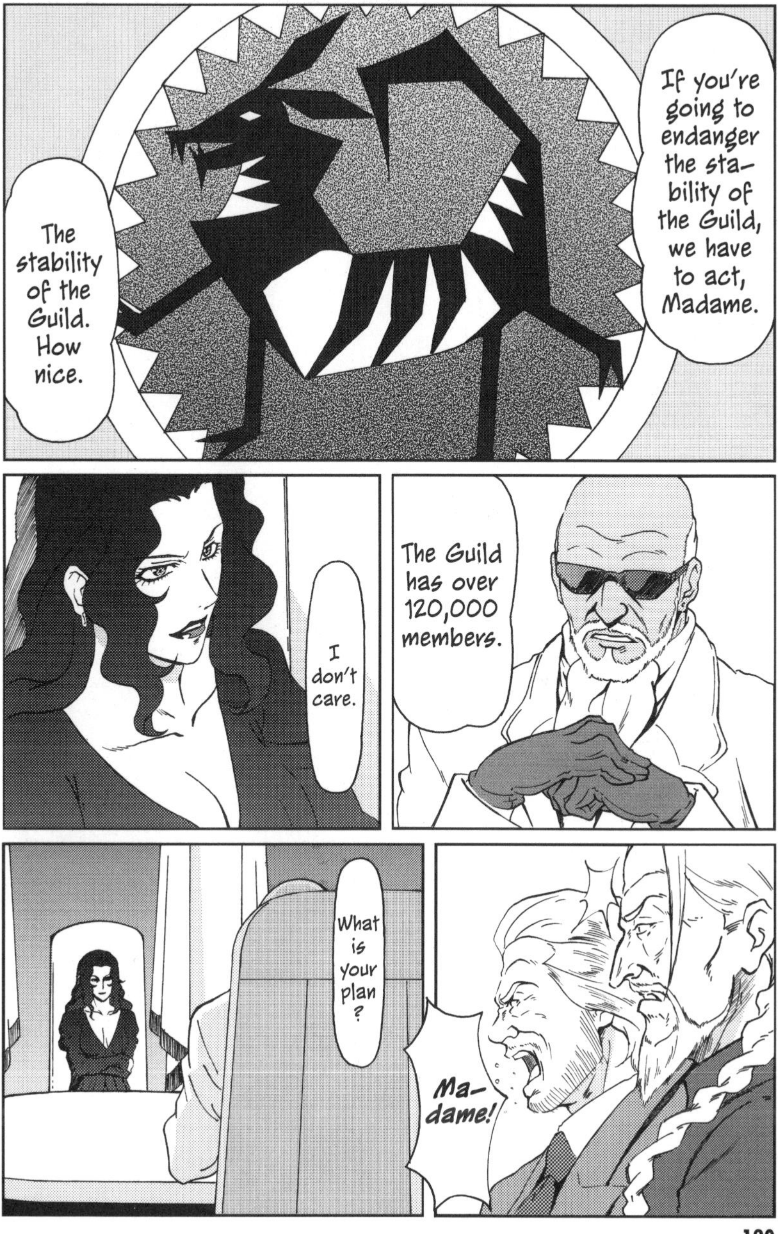
If you're going to endanger the sta-bility of the Guild, we have to act, Madame.
The stability of the Guild. How nice.
The Guild has over 120,000 members.
I don't care.
Ma-dame!
What is your plan?

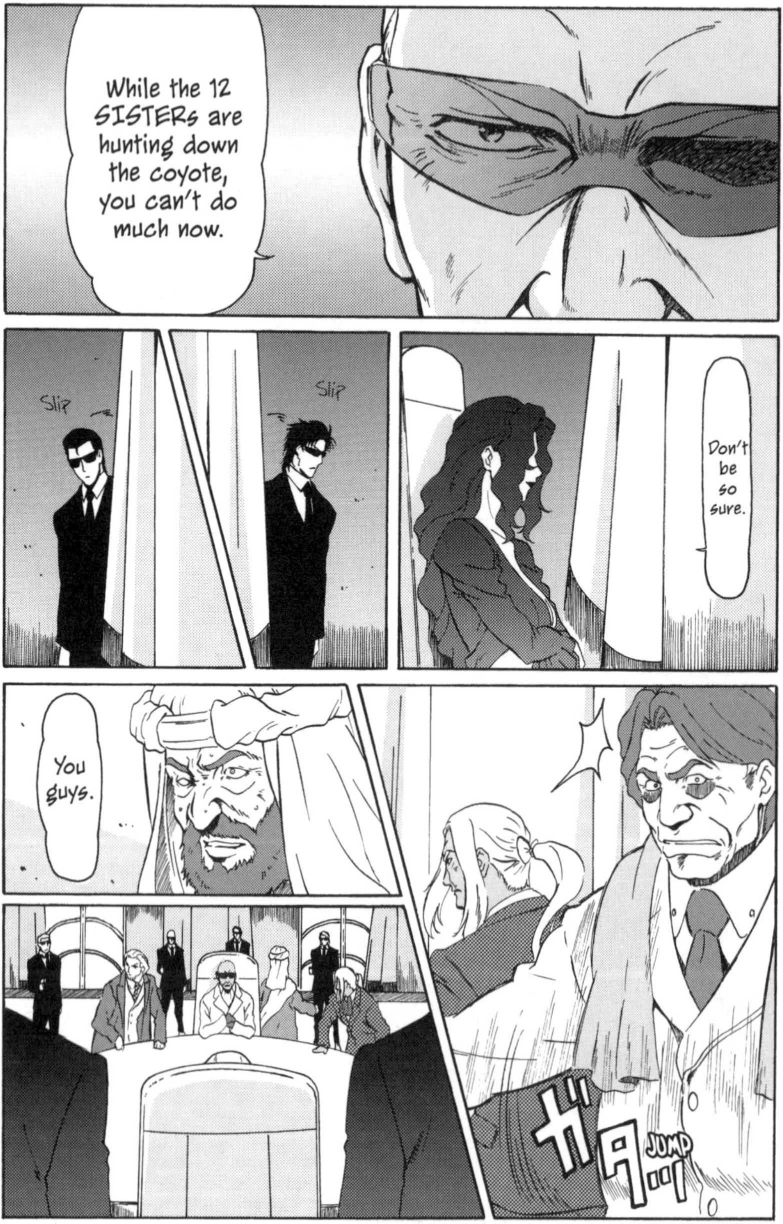
While the 12 SISTERs are hunting down the coyote, you can't do much now.
Don't be so sure.
Slip
Slip
ガタ
JUMP
You guys.

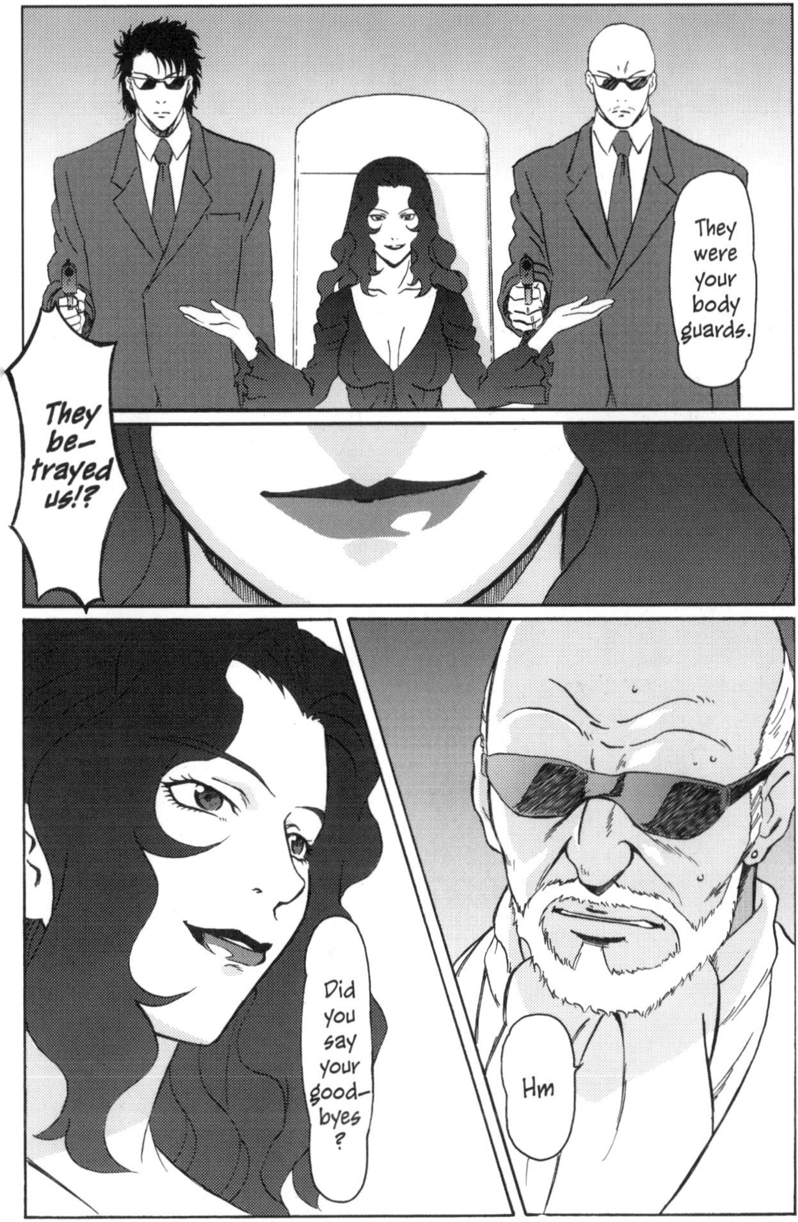
They were your body guards.
They be-trayed us!?
Hm
Did you say your good-byes?

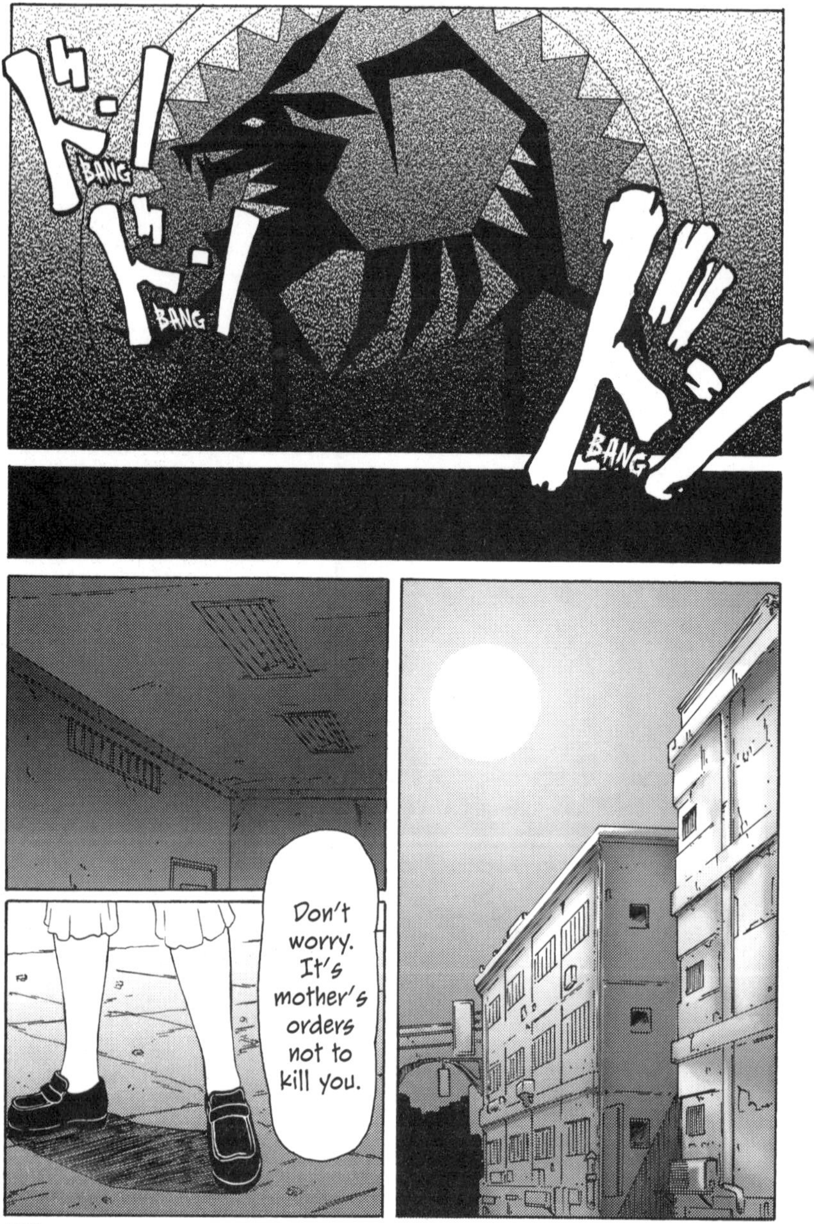
ドーン
BANG
ドーン
BANG
ドーン
BANG
Don't worry. It's mother's orders not to kill you.

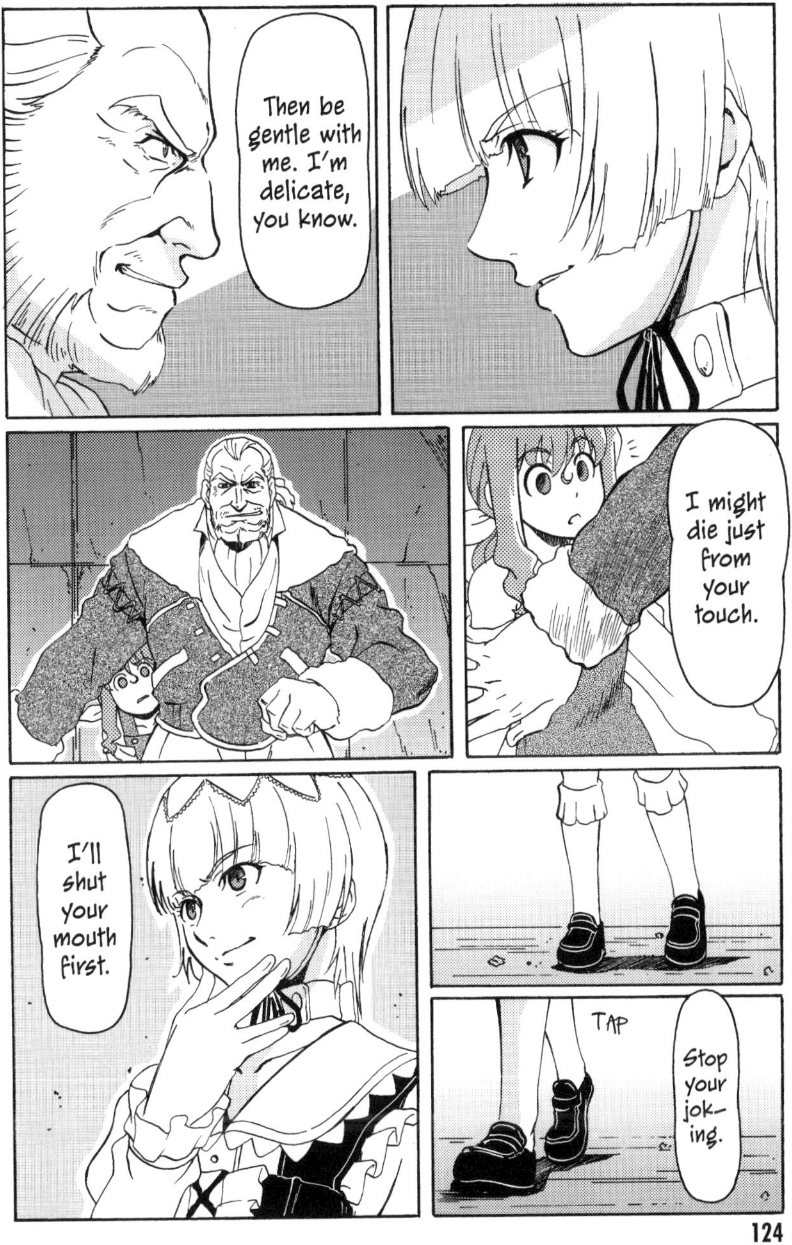
Then be gentle with me. I'm delicate, you know.
I might die just from your touch.
Stop your jok-ing.
TAP
I'll shut your mouth first.

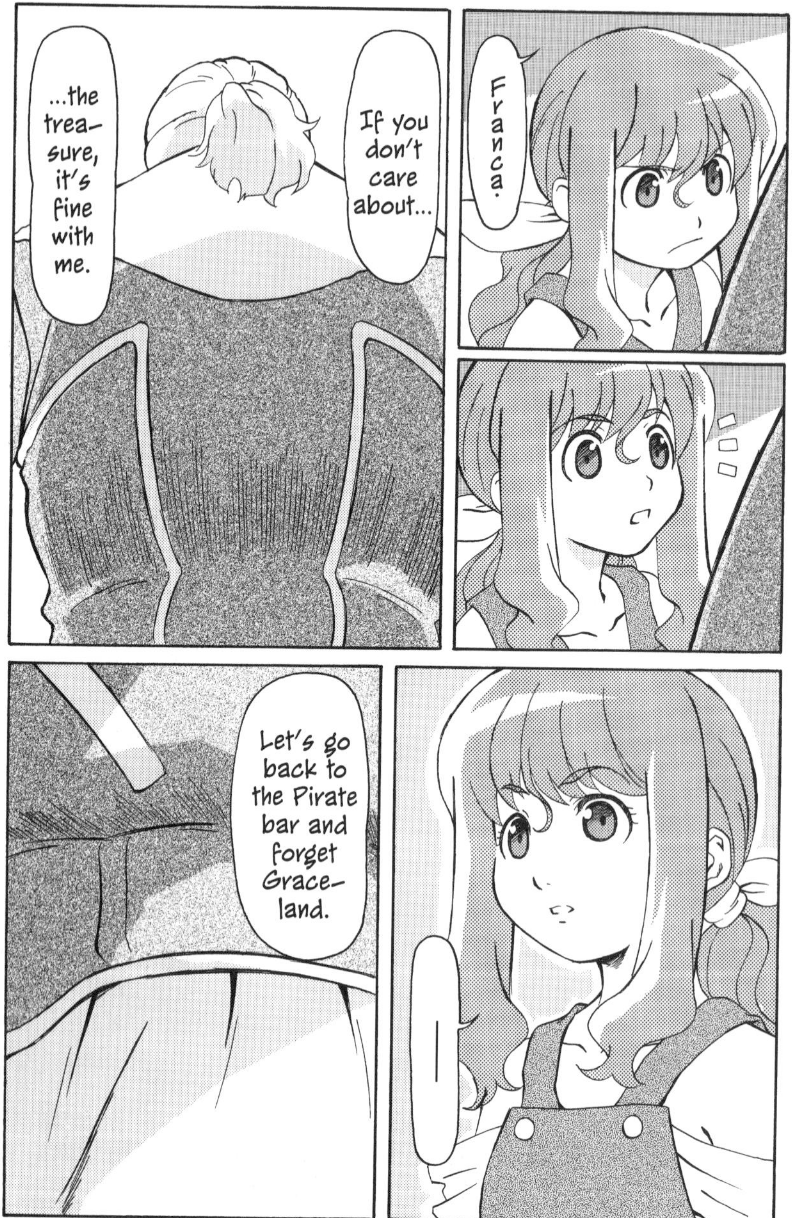
Franca.
If you don't care about...
...the trea-sure, it's fine with me.
...
Let's go back to the Pirate bar and forget Grace-land.

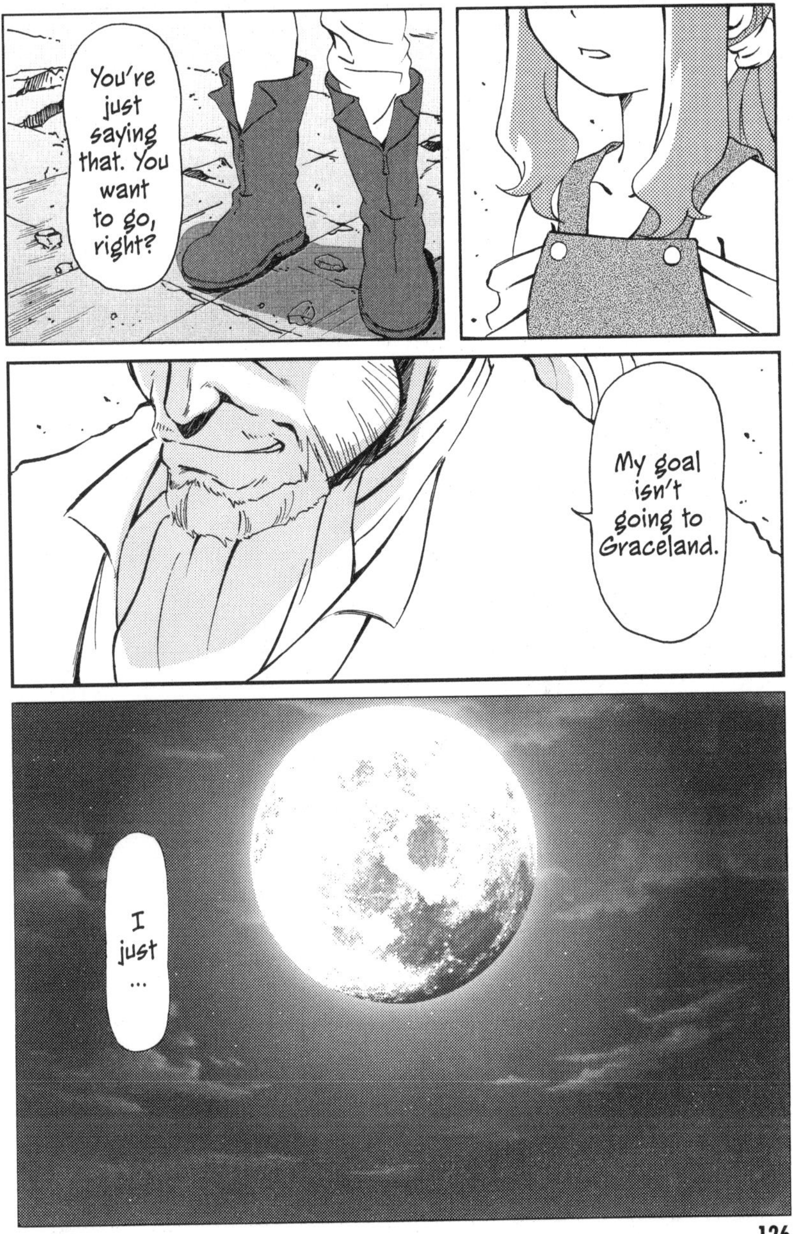
You're just saying that. You want to go, right?
My goal isn't going to Graceland.
I just ...

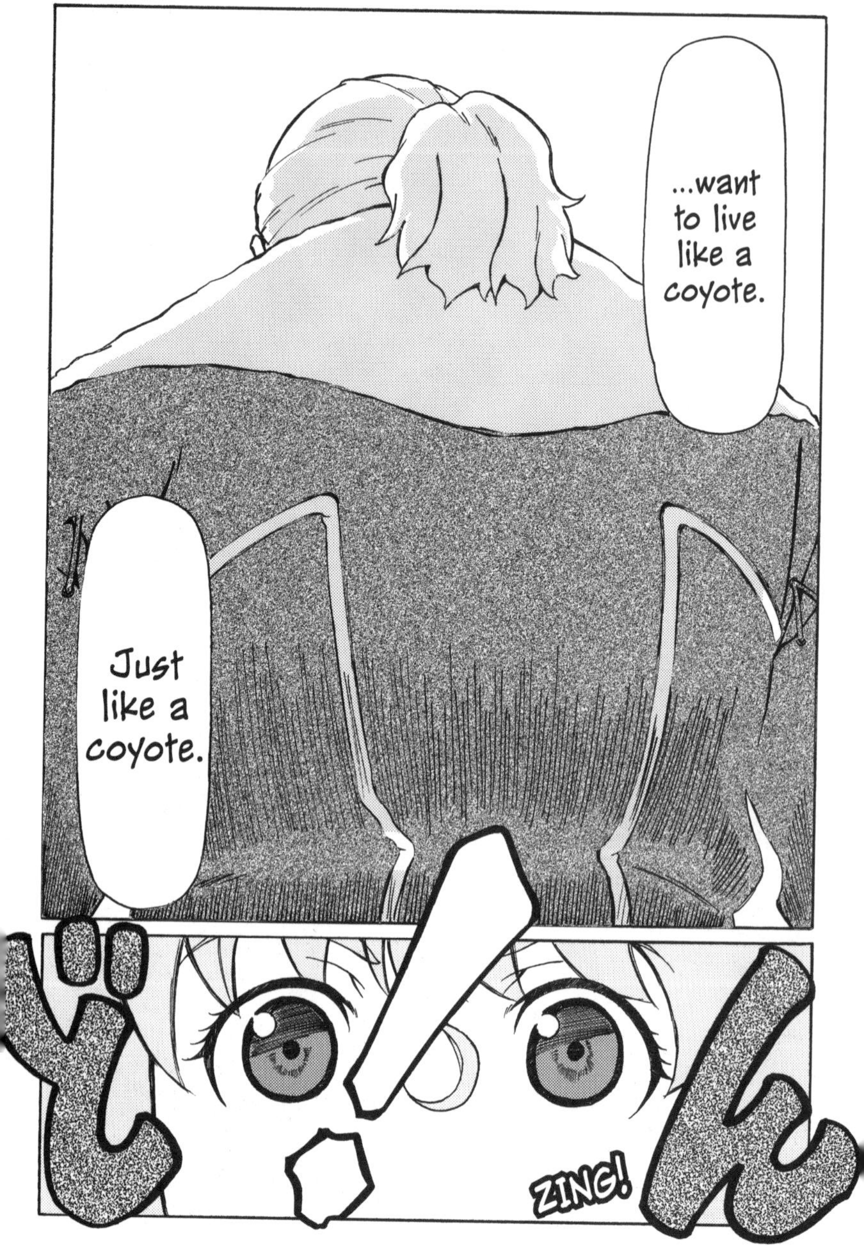
...want to live like a coyote.
Just like a coyote.
ZING!

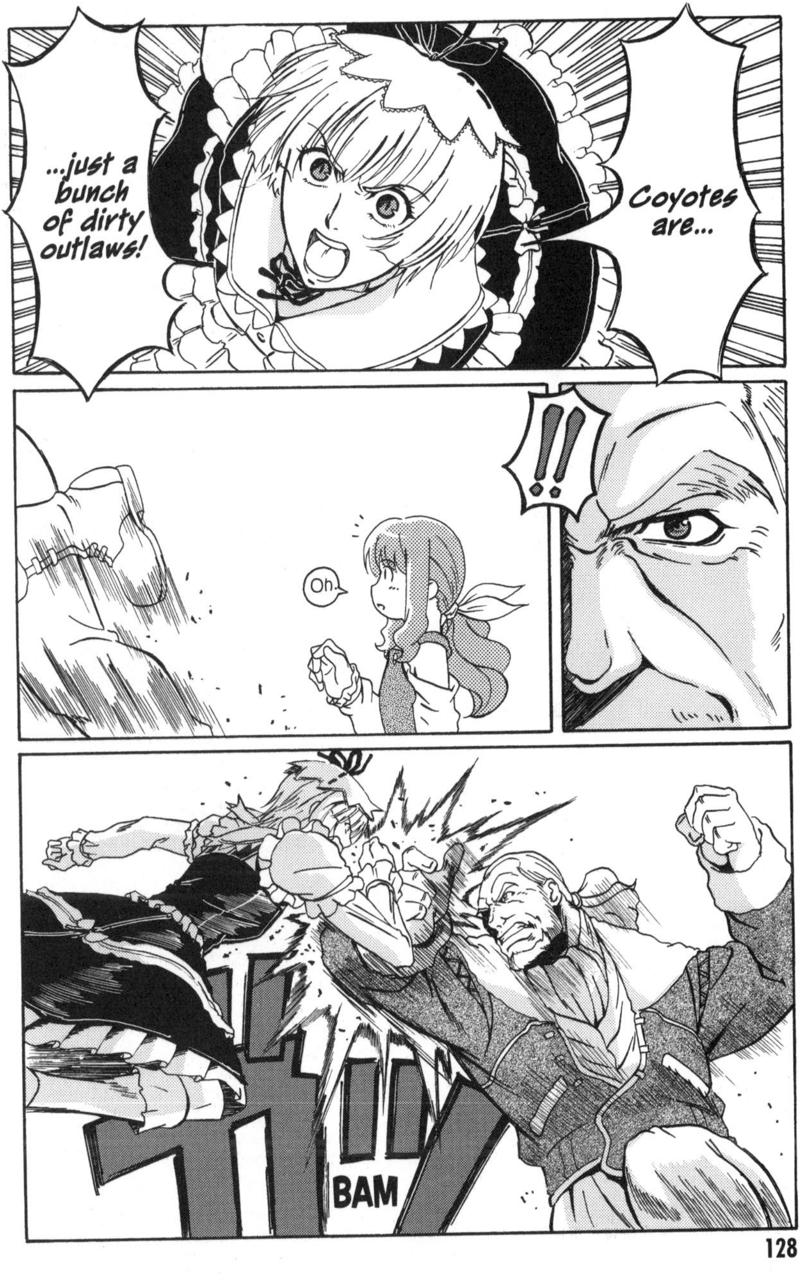
Coyotes are...
...just a bunch of dirty outlaws!
!!
Oh.
BAM

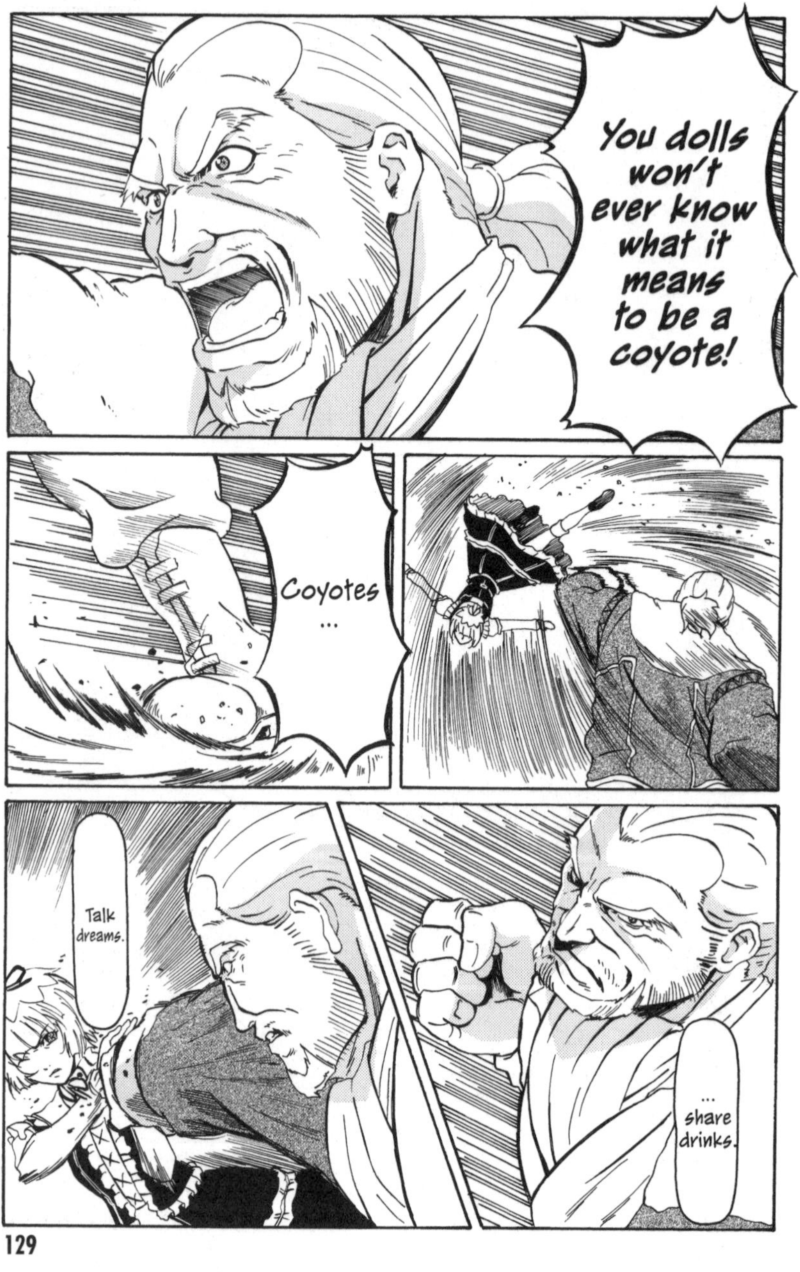
You dolls won't ever know what it means to be a coyote!
Coyotes ...
... share drinks.
Talk dreams.

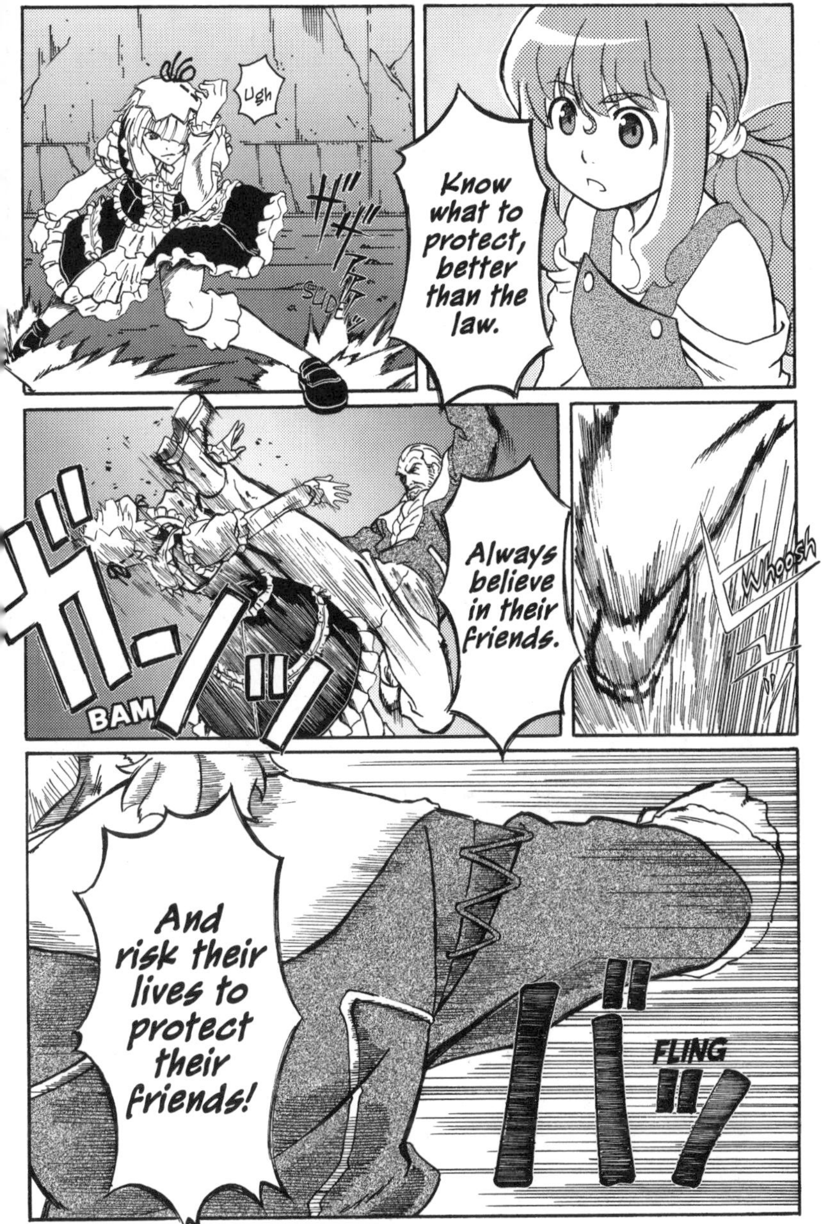
Know what to protect, better than the law.
Ugh
Whoosh
Always believe in their friends.
BAM
And risk their lives to protect their friends!
FLING

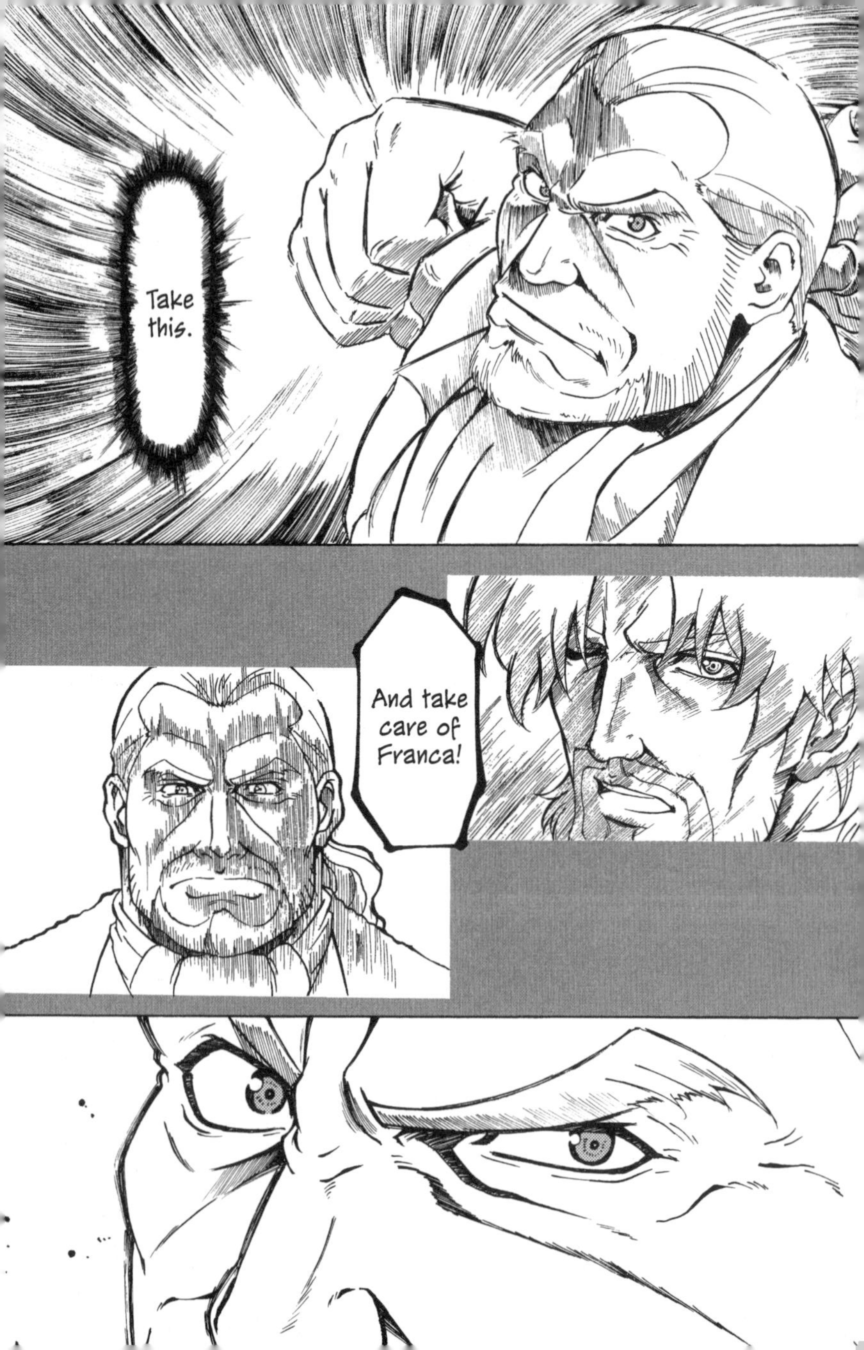
Take this.
And take care of Franca!

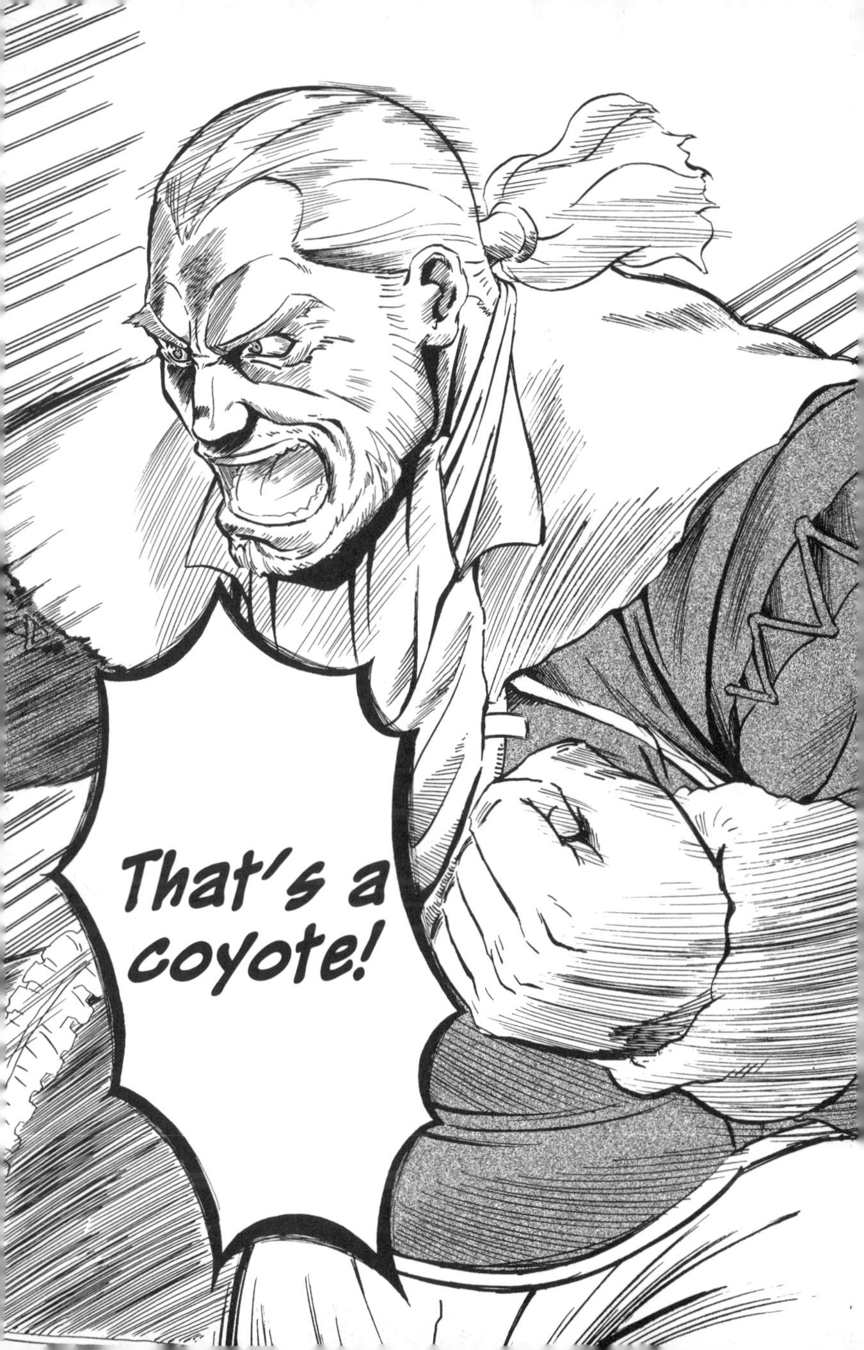
That's a coyote!

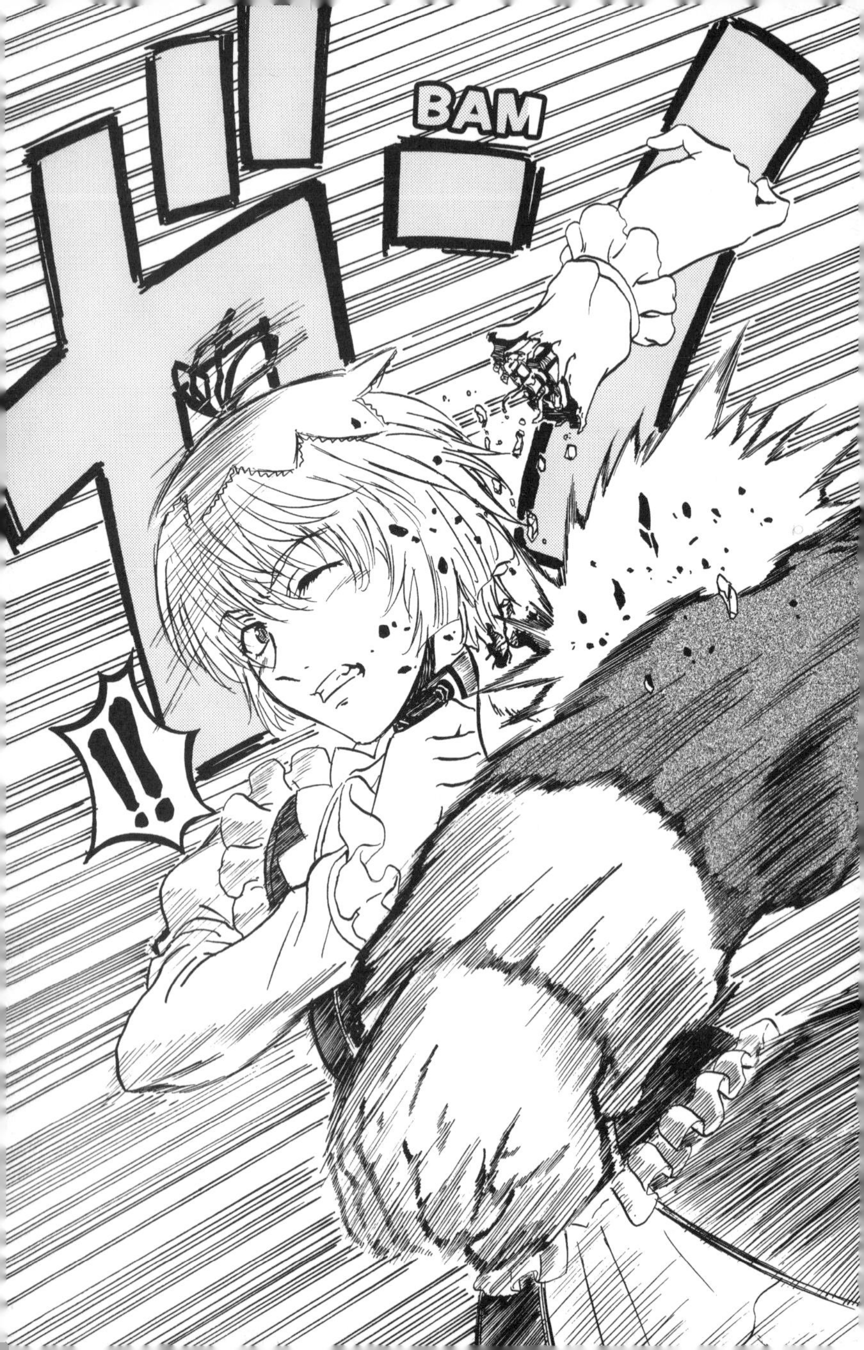
BAM
!!

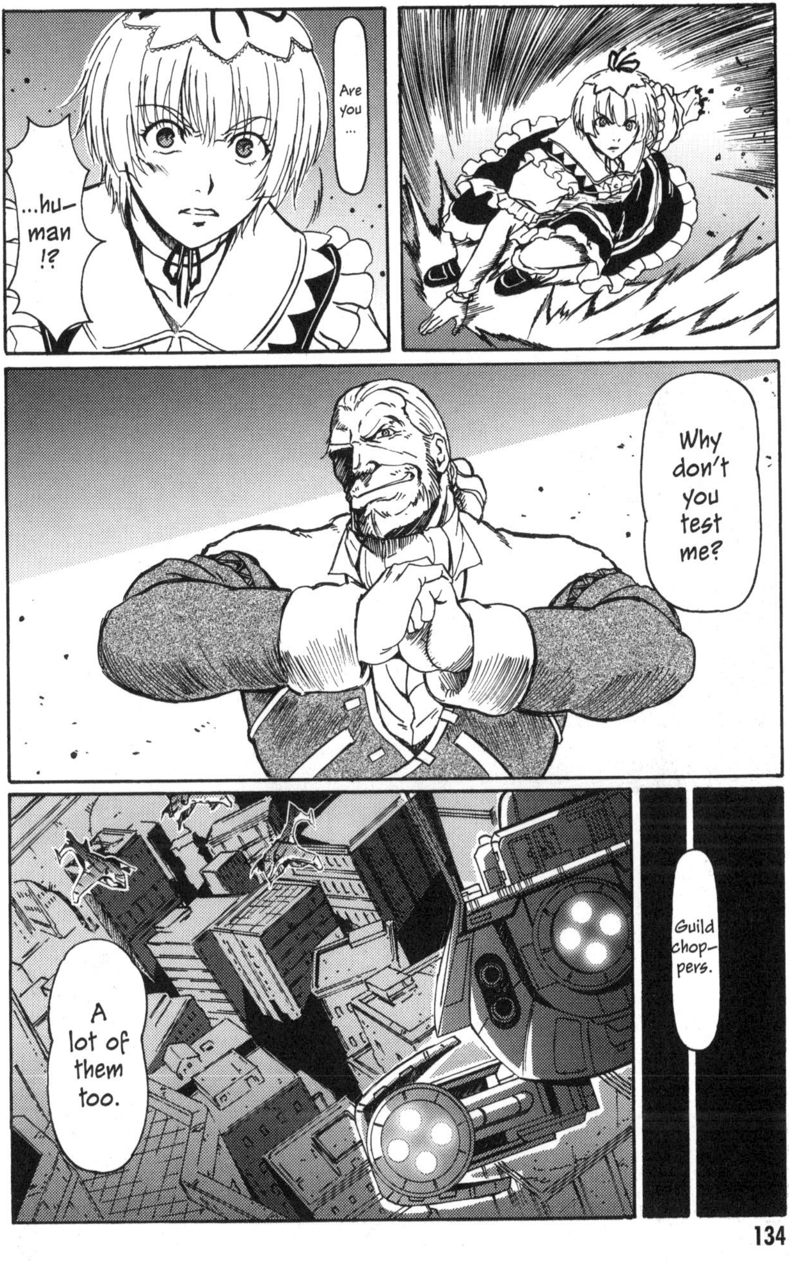
Are you ...
...hu-man!?
Why don't you test me?
Guild chop-pers.
A lot of them too.

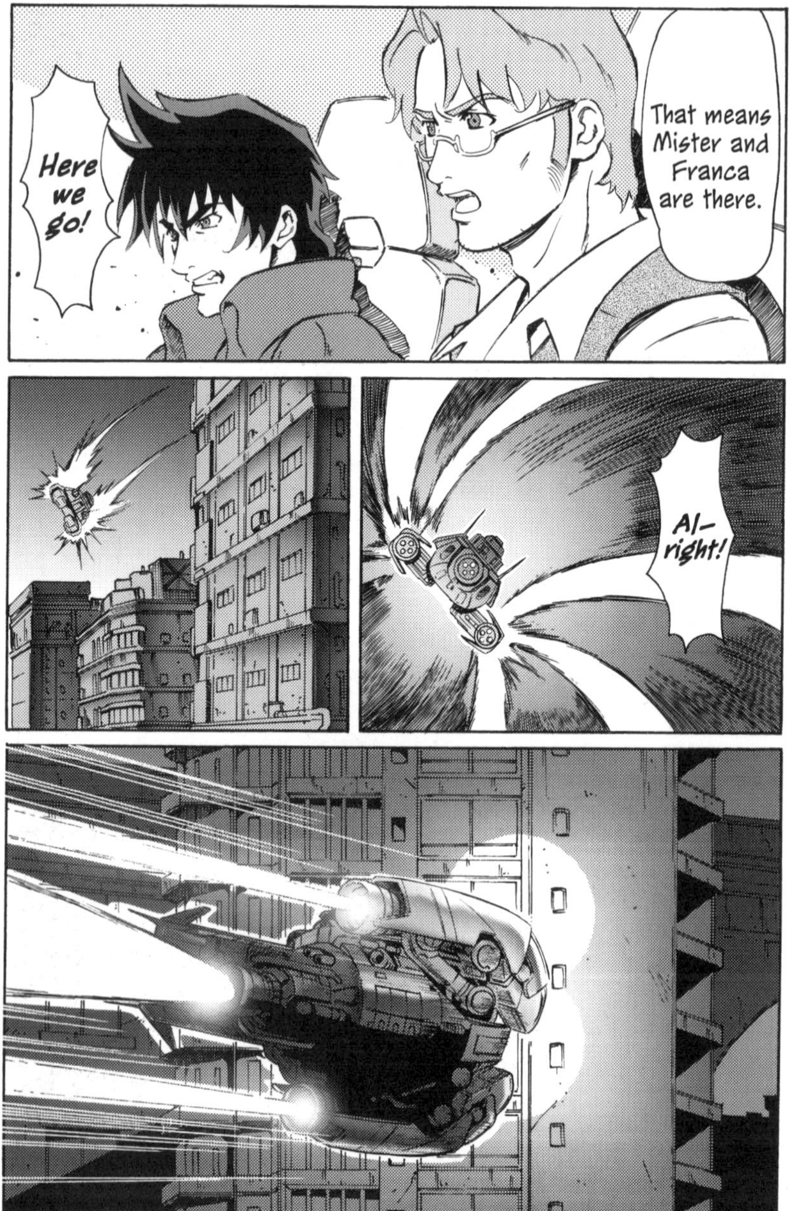
That means Mister and Franca are there.
Here we go!
Al-right!

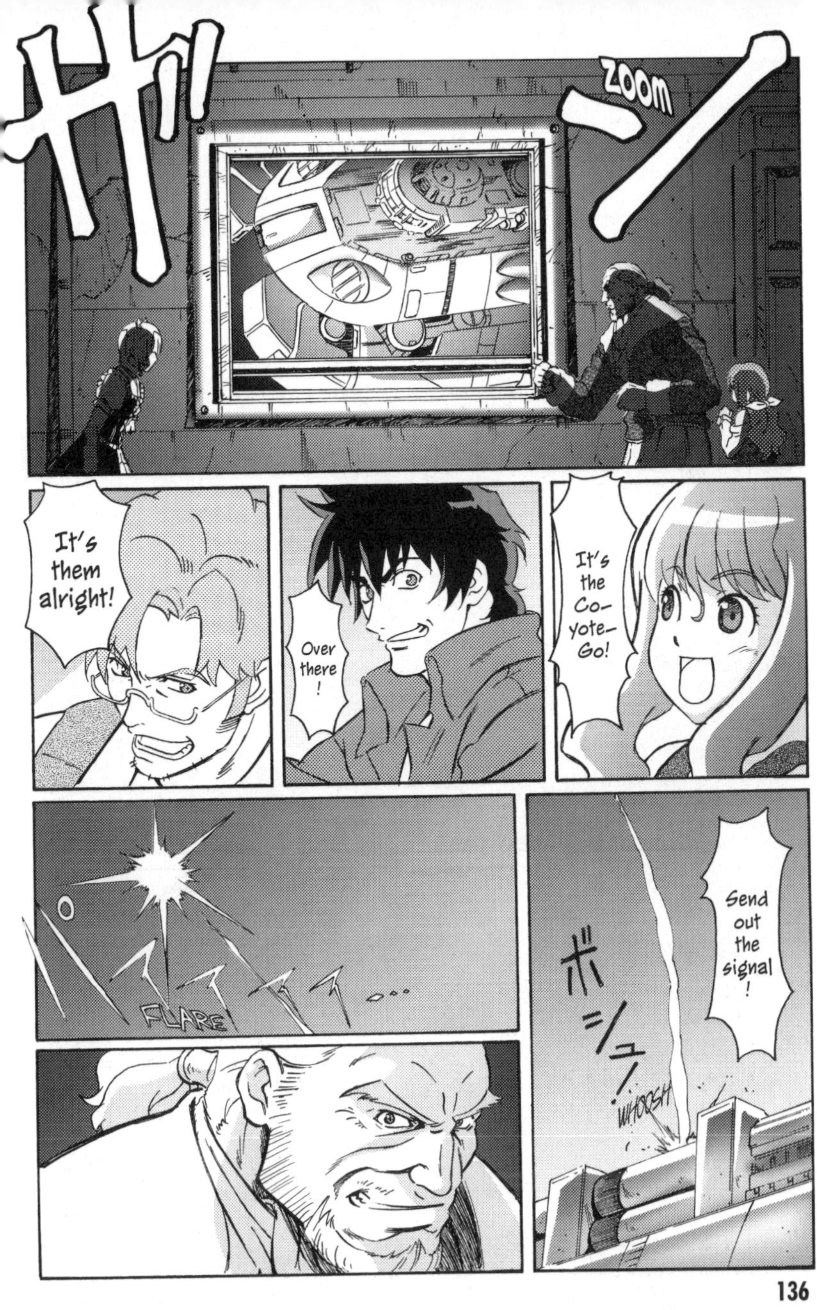
ZOOM
It's the Co-yote-Go!
Over there!
It's them alright!
Send out the signal!
WHOOSH
FLARE

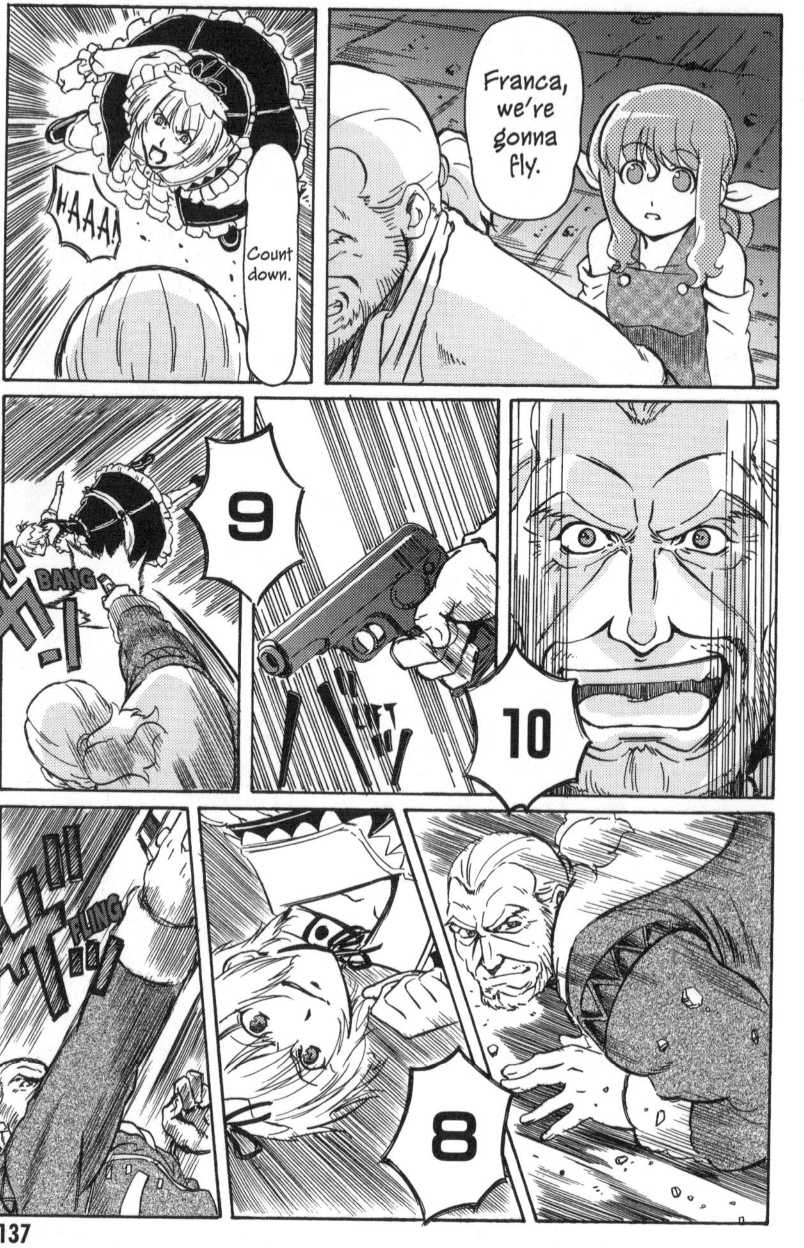
Franca, we're gonna fly.
HAAAA!
Count down.
10
9
LIFT
BANG
8
FLING

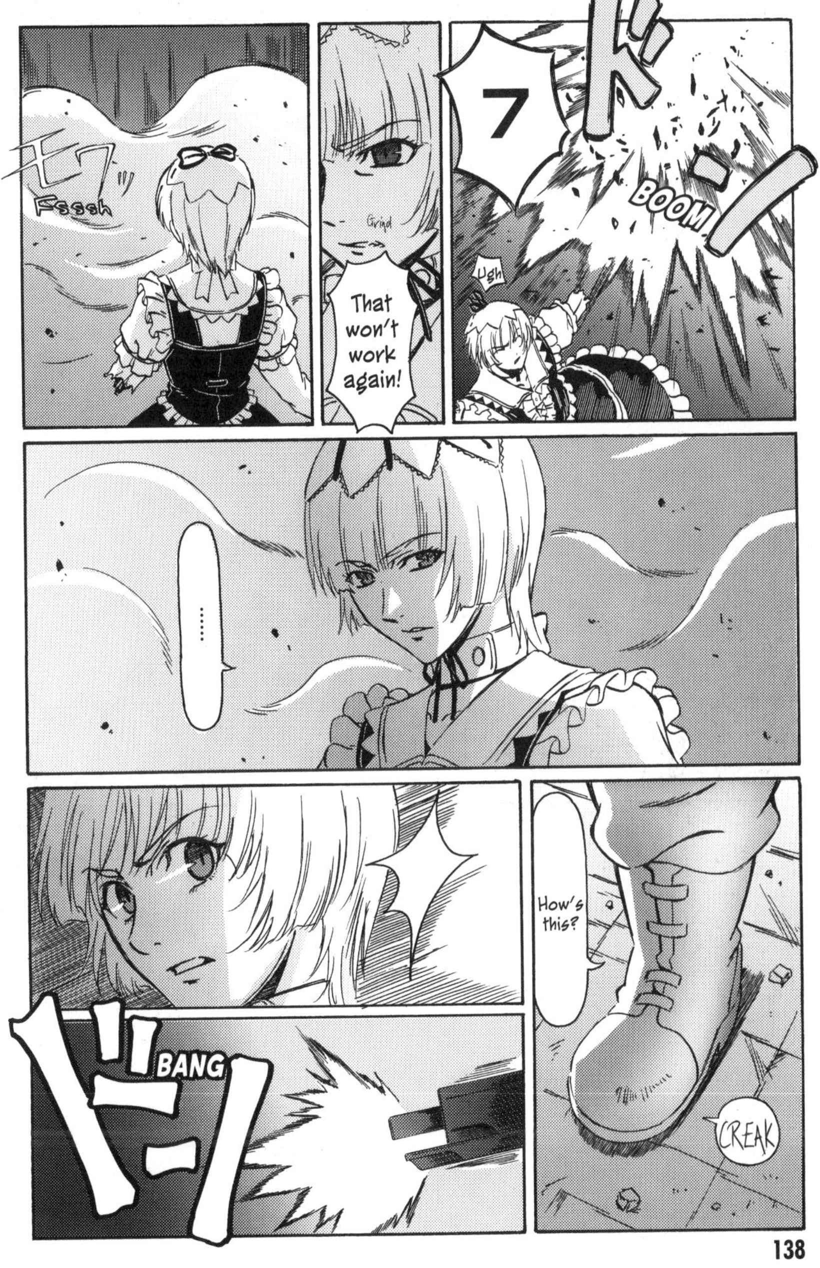
7
ドーン
BOOM
Ugh
Grind
That won't work again!
モフッ
Fsssh
......
How's this?
CREAK
ドーン
BANG

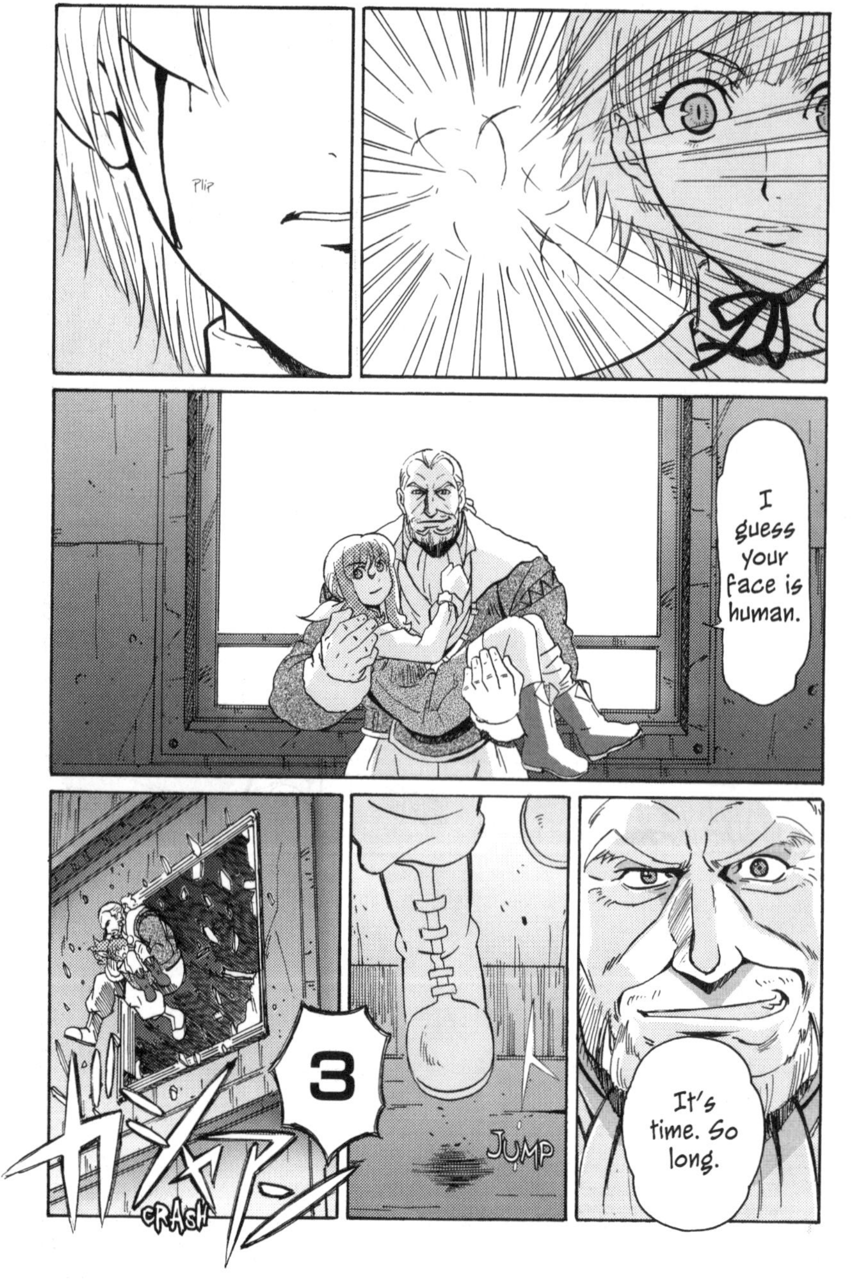
Plip
I guess your face is human.
It's time. So long.
JUMP
3
CRASH

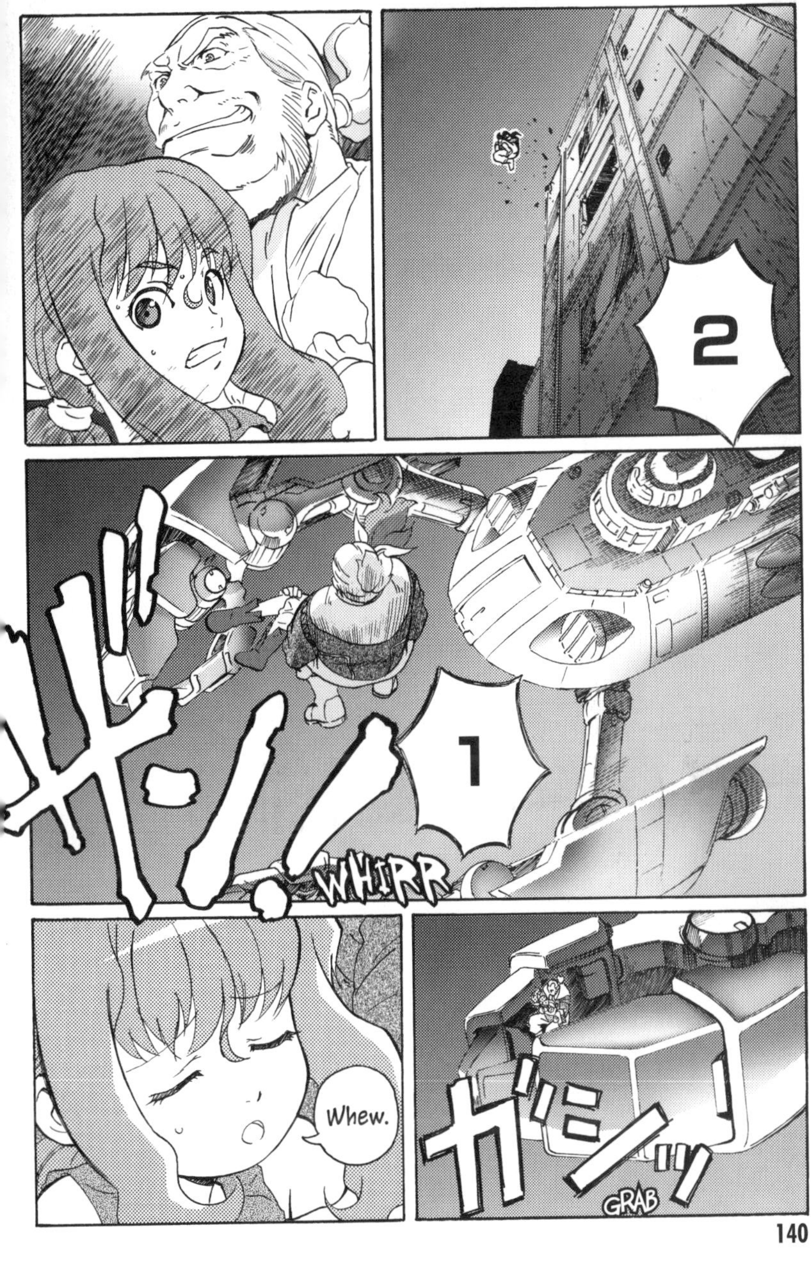
2
1
WHIRR
GRAB
Whew.

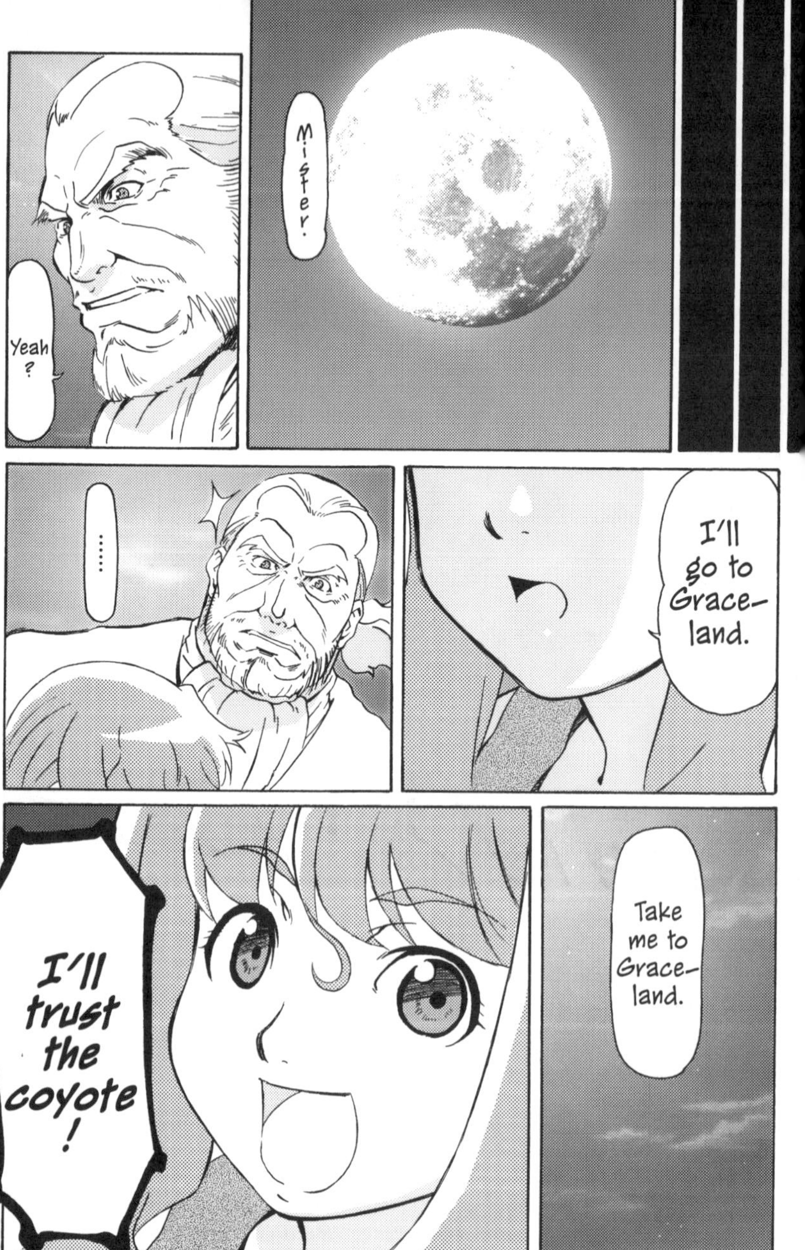
Mister.
Yeah?
I'll go to Graceland.
......
Take me to Graceland.
I'll trust the coyote!

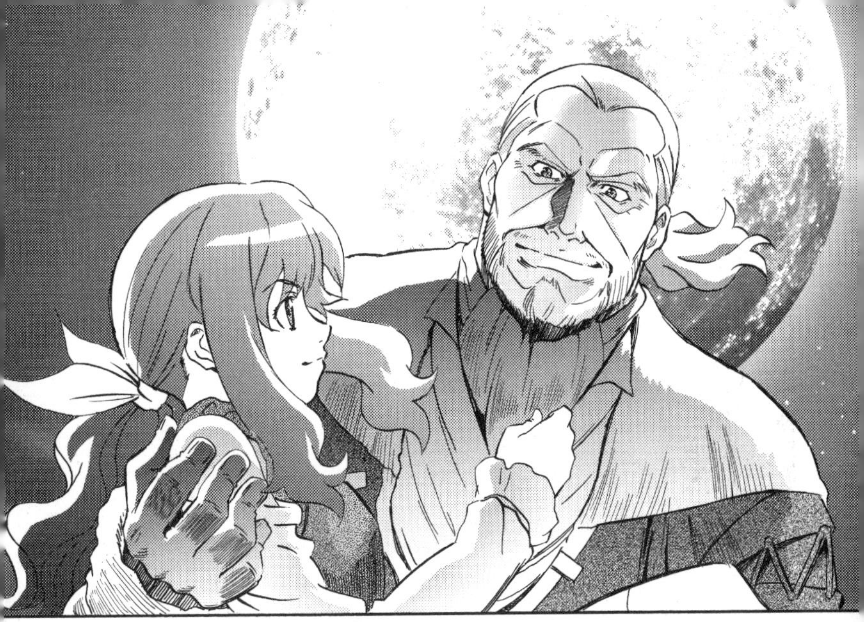
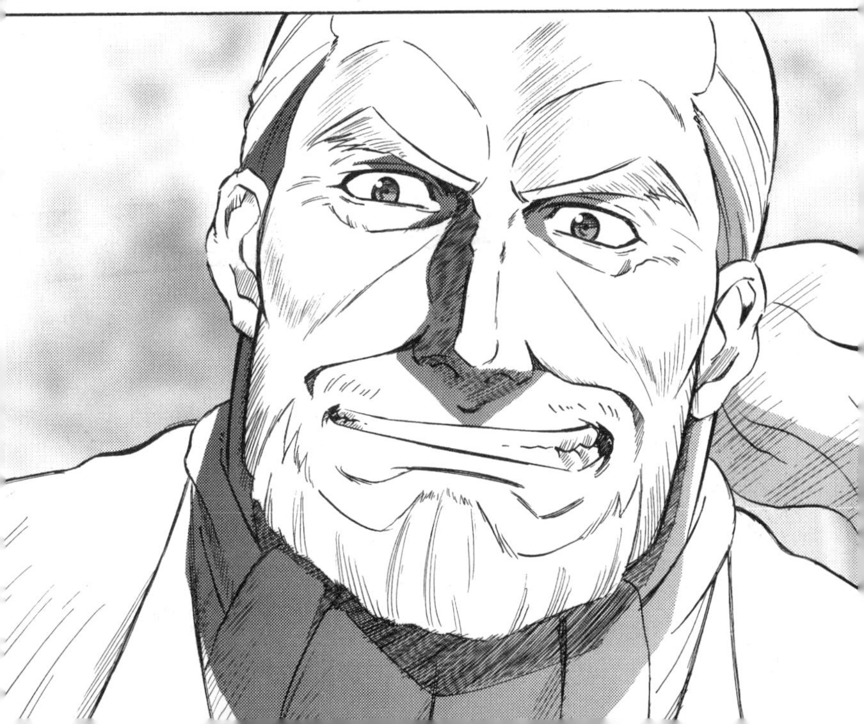

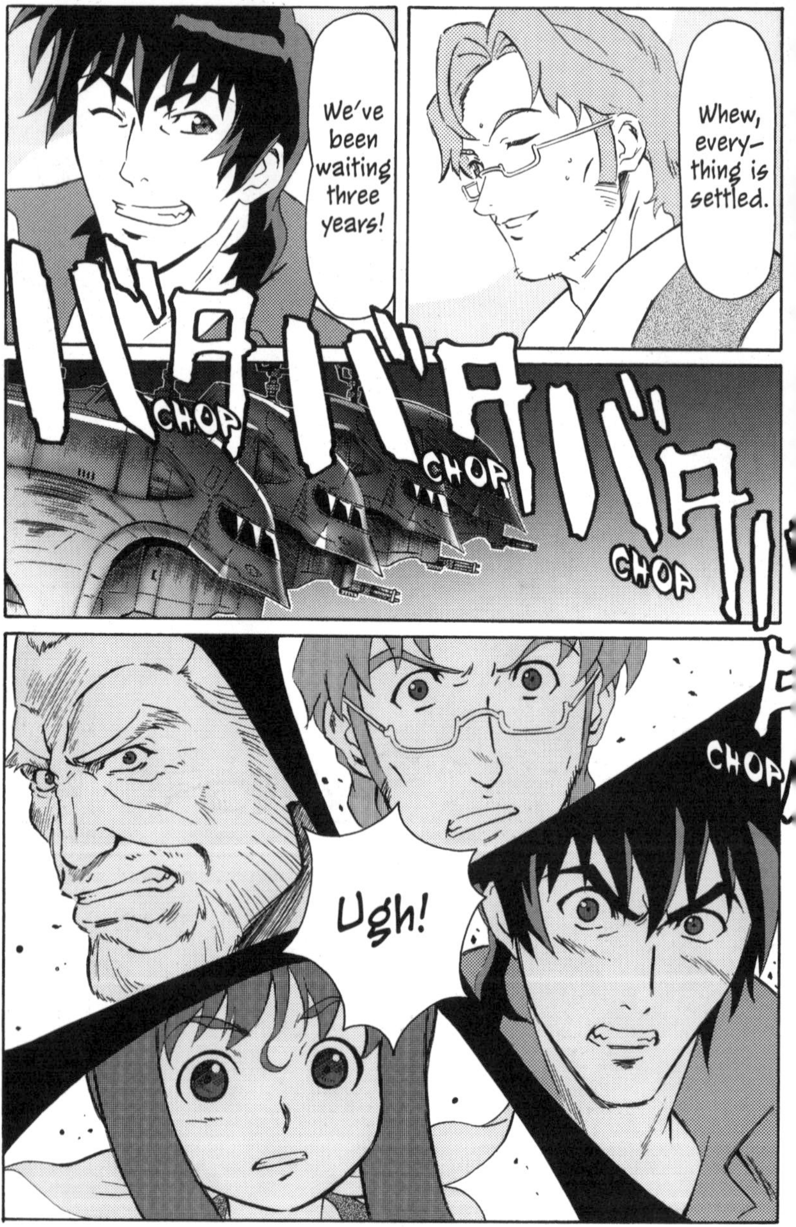
Whew, every-thing is settled.
We've been waiting three years!
CHOP
CHOP
CHOP
CHOP
Ugh!

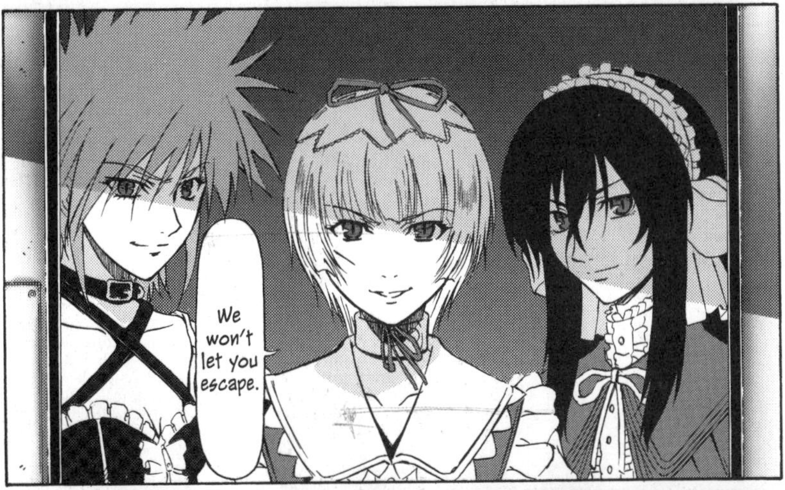
We won't let you escape.
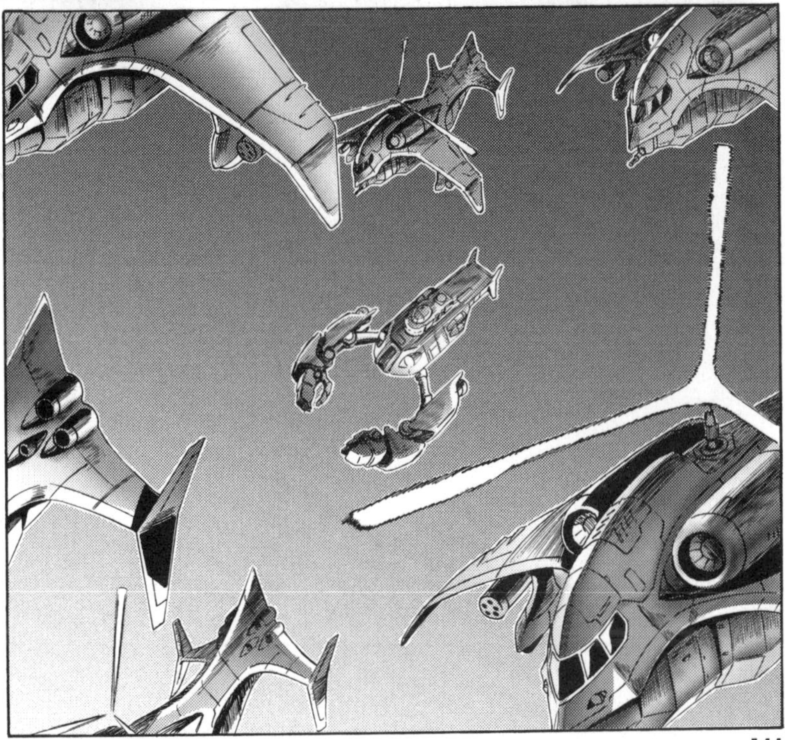

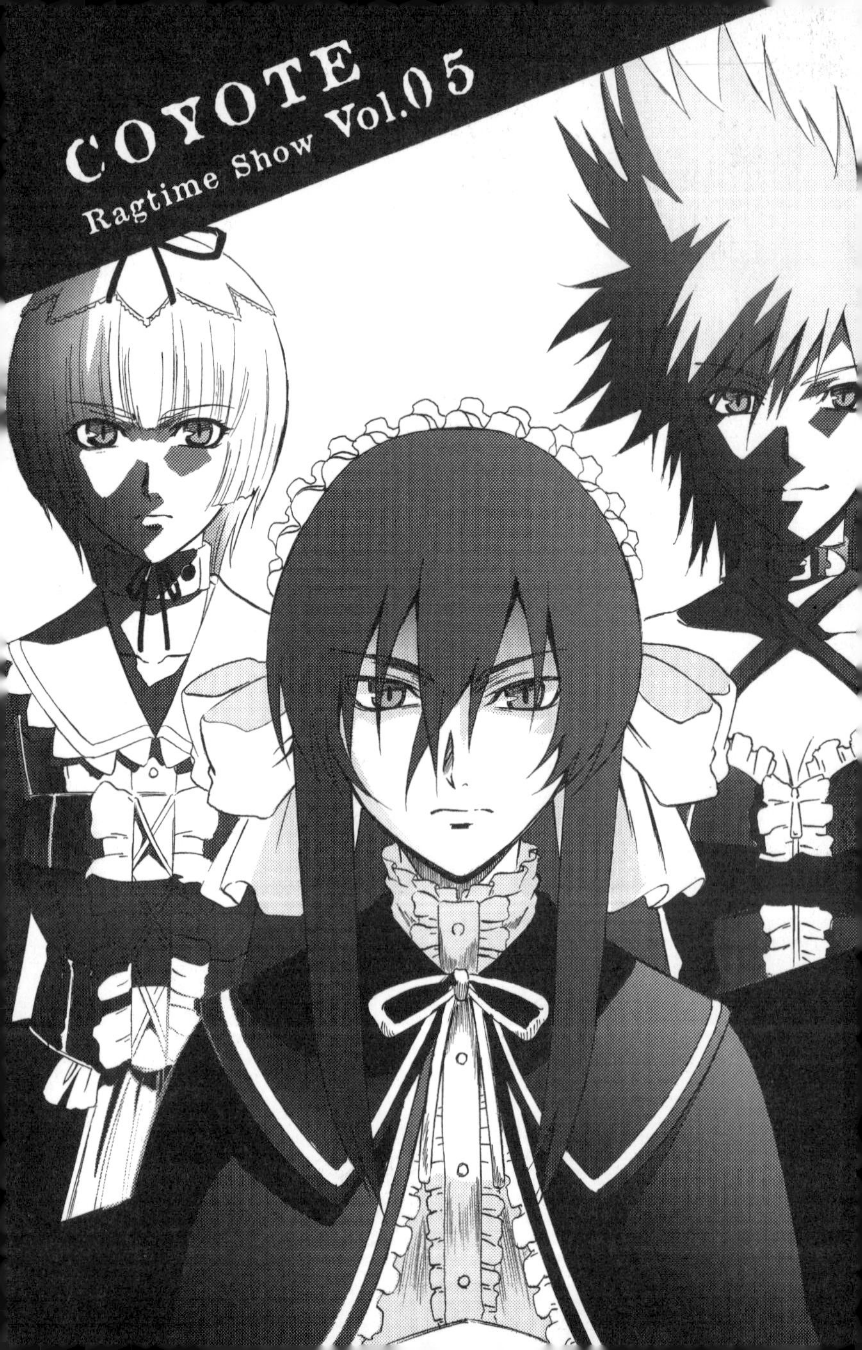
COYOTE
Ragtime Show Vol.05

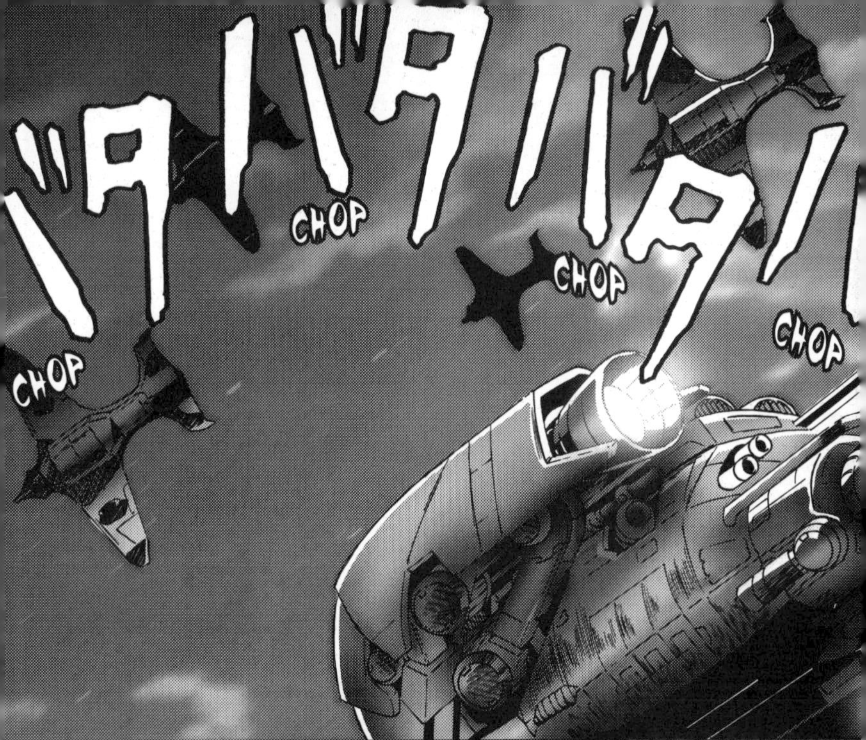
バタバタバタ
CHOP
CHOP
CHOP
CHOP

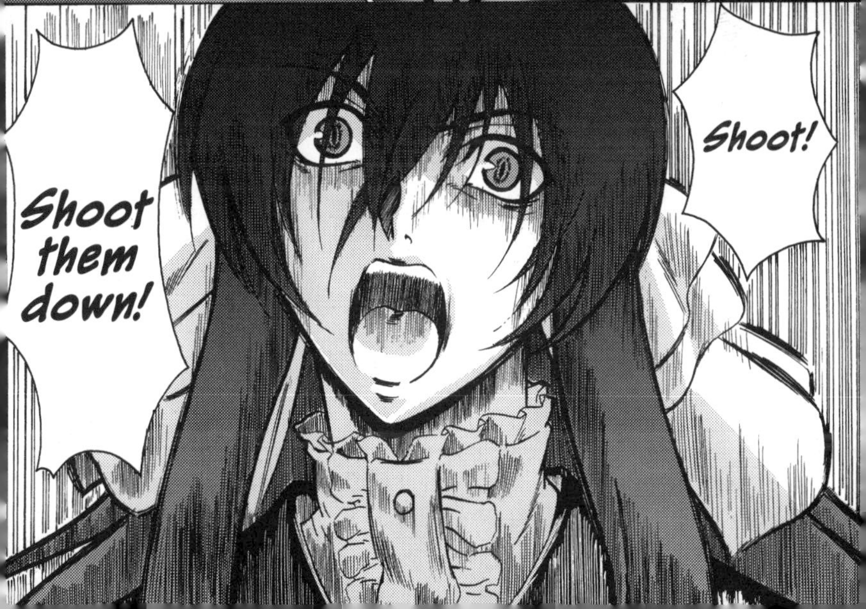
Shoot!
Shoot them down!

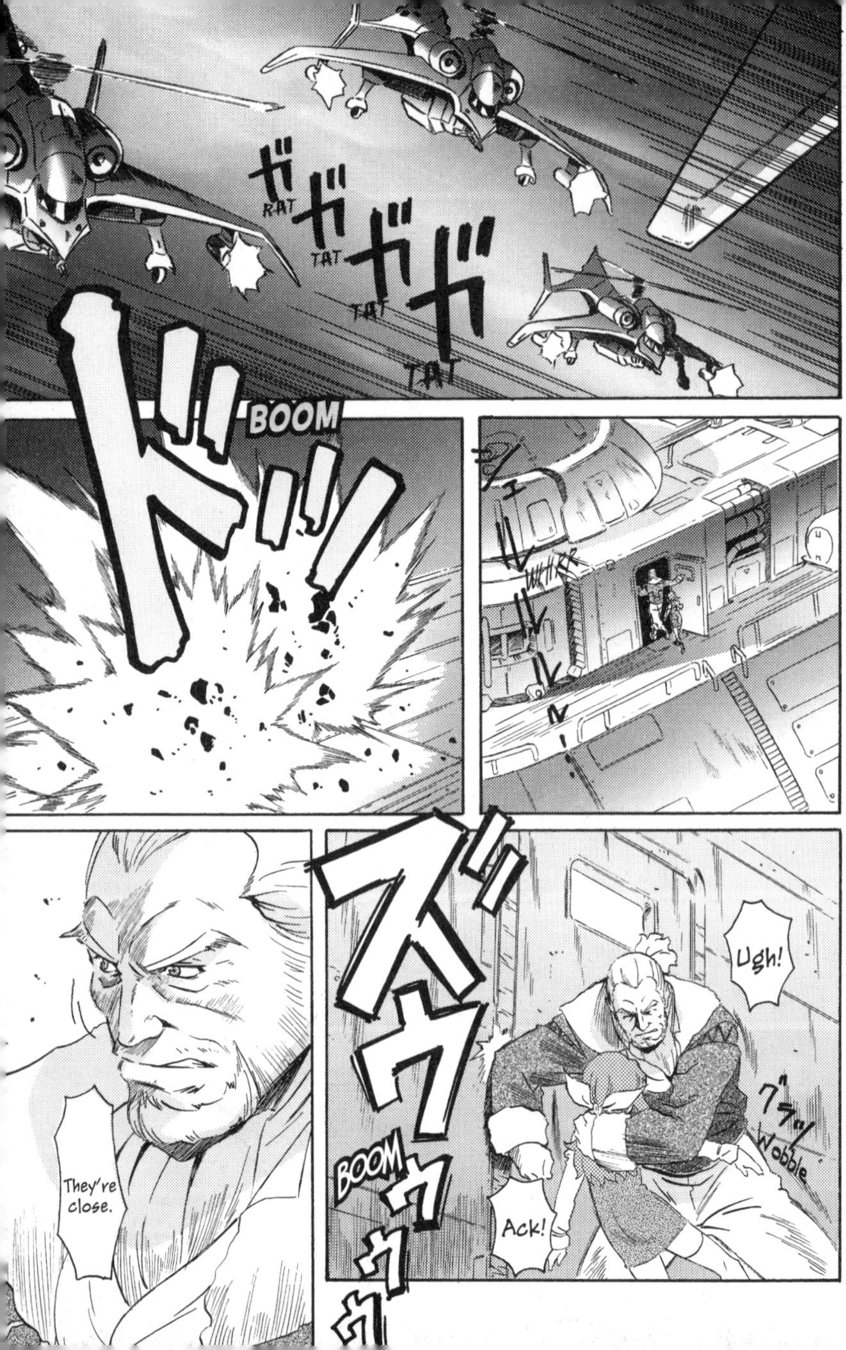

ガガガガ
RAT TAT TAT TAT
WHIRR
ドッ
BOOM
BOOM
Ugh!
グラッ
Wobble
Ack!
They're close.

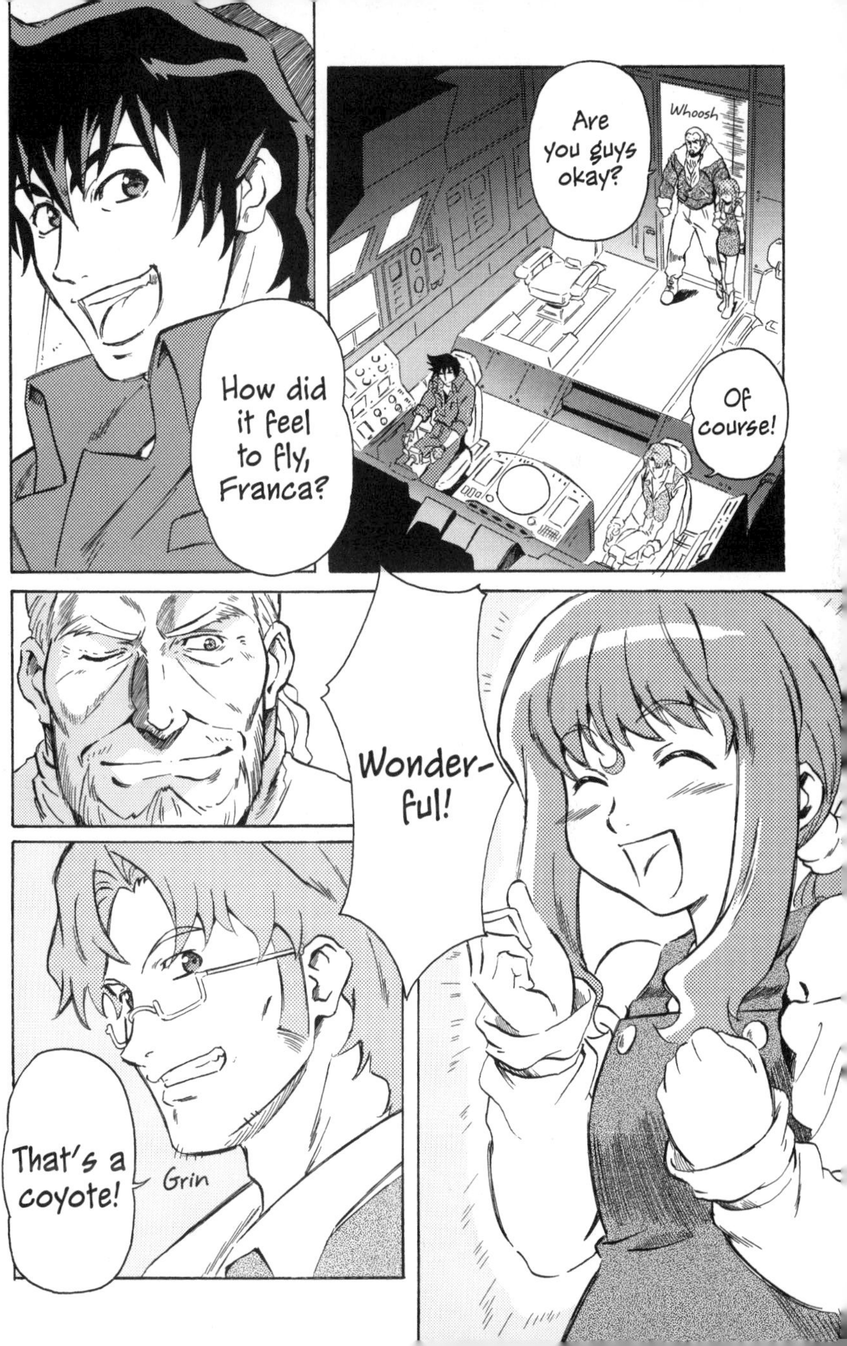
Whoosh
Are you guys okay?
Of course!
How did it feel to fly, Franca?
Wonder-ful!
That's a coyote!
Grin

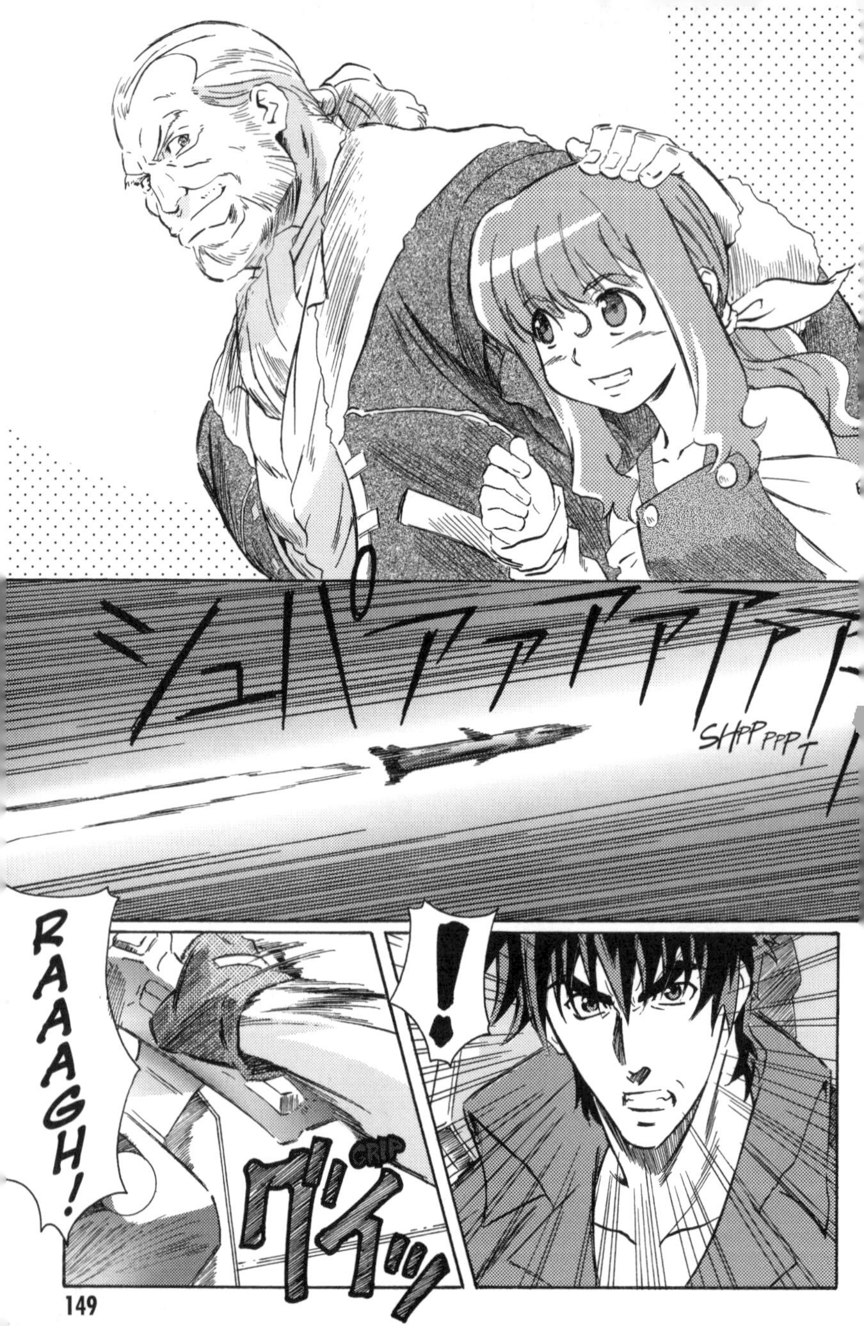
シュパァァァァー
SHPPPPPT
!
RAAAAGH!
グイッ
GRIP

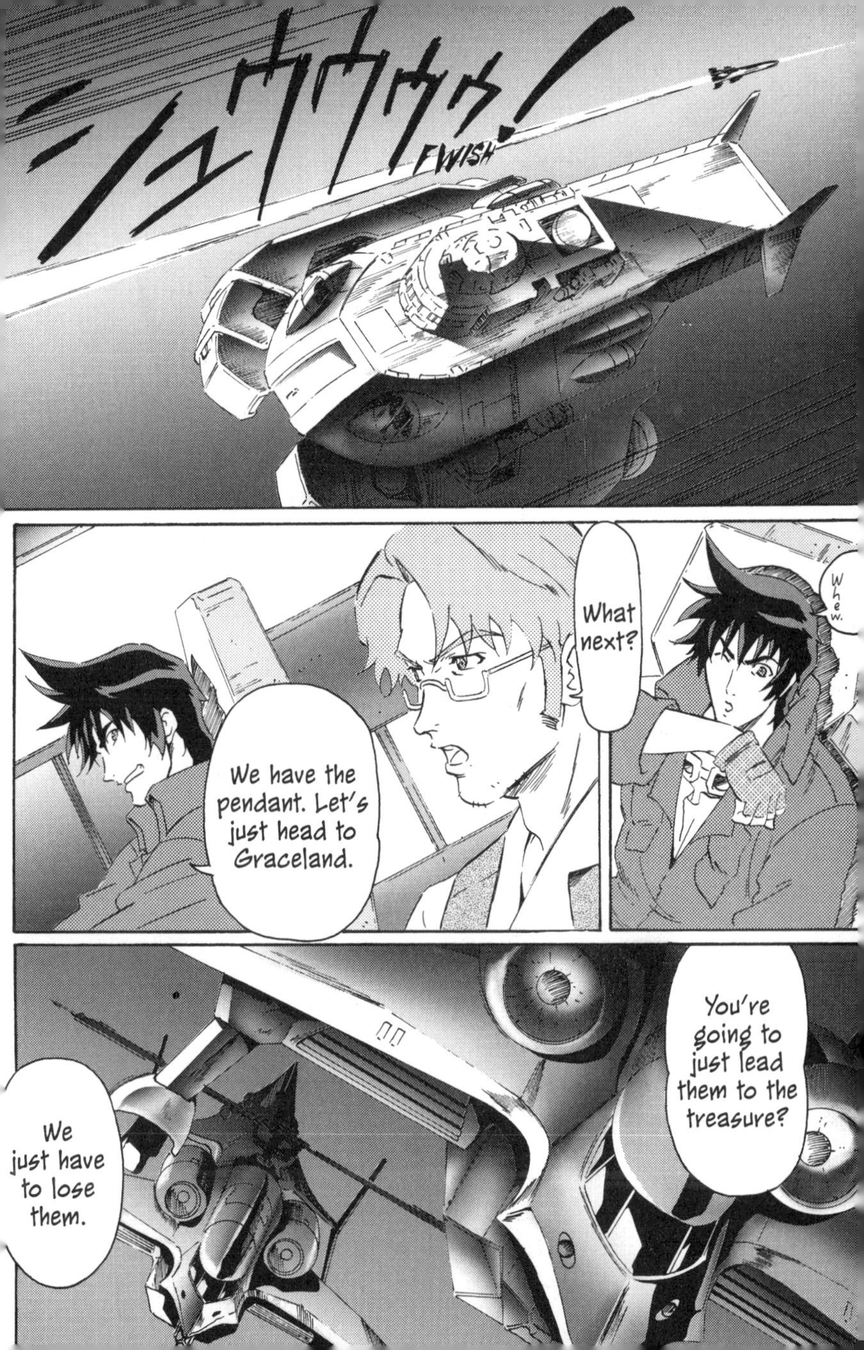
シュウウウウ!
FWISH
Whew.
What next?
We have the pendant. Let's just head to Graceland.
You're going to just lead them to the treasure?
We just have to lose them.

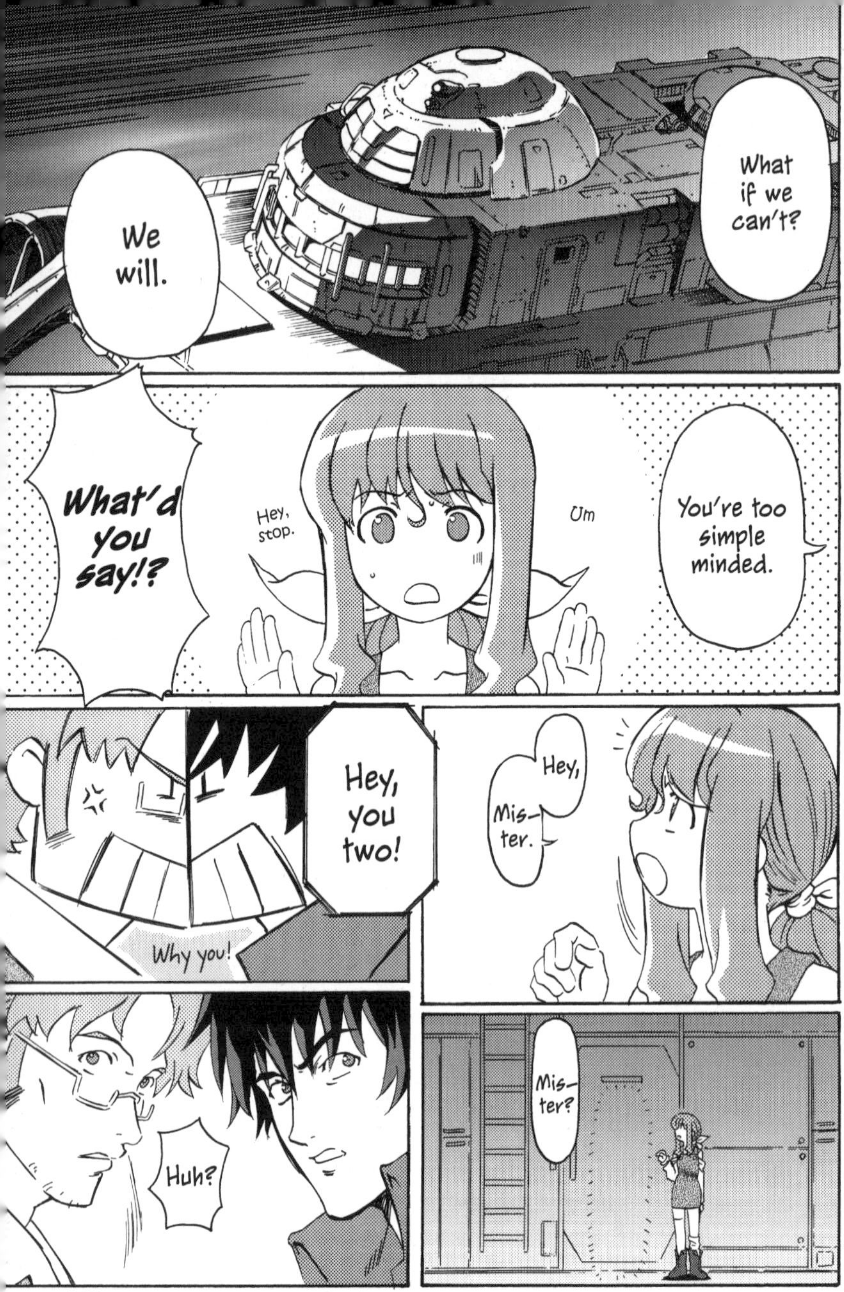
What if we can't?
We will.
You're too simple minded.
Um
Hey, stop.
What'd you say!?
Hey, Mister.
Hey, you two!
Why you!
Mister?
Huh?

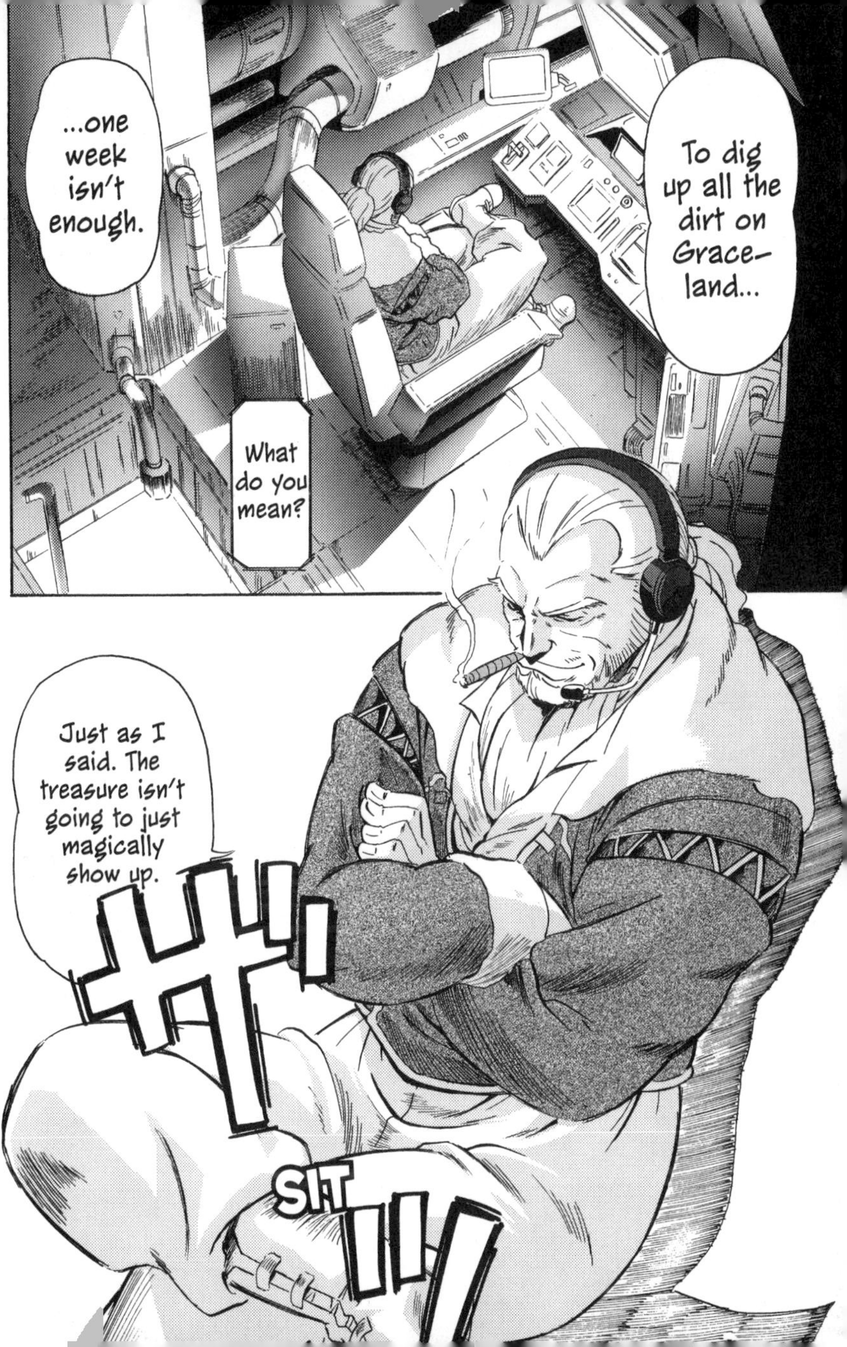
To dig up all the dirt on Graceland...
...one week isn't enough.
What do you mean?
Just as I said. The treasure isn't going to just magically show up.
SIT

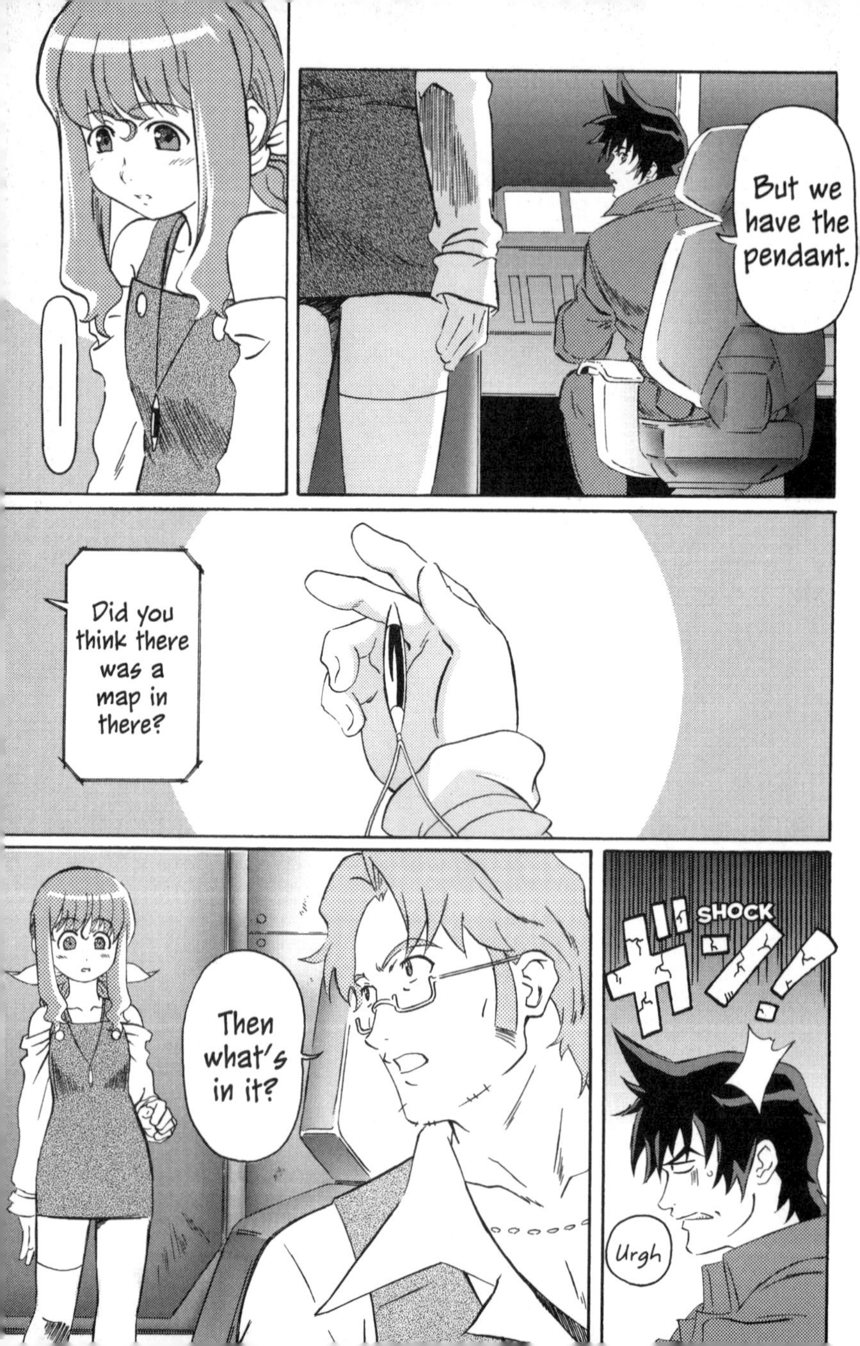
But we have the pendant.
Did you think there was a map in there?
SHOCK
Urgh
Then what's in it?

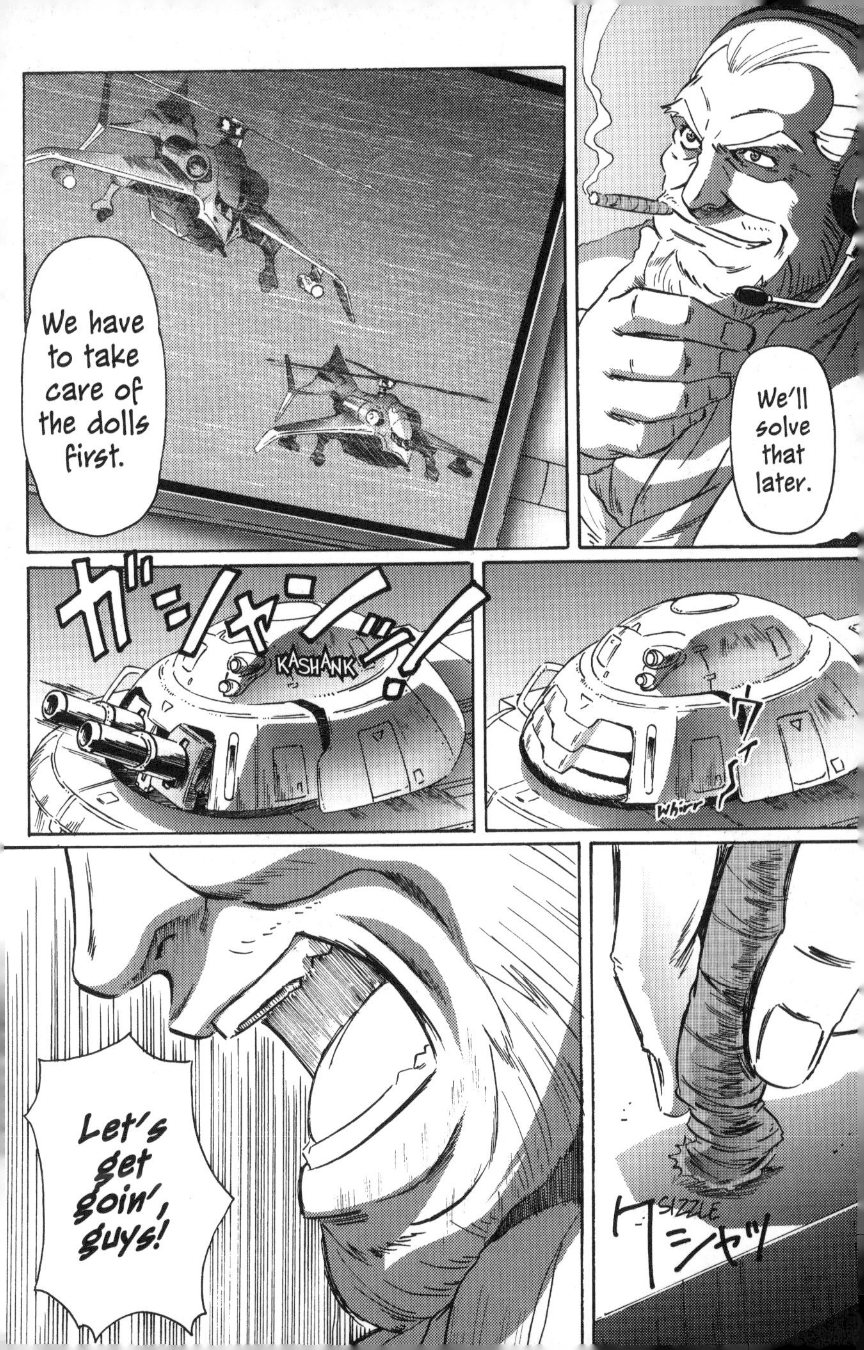
We'll solve that later.
We have to take care of the dolls first.
Whirr
KASHANK
SIZZLE
Let's get goin', guys!

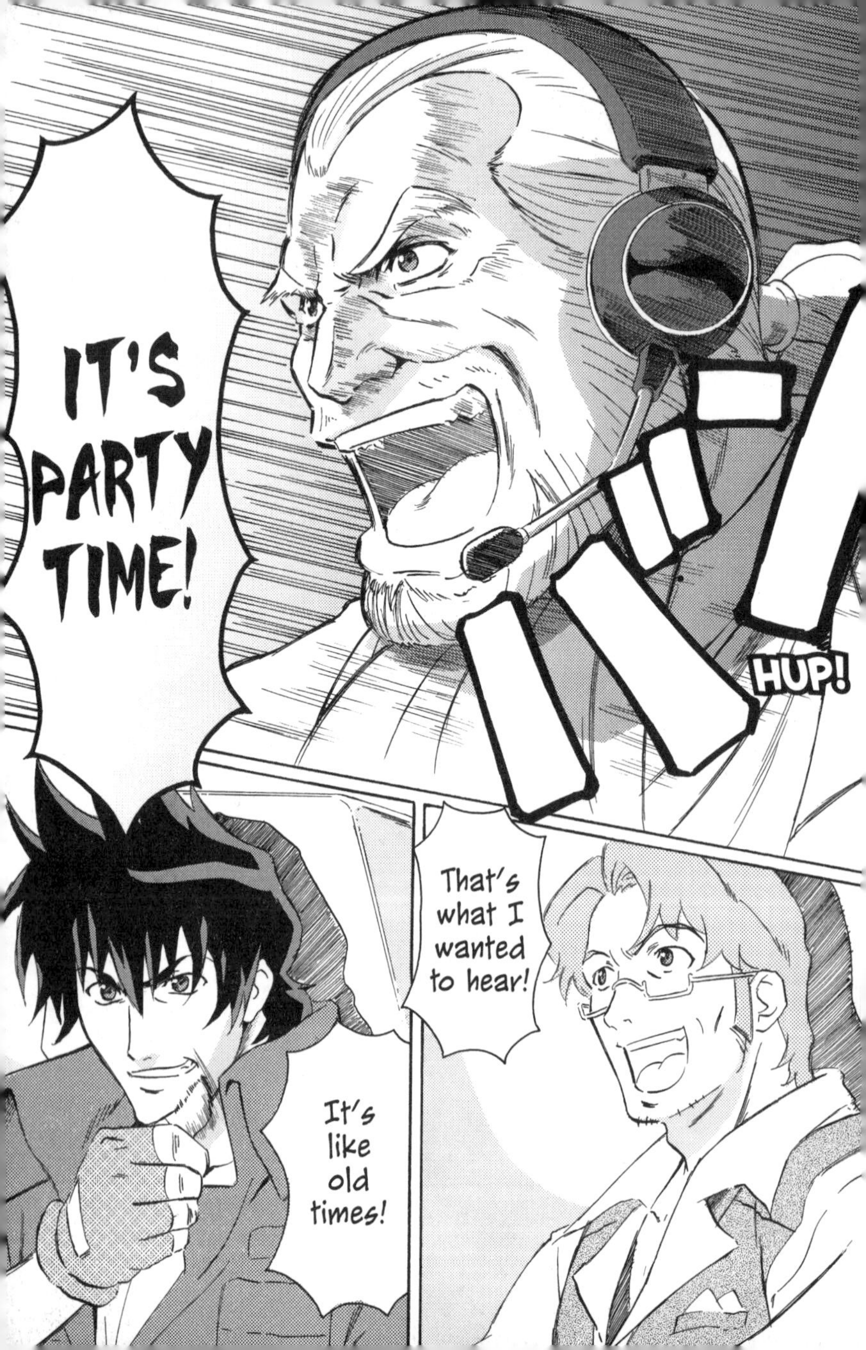
IT'S PARTY TIME!
HUP!
That's what I wanted to hear!
It's like old times!

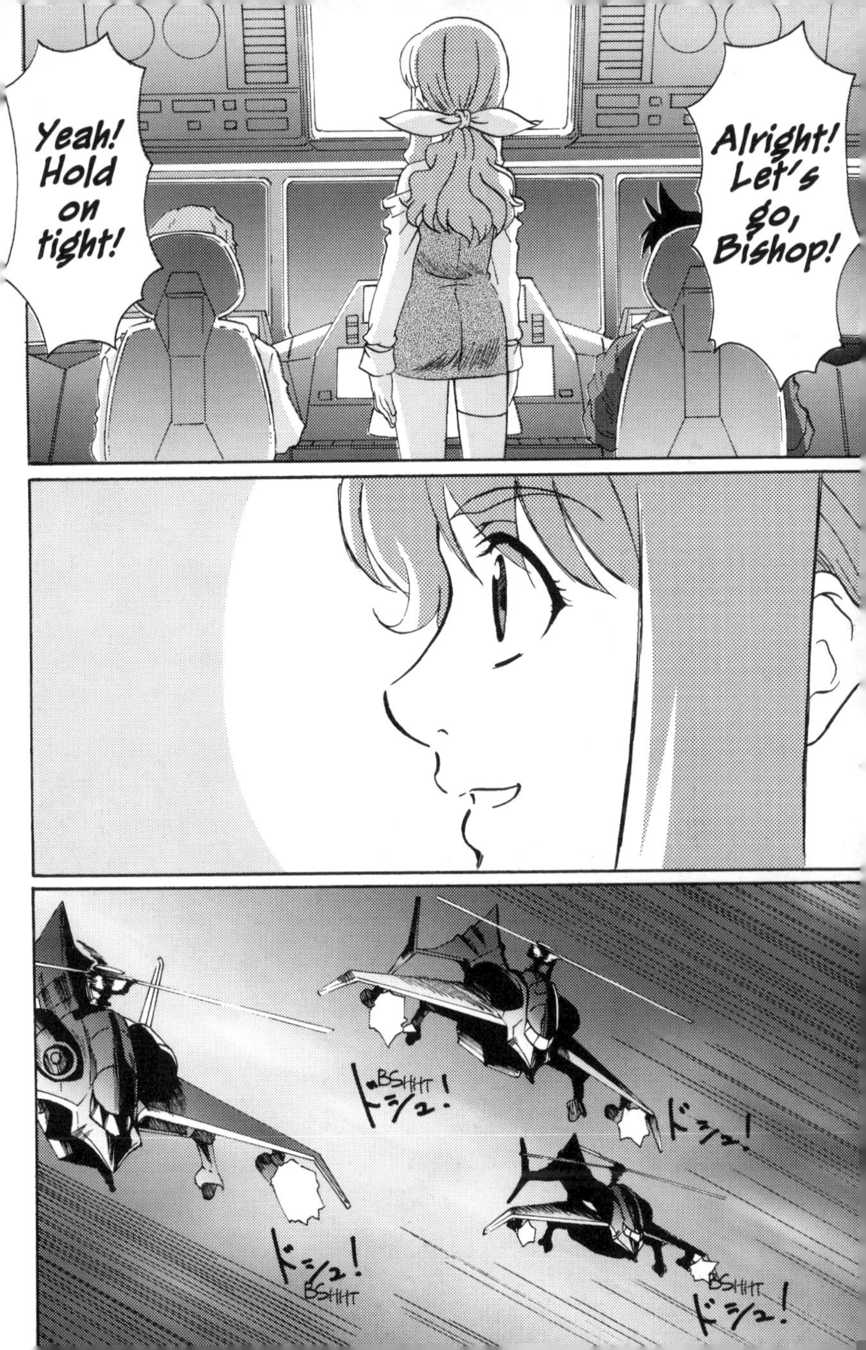
Alright! Let's go, Bishop!
Yeah! Hold on tight!
BSHHT! ドシュ!
ドシュ!
BSHHT ドシュ!
ドシュ! BSHHT

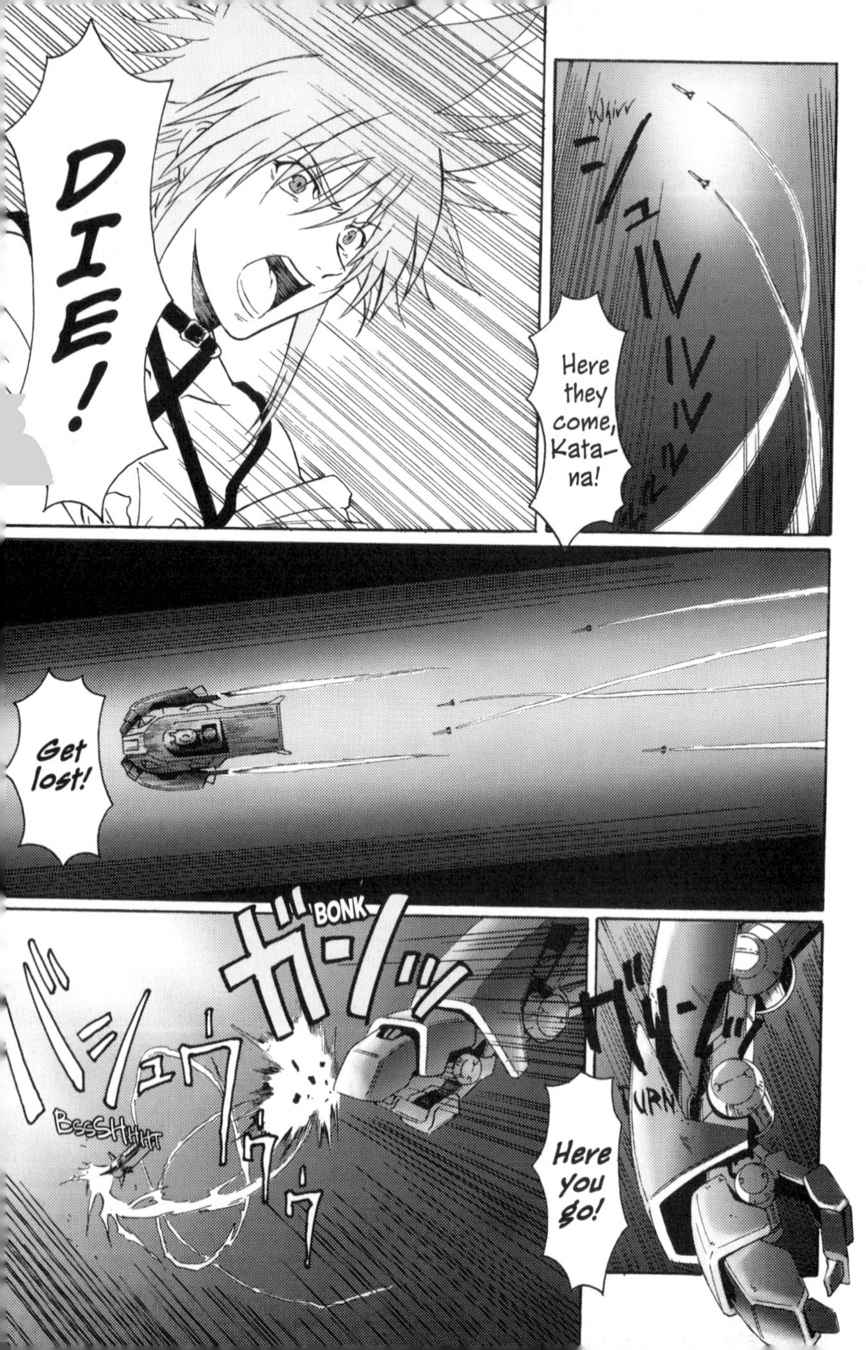
Whirr
Here they come, Katana!
DIE!
Get lost!
TURN
Here you go!
BONK
BssSHHHHT

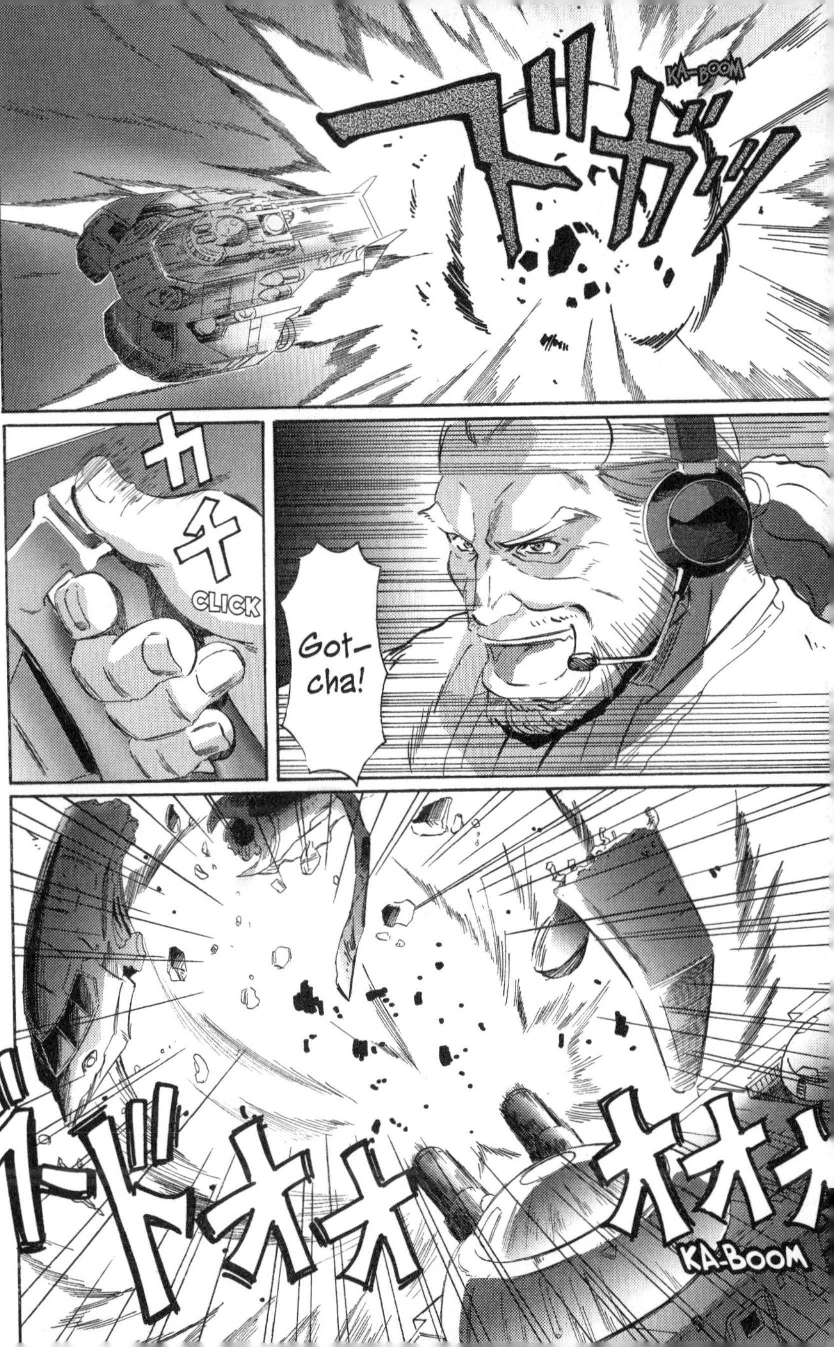
ドガッ
KA-BOOM
Got-cha!
カチ
CLICK
ドドオーオオ
KA-BOOM

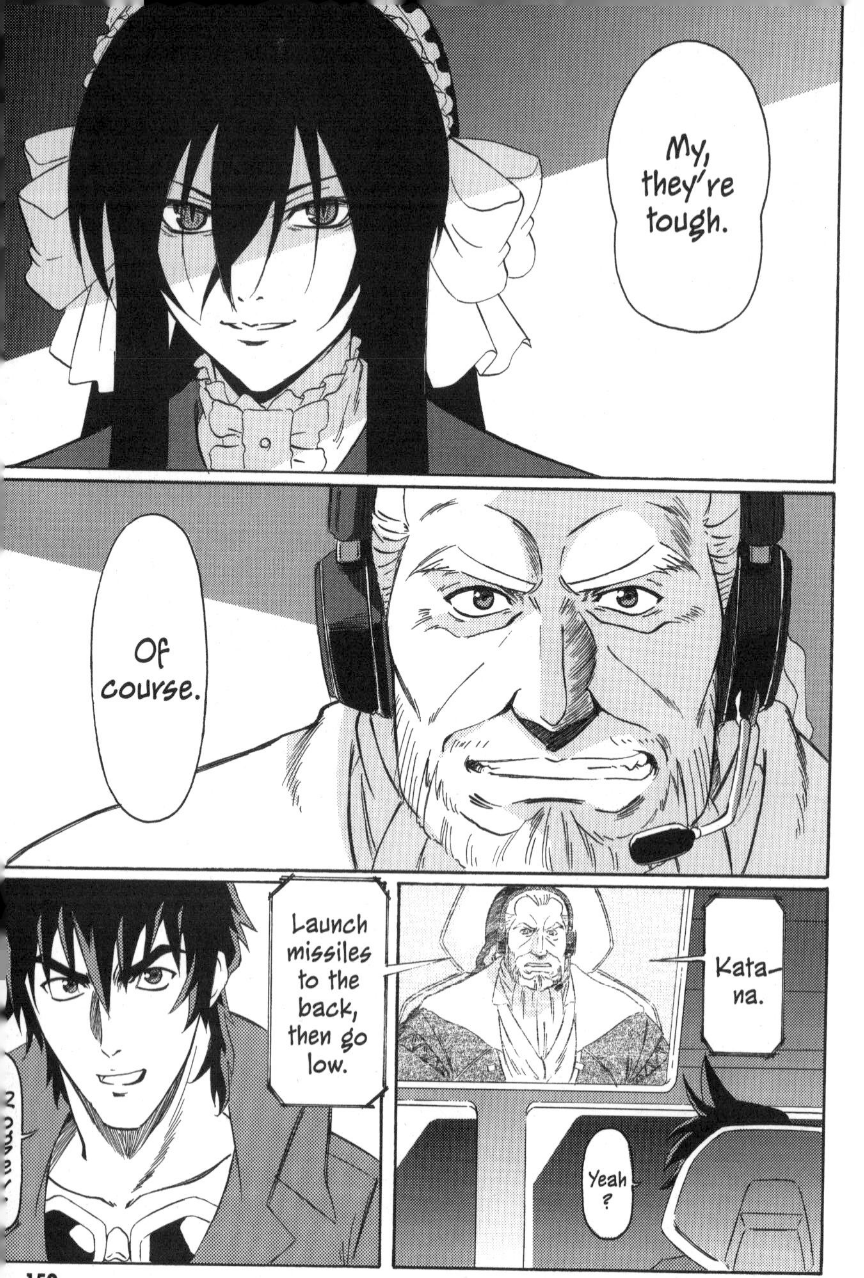
My, they're tough.
Of course.
Kata-na.
Yeah?
Launch missiles to the back, then go low.

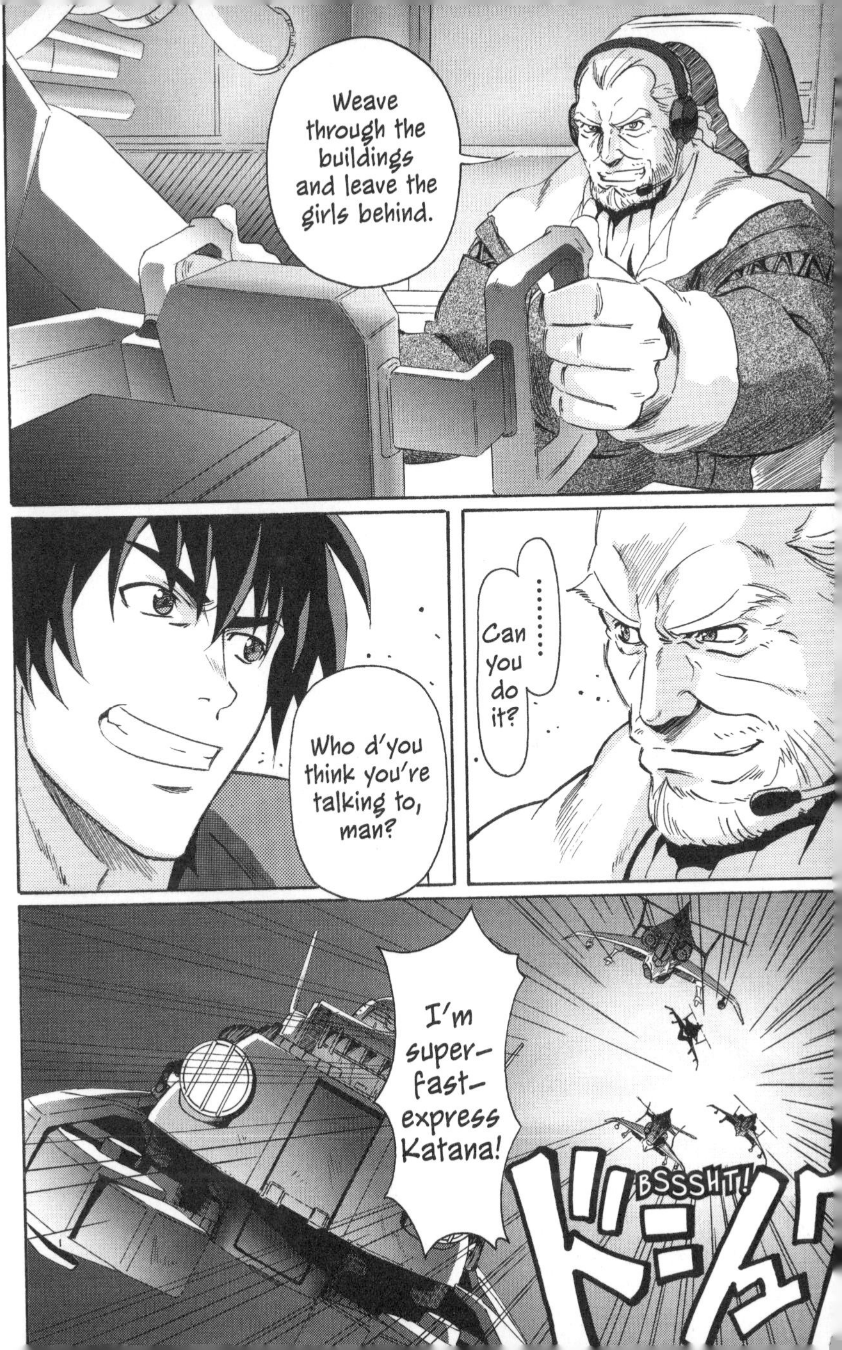
Weave through the buildings and leave the girls behind.
......
Can you do it?
...
Who d'you think you're talking to, man?
I'm super-fast-express Katana!
BSSSHT!

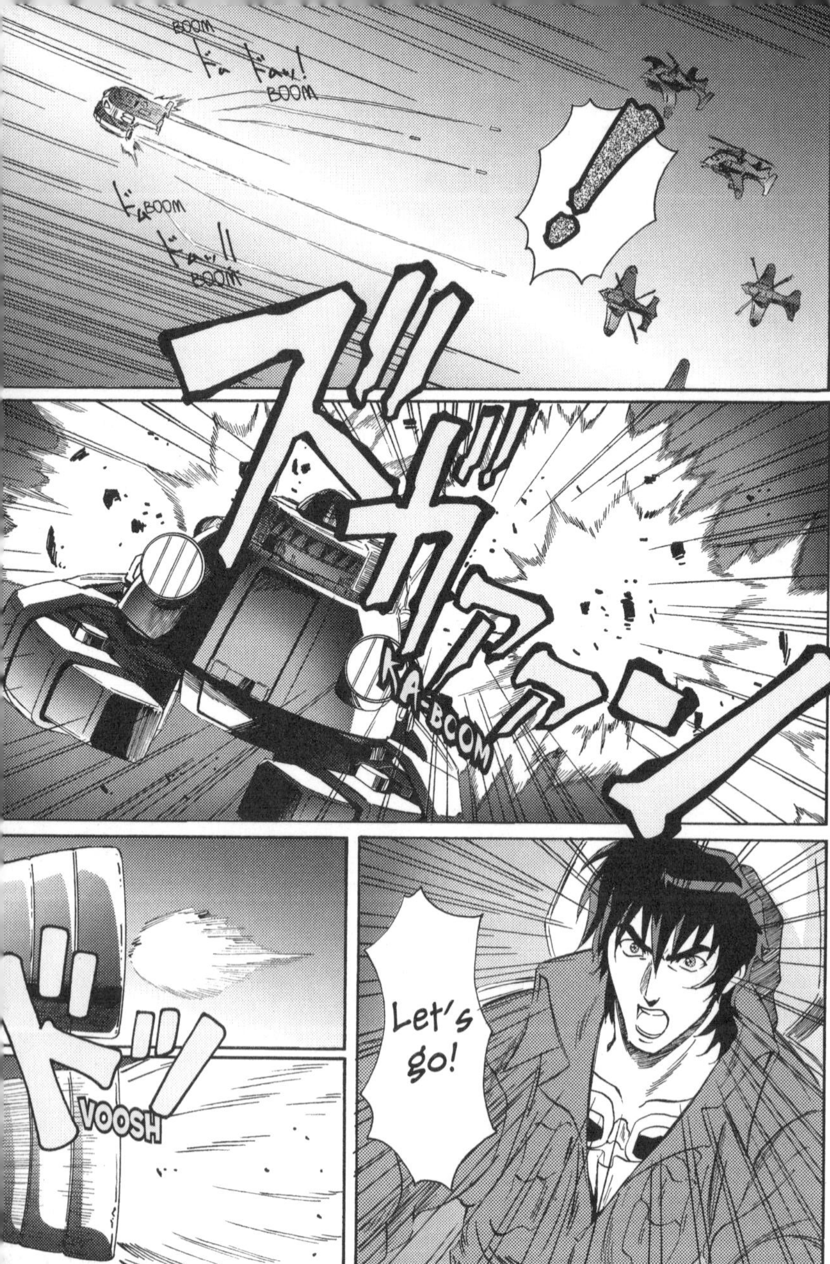
BOOM
BOOM
BOOM
BOOM
KA-BOOM
Let's go!
VOOSH

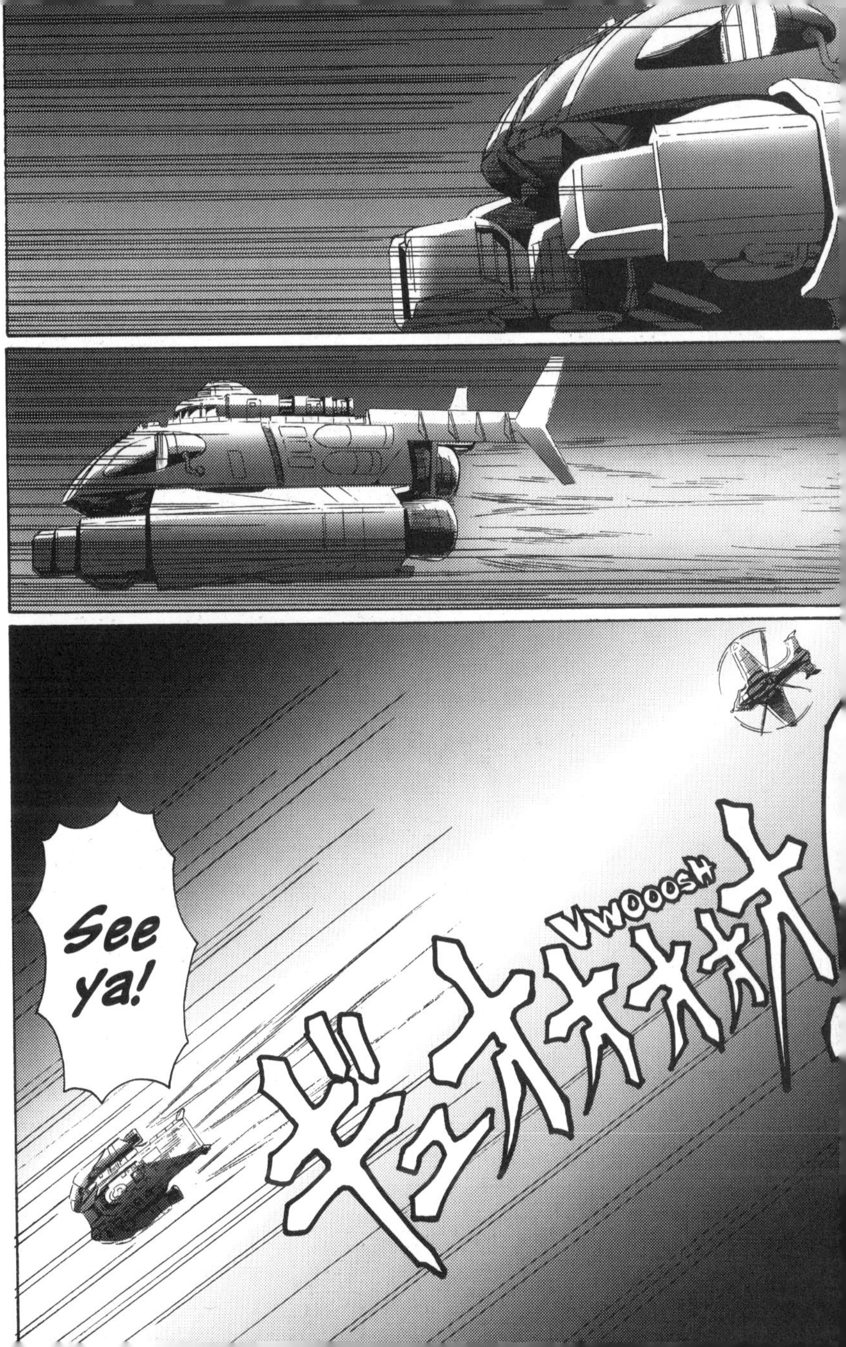
VWOOOSH
See ya!

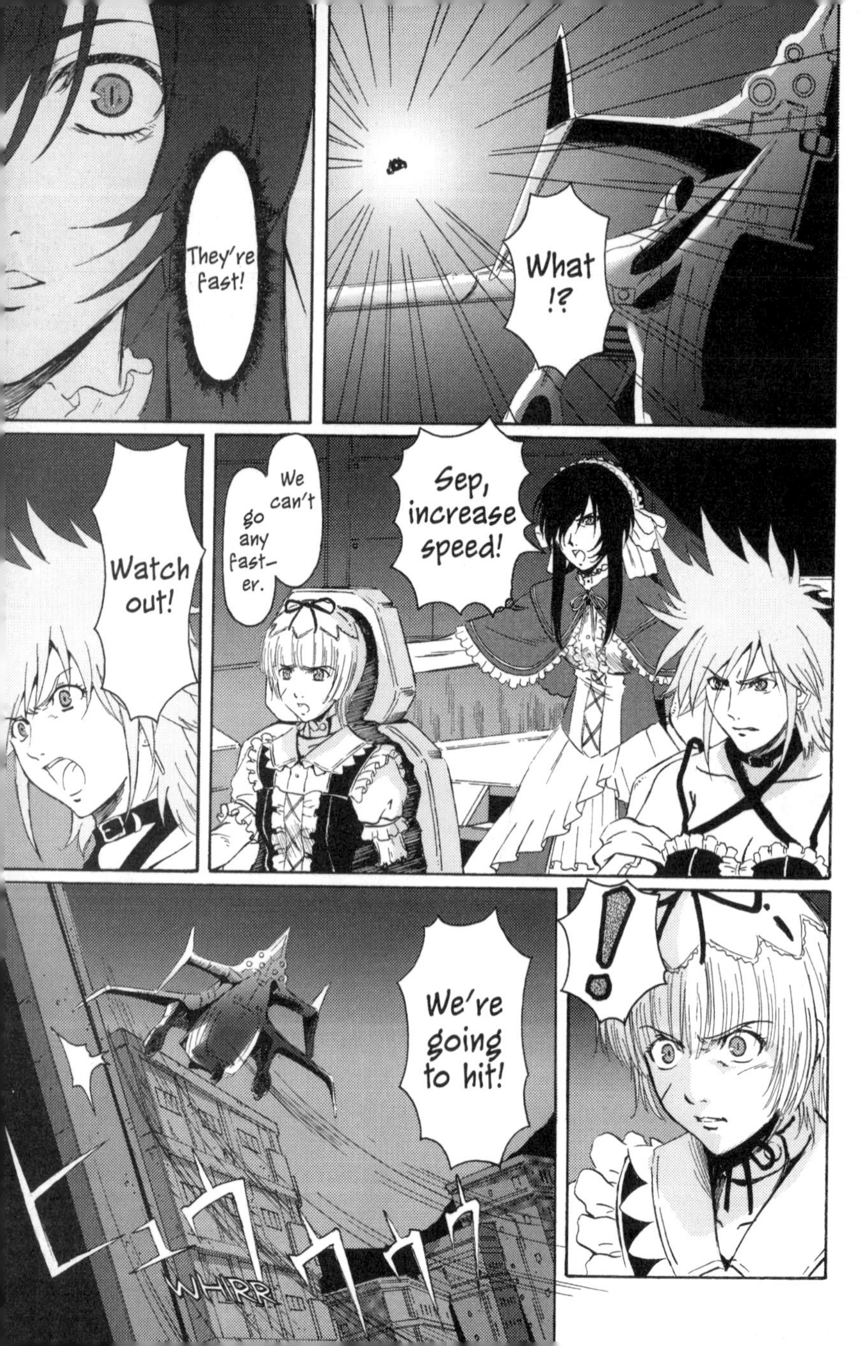
What !?
They're fast!
Sep, increase speed!
We can't go any faster.
Watch out!
!
We're going to hit!
WHIRR

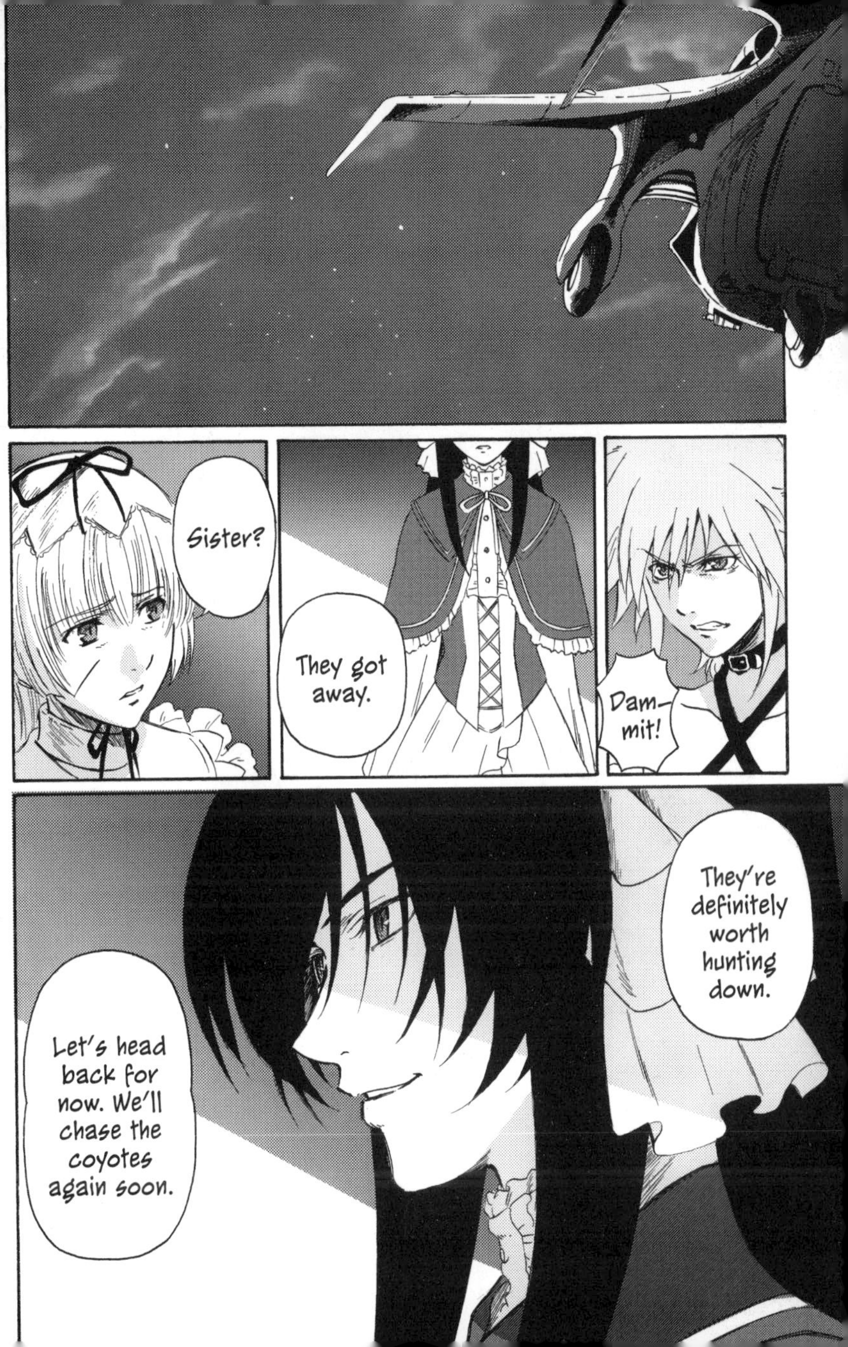
Dam-mit!
They got away.
Sister?
They're definitely worth hunting down.
Let's head back for now. We'll chase the coyotes again soon.

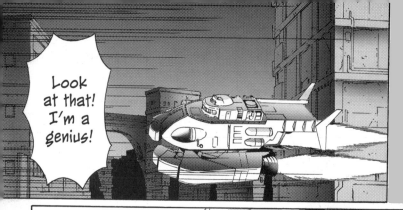

Look at that! I'm a genius!

It's at least three days to Graceland, even if we use the warp gates. And another half day to find the treasure and get it out of there.

How many more days until the photon bomb is dropped?

Six days and three hours.

Bi-shop.

Yeah?

165

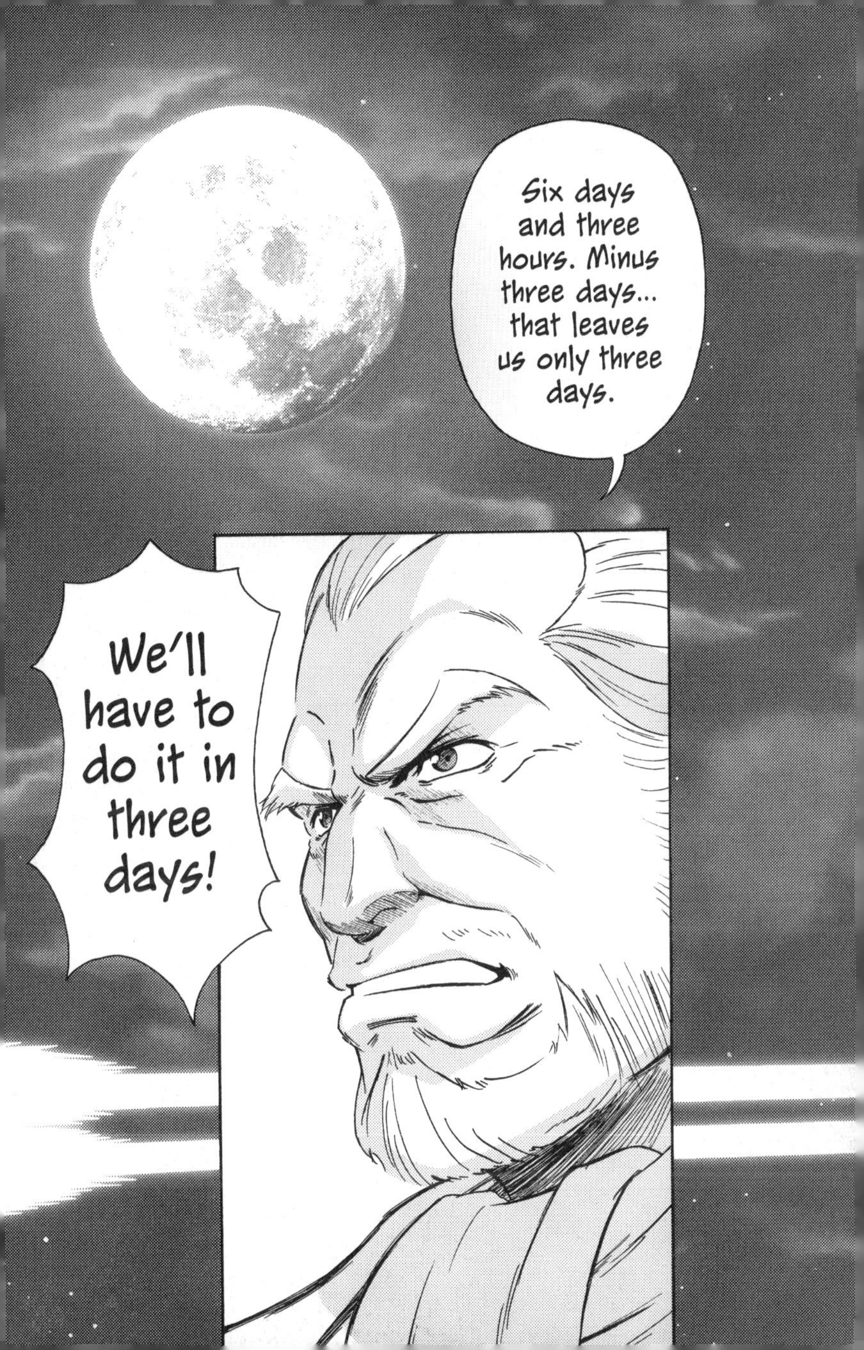
Six days and three hours. Minus three days... that leaves us only three days.
We'll have to do it in three days!

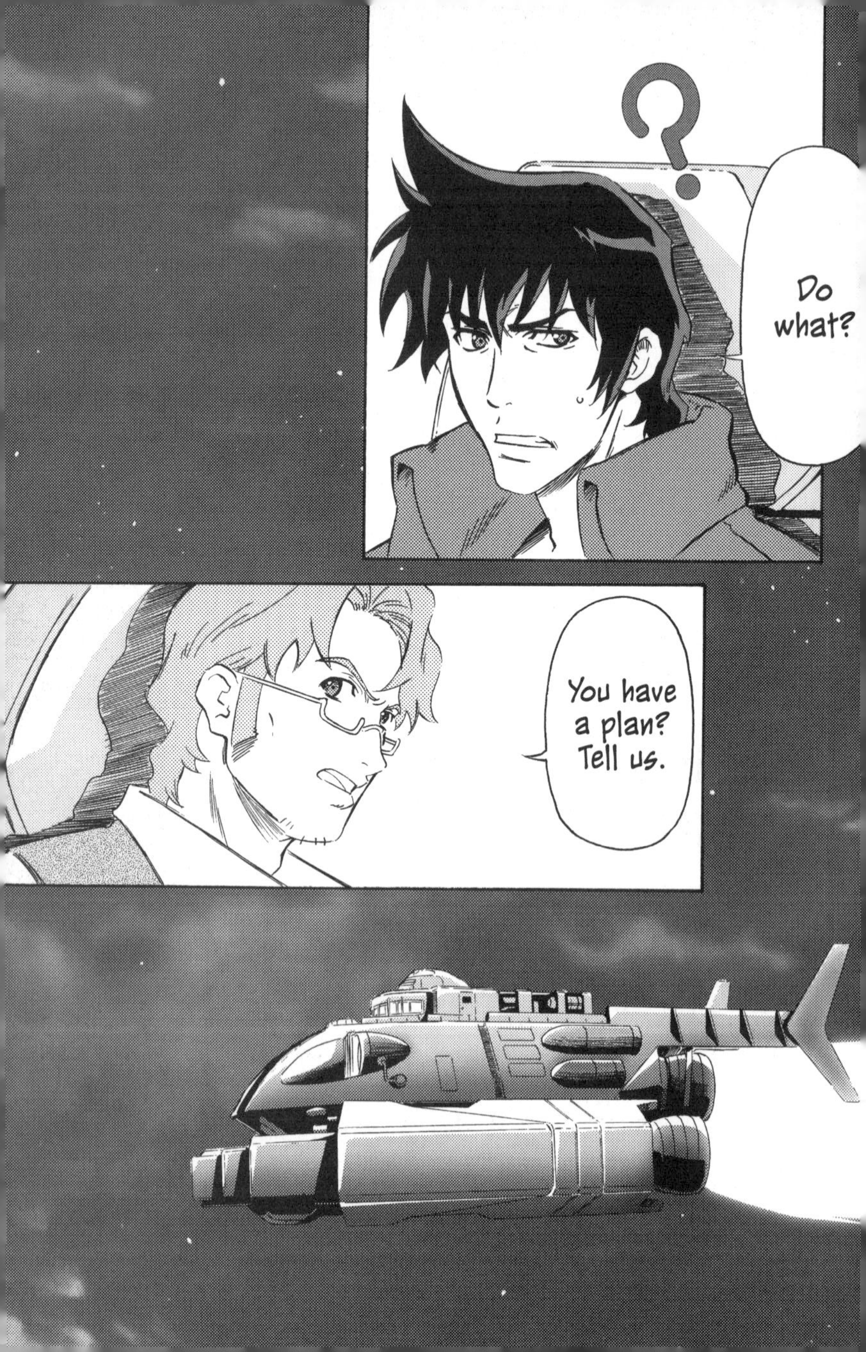
Do what?
You have a plan? Tell us.

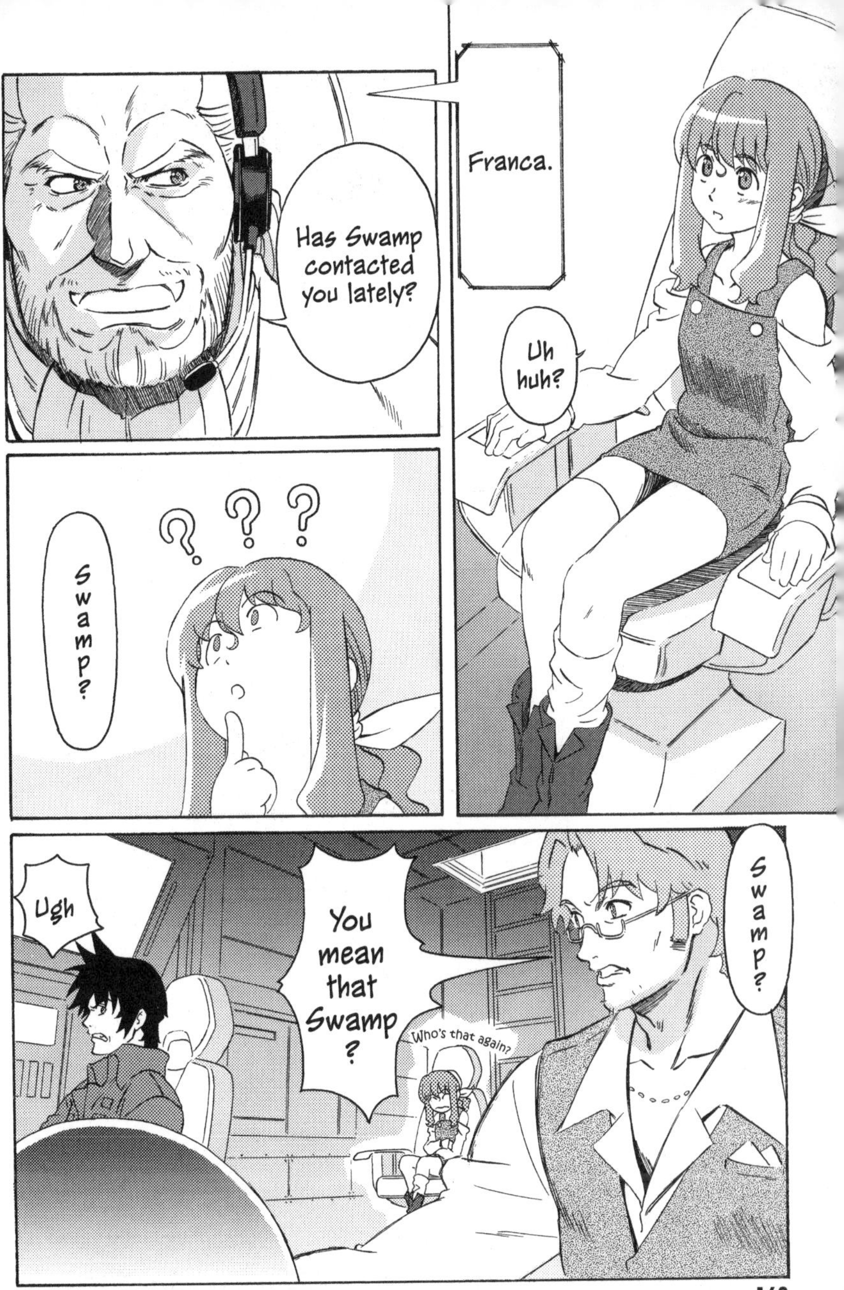

Franca.
Uh huh?
Has Swamp contacted you lately?
? ? ?
Swamp?
Swamp?
You mean that Swamp?
Who's that again?
Ugh

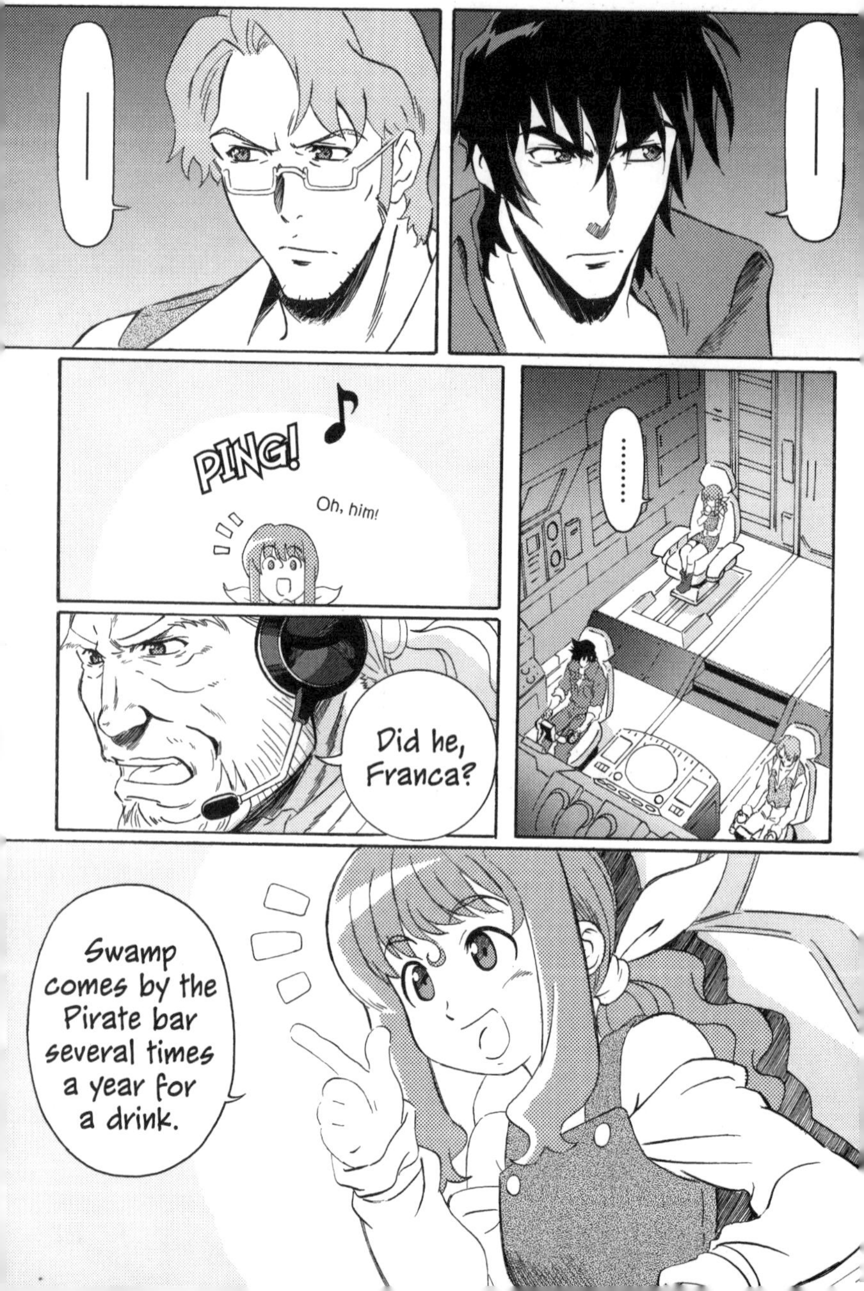
—
—
......
PING!
♪
Oh, him!
Did he, Franca?
Swamp comes by the Pirate bar several times a year for a drink.

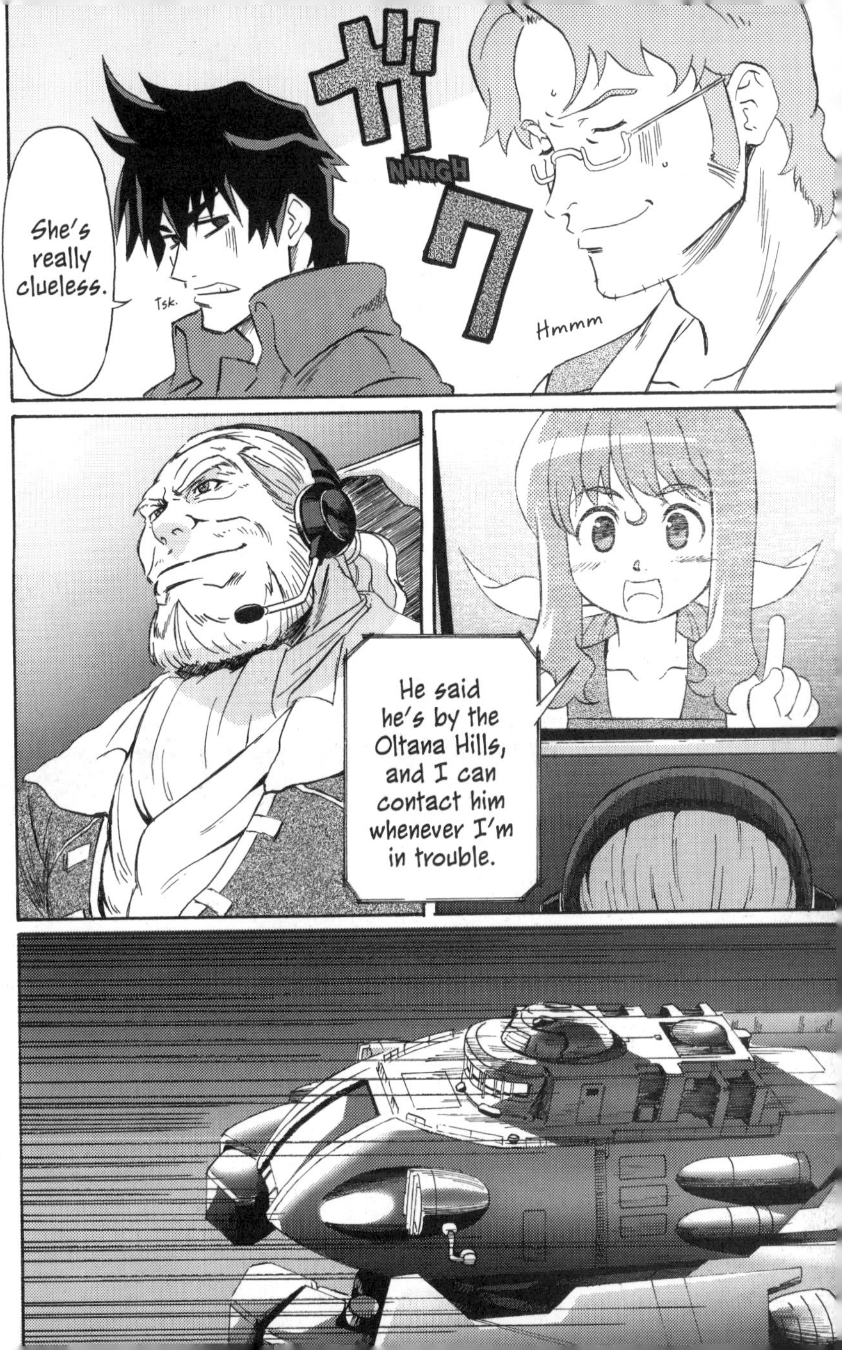
ガク
NNNGH
Hmmm
She's really clueless.
Tsk.
He said he's by the Oltana Hills, and I can contact him whenever I'm in trouble.

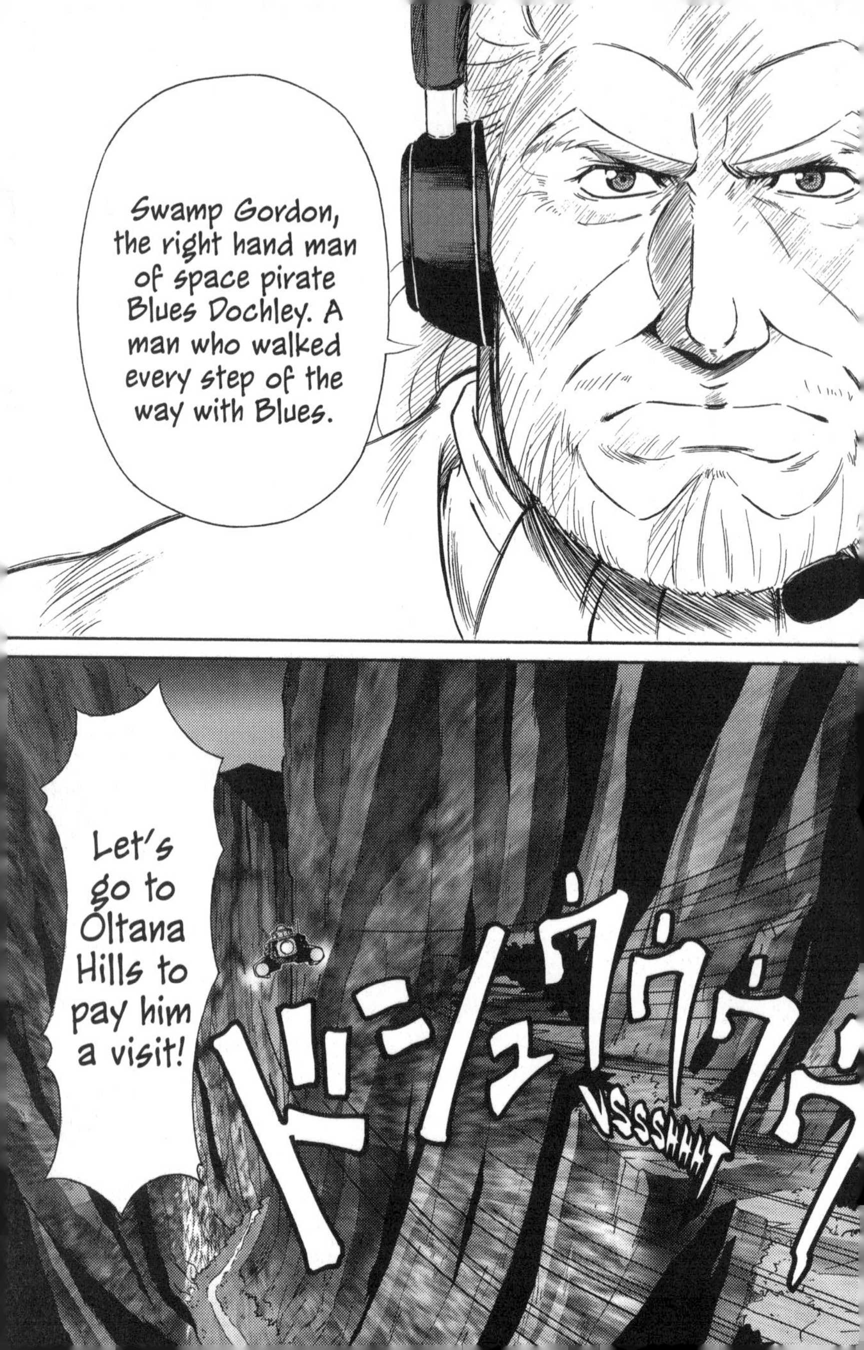
Swamp Gordon, the right hand man of space pirate Blues Dochley. A man who walked every step of the way with Blues.
Let's go to Oltana Hills to pay him a visit!
VSSSHHHT

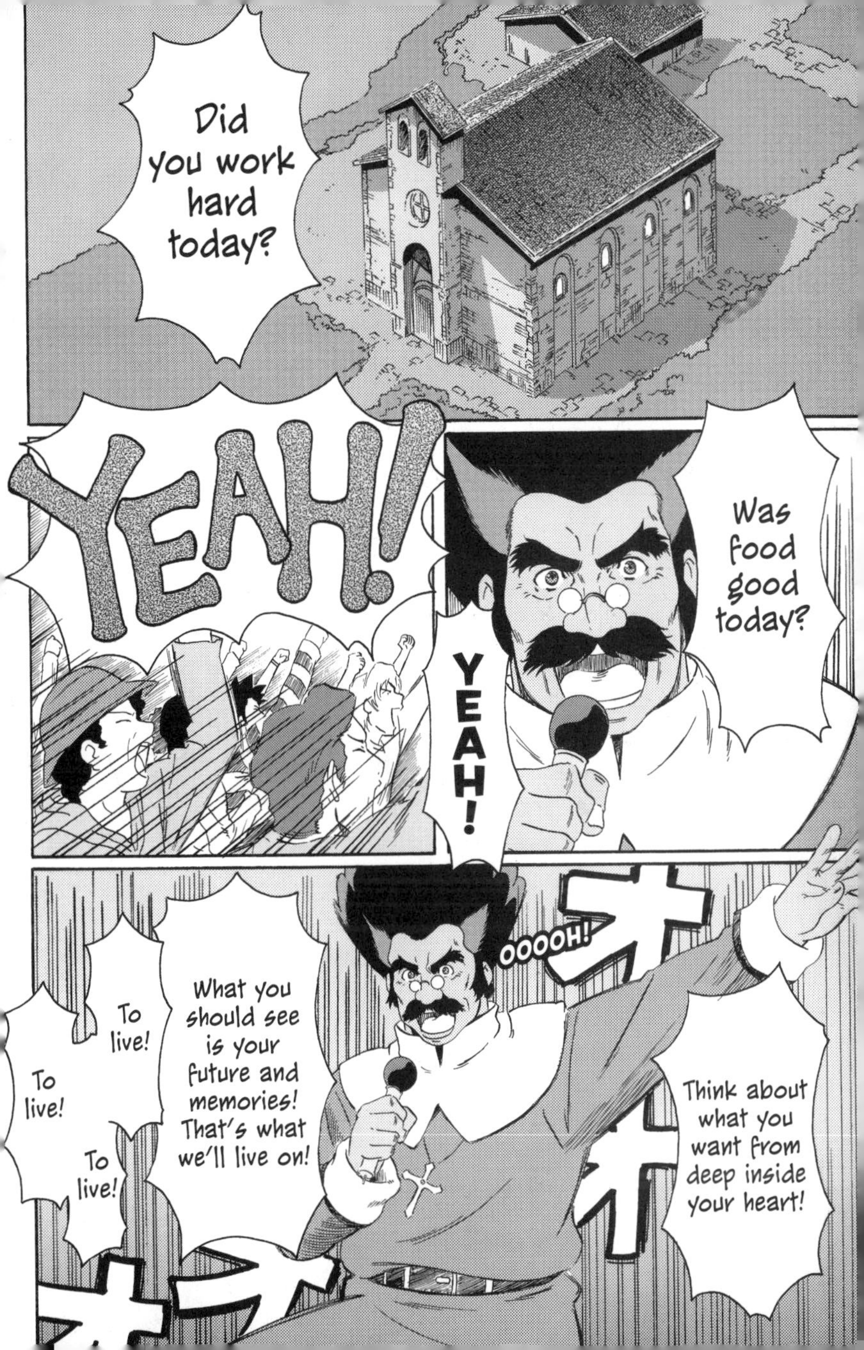
Did you work hard today?
Was food good today?
YEAH!
YEAH!
Think about what you want from deep inside your heart!
OOOOH!
What you should see is your future and memories! That's what we'll live on!
To live!
To live!
To live!

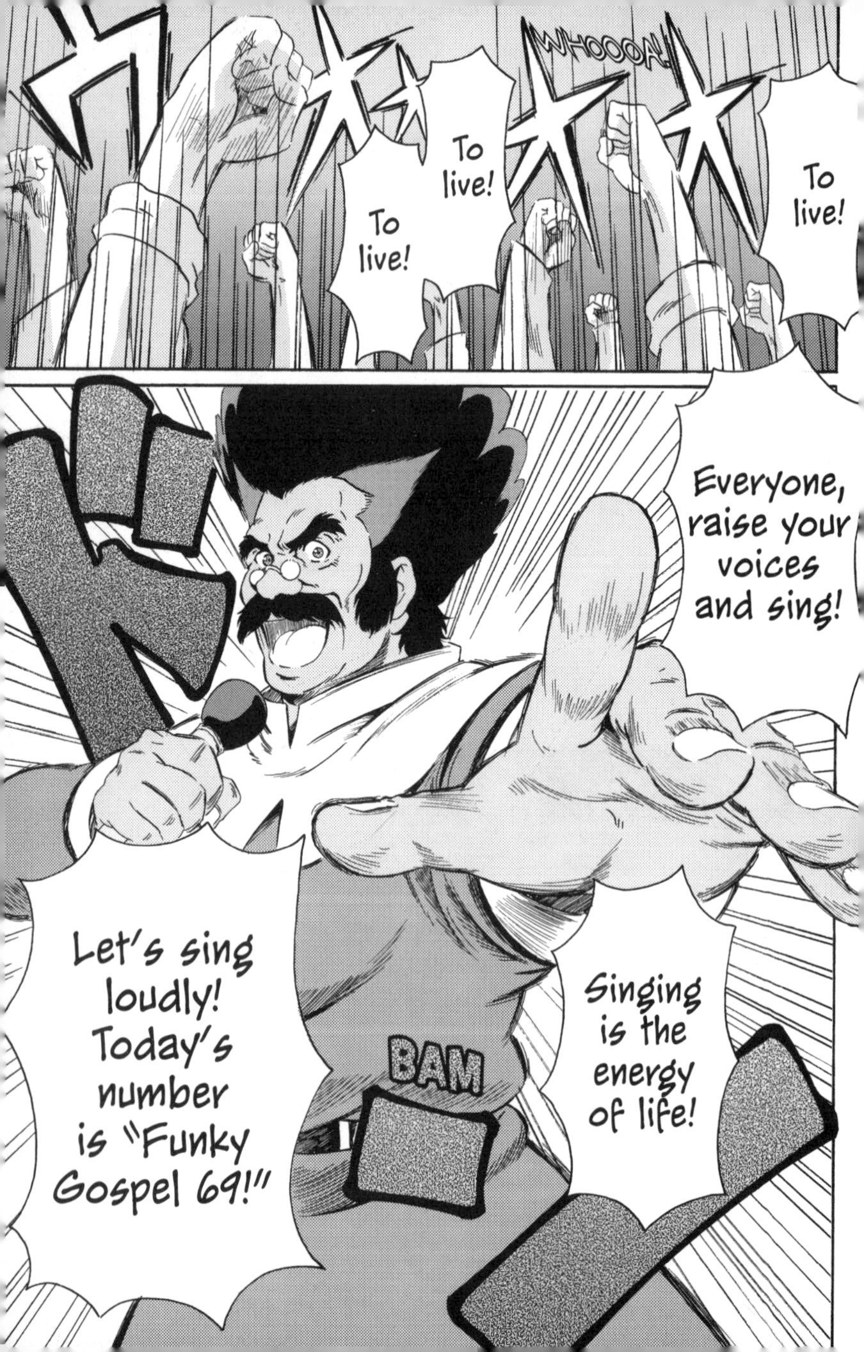
To live!
WHOOOA!
To live!
To live!
Everyone, raise your voices and sing!
Singing is the energy of life!
Let's sing loudly! Today's number is "Funky Gospel 69!"
BAM

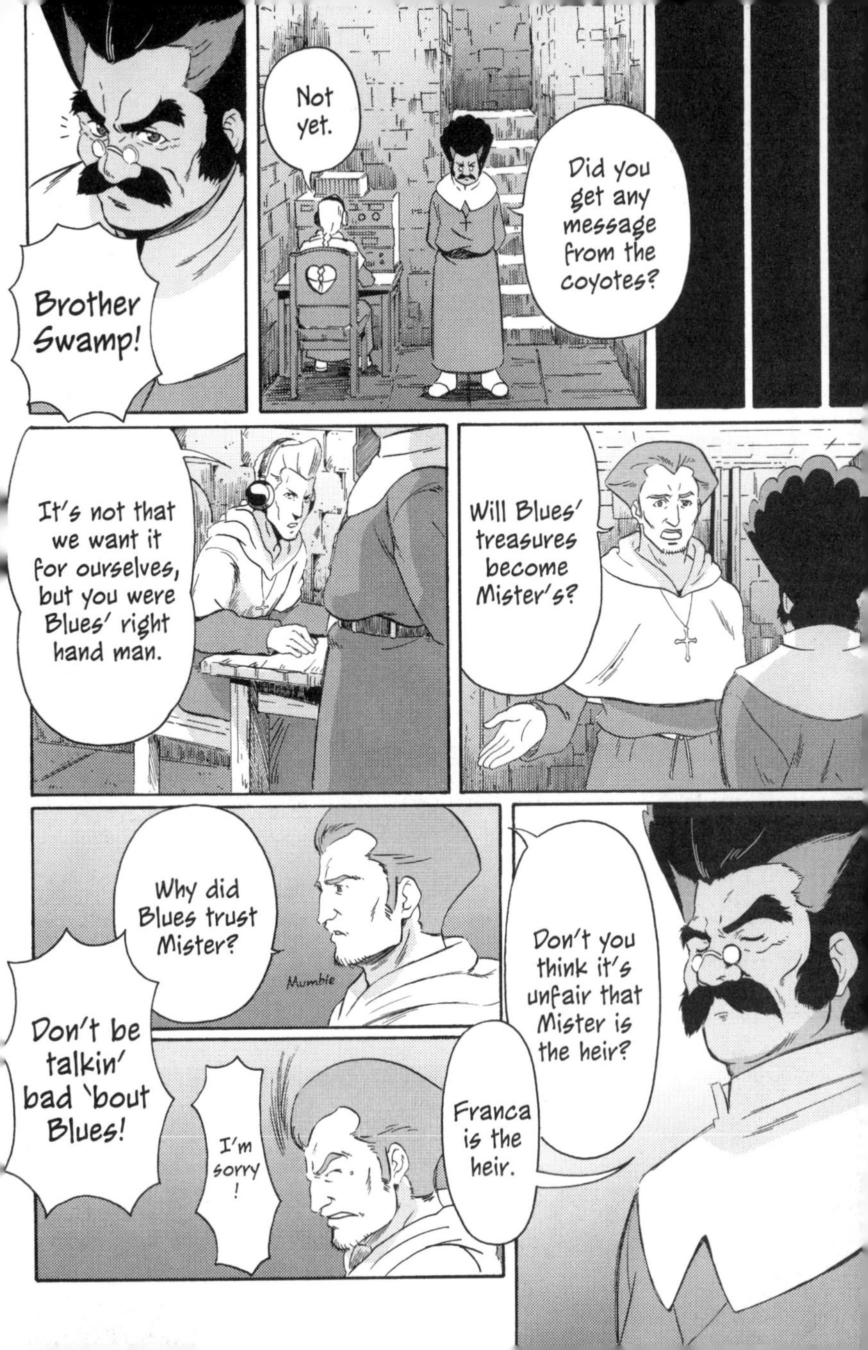
Did you get any message from the coyotes?
Not yet.
Brother Swamp!
Will Blues' treasures become Mister's?
It's not that we want it for ourselves, but you were Blues' right hand man.
Don't you think it's unfair that Mister is the heir?
Franca is the heir.
Why did Blues trust Mister?
Mumble
Don't be talkin' bad 'bout Blues!
I'm sorry!

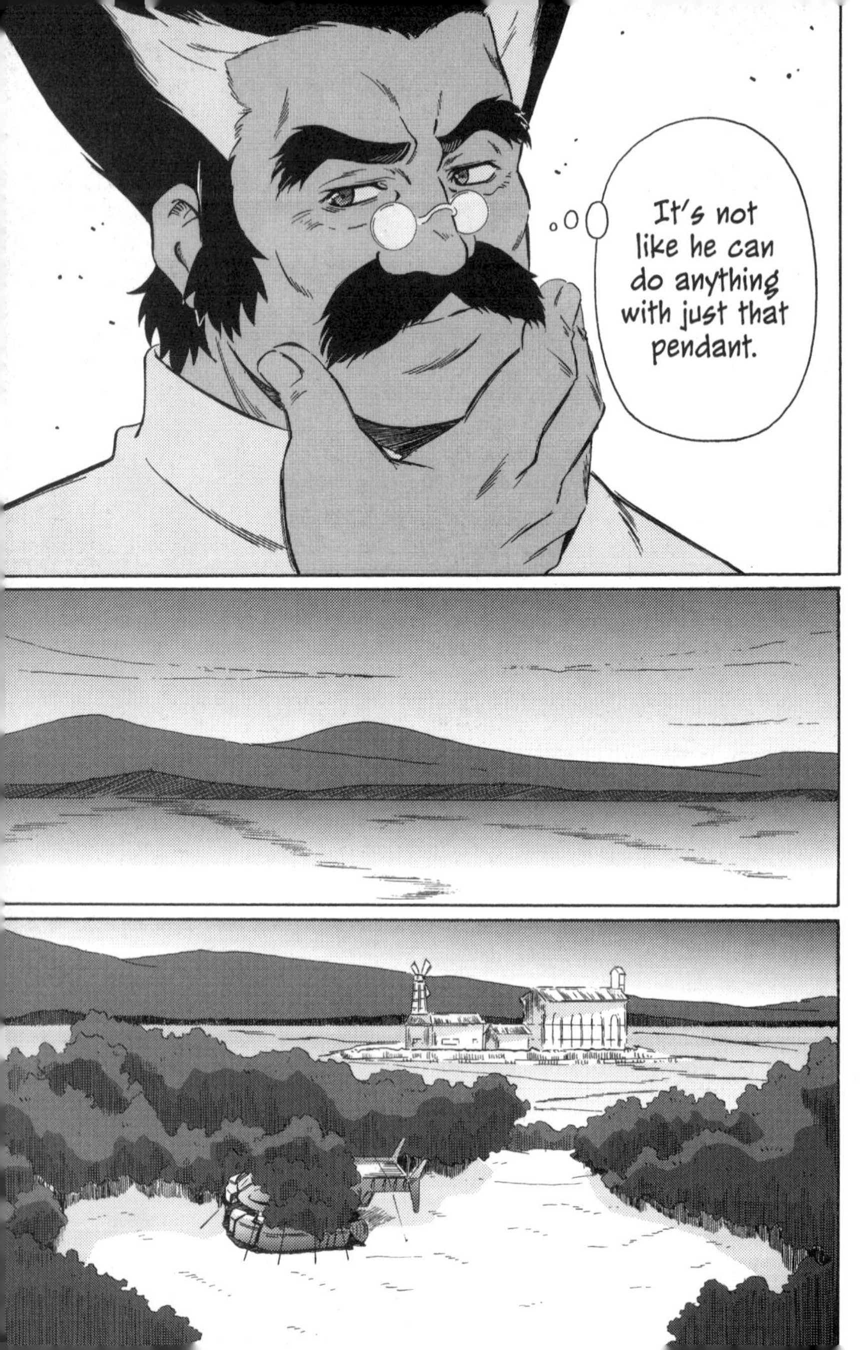
It's not like he can do anything with just that pendant.

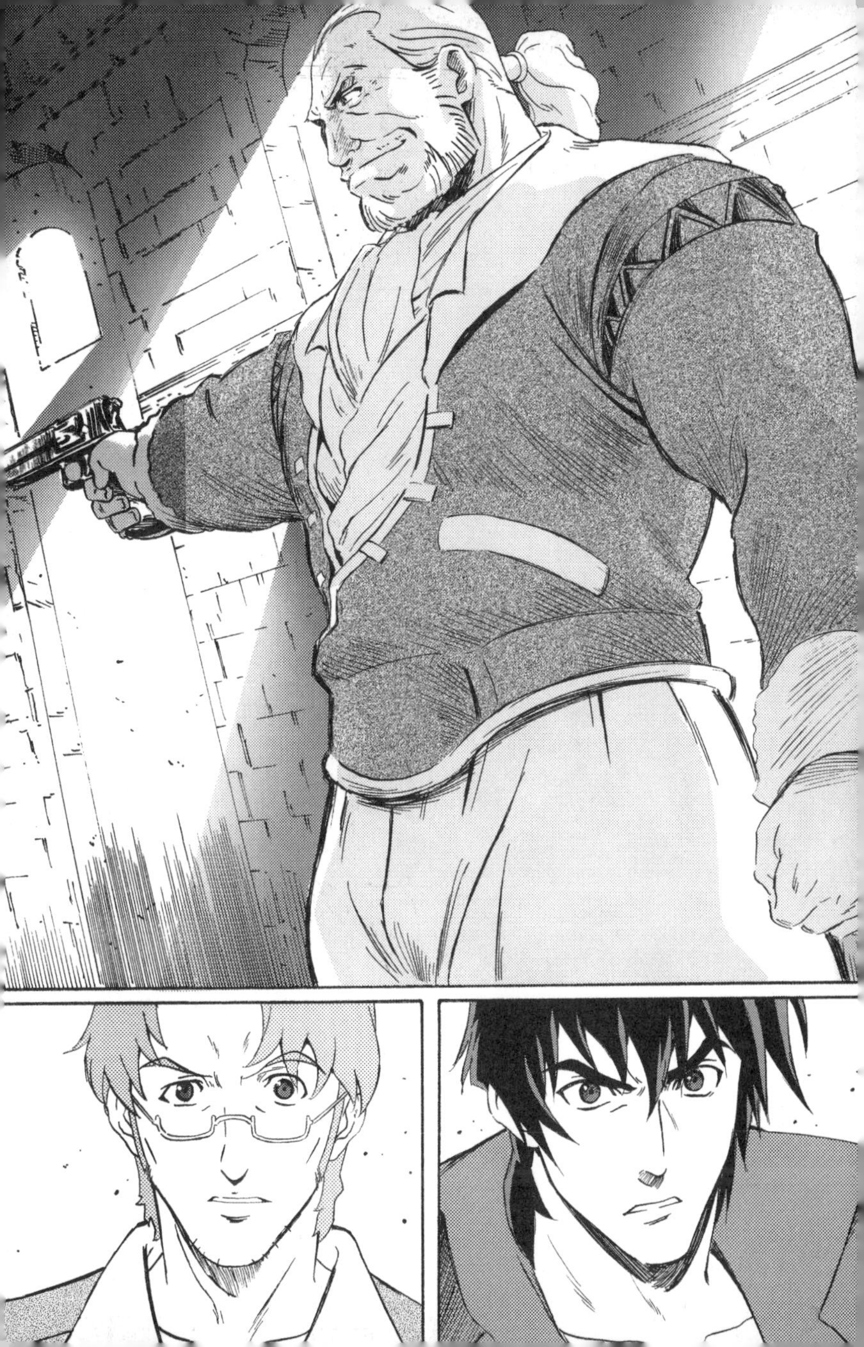

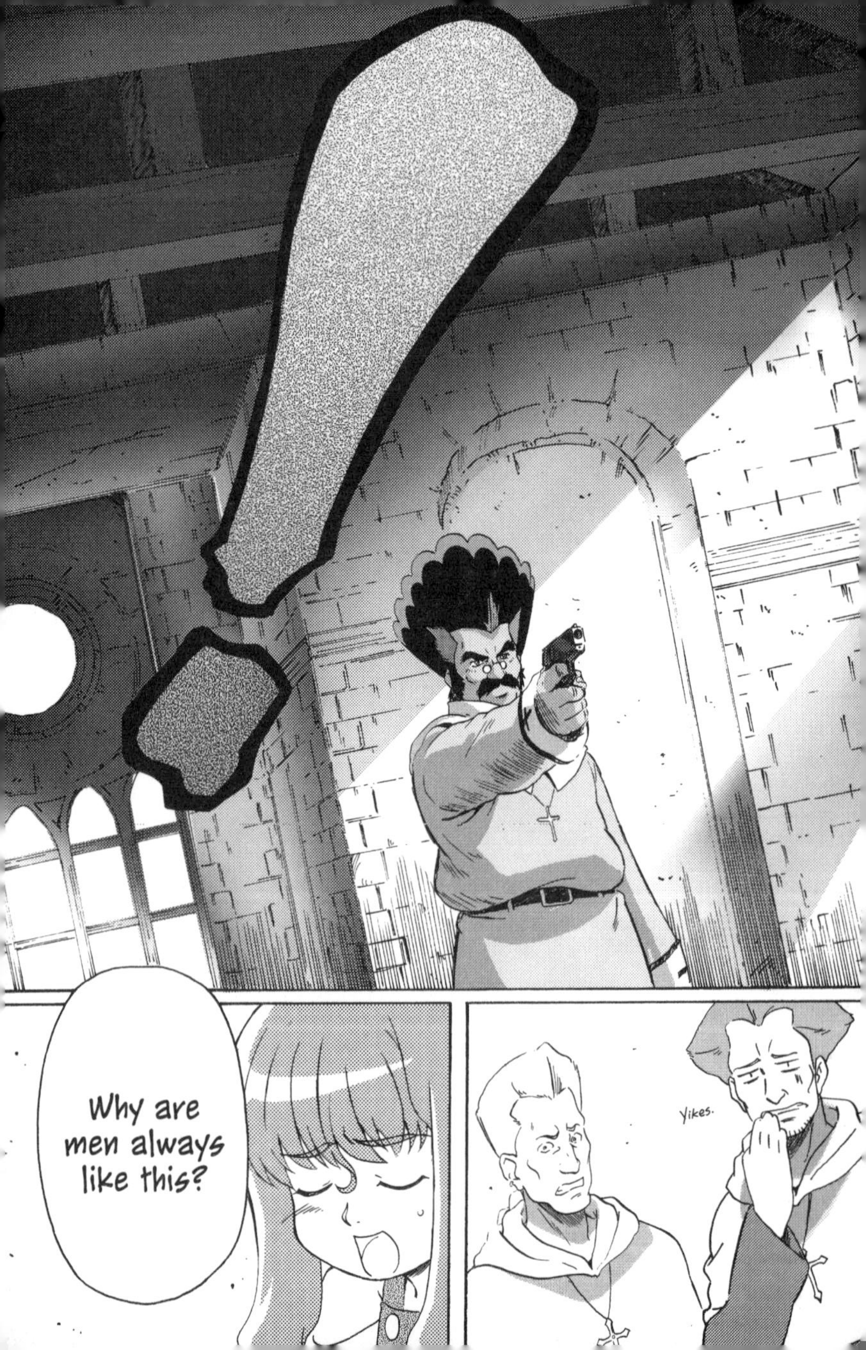
Yikes.
Why are men always like this?

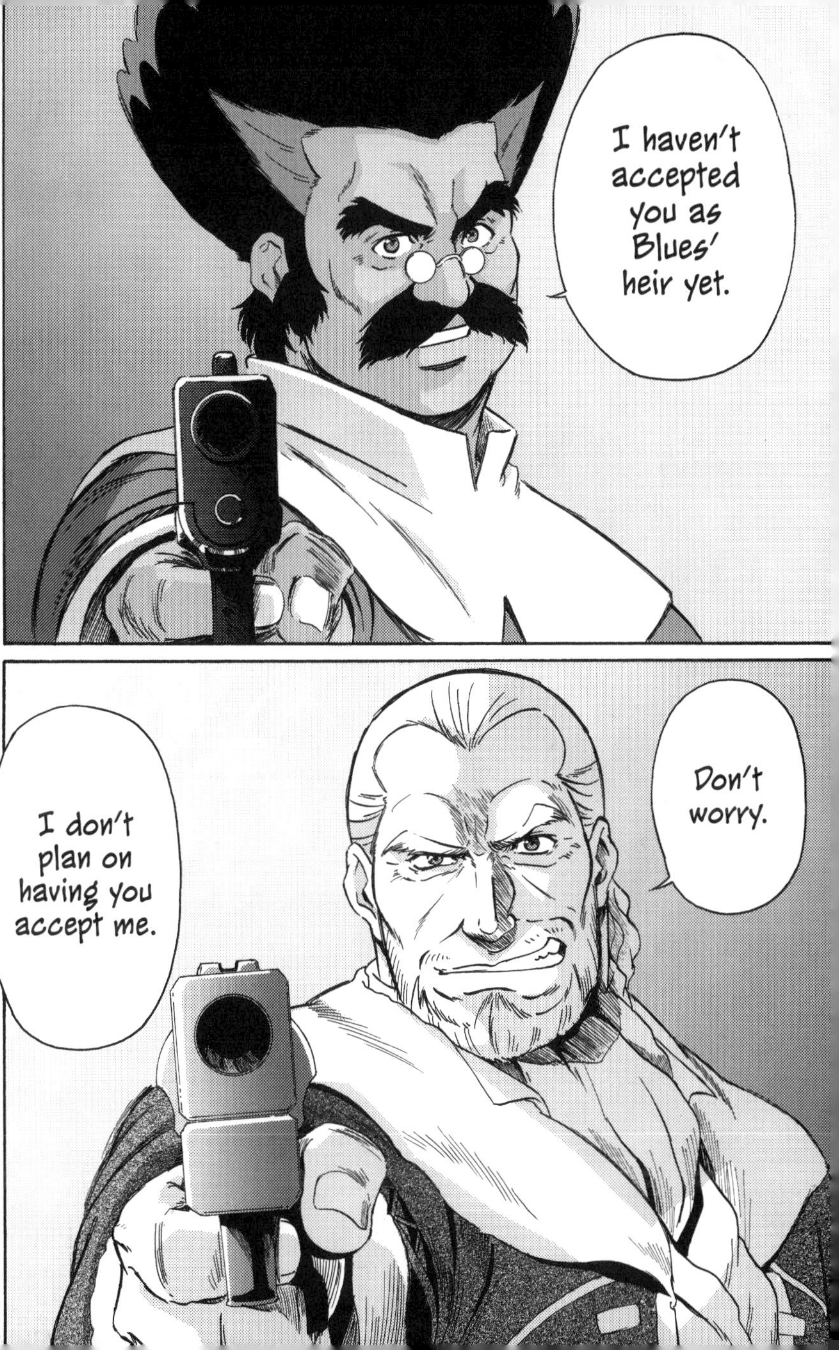
I haven't accepted you as Blues' heir yet.
Don't worry.
I don't plan on having you accept me.

COYOTE
Ragtime Show

COVER:
Illustrated by Seiya Numata
Color direction: Emi Chiba

COLOR PIN-UP (pg.01):
Illustrated by Tomonori Sudou
Color direction: Emi Chiba

COLOR PIN-UP (pg.02):
Illustrated by Haruo Sotozaki
Color direction: Emi Chiba

TITLE PAGE:
Illustrated by Haruo Sotozaki

COYOTE RAGTIME SHOW STAFF LIST CHAPTER 1
Base script: Ryunosuke Kingetsu
Comic script: Matsuri Ouse
Art director: Haruo Sotozaki, Seiya Numata
S part director: Tomonori Sudou
Draft writer: Takuro Takahashi, Teruo Shimotsukasa, Mitsuru Obunai, Yamato Kojima, Satoshi Takahashi, Mutsumi Kadekaru
Auxiliary art: Hitomi Odashima, Tan-Tan, Kawase Yu-ki, Atsushi Ogasawara
Digital process: Yuuichi Terao (chief), Saki Matsubara, Ko-ji Yokoi, Mikako Senzaki, Chihiro Ide, Shigeji Matsuda, Emi Chiba, Ryu Suzuki
Progress management: Kyousuke Nakazawa, Minoru Shimohara, Yasuyuki Fujii, Kumiko Ohori

COYOTE RAGTIME SHOW STAFF LIST CHAPTER 2
Base script: Ryunosuke Kingetsu
Comic script: Matsuri Ouse
Art director: Haruo Sotozaki, Seiya Numata
Digital process: Yuuichi Terao (chief), Saki Matsubara, Ko-ji Yokoi, Mikako Senzaki, Tan-Tan, Kawase Yu-ki

COYOTE RAGTIME SHOW STAFF LIST CHAPTER 3
Base script: Ryunosuke Kingetsu
Comic script: Matsuri Ouse
Art director: Haruo Sotozaki
Digital process: Yuuichi Terao (chief), Saki Matsubara, Ko-ji Yokoi, Mikako Senzaki, Yumi Aburaya

COYOTE RAGTIME SHOW STAFF LIST CHAPTER 4
Base script: Ryunosuke Kingetsu
Comic script: Matsuri Ouse
Art director: Haruo Sotozaki
Digital process: Yuuichi Terao (chief), Saki Matsubara, Ko-ji Yokoi, Mikako Senzaki

COYOTE RAGTIME SHOW STAFF LIST CHAPTER 5
Base script: Matsuri Ouse
Comic script: Matsuri Ouse
Art director: Haruo Sotozaki
Digital process: Yuuichi Terao (chief), Saki Matsubara, Ko-ji Yokoi, Mikako Senzaki, Yukiko Sugimoto, Rumiko Mizoguchi, Tan-Tan, No. 6

Producer: Hikaru Kondo
System manager: Kenichirou Kasahara

ufotable comic team tartan check

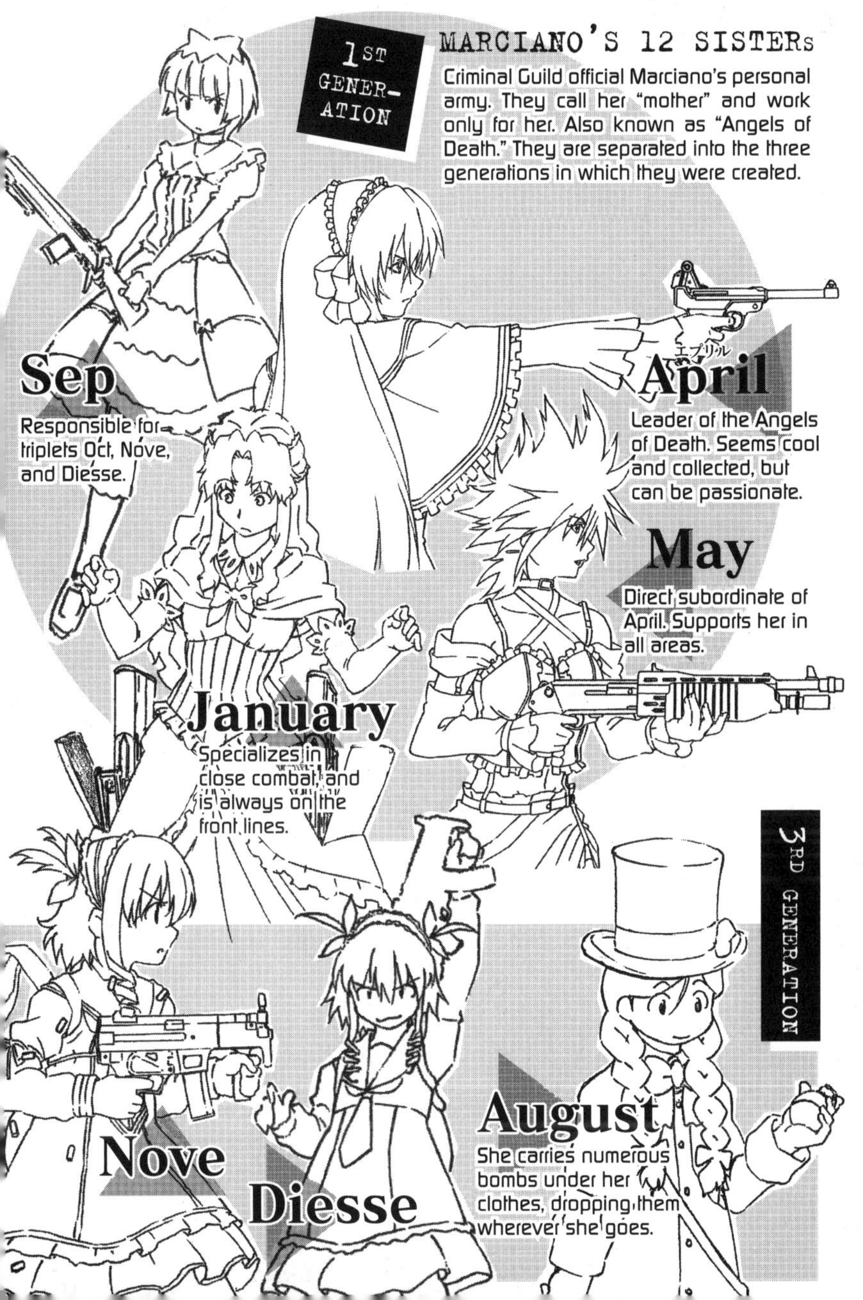
1ST GENERATION
MARCIANO'S 12 SISTERs
Criminal Guild official Marciano's personal army. They call her "mother" and work only for her. Also known as "Angels of Death." They are separated into the three generations in which they were created.
エプリル
April
Leader of the Angels of Death. Seems cool and collected, but can be passionate.
Sep
Responsible for triplets Oct, Nove, and Diesse.
May
Direct subordinate of April. Supports her in all areas.
January
Specializes in close combat, and is always on the front lines.
3RD GENERATION
August
She carries numerous bombs under her clothes, dropping them wherever she goes.
Nove
Diesse

COYOTE ENCYCLOPEDIA
-Marciano's12 SISTERs-

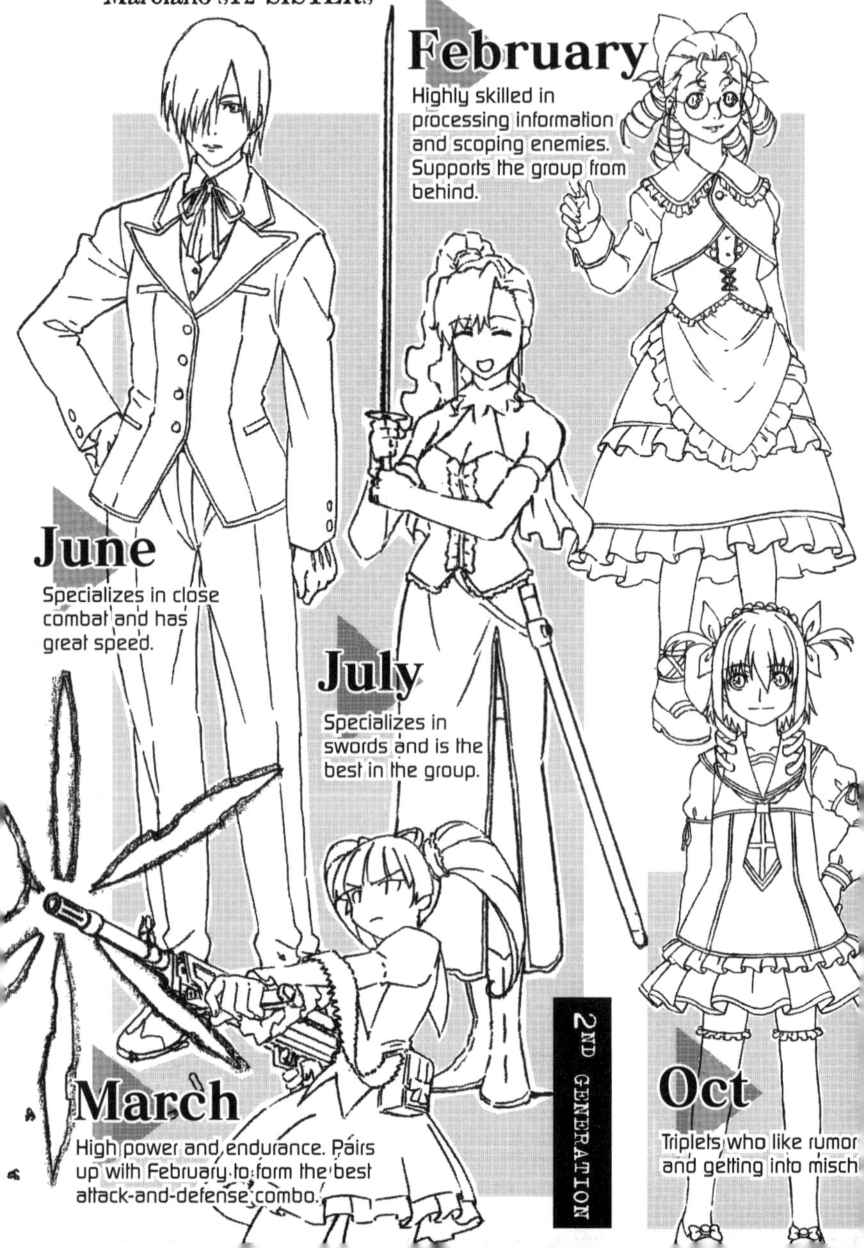
February
Highly skilled in processing information and scoping enemies. Supports the group from behind.
June
Specializes in close combat and has great speed.
July
Specializes in swords and is the best in the group.
March
High power and endurance. Pairs up with February to form the best attack-and-defense combo.
Oct
Triplets who like rumor and getting into misch
2ND GENERATION

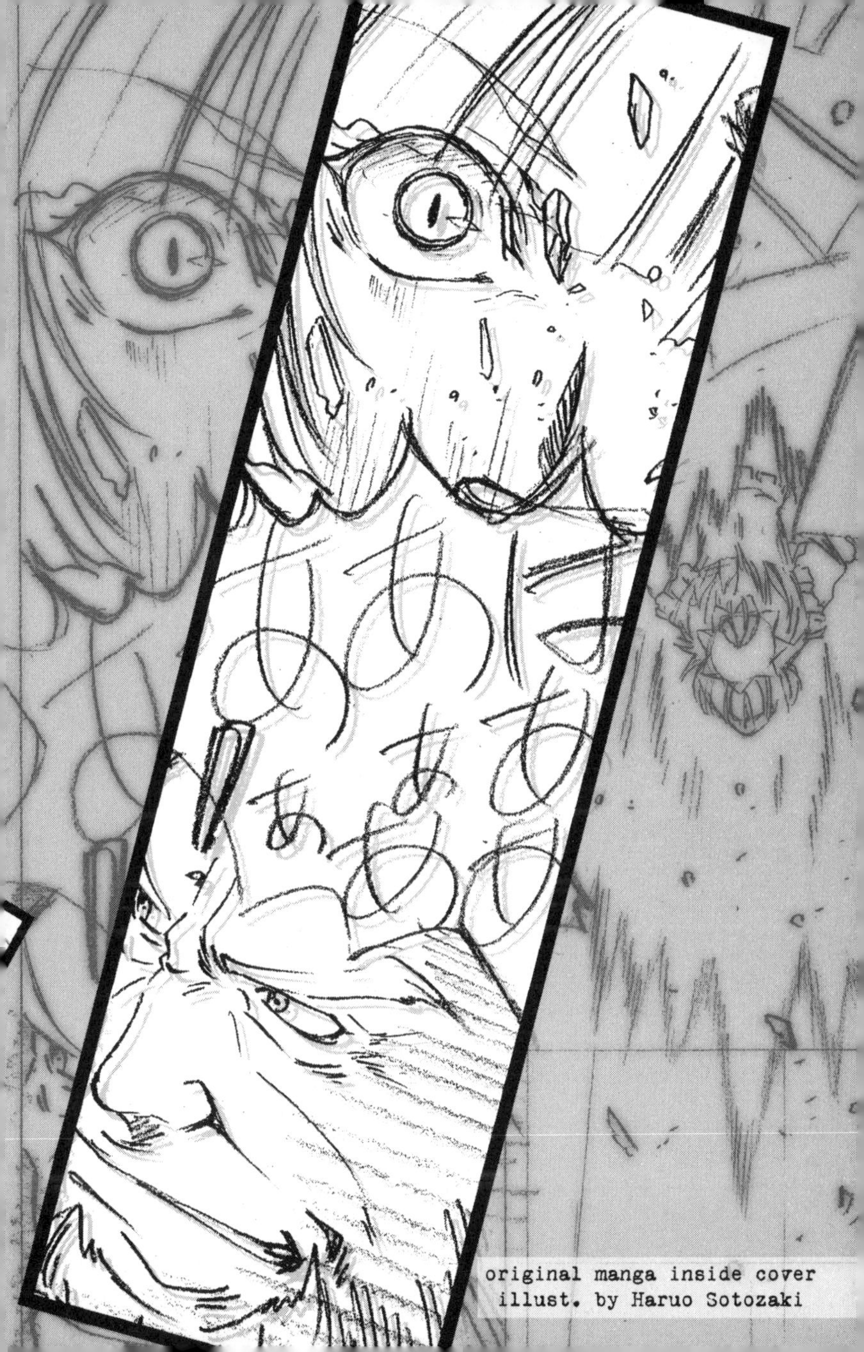

original manga inside cover
illust. by Haruo Sotozaki

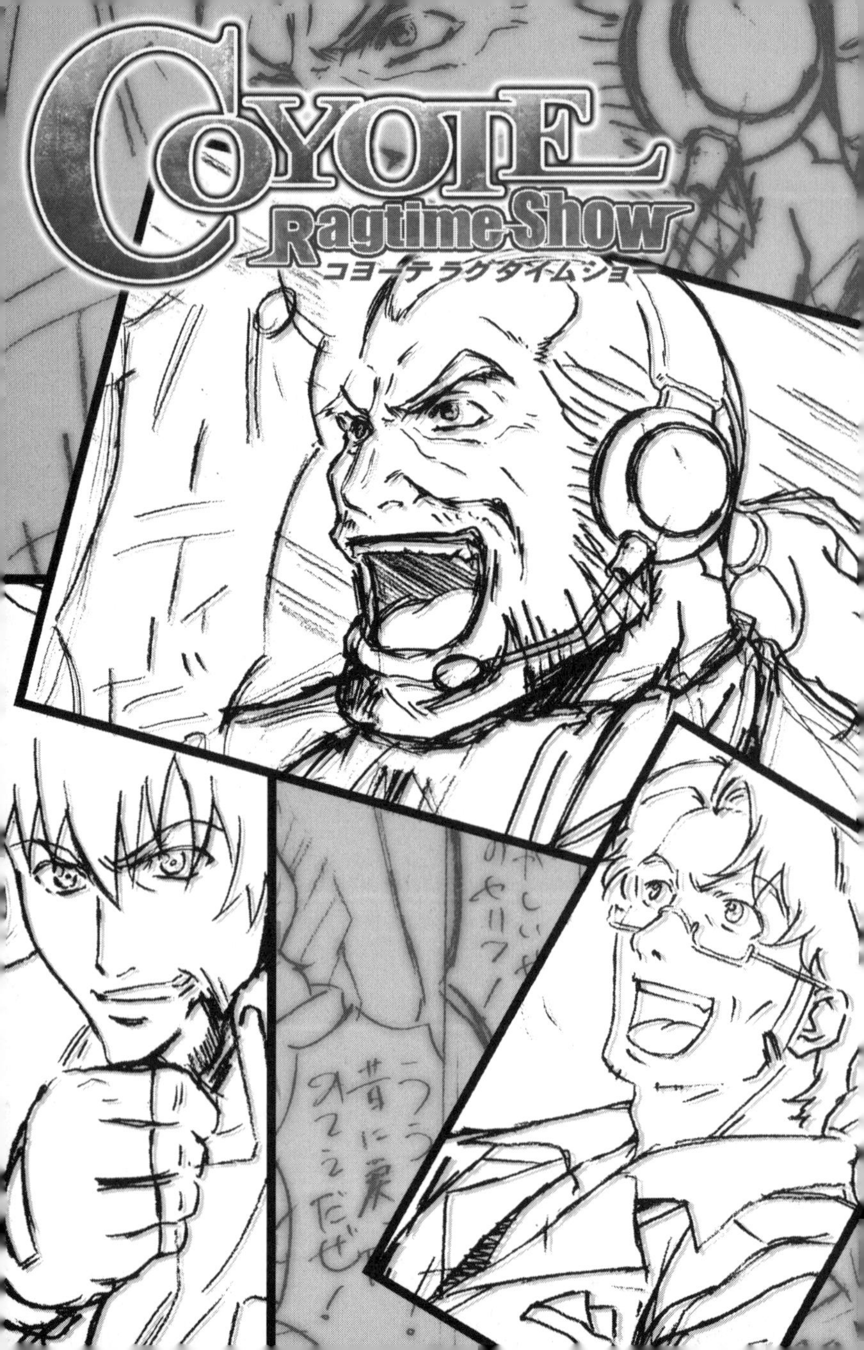
COYOTE
Ragtime Show
コヨーテラグタイムショー

translation notes

Pg. 19
MO - Modus operandi, Latin for "mode of operation," is a term used by law enforcement to describe a criminal's characteristic patterns.

Pg. 24
Criminal Guild - an organization that operates above the law and has significant influence in government affairs.

Pg. 60
Oolong-high - A mixed drink consisting of oolong tea and shochu, a Japanese alcohol.

Pg. 115
Moe - A Japanese term similar to "fetish" but without as much of the negative connotation. For instance, a person could have an attraction to, or could feel moe for girls or guys in glasses.

COYOTE Ragtime Show 2
コヨーテラグタイムショー

next volume preview

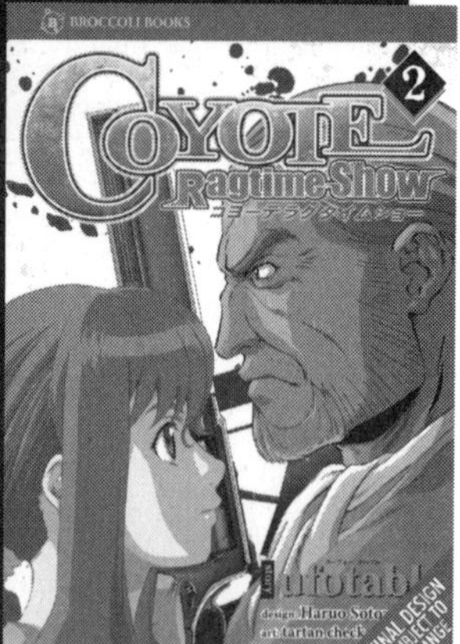
BROCCOLI BOOKS
COYOTE
2
Ragtime Show
コヨーテラグタイムショー
ufotable
design Haruo Soto
art tartan check
FINAL DESIGN SUBJECT TO CHANGE

When Mister and the crew of the Coyote go visit an old friend of the pirate king, they end up staring down the barrel of a gun. Grudges run deep, but so does their love for Franca. With just two days until Planet Graceland is destroyed, can an agreement be reached in time?

Meanwhile, Madame Marciano's memories are coming back to haunt her. It's time for her to keep old promises, but she might have to step into a trap to do it.

And all the while, the countdown continues ...

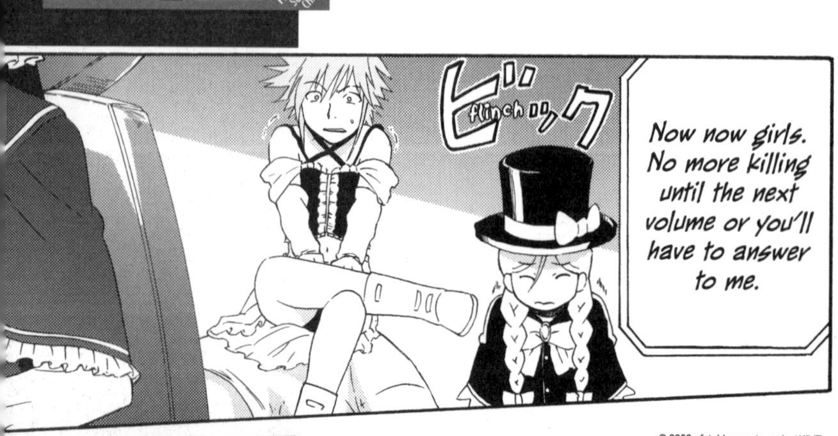
ビクッ
flinch
Now now girls. No more killing until the next volume or you'll have to answer to me.

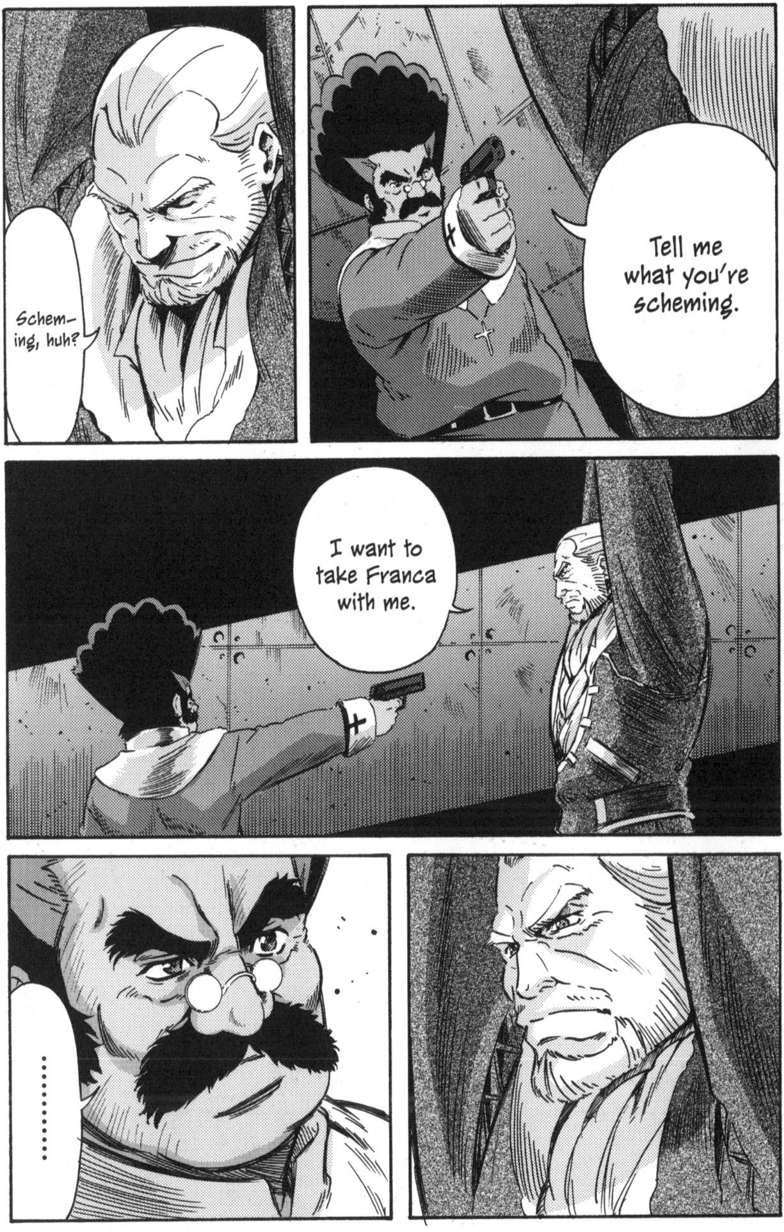
Tell me what you're scheming.
Schem-ing, huh?
I want to take Franca with me.
....

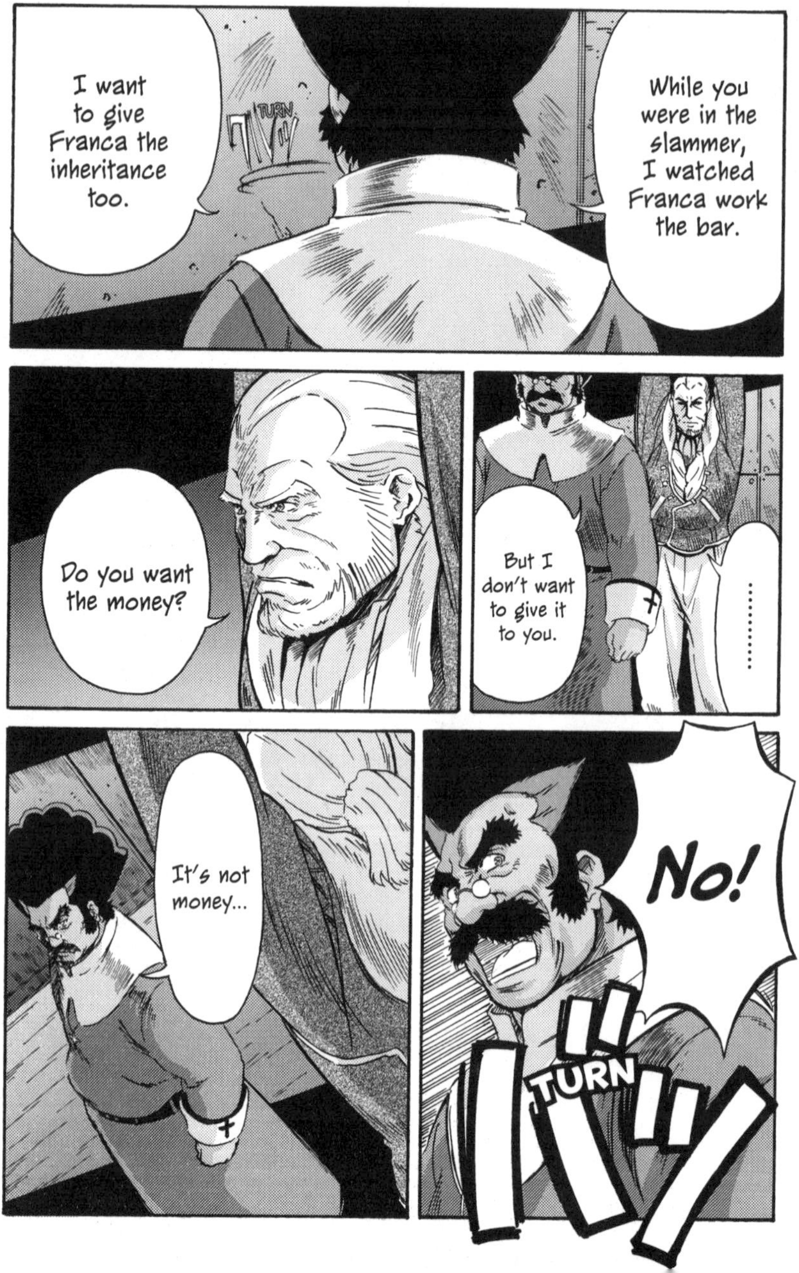
While you were in the slammer, I watched Franca work the bar.
TURN
I want to give Franca the inheritance too.
......
But I don't want to give it to you.
Do you want the money?
No!
TURN
It's not money...

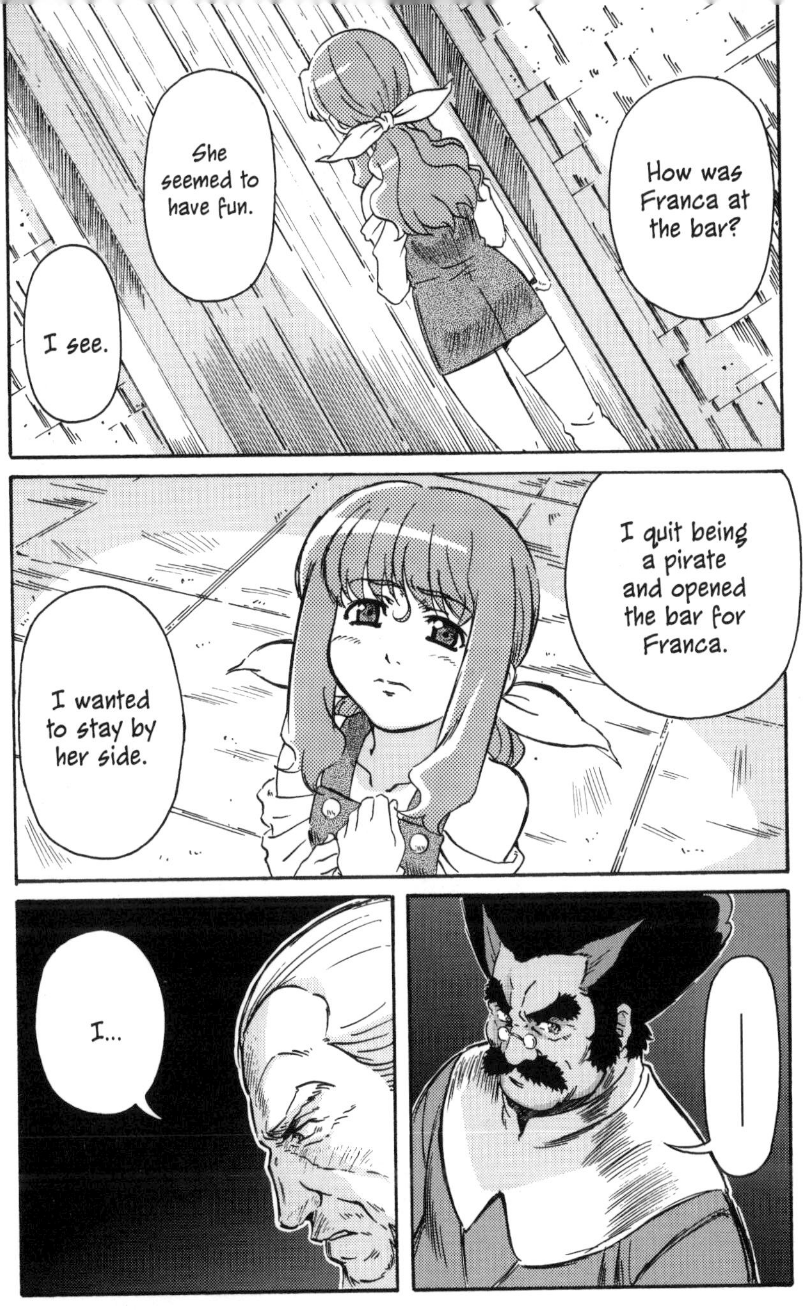
How was Franca at the bar?
She seemed to have fun.
I see.
I quit being a pirate and opened the bar for Franca.
I wanted to stay by her side.
I...

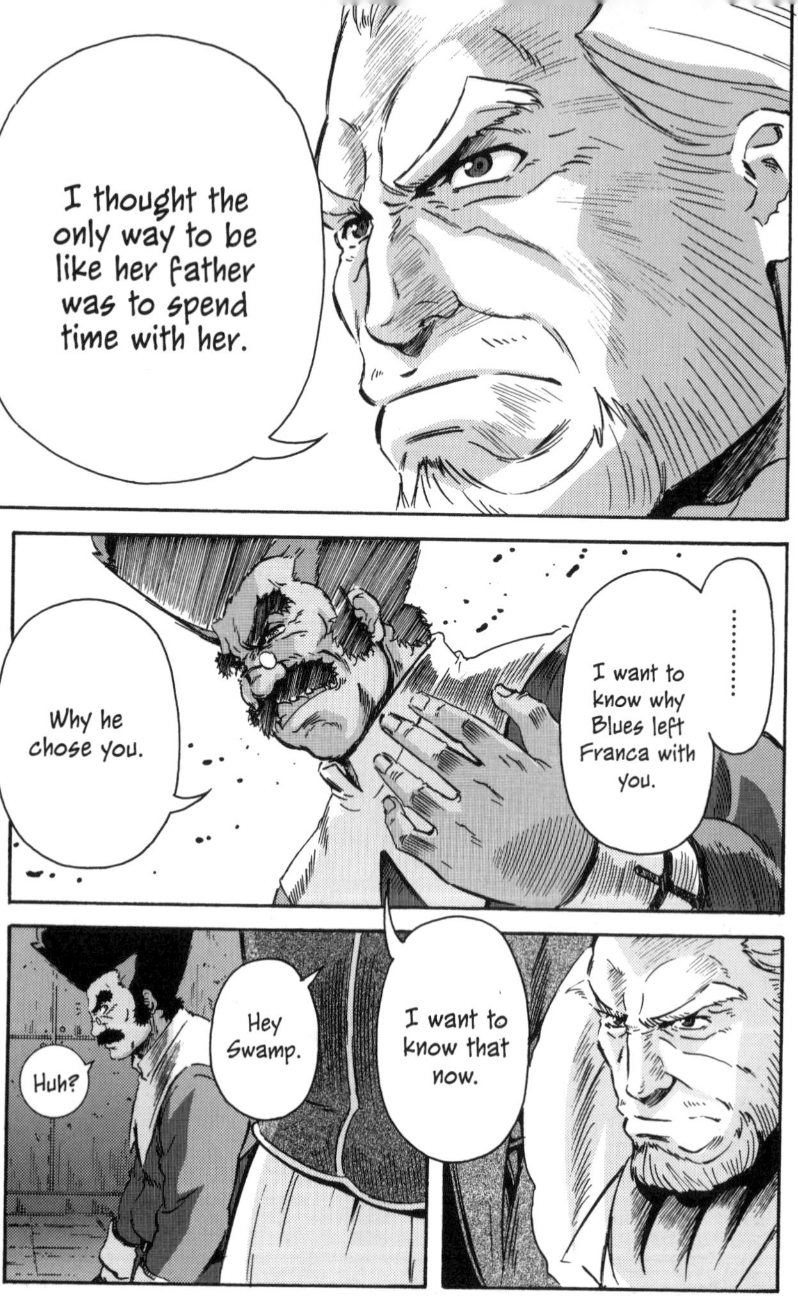
I thought the only way to be like her father was to spend time with her.
......
I want to know why Blues left Franca with you.
Why he chose you.
I want to know that now.
Hey Swamp.
Huh?

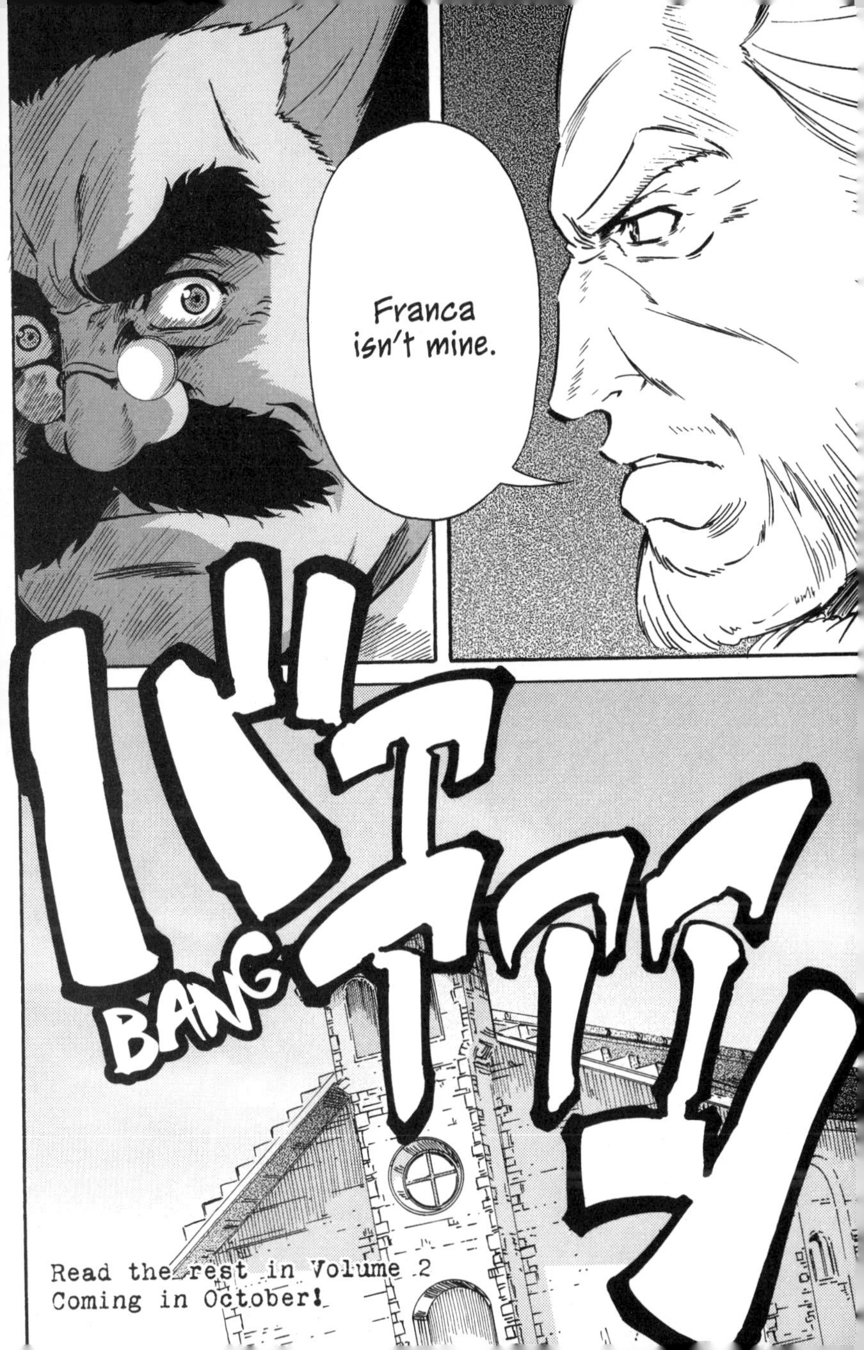
Franca isn't mine.
BANG

Read the rest in Volume 2
Coming in October!

A Book Fit for an Overlord.

The Disgaea Illustration Book
Filled with beautiful artwork as well as tons of info about your **favorite strategy RPG**!

Coming soon to a store near you!
For more information visit www.bro-usa.com

BROCCOLI BOOKS DELUXE
Galaxy II Angel
2
ORIGINAL CONCEPT BY BROCCOLI
BY kanan

Kai Kudou is part of an elite organization of psychics known as Ashurum. One day he is sent on a mission to take custody of other unregistered illegal psychics in the city of Gald. However, he strays from his companions and is taken in by Yuuki Tokugawa, an odd-job-man who is currently working for the guerillas who are in opposition to Ashurum. As Kai spends more time with Yuuki and his mysterious sister Asuka, Kai starts to wonder about the purpose of Ashurum—are they trying to protect the psychics or control them?

WHO DETERMINES WHAT MAKES US *HUMAN?*

Volume 3 available in July!

BROCCOLI BOOKS
KAMUI
OUT
7
SHINGO NANAMI

Spirits known as KAMUI are thrown into chaos when the sacred spirit Okikurumi is taken from Atsuma's village, and the imbalance threatens to destroy Earth. Infused with a spirit of an ancient sword, Atsuma must leave his village to reclaim Okikurumi.

He encounters NOA, an organization of youths who wield the power of the kamui, and who may hold the key to Okikurumi. Atsuma is recruited into NOA by Sumire, a young woman with an empty soul who yearns for a miracle. Atsuma and his new companions must work together to find Okikurumi before the world is destroyed.

SRP: $9.99

13+
Ages 13 & over

"Filled with attractive young men and women, intrigue, romance, and sexual tension as well as supernatural action, KAMUI is a good choice."
- Manga Jouhou

Voucher inside to receive a KAMUI dust jacket!

"It's like a Treasure game you read. The art is so Sin and Punishment I may have to get a tattoo."
- Play Magazine

KAMUI

Volumes 1-7 available now!

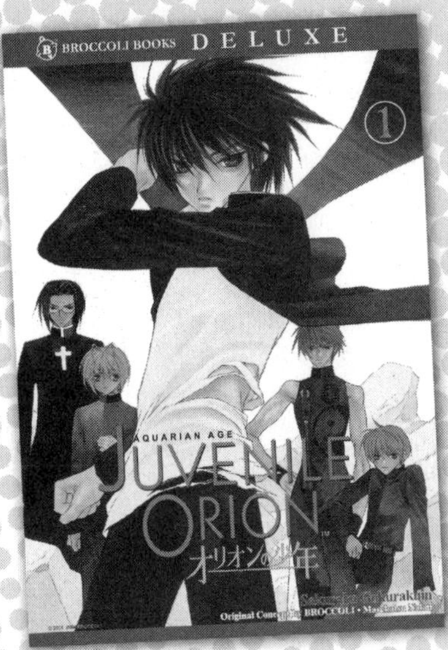
BROCCOLI BOOKS DELUXE
1
AQUARIAN AGE
JUVENILE ORION
オリオンの少年

Sixteen-year-old Mana returns to her hometown to unite with her childhood friend after 7 years. But Kaname seems to have changed during their years apart.

Mana's presence sets off a chain of events that changes the lives of Kaname and his best friend Naoya forever. Their classmates Isshin and Tsukasa, and their teacher Tomonori find themselves drawn to her as well.

They soon discover that they are all a part of the Aquarian Age–a secret war raging for thousands of years.

Now the fate of the world hangs in balance as one girl meets her destiny.

"From the great artwork to the intense shoujo action, this book has a lot to offer for just about anyone who reads it."
– AnimeFrontier.com

SRP: $9.99

13+
Ages 13 & over

AQUARIAN AGE
JUVENILE ORION
オリオンの少年

Limited Edition box with Volume 5 and keychain set also available.

Available now in stores everywhere!

Looking for more Broccoli Books? Just order directly from us!

Just photocopy this page, fill out neatly and mail with **money order** for the total amount to the address below:

I Love Broccoli Books!
c/o Anime Gamers
1728 S. La Cienega Blvd.
Los Angeles, CA 90035

SHIP TO:

NAME:_____

ADDRESS:_____

_____

CITY:_____ STATE:_____ ZIP:_____

EMAIL:_____

AGE:_____ GENDER: M / F

Would you like to be added to the mailing list? Yes / No

ITEM	VOLUME NUMBER	UNIT PRICE	QTY	EXTENDED TOTAL
Realm of Light, The Art of Aquarian Age— Juvenile Orion	N/A	$19.95		
The World of Disgaea Art Book	N/A	$19.95		
Aquarian Age – Juvenile Orion Volumes 1-5		$9.95		
Disgaea manga	N/A	$9.95		
Disgaea 2 Volumes 1-2		$9.95		
E'S Volumes 1-2		$9.95		
Galaxy Angel II Volumes 1-2		$9.95		
KAMUI Volumes 1-7		$9.95		
My Dearest Devil Princess Volume 1		$9.95		
Murder Princess Volume 1		$9.95		
Shipping is FREE for domestic orders. For Canadian orders, add $3.00 for the first BOOK, and $1.00 for each additional BOOK.				
			Shipping to Canada:	
			TOTAL:	

Only Money Orders made out in US funds will be accepted using this order form. Make Money Orders out to Anime Gamers. Checks will not be accepted. Credit card payments are accepted, but only for online orders. There is no shipping charge for domestic orders. For Canadian orders, add $3.00 for the first BOOK, and $1.00 for each additional BOOK. All shipping is via US Postal Service. This order form is valid for the United States and Canada only. For international orders, please visit: **www.animegamersusa.com**

Shipping within the USA - FREE

FLCL ULTIMATE EDITION

FLCL: The Ultimate Edition

collects all 6 episodes of the groundbreaking anime series with new extras including the FLCL Ultimate Book, FLCL Test Type, and MORE!

Features:
- Collector's box
- All 6 episodes on 3 DVD discs
- Director's Commentary
- Storyboard Comparison
- Image Gallery
- FLCL Test Type
(Animation from FLCL, music by the pillows)
- And MORE!

Bonus items include:
- FLCL T-Shirt Postcard
(Redeemable for one (1) t-shirt, size S-XL)
- Sticker Sheet featuring FLCL Logos
(9 stickers)
- Postcard Set featuring robots from FLCL
(6 postcards)
- FLCL Ultimate Book featuring translation notes, English voice actor interviews, manga scenes, and more!

AVAILABLE NOW!

YOU'RE READING THE WRONG WAY!

This is the end of the book! In Japan, manga is generally read from right to left. All reading starts on the upper right corner, and ends on the lower left. American comics are generally read from left to right, starting on the upper left of each page. In order to preserve the true nature of the work, we printed this book in a right to left fashion. Those who are unfamiliar with manga may find this confusing at first, but once you start getting into the story, you will wonder how you ever read manga any other way!

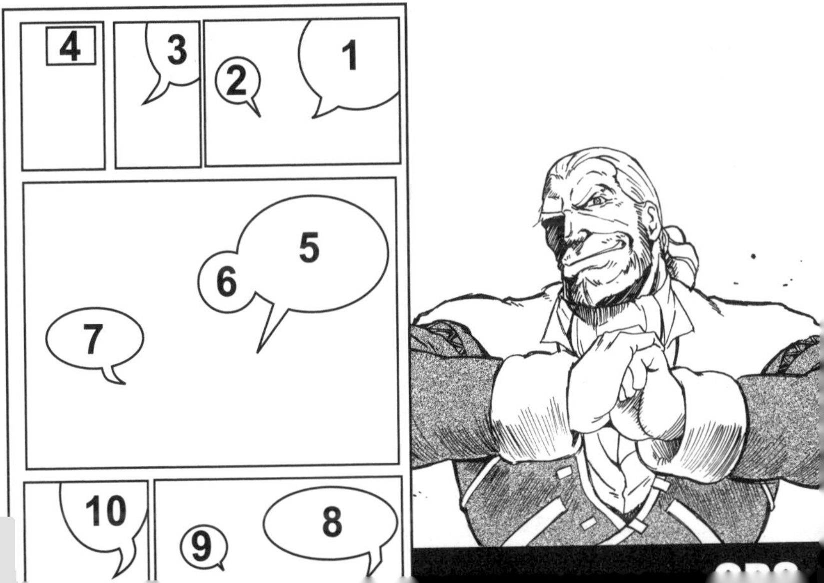
1
2
3
4
5
6
7
8
9
10

THIS QUESTIONNAIRE IS REDEEMABLE FOR:

Coyote Ragtime Show Volume 1 Sticker

Broccoli Books Questionnaire
Fill out and return to Broccoli Books to receive your corresponding sticker!*

PLEASE MAIL THE COMPLETE FORM TO:**

Broccoli International
Attn: Broccoli Books Dust Jacket Committee
1728 S. La Cienega Blvd
Los Angeles, CA 90035

(Please write legibly)

Name: _____

Address: _____

City, State, Zip: _____

E-mail: _____

Gender: ☐ Male ☐ Female **Age:** _____

(If you are under 13 years old, parental consent is required)

Parent/Guardian signature: _____

Where did you hear about this title?

☐ Magazine   ☐ Convention

☐ Internet   ☐ Club

☐ At a Store   ☐ Other

☐ Word of Mouth

Where was this title purchased? (If known)

_____

Why did you buy this title?

_____
_____
_____
_____

How would you rate the following features of this manga?

	Excellent	Good	Satisfactory	Poor
Translation	☐	☐	☐	☐
Art quality	☐	☐	☐	☐
Cover	☐	☐	☐	☐
Extra/Bonus Material	☐	☐	☐	☐

What would you like to see improved in Broccoli Books manga?

____

Would you like to join the Broccoli Books Mailing List? ☐ Yes ☐ No

Would you recommend this manga to someone e ☐ ☐ No

What related products would you be interested i

D1536928

☐ Apparel ☐ Art Books

☐ Posters ☐ Stationery

☐ Figures ☐ Trinkets

☐ Plushies ☐ Other

Favorite manga style/genre: (Check all that apply)

☐ Shoujo ☐ Anime-based

☐ Shounen ☐ Video game-based

☐ Yaoi

Final comments about this manga:

____

____

____

Thank you!

* While supplies last.
** For residents of Canada, please send an International Reply Coupon (IRC) of $3.00 US made out to "Broccoli International."

All information provided will be used for internal purposes only. We will not sell or otherwise divulge any of the information.

Requests not in compliance with all terms of this form will not be acknowledged or returned. All submissions are subject to verification and become the property of Broccoli International USA. Fraudulent submission, including use of multiple addresses or P.O. boxes to obtain additional Broccoli International USA information or offers may result in prosecution. Broccoli International USA reserves the right to withdraw or modify any terms of this form. Void where prohibited, taxed, or restricted by law. Broccoli International USA will not be liable for lost, misdirected, mutilated, illegible, incomplete, or postage-due mail. Sticker offer is only available to residents of the United States and Canada. For updates to the rules and regulations, please see www.broccolibooks.com.